THE
DISCRETIONARY
ECONOMY

THE DISCRETIONARY ECONOMY

A Normative Theory of Political Economy

Marc R. Tool

With a new introduction by the author

Transaction Publishers
New Brunswick (U.S.A.) and London (U.K.)

New material this edition copyright © 2001 by Transaction Publishers, New Brunswick, New Jersey. Originally published in 1979 by Goodyear Publishing Company.

Library of Congress Catalog Number: 00-061988
ISBN: 0-7658-0693-2
Printed in the United States of America

Library of Congress Cataloging-in-Publication Data

Tool, Marc R.
   The discretionary economy: a normative theory of political economy /
Marc R. Tool.
      p. cm.
   Originally published; Santa Monica, Calif. : Goodyear Pub. Co., c1979.
   Includes bibliographical references and index.
   ISBN 0-7658-0693-2 (pbk: alk. paper)
   1. Economics—Moral and ethical aspects. I. Title.

HB72 .T67 2000
330—dc21   00-061988

for
Lillian
Laurence
Marilyn

and

J. Fagg Foster

CONTENTS

VALUE AND GOALS

ILLUSTRATIONS

INTRODUCTION TO THE TRANSACTION EDITION

This volume introduces students to the substance and complexities of social, political, economic, and ecological problems, to scientifically warranted ways of understanding their causal determinants, and to finding and judging institutional remedies that show promise of resolving such problems.

The revolutionary pressures for social change, and their examination through social inquiry, that prompted the initial appearance of *The Discretionary Economy,* are perhaps even more substantive, vital, and pressing now than they were some two decades ago when identified and explored in the 1979 edition of this volume, which I refer to throughout as the first edition. The pressures for social change identified therewith as the Economic Productivity Revolution, the Political Participatory Revolution, the Racial and Sexual Revolutions, and the Ecological Crisis appear to have increased over the intervening years. They are expanding as foci of interest, objects of analysis, and sources of policy considerations around the globe. Without intending any ranking as to comparative significance, examples of continuing problem areas include: the tortured efforts to transform the Soviet economy into a quasi-capitalist system; the pressures to democratize authoritarian politics in developing countries; the continuing efforts in the United States to erode remaining manifestations of race and gender discrimination; the international efforts to promote inquiry into, and develop remedies for ecological crises (global warming, loss of species, genetic manipulation).

None of these "revolutions" can be considered as having significantly abated, and certainly not the last named, although constructive institutional adjustments have indeed been introduced in some areas. Yet they will continue to constitute an encompassing agenda for critical analysis and further institutional adjustments. They continue to identify areas for which instrumental inquiry and democratic policy making provide fresh approaches to problem resolutions.

In current considerations, given the interval since the first edition, the data may be different, the settings may be different, the loci of control may be different, the defense mechanisms of those insisting on the status quo may be different. But the inquiry approach to social problem solving herein introduced will, I believe, continue to apply perhaps even more pertinently and extensively than it did earlier.

The neoinstitutionalist's theory of instrumental value, and its undergirding analytical structure as developed in the first edition (especially in the last section on "Social Value and Goals") has, since then, been a continuing focus in my own work. While I have not found it necessary to "recant" on theoretical positions set forth in the first edition, I have found and developed additional theoretical support for these positions. This extension and refinement have made possible the application of the theory of instrumental value to new issues and areas. The economic, social, political, and philosophical theory embodied in instrumental value has been extended and employed in my *Essays in Social Value Theory* (1986), in *Pricing, Valuation and Systems* (1995), in *Value Theory and Economic Progress* (2000), and in a number of contributions to journals and collected volumes.

While the dominion of neoclassically trained orthodox economists over graduate programs in economics, and over national policy initiatives, remains largely intact, in the "nooks and crannies" of the discipline, heterodox economists are emerging evidently in increasing numbers. The current spectrum of the latter is broad: included are Original Institutional Economists (OIE), Neoinstitutionalists, New Institutionalists (NIE), PostKeynesian Economists, Feminist Economists, Social Economists, Heterodox Economists, Environmental Economists, Regulatory Economists, et al. Each of these groups now has its own professional association. New associations of institutional economists have developed in Europe, Japan, and elsewhere. Moreover, a greater number of publishers have accepted the responsibility of enhancing alternative approaches to economic inquiry by publishing the work of heterodox scholars (Transaction Publishers, Edward Elgar, Kluwer Academic Publishers,

M.E. Sharpe, Routledge, Greenwood, Polity, Westview, et al.). It is my hope that the reappearance of this volume will be of interest and use to these emerging heterodox scholars and their students.

Meanwhile, the major political economies continue to confront problems and issues of generating warranted knowledge, of enhancing democratic accountability, of improving economic performance, of advancing technological development, of achieving distributional fairness, of reducing invidious discrimination, of providing for industrial expansion, and of ensuring ecological sustainability. In democracies, problem resolution is an omnipresent obligation of those holding discretionary power on behalf of their community. Indeed, participation in problem solving is also a continuing obligation of the public citizen. It is the special responsibility of scholars to help the community and its students understand the reality of the problems confronted and the options that can be made available to provide for their resolution. It is the special responsibility of students of all ages, through whatever avenues available, to accept scholarly and participatory responsibilities and to become empowered agents for instrumental, noninvidious, social policymaking.

Finally, I wish to thank Michael Keaney, Mecuria Business School, Vantaa, Finland, Phillip Anthony O'Hara, Curtin University of Technology (Perth), and Paul Dale Bush, California State University, Fresno, for their support for the republication of *The Discretionary Economy*. I wish to thank Irving Louis Horowitz, Rutgers University and Transaction Publishers, for agreeing to publish this new edition.

Sacramento, July 1999   Marc R. Tool

PREFACE TO THE
1985 EDITION

Once published, a book takes on a life of its own. So it has been with *The Discretionary Economy*. As one of a small number of recent attempts to set forth a paradigmatic statement on the neoinstitutionalist perspective on political economy, it has served as an introduction to institutional theory and policy. The special focus of the work is the theory of social value and its applications to economic policy.

In the six years since its publication, *The Discretionary Economy* has been cited frequently in articles and books, with most attention given to sections on social value and its corollaries. I am pleased that others have found the work useful. In recent years, a number of institutional scholars have done extensive research and writing addressing problems, theories, and policies that were touched on only briefly in this book. Several of these important contributions come immediately to mind. The special policy issue of the *Journal of Economic Issues* (March 1984) presented papers analyzing the need for changes in some ten different areas of national economic policy—this volume was later published by M. E. Sharpe under the title *An Institutionalist Guide to Economic Theory and Policy*. William M. Dugger's *An Alternative to Economic Retrenchment* provides a systematic analysis of the quest for corporate accountability. Wallace C. Peterson's *Our Overloaded Economy* offers an insightful discussion of the route to greater economic stability and more equitable distribution of income. Baldwin Ranson and others have made important contributions to the debt theory of capital formation in the *Journal of Economic Issues*. These works, among others, have extended the kind of analysis set forth in this book.

The fundamental concern to which *The Discretionary Economy* and other institutional writing is directed is, if anything, more critical now than when it was first published. That concern is to develop a comprehensive analytical approach to political economy, especially as an alternative to orthodox, mainstream analysis. The need for greater realism and relevance in economic theory has not waned—indeed, it has increased. The conservative counterrevolution of the 1980s continues to elicit substantial support, both political and academic. This support has not yet been significantly eroded by the evident inadequacies of analysis and prescription found in supply-side, monetarist, rational expectations, and libertarian theories and policies. Too many still defer too often to alleged "market solutions" as the optimum response to virtually all economic issues and policy questions.

The renewed availability of this book is a response to that concern. It is intended to provide continuing and convenient access to institutional thinking for students and to contribute to the ongoing effort of an increasing number of scholars to produce a more definitive and comprehensive institutionalist paradigm in political economy.

Sacramento, April 1985   Marc R. Tool

PREFACE TO THE
FIRST EDITION

This book offers a theory of political economy based mainly on economic, political, and philosophical writings of American (U.S.) contributors. It presents a normative and evolutionary point of view— technically a neoinstitutionalist perspective. It offers a conceptual frame for the continuing analysis of problems of political economy. It encompasses theories of an evolving, functional economy and of a participatory, democratic polity. As an approach to the comparative study of economic and political ideologies and systems, it is intended to facilitate constructive analysis apart from the molds, models, and methodologies of major ism-ideologies of the last two centuries—capitalism, Marxian socialism and communism, and fascism.

The continuing manifestations of revolutionary unrest around the world which arise from endemic poverty, protracted unemployment, and rampant inflation; from political oppression and elitist control; from bitter racism and imbedded sexism; and from environmental pollution and resource competition prompt thoughtful people to give critical attention to the frames of reference, the social perspectives, the belief systems with or through which such problems are seen. Sometimes, the conventional isms appear to provide the only available perspectives. Such perspectives often define and delimit how problems will be identified and which policies will be proposed as "solutions."

Presented here is a different kind of perspective with which to engage in the continuing exploration of what to do about conditions which engender revolutionary unrest. As problems are appraised, as policies are reviewed, as systems are compared, and as performance is judged, how do we determine "which direction is forward"? How do we decide what "reform" will mean? This work is addressed to such questions.

The approach here is distinctive in several respects: underlying assumptions are made explicit and their significance is noted; the analysis is evolutionary and open-ended; economic and political elements are fully integrated; the social value problem is addressed directly and continuously as the central and frontier question in inquiry in political economy—that is, the "ought" as well as the "is" is included in this study.

The approach has historical roots in American experience and in American scholarship. Aspects of that experience include the diversity of origin and the heterodoxy of belief of immigrants, the pressures and exigencies of frontier living, the conditioned irreverence for status and rank, the insulation from older power systems abroad, among others, as Henry Bamford Parkes and others have noted. The American experience has been characterized in part by its practicality; its optimistic reworking of its heritage of creed, custom, and skill; and its problem-oriented adaptability to change. This book draws on and is reflective of that experience.

This work reflects American scholarship of the late nineteenth and twentieth centuries as well. Readers will find references to John Dewey and instrumental philosophy and to Thorstein Veblen and institutional economics. The book reflects some of the concerns and ideas of contemporaries including John Kenneth Galbraith, Clarence E. Ayres, Gardiner C. Means, and others. Some may see this effort as a revival of the critical voice of early twentieth-century Progressive thought; others may see it more as a contemporary reformulation of principles of reformistic policy making. Certainly its concern with the normative aspects of public policy is a departure from the pursuit of a "value-free" social science and economics in recent decades. It is, then, a response to the long-standing call of Nobelist Gunnar Myrdal for the inclusion of explicitly stated value premises in social and economic inquiry.

The book is addressed to college students in economics, political science, social science, and social philosophy. Since technical language has in the main been avoided, the material should be accessible to students at all levels. This work is both a text and a treatise. It is written, as are all texts, from a point of view. That point of view is made explicit here; value judgments are made in order to set dialogue in motion with the reader. The concern is to open inquiry and suggest a focus that students may find provocative and productive.

For students of institutional or evolutionary economics, the work offers a synthesis of the neoinstitutional paradigm in economic analysis. For students of comparative economic and/or political systems, it provides an analytic exercise in comparative ideology. For students of political economy, it offers an integrative theory of a participatory democracy. For students of economic planning, it suggests a conceptual frame, a philosophic basis, for the conduct of inquiry. For students of social philosophy, it includes an explication and application of instrumental social value theory.

If this book is helpful to my colleagues who have been lamenting the absence of normative analysis in more conventional materials, I would be most pleased. In addition, I hope that this work might also be of assistance to citizens generally in their public lives as they seek fresh perspectives with which to appraise the flood of opinion, advice, and conjecture to which the mass media and other sources expose them.

As is commonly the case, I am indebted to countless students and many colleagues who have punctured my certitude and disturbed my sleep. I am grateful to John C. Livingston, Thomas R. Williams, Brian D. Comnes, Norris C. Clement, Albert R. Gutowsky, Emanuel Gale, Angus L. Wright, William C. Kirby, John G. Ranlett, and the late Robert M. Robinson for comments on early drafts of selected parts of the work or for other assistance. John Livingston offered encouragement and insights over several years. I have drawn liberally upon his own work. My son, Laurence A. Tool, read the entire work and made numerous suggestions for improvement of form and substance. His critique of the sections involving political theory and philosophy was especially helpful. Paul Dale Bush also reviewed the entire manuscript and contributed significantly to the clarity and integrity of the analysis. His enthusiasm for the project has been invaluable. As a student of J. Fagg Foster years ago, I was introduced to an evolutionary point of view on political economy. As will be evident, his contribution to my thinking has been substantial. The conceptual frame for this study in part reflects his excellent instruction. Suggestions of reviewers engaged by the editors and by me were also most helpful. Goodyear editors Jim Boyd and Steve Lock provided needed support and assistance.

I wish most sincerely to thank my wife, Lillian, for her continuing confidence, her patience, and her editorial contributions. My daughter, Marilyn L. Tool, assisted with editing and proofreading. Carol Brainard typed the work with great skill and good humor. Highly competent and thoughtful copy editing was provided by Jean Sedillos.

Remaining ambiguities, misrepresentations, and inaccuracies are of course my own responsibility.

Sacramento, July 1978   Marc R. Tool

INTRODUCTION

Chapter 1

REVOLUTIONS AND IDEOLOGISTS

I suppose we are all aware of the fact that we live in the most catastrophically revolutionary age that men have ever faced. Usually one thinks of a revolution as one event or at least as one interconnected series of events. But we are in fact living with ten or twenty such revolutions—all changing our ways of life, our ways of looking at things, changing everything out of recognition and changing it fast.

BARBARA WARD*

In my judgment all the received systems are but so many stageplays, representing worlds of their own creation after an unreal and scenic fashion.

FRANCIS BACON**

---

*Barbara Ward, *The Rich Nations and the Poor Nations*, W. W. Norton & Co., Inc. 1962, p. 13.

**Francis Bacon, *Novum Organum*, in John M. Robertson (ed.), *The Philosophic Works of Francis Bacon*, George Routledge & Sons, London, 1905, p. 264.

T here is nothing more practical than theory, folklore notwithstanding. Theory helps people understand and cope with the
realities faced daily. Here, the concern is to formulate, and to explain
the relevance of, a normative theory of political economy with which to
confront current problems.

In order to provide a setting or context for this formulation, it will
be useful to explore some aspects of this "most catastrophically revolutionary age that men have ever faced" and some conventional ideological responses to it. Why, or in what way, are these times revolutionary?
Are responses of "received systems"—ideological commentaries—
helpful? Do they provide relevant guidance, or are they "unreal and
scenic"?

I. REVOLUTIONARY PRESSURES

It is not altogether clear just which "ten or twenty such revolutions"
Barbara Ward is referring to in the quotation above, but for present
purposes, four areas of change seem so apparent, so dramatic, and
comprehensively significant that they require inclusion and explication
here. They are (1) the economic productivity revolution, (2) the political
participatory revolution, (3) the racial and sexual revolutions, and (4)
the ecological crisis. [1]

With regard to each of these areas of fundamental change in the
social process, ideologists have emerged to comment, to admonish, to
demand, and/or to recommend policy. In the following pages, we
briefly examine dimensions of revolutionary pressure and provide some
examples of ideological response.

The Economic Productivity Revolution

In the last two centuries, the capacity to produce and distribute real
income in increasing volume and variety in countries with the requisite
growth potential—motivation, manpower, resources, technology, organization—has repeatedly been demonstrated. In the industrialized
nations of North America, Western Europe, and Japan (the first world)
relatively high levels of gross output and per capita income have been
achieved. In the Eastern bloc of the Soviet Union and Eastern Europe
(the second world) substantial improvement has occurred in most areas,
but levels of gross output and per capita income are generally below
those of the Western bloc. In the third-world countries of India,
Mainland China, Africa, and most of Latin America, improvements are
more modest; levels of output and per capita income are generally

---

1. Compare with the position of the Ad Hoc Committee on the Triple Revolution in
   Arthur K. Blaustein and Roger R. Woock (eds.), *Man Against Poverty: World War III,*
   Random House, Inc., New York, 1968, pp. 161-70. Also see Robert Perrucci & Marc
   Pilisuk, *The Triple Revolution Emerging,* Little, Brown & Co., Boston, 1971.

below, except for oil-rich countries, those of the more industrially developed countries.[2] When growth rates in real output are higher in industrially developed countries than they are in newly developing agrarian countries, the gap between rich and poor obviously tends to widen.

In the last decade, economic relations between the richer developed countries and the poorer less developed countries appear to have taken on a North-South split. Most third-world economics are in the Southern Hemisphere; most developed countries are in the Northern Hemisphere. Third-world economies are seeking increased economic assistance from developed economies and a much increased political role in determining the shape and character of an emerging interdependent world economy in the next several decades.[3]

This emerging North-South agitation reflects the fact that a major contributor to contemporary unrest is the continuing income gap between rich and poor nations. Difficult and sensitive questions remain: Was and is development of rich countries occurring at the expense of poor countries? Can resource-rich, but otherwise poor, countries force resource-dependent, but otherwise rich, countries to increase overseas economic assistance? Should debts owed by poorer countries to rich countries be forgiven? Should there be increased transfers of technology from rich to poor countries? Relative poorness is at issue.[4]

But the productivity revolution is not just an issue between rich and poor nations. It is, of course, a domestic issue in most major economies —rich and poor. Differential patterns of income sharing which permit a tenth, a fifth, a third, a half, or more of the people in an economy to live in poverty while the remainder are comfortably well off are major sources of pressure for social and economic change. Those who write from or about the core cities of the United States, the Italian south, or the Brazilian northeast address the fact of poverty and its consequences.

Poverty is no longer viewed, as it was for ages past, as a condition fatalistically to be endured, as a divinely sanctioned circumstance, or as a superior, because ascetic, life style. Poor countries seek to emulate the ability of comparatively rich countries to produce relative affluence for most of their people. The United States, for example, may well have the "highest standard of low living in the world" (H. J. Muller, referring to the preponderance of mass-produced consumer goods), but it is, for

---

2. United Nations, *Statistical Yearbook 1974*, United Nations, New York, 1975, pp. 644-49.

3. Clyde H. Farnsworth, "North-South Talks: Pianissimo, But Still Going," *The New York Times*, November 28, 1976, p. E3; Peter Grose, "The Third World's Clamor Grows," *The New York Times*, January 30, 1977, Sec. 12, p. 1.

4. Gunnar Myrdal, *The Challenge of World Poverty*, Vintage/Random House, New York, 1970. See also Jogdish N. Bhagwati (ed.), *The New International Economic Order: The North-South Debate*, The MIT Press, Cambridge, Massachusetts, 1977.

good or ill, much sought after. And this quest for rising real income accelerates with the maldistribution effects of rampant inflation in richer economies and with population pressure and food crises in poorer countries.

The productivity revolution has exposed a wide gap between the "is" of residual poverty and the "ought" of comparative affluence. The world-wide recognition of this fact cannot be blinked away or ignored. Politicians must pronounce in favor of improved levels and better distribution of real income. And their listeners view with dismay the continuing shortfall between promised gains and modest accomplishments.

The Political Participatory Revolution

A second revolutionary condition which contributes dramatically to the ferment of our day is the world-wide acknowledgement that only consent of the ruled provides legitimacy for political institutions and processes. Democracy is the spelling on nearly every national banner.[5] Virtually all current ruling groups claim, although in markedly different ways, the right to govern by purporting to rule by consent, tacit or overt, of the people generally.

Meanings of "democracy" and of "consent" vary widely. Indeed, some meanings and usages are incompatible with others. Some governing bodies, claiming to be popularly based, see "consent" accorded through genuine elections which offer real alternatives, establish accountability, and implement democracy. Other governing bodies which are inherently authoritarian will often seek to demonstrate by symbol and form, if not in substance, that they have popular support. The demonstration may be more apparent than real, but popular support is the alleged basis of the claim to credibility in the eyes of others.

Thus, we have, in recent decades, been witness to "peoples' democracies" in the Communist world, to the "democratic centralism" of Lenin, to the "guided democracy" of Sukarno, to a "people's democratic dictatorship" of Mao Tse-Tung,[6] to a "democracy of a new kind" via plebiscite of Franco,[7] to a "plebiscitory democracy" of DeGaulle,[8] and to a "participatory democracy" of Switzerland, and to a degree also of England.[9] A Spanish editor, following the demise of the Franco regime, remarked,

5. J. Fagg Foster, "The United States, Russia and Democracy," (mimeographed), University of Denver, 1949.

6. Anne Fremantle (ed.), *Mao Tse-Tung: An Anthology of His Writings*, New American Library (Mentor), New York, 1962, p. 267.

7. *New York Times*, March 11, 1963, p. 2.

8. R. H. S. Crossman, "Politics of Viewing," *New Statesman*, October 25, 1968, pp. 525 ff. See also *New York Times*, February 9, 1968, p. E3.

9. Ibid.

It isn't easy to build a democracy. There are only a score or more countries in the world which have managed to achieve it. I know there will be a lot of difficulties, but our society has matured now and that is what we want.[10]

There is, we believe, profound significance in this nearly universal acceptance of the normative view that warrantable rule making is dependent at bottom on popular consent. Although the claim to legitimacy through consent may prove to be fraudulent, the fact that such a quest for legitimacy in the eyes of others is made is most instructive.

The pressure for participatory involvement contributes significantly to the revolutionary tenor of the age.

The Racial and Sexual Revolutions

Heavily overlaid upon the economic revolution of productivity and the political revolution of participatory involvement are the racial and sexual revolutions. At an accelerating rate, it seems, the black, brown, yellow, and red segments of humankind are saying to each other and to the white segment, the determination of a person's worth may no longer be established by race or skin color. Women, especially in the West, are asking why sex differences should, a priori, define economic and political access and roles. To use race or color as an index of worth is to discriminate on grounds which, many believe, are no longer admissible. To use sex differences as an index of worth is thought to demean and cripple unwarrantably.

The conflict between those who want to abandon and those who retain beliefs and structures grounded in whole or in part on discrimination appears now to be epidemic and world-wide. The remnants of institutional racism and sexism, racial imperialism, masculine prowess and dominion, "separate-but-equal" doctrines, the "white man's burden," and the like, face an accelerating pressure from those who see the "is" as a racist and sexist society,[11] and the "ought" as a society in which race, color, and sex are not admissible measures of human significance. This hiatus between the "is" and the "ought"—between the real and the possible—contributes generously to the revolutionary demands for revamping political, economic, and other institutions.

In sum, the day when one can attempt to establish one's own identity, one's own sense of place and purpose, one's personal relationships and demeanor with others, by denigrating the visible but generally nonsignificant differences of others, seems to be rapidly passing.

10. Quoted by Flora Lewis, "After Decades of Repression, Democracy is Still the Wish," *The New York Times*, November 16, 1975, p. E4. © 1975 The New York Times Company. Reprinted by permission.

11. See, *Report of the National Advisory Commission on Civil Disorders*, (Otto Kerner, chairman), Bantam Books, New York, 1968. Also, Kirsten Amundsen, *The Silenced Majority*, Prentice-Hall, Englewood Cliffs, New Jersey, 1971.

The Ecological Crisis

A fourth facet of this generated pressure for substantial social change is the mounting concern with environmental pollution, ecological imbalances, and the population explosion. People around the globe are rapidly being faced with an increasing threat to their habitual modes of thought and behavior by pollution of air, fresh water, and sea water; by wanton destruction of remaining natural areas; and the like. The demands for new ideas, new institutions, new plans to preserve and protect the environment from preventable destruction are nearly everywhere in evidence. There is a rapidly growing recognition that uncontrolled population growth may well make ordered society impossible, that unrestrained consumption of known resources may force a drastic reconstitution of the character of real income, that environmental pollution—"man's fouling of his own nest"—may literally imperil the continuity of his own species (to say nothing of the continuity of other life forms). The Americans have polluted Lake Erie; the Russians have polluted Lake Baikal; the Mediterranean is threatened.

The gap between the "is" of the deteriorating environmental quality of life and the "ought" of rational planning to assure resource expansion, environmental restoration, and population control is perceived by some to be widening. The clamor for social change, for rewriting the rules, seems to get more vigorous. There are elements of obviousness and immediacy about it. Thousands of tons of heavy, black oil blanketing the beaches of Southern California, Nova Scotia, Massachusetts, or the southwest coast of England are difficult to ignore. [12] The surface devastation caused by massive strip mining for coal into the Mountain West (Wyoming and Montana) are alarming environmentalists. [13] Many, with reason, fear that efforts to cope with the rising energy demands of the next generation will bring increased radiation hazards from nuclear power plants, [14] environmental havoc from oil spillage from the Alaska pipeline [15] and giant tankers, and continuing air pollution from internal combustion. "Doomsday" predictions of "points of no return" have been accorded credibility through computer projections by researchers at MIT [16]. Pressures for doing something about the ecological

---

12. See, e.g., Ross MacDonald and Robert Easton, "Santa Barbarans Cite an 11th Commandment: 'Thou Shalt Not Abuse the Earth'," *The New York Times Magazine*, October 12, 1969, pp. 32ff. Also Wesley Marx, *Oilspill*, Sierra Club, San Francisco, 1971.

13. John F. Stacks, *Stripping*, Sierra Club, San Francisco, 1972.

14. E.g., Ralph E. Lapp, *A Citizen's Guide to Nuclear Power*, The New Republic, Washington, D.C., 1973; Sheldon Novick, *The Electric War*, Sierra Club, San Francisco, 1976.

15. Tom Brown, *Oil on Ice*, Sierra Club, San Francisco, 1971.

16. D. H. Meadows, D. L. Meadows, J. Randers & W. W. Behrens III, *The Limits to Growth*, New American Library, New York, 1972.

crisis continue. But "which direction is forward"? What institutional changes (beliefs and behaviors) might be proposed to cope with this crisis?

II. IDEOLOGICAL RESPONSES

In a period of rapid social, economic, and political change, those who challenge what is and those who defend it are likely to do so on the basis of established belief systems—ideological views of the organization of society which have gained some credibility either in the above-ground realm of acceptance and reinforcement or in the underground realm of disenchantment and dissent. Such ideological belief systems, whether conservative or radical, consist of ideas, myths, institutions, and symbols. [17] These systems offer conceptual windows from which to view the human experience. They are designed to "explain" economic and political phenomena and to guide or direct conduct.

The current revolutionary era is not an exception. The following selections are examples of, or commentaries upon, ideological views regarding various incidents of and pressures for revolutionary change. [18]

Concerning the Productivity Revolution

A graduating class in Massachusetts is told by one of the country's leading socialist writers that

> To have meaning, our rebellion in the United States must be joined to the world revolutionary movement whose objective is to overthrow the global system of capitalism and replace it with an equally global system of social ownership and production for people's needs, not for private profit. And our task in the United States can only be what is perhaps the most difficult one assigned to revolutionaries anywhere—to find ways and means to make a revolution right here at home. [19]

Thus, the recommended economic cure for contemporary unrest is the far-reaching application of an essentially Marxian doctrine to problems of development and social justice.

---

17. A more extensive and definitive discussion of the meaning of *ideology* can be found in part II of chapter 2.

18. These selections have in common only the fact of their illustrating in public print the application of, or comment upon, one or another ideological perspective on an issue of public concern. They are intended to be indicative of the continuing recourse among some scholars, political figures, and others to the use of ideological belief systems.

   For an insight on the impact of holding power on ideological convictions, see Flora Lewis, "Power and Its Effect on Socialist Ideology," *The New York Times*, December 12, 1976, p. E2.

19. Paul M. Sweezy, "Where Are We Going?", *Monthly Review*, September, 1969, p. 48.

When the question of extending economic aid from the United States to poor countries was examined by a presidential study committee a few years ago, their report reflected the application of long-held beliefs about the nature and virtues of "our own economic system" viewed ideologically.

Said the report:

> We must be clear . . . as to the kind of economic systems we attempt to foster and assist. Our aid should help create economic units which utilize not only limited governmental resources wisely but mobilize the great potential and range of private, individual efforts required for economic vitality and rapid growth. The broad encouragement of these efforts requires incentives. . . . However, there have been too many instances in which foreign economic aid has been given without regard to this fact and to the historic form, character, and interest of our own economic system. We believe the U. S. should not aid a foreign government in projects establishing government-owned industrial and commercial enterprises which compete with existing private endeavors. While we realize that in aiding foreign countries we cannot insist upon the establishment of our own economic system, despite its remarkable success and progress, we should not extend aid which is inconsistent with our beliefs, democratic tradition, and knowledge of economic organization and consequences.[20]

The committee appears concerned about the violation of an ideologically grounded preconception that government enterprise is "in principle" an erroneous structure with which to promote development if it interferes with private enterprise. The questions of whether aid should be extended and for what purposes, of course, must be answered, but the answers which appear to emerge as a reflection of the orthodox capitalist ideology seem quaintly out of date.

The approval by the Senate in 1974 of Alan Greenspan as chairman of the Council of Economic Advisors brought into government a confirmed ideologist. As a twenty-year associate of Ayn Rand, he joins her in the advocacy of the efficiency, practicality, desirability, and morality of "complete laissez faire capitalism" and its embodied "rational selfishness."[21]

His analysis of inflation—the economic plague of the 1970s—was to attribute its cause to "excessive Federal borrowing in the financial markets." He proposed to curb spending and to achieve a budget surplus

20. Report to the President of the United States from the Committee to Strengthen the Security of the Free World, *The Scope and Distribution of United States Military and Economic Assistance Programs*, Government Printing Office, Washington, D.C., March 20, 1963, pp. 5-6.

21. Soma Golden, "Why Greenspan Said 'Yes'," *The New York Times*, July 28, 1974, Sec. F., pp. 1 & 7. © 1974 The New York Times Company. Reprinted by permission. See also, Richard L. Strout, "Chairman Greenspan," *The New Republic*, September 14, 1974, pp. 13-14.

as primary policy aims. He opposed antipoverty programs and the "orgy of short-term solutions" to inflation such as wage and price controls.

As a self-styled "free enterpriser," Greenspan is neither a Keynesian nor a monetarist economist. He opposed the "fine tuning" activistic monetary and fiscal management practiced by Democratic advisors in the 1960s. "At the end of the activist road is economic regimentation," he insisted. [22]

To the degree that Greenspan was able to influence the course of federal economic policy was the degree to which the community had a test of the effectiveness of his variant of capitalist ideology for the curtailment of inflation and the enhancement of the economy.

Concerning the Participatory Revolution

At a time when Mr. Krushchev was premier of the U.S.S.R. and had occasion to address the Twenty-First Party Congress, he spoke expansively of the competition between his country and the United States and of the need to allow the world to choose between models of political economy in pursuit of economic growth. The *choosing* of systems was to be left to the people.

> We want to compete with the capitalist countries in peaceful pursuits, to compete in the development of productive forces, in the development of the economic potential of the country and in advancing the material and cultural well-being of the people. We want each country to exhibit its economic and spiritual forces in this competition. To speak in commercial terms, which are apparently more intelligible to the representatives of the capitalist world, let us spread out our "wares" and show what the socialist world has and what the capitalist world has. . . .

> We believe that the social order which gives the people greater material benefits, the system that makes available to the people limitless opportunities for spiritual development, is a progressive system and the future belongs to it.

> Who will be the judge, who will decide which social system is the better and more progressive? Of course we shall not consent to have the ideologists of the capitalist world be the judges. Nor can we expect the bourgeois ideologists to consent that we should be the judges. It must be assumed that both groups will cling to their positions. Who, then, will be the judges? The peoples. They will decide which system is better. [23]

Clearly, the Soviet occupation of Czechoslovakia in 1968, in part to forestall and reverse reformist measures, eroded confidence in Soviet

22. Ibid.

23. Nikita S. Khrushchev, *The Current Digest of the Soviet Press*, Vol. XI, No. 19, June 10, 1959, p. 25. Translation copyright, June 10, 1959, by THE CURRENT DIGEST OF THE SOVIET PRESS, published weekly at The Ohio State University by the American Association for the Advancement of Slavic Studies; reprinted by permission of the Digest.

rhetoric about the "people" making an uncoerced choice of their own "social system." And the nervousness with which the Soviet Union, for the last third of a century, has watched the development of diverse patterns of economic reform elsewhere in Eastern Europe, especially with regard to economic planning and agricultural organization, may also lead one to question the credibility of Mr. Krushchev's contention.

What surely must be regarded as one of the most critical domestic political crises of the century—as revealed in the Watergate hearings of the Select Senate Committee on Presidential Campaign Activities and the impeachment investigation of former President Nixon by the Judiciary Committee of the House—also provides some examples of an essentially ideological perspective applied by those in power to the nature and conduct of the political process. That perspective included elements of fascistic beliefs. That such attitudes became reflected in the administration's policies, programs, and behavior needs no elaboration in this context.

The habits of mind and habits of behavior exhibited by members of the Nixon administration have been widely reported and recorded in the Watergate Hearings, [24] in transcripts of recorded White House conversations, [25] in narratives regarding the administration and its members, [26] and in materials published by the House Judiciary Committee in the conduct of its investigation into impeachable offenses as charged by the House of Representatives under the latter's Constitutional responsibilities. [27] Probably no brief selection of examples will be regarded as wholly fair. But since our intent here is to *open* the question of ideological perspectives and not to *settle* questions of ideological identification and attribution, a few statements are cited to suggest the character and flavor of attitudes of some in or associated with the Nixon Administration.

President Nixon and John W. Dean, III, (counsel to the president):

> *President:* I want the most comprehensive notes on all those who tried to do us in. They didn't have to do it. If we had had a very close election and they were playing the other side I would understand this. No—they were doing this quite deliberately and they are asking for it and they are going to get it. We have not used the power in this first four years as you know.

24. United States Congress, Senate Select Committee on Presidential Campaign Activities, *Presidential Campaign Activities of 1972* (Hearings & Report), U.S. Government Printing Office, Washington, D.C., 1973.

25. *The White House Transcripts*, (Submission of Recorded Presidential Conversations to the Committee on the Judiciary of the House of Representatives by President Richard Nixon), Bantam Books, New York, 1974.

26. Carl Bernstein & Bob Woodward, *All the President's Men*, Simon and Schuster, New York, 1974; Carl Bernstein & Bob Woodward, *The Final Days*, Simon and Schuster, New York, 1976.

27. U.S. Congress, House of Representatives, Committee on the Judiciary, *Hearings and Report*, [The Impeachment of Richard M. Nixon.] U.S. Government Printing Office, Washington, D.C., 1974.

We have never used it. We have not used the Bureau [FBI] and we have not used the Justice Department but things are going to change now.

Dean: What an exciting prospect.[28]

Egil Crogh, Jr. (deputy assistant to the president for domestic affairs, aide to John D. Ehrlichman, head of Special Investigations Unit —"the plumbers"):

> Anyone who opposes us, we'll destroy. As a matter of fact, anyone who doesn't support us, we'll destroy.[29]

Charles W. Colson (special counsel to the president in an interview concerning his work for the president):

> You tend to become ethically insensitive when your goal—I don't want to use the old cliché that the ends justify the means, but when a goal becomes so important to you . . . You know, I was really totally convinced that the most important thing in this country was to get President Nixon re-elected. I would not run over my grandmoth[er] to do it except to the extent that that became a fun catch phrase, but there wasn't much else I wouldn't have done to get him reelected and that obviously is not a healthy attitude.[30]

Hugh W. Sloan, Jr. (treasurer of the Committee to Reelect the President, former aide to Haldeman, as reported by *Washington Post* reporters):

> People in the White House believed they were entitled to do things differently, to suspend the rules, because they were fulfilling a mission; that was the only important thing, the mission. It was easy to lose perspective.[31]

President Nixon (in conversation with John Mitchell, campaign director, Committee to Reelect the President, former attorney general, and others concerning the White House posture regarding the Senate Watergate Hearings):

> I don't give a [expletive deleted] what happens. I want you all to stonewall it, let them plead the First Amendment, coverup or anything else, if it'll save it—save the plan. That's the whole point.[32]

28. *The White House Transcripts*, op. cit., p. 63.
29. Quoted in J. Anthony Lukas, "The Story So Far," *The New York Times Magazine*, July 22, 1973, p. 13. © 1973 The New York Times Company. Reprinted by permission.
30. Seymour M. Hersh, "Colson Says He Thought He and Colleagues Were 'Above the Law'," *The New York Times*, July 7, 1974, p. 29. © 1974 The New York Times Company. Reprinted by permission.
31. Bernstein & Woodward, *All the President's Men*, op. cit., p. 84.
32. U.S. Congress, House of Representatives, Committee on the Judiciary, *Hearings* (March 22, 1973 tape transcription), [Impeachment of Richard M. Nixon], U.S. Government Printing Office, Washington, D.C., 1974.

Thus, to the extent that these remarks are representative, there are elements of a crypto-fascist ideological view in the Nixon administration. Getting and retaining office was the paramount criterion for behavior; the abuse of power was threatened; and the participants, seeing their mission as worthy, considered themselves to be accountable to no one but the president. [33] Fortunately, the manic nationalism found in European fascism was missing. The president's reelection in 1972, often characterized as a "mandate," came, it appears, increasingly to be thought of as a plebiscite sufficient to justify a de facto undemocratic administration. Based on this "justification" and other grounds, of course, the impeachment was pursued and resignation forced upon the president.

Concerning the Racial and Sexual Revolutions

The propensity to view the question of racial discrimination in ideological terms is well illustrated in the remarks of Eldridge Cleaver, a former minister of information of the Black Panther Party, in an address to college students. In the course of a commentary on the repressive characteristics and personalities of the American culture, Mr. Cleaver said:

> The exploitive businessmen who control this capitalistic system are criminals. The politicians who defend their interests are criminals. The racist Gestapo occupying armies that back them up are criminals and they have no right which the people are bound to respect. The capitalistic system [which] controls this country is the chief obstacle to progress in the world today. Bankrolling depression all over the world, financing armies, every repressive, oppressive regime on the place on planet earth, from South Africa to the puppet regime of South Viet Nam to the occupying regime in the black communities right here in Babylon [sic]. It is this government, this economic system that has to be changed. It has to be changed or the world is going to go up in flames. . . . the world has to be liberated from an anarchistic system that is not capable of fulfilling the desires and needs of the people. We need an economic system that functions on the basis of the needs of the people, not one that struggles along crippled, rumbling along according to the margin of profit laws of some fat, funky business man laying up in the white suburbs. That is not what we need. . . . we need a specific application of universal principles of socialism of home-grown Yankee Doodle Dandy American version of socialism that can provide a life, a good life. . . . The people have a right to that. . . .[34]

33. Tom Braden, "Have We Escaped Fascism?" *The Sacramento Bee*, May 31, 1973, pp. 8-9. See also, Clayton Fritchey, "Fuehrer Principle Among Nixon Aides," *The Sacramento Bee*, July 19, 1973, p. B9; Hans J. Morgenthau, "The Aborted Nixon Revolution," *The New Republic*, August 11, 1973, pp. 17-19.

34. Eldridge Cleaver, "Racism in America," an address at Sacramento State College, September, 1968. Printed in *A Symposium on Racism in America*, edited by Student Co-Operative, Sacramento State College, Sacramento, California, 1969, pp. 69-70. Since his return from seven years abroad, Mr. Cleaver has evidently modified his

Clearly, Eldridge Cleaver's remarks reflect the deep bitterness and rage which many blacks share with regard to a system they hold responsible for their relatively deprived condition.

Note now a more general statement concerning the relation between racism and capitalism. Few exceed Milton Friedman in offering ideological praise to the latter:

> It is a striking historical fact that the development of capitalism has been accompanied by a major reduction in the extent to which particular religious, racial, or social groups have operated under special handicaps in respect of their economic activities; have, as the saying goes, been discriminated against.
>
> . . . The maintenance of the general rules of private property and of capitalism have been a major source of opportunity for Negroes and have permitted them to make greater progress than they otherwise could have made. To take a more general example, the preserves of discrimination in any society are the areas that are most monopolistic in character, whereas discrimination against groups of particular color or religion is least in those areas where there is the greatest freedom of competition.[35]

The adequacy of Eldridge Cleaver's view or that of Milton Friedman remains at this point in our inquiry an open question; the analysis to follow will suggest ways of testing for adequacy. But there can be no doubt about the willingness of each man to view racial discrimination from the windows of conventional ideologies.

Sexual discrimination also is sometimes viewed as being an expression or application of an ideology. A recent study of economic discrimination against women included the following observations:

> Many of us are now aware that the average American working woman earns less than the average working man. To be exact, she earns only 58 percent of what an equally qualified man would make.
>
> . . . discrimination often is justified in terms of an ideology or set of values. In the case at hand, an achievement ideology is used to justify unequal salaries. The argument runs as follows: 1. unequal pay is legitimate when there is unequal achievement; 2. women achieve less than men; thus it is legitimate, not discriminatory, to pay them less; and 3. women who achieve as much as men can expect to earn as much as men.
>
> Such reasoning is common—and it is faulty. We have clear evidence that women do *not* receive pay and benefits commensurate with their achievement. They are far worse off than equally qualified men.[36]

---

views substantially. See T. D. Allman, "The 'Rebirth' of Eldridge Cleaver," *The New York Times Magazine*, January 16, 1977, pp. 10ff.

35. Milton Friedman, *Capitalism and Freedom*, The University of Chicago Press, Chicago, 1962, pp. 108-09.

36. Teresa E. Levitin, Robert P. Quinn, & Graham L. Staines, "A Woman is 58% of a Man. . . ," *Psychology Today*. Reprinted in *Annual Editions, Readings in Economics, 1973-1974*, Dushkin, Connecticut, 1973, p. 187. Reprinted by permission of *Psychology Today Magazine*. Copyright © 1973 Ziff-Davis Publishing Company.

The "achievement ideology" is, as many are aware, a derivative from the more inclusive capitalist ideology and its presumptions of equal pay for equal work through an equilibrating market mechanism.

Concerning the Ecological Crisis

Growing sensitivity to the environmental and ecological crisis has produced expected responses, many of which are ideologically grounded.

An ideological response to the pollution problem from an uncommon source is contained in a press release out of Hong Kong:

> Communist China reported . . . that it, too, faced problems of industrial pollution, but it said that they were being solved by frugality and Maoist ingenuity. . . .
>
> Predicttably [sic], they placed the blame for pollution on "laissez-faire capitalist-revisionist attitudes" and the operation of enterprises for profit.
>
> The report, which dealt with pollution in Shanghai, Communist China's major industrial city, said the problem had not been solved there until "the counter-revolutionary trash" of "putting profit in command" had been overcome in "a sharp struggle."[37]

A few years later the party line remained virtually unchanged. A report in *The Peking Review* discusses pollution in the West:

> Factories discharge industrial wastes and natural resources are exploited at will, cities develop even more abnormally and the environment suffers even worse pollution and harm, and the health of the masses of the laboring people is seriously endangered.
>
> All these facts, past and present, point to the conclusion that pollution and destruction of the environment in these countries is a social phenomenon of capitalism and a manifestation of the sharpening contradiction between the private ownership of the means of production and the social character of production.[38]

But the Marxists and Maoists have no monopoly on concern. A considerably more sober and reflective view is held by students of the ecology crisis in the United States. Some are attempting to probe the accepted beliefs of the "American system." Says Cliff Humphry, founder of Ecology Action in Berkeley,

> Everywhere I speak I say we have a vested interest in our own destruction. . . . When the stock market goes up it is a signal device warning us of the imminent destruction of some part of the environment. Capitalism is predicated on money and growth, and when you're only

---

37. Tillman Durdin, "Chinese Report Cut in Pollution," *The New York Times*, February 23, 1970, p. 12 © 1970 The New York Times Company. Reprinted by permission.

38. Quoted by John Burns, "China is Plagued by Pollution, Too," *The New York Times*, August 19, 1973, p. 8 © 1973 The New York Times Company. Reprinted by permission.

interested to maximize profits, you maximize pollution. We need a system that takes maximum care of the earth. . . .

You can't really blame the stock market. . . . Our culture evolved in almost total ignorance of the ecological absolutes. The New Left rhetoric is so simplistic. There was no conspiracy to get us into this mess. People in the establishment never had a choice. . . .[39]

Steve Cotton, a law student working on ecological problems, adds this disquieting comment,

Many people saw Vietnam as a tragic mistake in American foreign policy, but the more radical kids are saying that it was a natural outgrowth of a system that doesn't care about people, just about profits, about its own expansion and nothing else. There has been a lot of thinking about the system, where it's going and what the alternatives are. Some of it is heavily ideological, but a lot is just a vague sense of unease, of disquiet, that the whole thing is rushing pell-mell in the wrong direction. Environment as the kids conceive it is an expression of that. They're not saying this is a sanitation job, that if we spend enough money we'll scrub it all clean. . . . The state of the environment is just another symptom of society's corruption, it's what the system is all about.[40]

In sum, for good or ill, we do live in an era of revolutionary change. Barbara Ward is right about that. And the multiple facets of these revolutionary pressures for social, political, and economic change continue to be discussed, analyzed, and defended in part on ism-ideology grounds. We have noted examples of the affirmations, admonitions, and apprehensions of ideologists. Doubts will probably have arisen concerning the adequacy of ideological views of these problem areas. This study is directed to the formulation of a more defensible and more applicable perspective with which to view these and other social pressures.

III. PLAN OF THE BOOK

The foregoing observations of ideologists and commentators on the revolutionary pressures of the age are, in the main, expressions of basic comprehensive belief systems which provide conceptual equipment to identify what is and to recommend what ought to be in problematic situations. Any presentation of a fundamentally different position to that of these Grand Alternatives must also then constitute a basic, comprehensive belief system.

The following questions probe for and delineate basic components of such a comprehensive belief system in political economy. They are

39. Quoted by Steven V. Roberts, "The Better Earth," *The New York Times Magazine*, March 29, 1970, p. 53 © 1970 The New York Times Company. Reprinted by permission.

40. Ibid., p. 56.

the questions with reference to which this presentation of a normative theory of political economy is organized; responses to these questions, then, constitute the substance of the book. They are also questions to be addressed to the ism-ideologies when they are called to account as problem-solving perspectives.

(1) Upon what idea of inquiry does the belief system rest? What are the theories of knowledge and reality incorporated?

(2) What assumptions are made about men and women and the determinants of their beliefs and behavior? What theory of human nature is provided or implied?

(3) What kind of an economic system is recommended? Of what institutions does it consist? How is it to be changed? What is the meaning of an economic problem?

(4) How is public policy to be determined? What kind of a political system is recommended? By whom and for what purposes is policy determined? Where is the locus of power, and what is the basis for its legitimacy?

(5) What is the criterion of judgment in social, political, and economic policy making? What principle of social value is recommended?

(6) What is the meaning of freedom, of equality, and of justice? How are they perceived? Will they serve as guides to conduct?

Responses to these questions in the chapters which follow will provide, in the aggregate, the main elements of a normative theory of political economy—an alternative to the isms of yesterday. It is a perspective *different in kind* from these Grand Alternatives. It is offered as one approach which seeks to open minds and to keep them open.

Clearly, the reader will find here no blueprint for a society of the future. We envision no twentieth- or twenty-first-century utopia. This is no appeal for modern communes or communitarian orders. (It *is* an appeal for the continuing re-creation of community.) We shall not emerge from our analysis with a position which unfailingly prophesies future events, generates eternal answers, or sees an end to the need for progressively more mature and insightful inquiry. We do not seek to turn off revolutionary ardor; we wish to help provide it with appropriate theoretical direction. We offer no shortcuts to hard work or hard thinking. We have no Bibles, no answer sheets, no "all-in-one-lesson" analysis. We offer no manifesto penned in undying prose. We have no elixirs to turn hate into love or violence into peace. We have no panaceas for the ills generating revolutionary unrest.

We intend, simply, to suggest a constructive way of viewing demands for revolutionary, that is to say, extensive and substantive, social, political, and economic change. We do offer a kind of handbook, a preliminary guide to some important and continuing considerations. But hopefully, and mainly, we explore a somewhat different way of posing questions. For example, we attempt to dispel interest in the query of whether or not we are headed "down the road" to one or another ism. We suggest that asking whether we are moving toward or away from (say) a capitalist economy is not a very important question. Congruity or convergency with a doctrinaire ism-ideology does not adequately define "which direction is forward."

We seek an approach, an orientation, and a methodology which, because of a tendency toward an internal correction of error, ought to be more continuously relevant as a theory-building and problem-solving perspective. When existing tools or modes of inquiry are demonstrably inadequate, they must be redesigned and/or new ones must be fashioned. Drawing heavily on the work of other scholars, we try to do this. [41]

Perhaps more importantly, we attempt to reintroduce into inquiry about political economy the notion of social value in the philosophical sense. We do not believe that scholars can continue the posture of "eschewing value judgments" in their analyses of social, political, and economic problems. Whether or not we succeed in formulating an analysis of social value which is, as we intend, largely devoid of ism-ideology and ethnocentric characteristics remains for the reader to judge. But we do address directly and continuously the task of choosing a criterion (or criteria) of judgment to employ in deciding "which direction is forward" in a period of revolutionary unrest.

Throughout, we shall try to be mindful of Albert Guerard's insightful admonition: "By thought ye shall *seek* the truth; and the *quest* shall make you free." [42] And the reader should be mindful that "thought" here means a running dialogue between reason and experience.

---

41. A similar approach is suggested by Robert L. Heilbroner in "On the Possibility of a Political Economics," *Journal of Economic Issues*, Vol. IV, No. 4, December, 1970, pp. 1-22.
42. Albert Guerard, *Testament of a Liberal*, Harvard University Press, Cambridge, Massachusetts, 1956, p. 10. (Emphasis added.)

FOUNDATIONS

Chapter 2

SOCIAL INQUIRY AND REALITY

Upon this first, and in one sense this sole, rule of reason, that in order to learn you must desire to learn, and in so desiring not be satisifed with what you already incline to think, there follows one corollary which itself deserves to be inscribed upon every wall of the city of philosophy:

Do not block the way of inquiry.

CHARLES SANDERS PEIRCE*

We ought to act in such a way that what is true can be verified to be so.

J. BRONOWSKI**

*Charles Sanders Peirce, "The Scientific Attitude and Fallibilism" in Justus Buchler (ed.), *Philosophical Writings of Peirce*, Dover Publications, New York, 1955, p. 54. Quoted by Thomas Landon Thorson, *The Logic of Democracy*, Holt, Rinehart and Winston, New York, 1962, p. 120.

**J. Bronowski, *Science and Human Values*, Harper & Brothers, New York, 1956, p. 74.

"Do not block the way of inquiry" is the admonition. Why not? Because only through inquiry can we come to understand the complexities of revolutionary unrest and to reduce uncertainties regarding our personal and communal behavior arising from that unrest. The development of a belief system, a perspective, relevant to this age must begin then with attention to the matter of inquiry itself. How do we come to "know" something pertinent? What are the real problems? How do we avoid the limitations of the ism-ideologies which in different ways do "block the way of inquiry"?

I.   DOUBT AND ITS REMOVAL

All social inquiry originates with doubt. Some event, an experience, or contact with another mind brings into question an idea held, a behavior habitually practiced, an expectation of an outcome, or a prediction of a future occurrence. Questions are posed: Why did that happen? How do you account for those results? Why did they make that judgment? What ought we to do next? How can that be true?

Inquiry is undertaken to explain phenomena, to remove doubt, to restore confidence in expectations, to reintegrate, reconstitute, rehabilitate, or reorder that which has been questioned, has become problematic, has become of some urgent concern.

Inquiry results from the glory of consciousness, from our becoming aware of our own identity and capacity in a cultural context and of the complexities and problems which arise in our interaction with each other and with the environment.

The appearance of doubt concerning the social order is a reflection of our capacities for perceiving relations between means and consequences, between events and their causes. Inquiry is initiated by persons when something in their lives intrudes upon their proclivities to think and act along previously established lines.

Scholars (professional inquirers) deliberately seek out areas of individual or community doubt for scrutiny and analysis. Doubt about the structural character or functional adequacy of the social order is resolved through social inquiry. Scholars seek to explain, to account for what is observable and understandable in the social process. Social inquiry consists of a quest for knowledge, for reliable knowledge, for knowledge in which confidence can be placed and on which judgments to alter the fabric of society may be based.

Social inquiry is significant because it is addressed directly or indirectly to the resolution of social problems, the appearance of which initiated the doubts about current conditions and practices. *The inclusive and continuing function of social inquiry is to assist the community to resolve an unending series of problems with which it is confronted.*

For example, with regard to the productivity revolution: Why does the price level continue to rise when the level of employment continues to fall? Why is the real income gap between the rich and poor tending to widen? Will a tight money policy—"that old-time religion"—successfully control "double-digit" inflation?

With regard to the participatory revolution: Did the political turmoil of the 1960s and 1970s adversely affect the viability of political parties in the United States? Ought the electoral college to be abolished? Does planning destroy freedom?

With regard to the racial and sexual revolution: Are black or brown "liberation" movements a serious threat to established centers of political and police power? Is school integration an effective instrument to achieve greater racial equality? Should women be given preferential consideration for jobs in male-dominated professions and occupations?

With regard to the ecological crisis: Are federal incentives and controls required to end industry-originating environmental pollution? What are the structural (institutional) impediments to the rapid development of urban mass transit systems? Ought foreign economic aid to be made conditional upon the adoption by the recipient country of effective population control measures?

In each of the foregoing questions there is a manifestation or emergence of doubt and an explicit or implicit reflection of a difference between "is" and "ought." In each area of doubt, attention is invited to the fact of a probable structural infirmity or judgmental inadequacy or both. With reference to each of the foregoing questions, the reader probably formulated a preliminary response that would set inquiry in motion to remove doubt. It might even constitute a hypothesis with which the inquiry could be guided initially.

Our point is a simple one. The *significance* of social inquiry is and always has been a function of its relevance for genuine problem solving. No other "purpose" can approach it in degree of de facto acceptance. Occasionally someone may argue that his inquiry is grounded merely in idle curiosity; others may contend that their concern with inquiry is prompted by a need for reaffirmation of belief, for providing apology for established power systems, or for establishing or maintaining a position of rank or status. However accurate these reasons for inquiry may appear to be in individual cases, the community (where it has any significant say in the matter) will generally not support social inquiry on such grounds.

Deliberately pursued social inquiry is purposive; it derives its significance from its relevance to problem solving. That this conclusion embodies assumptions concerning a position on social value is obvious. To this matter we return.

II.   INQUIRY, THEORY, AND IDEOLOGY

Ism-ideologies, we said above, are systems of belief comprised of ideas, myths, institutions, and symbols held by some discernible group of people—economic class, elite fragment, ethnic segment, and the like. Ism-ideologies are alleged to be relevant to experience and social action and to have pertinence for problem solving.

"Ideology is conversion of ideas into social levers," says Daniel Bell. [1] An ideology is "any system of beliefs publicly expressed with the manifest purpose of influencing the sentiments and actions of others," according to a group of scholars who examined the ideology of American businessmen. [2] These general attributions of purposiveness to ideology (belief systems to promote and justify social action) we accept. But they are not sufficiently inclusive for our purposes.

We join James Gregor in choosing a somewhat more comprehensive characterization of the meaning of ideology. In his view,

> An "ideology" is understood to be an implicit or explicit value system accompanied by a relatively coherent system of doctrinal beliefs about nature, society, and man that a group offers in justification of the issuance of social and political directives, prescriptions, and proscriptions, as well as the directives, prescriptions, and proscriptions themselves. [3]

Although in this study we do not order the analysis in quite the same way, the elements considered crucial and central by Gregor (social philosophy, doctrine, formal and informal imperatives) are, in the main, those given emphasis here.

Thus, for present purposes we define an ism-ideology as a system of beliefs to guide and sanction social action, a system which affirms the efficacy of a *particular* set of (mainly) political and economic institutional forms together with the underlying assumptions about knowledge, reality, people, society, and value which purport to validate and justify that affirmation. Capitalism, Marxian socialism and communism, and fascism are ism-ideologies in this sense.

Consider now some distinctions between *inquiry*, *theory*, and *ideology*.

Inquiry directed to social problem solving has as its central purpose the formulation of hypotheses purporting to explain the causal linkages of phenomena under review. Tentative confirmation of hypotheses constitutes *theory*. A theory is a demonstrable explanation in causal terms of observable phenomena.

Ism-ideologies rest upon theoretical premises. They are belief systems which draw ideational substance from assumptions and propositions believed to be theoretically defensible or a priori self-evident. Ism-ideologies are efforts to apply certain theoretical formulations to

---

1. Daniel Bell, *The End of Ideology*, Collier Books, New York, 1961, p. 394.
2. Francis X. Sutton, Seymour E. Harris, Carl Kaysen, James Tobin, *The American Business Creed*, Schocken Books, New York, 1962, p. 2.
3. A. James Gregor, *Contemporary Radical Ideologies*, Random House, New York, 1968, p. 8.

influence the sentiments and actions of persons to bring them into congruity or conformity with those sentiments and actions espoused by the ideologists. For the unwary or naive, ism-ideologies may become coercive of thought and behavior.

Once embodied in an ism-ideology theoretical material typically is removed from the universe of inquiry and truth-seeking from which it allegedly emerged. Such ideas become encapsulated in protective casings of familiar language forms. They frequently appear reduced to jargon, clichés, and symbolic utterances. Ideologists using such language forms appear to assume the role of reciters of catechismal verities. These ideational forms come to define the mind set with which problems are seen. The forms tend to take on the status of "first principles," "eternal truths," or "basic postulates," which are rarely subjected to further critical scrutiny through inquiry.

Ism-ideologies consist, in the main, of particular sets of habits of mind and habits of behavior which constitute instutions. These are what James Gregor calls "legislation, the institutions and social sentiments codified, instituted, or fostered by a regime committed to a given social and political philosophy and its doctrinal derivatives."[4] Indeed, ism-ideologies affirm the perpetual efficacy and efficiency of such ideas and institutions. These institutional forms, "validated" by theoretical under-pinnings, are offered as recipes for social action or social control.

The body of classical and neoclassical politico-economic theory,[5] as nearly everyone knows, provides the basis for the ism called capitalism. Capitalism is the ideological derivative primarily of traditional, ortho-dox, or standard economic theory. The philosophical, political, and economic writings of Marx and Engels (and Lenin) provide most of the theoretical materials for the ideologies of Marxian socialism and com-munism. The case of fascist ideology and its theoretical underpinnings is

4. A. James Gregor, *Contemporary Radical Ideologies*, op. cit., p. 10.

5. For those less familiar with the development of economic thought, an additional comment may be helpful. *Classical economic theory* refers to the body of analysis developed in England in the late eighteenth and the first half of the nineteenth century. Adam Smith, David Ricardo, Thomas Malthus, and John Stuart Mill were perhaps the major contributors. This theory explained a self-adjusting economy, organized with natural capitalist institutions which operated to produce products and distribute shares to capitalists, workers, and landowners according to their real cost (labor) contributions. Consumers' real income was the goal; utility (the ability or capacity of goods and services to satisfy wants) was the meaning of value; labor em-bodied in goods was the measure of economic worth.

Neoclassical economics is a mainly English development of the last half of the nineteenth century and the twentieth century. Beginning with Stanley Jevons (among others), its major figures include Alfred Marshall, A. C. Pigou, Lionel (now Lord) Robbins, and such contemporaries as Milton Friedman and George Stigler. This school builds on and modifies the classical position. The focus narrows to the examina-tion of the allocation of scarce means among unlimited ends; the price system in competitive markets is the efficient allocator. The meaning of value is utility; *price* becomes the measure of economic worth. An extensive marginal mode of analysis provides for greater precision in explaining price behavior. Reference in this work to

somewhat less obvious. Theoretical antecedents for Italian fascism may be found in the works of Giovanni Gentile and others,[6] for German Nazism in that of Ludwig Woltmann and some social Darwinists,[7] and for French fascism in the writings of Charles Maurras.[8] But because these and other writings erode the case for reasoned reflection and rational judgment, it is difficult to identify a paradigmatic fascism as a simple derivative of a coherent body of theory.

In the continuum of contemporary social inquiry, particular hypotheses are formed, tested (insofar as they are amenable to empirical and logical test), affirmed, and constituted as theoretical truths (with a lowercase t). Such theories have a tentative acceptance status; they explain what they purport to explain. They retain their explanatory significance only so long as that capacity to explain is not seriously eroded or faulted by new evidences or more adequate or inclusive formulations.

Ism-ideologies, in contrast, have little or no capacity to accommodate to change in facts or conditions. The theoretical material buttressing ideologies tends to be frozen. Ideological use renders supporting theories largely immune to the forces of change. As belief systems, ism-ideologies are largely finished and final in fundamental form and content. They rapidly take on a creedal quality and become matters of faith. Ideological "saints" appear, and "sacred texts"—a hagiologic literature—are written. The quest for ideological followers becomes a search for converts and disciples, not for students of inquiry.

Theory, while it lives to serve men, out of reverence for truth bows to no earthly master; ideology, who is no worshipper of truth, falls prey to idolatry—of men, institutions, processes of history, and the like.[9]

"traditional," "orthodox," "standard," or "mainstream" analysis refers generally to this tradition of classical, and especially neoclassical, thought. David Hamilton, in his *Evolutionary Economics*, (University of New Mexico Press, Albuquerque, 1970) provides an excellent comparative analysis of neoclassical and evolutionary approaches to economic inquiry.

Perhaps the following will also be helpful: We assume that most economists make greater or lesser use of this orthodox tradition, but we do not presume that all such users are necessarily ideologists. Economists generally appear to be eclectic in their approaches to theory and policy. While many profess to have "market mentalities," they often seem to be well aware of "market failures" and to seek policy options which may not always fit the orthodox perspective. Accordingly, in what follows, we occasionally offer critiques of the ideological use of orthodoxy, but we do not therewith intend the criticism necessarily to extend to individuals themselves. We are interested in belief systems and their relevance; we are less interested in individual scholars and their consistency and stature. Similar observations apply also to Marxist and fascist writers.

6. H. S. Harris, *The Social Philosophy of Giovanni Gentile*, University of Illinois Press, Urbana, 1960, pp. 160-223.

7. A. James Gregor, *Contemporary Radical Ideologies*, op. cit., pp. 181ff.

8. Ernst Nolte, *Three Faces of Fascism*, Holt, Rinehart and Winston, New York, 1966, Part II.

9. Contributed by reviewer, L. A. Tool.

In sum, inquiry modes of ism-ideology belief systems must be distinguished from the processes of evidentially grounded, logically consistent social inquiry. In marked contrast to evolutionary theory building in social inquiry, ideological positions are characteristically rigid. After initial affirmation, such positions are not themselves the object of inquiry. They reflect an arrest of inquiry; they are essentially static constructs; they are time and culture bound. Notwithstanding this characteristic, such ideological views are thought to be both true and relevant as maxims to be applied to the continuing flow of experience, including areas of revolutionary unrest.

A brief excursion into these modes of inquiry will undergird the foregoing contentions.

III. MODES OF INQUIRY

The trouble with the ism-ideologies' preconceptions regarding knowledge and reality (and hence, the inquiry process by which knowledge is addressed to reality), is, as we said above, that, ironically, their adoption does "block the way of inquiry." We shall see that each ism-ideology as a belief system either arrests inquiry by its static design or distorts inquiry by excluding crucial elements or both.

Capitalism

The inquiry method provided by orthodox capitalists tends to offer students only part of the conceptual tools they need; half a loaf is provided when a whole loaf is required. The approach to inquiry of classical and neoclassical theorists, of which the capitalist ideology is a derivative, was an effort to formulate a scientific approach comparable to the highly successful pursuits of the Newtonian physical scientists in earlier periods. To explain in causal terms the regularities of nature was the main mission. In the hands of the economists, this inquiry became rationalistic and deductivistic, episodic, positivistic, and primarily focused on price and market phenomena. Consider these characteristics briefly.

Rationalism, as here used, is the view that knowledge can be derived via deduction from a priori assumptions or postulates. Rationalism consists mainly of deductive inference—the logical extraction or distillation of particulars from general propositions. Assuming a utility maximization principle (receiving maximum satisfaction from consumption of goods), one can deduce principles of effective demand, substitutability of goods for each other, a market price system, and the like. [10] "Pure economic analysis is a deductive form of explanation." [11]

10. Lionel Robbins, *The Nature and Significance of Economic Science*, (2nd ed.), Macmillan and Company, London, 1952, p. 75.

11. Sherman Krupp, "Analytic Economics and the Logic of External Effects," *American Economic Review*, Vol. LIII, No. 2, May, 1963, p. 220; & Krupp, "Axioms of Economics and the Claim to Efficiency," *Journal of Economic Issues*, Vol. II, No. 3, September, 1968, pp. 275-82.

The general propositions or assumptions of orthodoxy were re-garded as commonplace and virtually self-evident. What the orthodox writers did, observes Overton Taylor, "was to 'reason' from or upon simple, plausible, general assumptions arising from or suggested by their limited amounts of informal, casual, 'everyday experience and observa-tion' and their 'common sense.'[12] These assumptions—utility maximiza-tion, profit motive, private property, competition—were taken as given. They were not the object or product of inquiry.

Through this mode of inquiry, then, human reason would identify the connecting linkages, the observable regularities in nature, the nat-ural laws (law of markets, of demand, of diminishing returns, etc.) governing relations in the naturally ordered universe. Deductive, rationalistic inquiry discovered the laws; proper public policy was to seek congruity with such laws. Although contemporary mainstream writers no longer talk of natural laws as such, analyses are replete with reference to "market forces," "movements toward equilibria," "inherent tendencies," and the like. Modern inquiry, in contrast, searches for regularities of *experience* through modes involving deductive and in-ductive tools.

Orthodox deductivistic inquiry is episodic rather than processional or evolutionary. The inquiry episode has a beginning—taking premises as given. The episode has a middle—drawing of inferences. The episode has an ending—application to experience and (with luck) prediction of outcomes. Inquiry affirms that with which inquiry began—its assump-tions. The episode is set off; it is not distracted or forestalled by unexpected inferences; it is not diverted by unexplained evidence. Logically elegant, it has no awkward facets and no ungainly handles; it is discrete; it sets no questions for further inquiry. In contrast, modern inquiry is processional, not episodic.

Orthodoxy, in design, is positivistic. It addresses what is, not what ought to be.[13] Since this matter is discussed at length in a later chapter, it will suffice here to note that inquiry cannot be purposive *and* positivistic. To conceive a problem is to perceive a difference between is and ought, that is, to apply value theory embodying normative prin-ciples. Orthodoxy, in application, *is* normative, the protests of its advocates to the contrary notwithstanding.

Finally, the examination of price phenomena in markets is the primary inquiry interest of orthodox capitalists; it normally defines the scope of their inquiry. The case is built on the assumptions of unlimited wants and limited means to satisfy wants; the price system becomes the

12. Overton Taylor, *History of Economic Thought*, McGraw-Hill Book Co., Inc., New York, 1960, pp. 4-5.

13. It is true, of course, that neoclassical welfare economics (e.g., Paretian Optimality) is addressed to normative questions. But it involves no abandonment of utility as the normative principle.

allocative instrument to distribute limited means to unlimited ends. The focus, then, is on pricing in markets; the price system accomplishes the allocation. While such matters are, of course, important, political economy must include many additional factors which bear on the production and distribution of real income—technology, private and public power, motivations and their origin and character, nonmarket institutions, and the like.

In sum, orthodox inquiry tends to be overly rationalistic, episodic rather than evolutionary, and positivistic rather than normativistic. It is generally limited to market phenomena in its sweep and applications and is concerned with approaches to or departures from a natural order political economy. It will not suffice as a belief system in these revolutionary times.

Marxism

Marx and Engels struggled mightily also to construct a comprehensive view of the human condition wholly on what they conceived to be scientific grounds. They rejected equally the fatalistic contentions that human affairs were not rationally examinable and the idealistic contentions that these human affairs were explainable in supernatural, non-materialistic terms. They believed that they had found in the construct of the dialectic the master logical and analytical tool with which to pursue inquiry into the problems of providing the material means of life.

The specific idea of the dialectic—that reality is exhibited as a constantly unfolding process of contradiction and resolution—was, as is generally known, not original with Marx and Engels. They drew on Hegel for this construct, although the germ of the idea, evidently, is traceable to the Greeks.

The dialectic consists of a fixed, three-phase pattern which relates items in sequence. It is presumed to constitute a method of logical analysis superior to that of formal or Aristotelian syllogistic reasoning alone. The dialectic (where necessary buttressed by formal logic) is the design for inquiry. Phenomena occur in processional form; the dialectic explains that process. ". . . all nature, from the smallest thing to the biggest, from grains of sand to suns, from protista to man, has its existence in eternal coming into being and going out of being, in ceaseless flux, in unresting motion and change." [14]

The dialectic consists of an assertion or stipulation of an item or condition—the thesis; the self-generation of an opposite or contrary stipulation or assertion—the antithesis; and the consequent stipulation or assertion which incorporates the "truth" of the thesis and the antithesis into a synthesis. When the new synthesis is formed and subjected

14. Engels, "Introduction to *Dialectics of Nature*," in Marx & Engels, *Selected Works*, Vol. II, Foreign Languages Publishing House, Moscow, 1958, p. 71.

to examination, it constitutes a new thesis, is discovered to be "deficient," prompting the formation of a contradictory premise or condition—its antithesis, which leads necessarily to a new synthesis which "resolves" the contradiction.

To illustrate, in Marxism, economic classes in societies employing private property will stand in dialectical opposition to each other. The feudal conflict between lords (thesis) and serfs (antithesis) evolves into a synthesis, the emergent bourgeoisie or capitalists. The bourgeoisie come to constitute a thesis standing in dialectical conflict with the proletarian workers as an antithesis. This conflict is ultimately resolved through the communist revolution and the appearance of a state under the aegis of the dictatorship of the proletariat, the new synthesis.

The dialectical movement, however, is not merely a processional or mechanical affair; clearly explicit is the contention that each new synthesis is a "progressive" shift to a "higher" or "truer" state, condition, or premise, than was characteristic of either the thesis or the antithesis. This dialectical process is thought to characterize "That process of conflict and reconciliation which goes on within reality itself, and within human thought about reality."[15] Or again, "dialectics is nothing more than the science of the general laws of motion and development of Nature, human society, and thought."[16]

Marxists, of course, believe that the significance of acquiring knowledge through dialectical methods is to guide human action. Scientific laws, derived dialectically, should be regarded as guides for study and conduct. "Communism proceeds not from principle, but from facts. It is no doctrine, but a movement."[17]

The Marxist inquiry mode suffers from four fundamental flaws: First, dialecticism, too, has a rationalistic cast. The dialectic is not an inductive instrument through which to discover the complexity of causal relations and from which to distill and sustain observed regularities of experience; it is, on the contrary, a rationalistic affirmation of conflict in phenomena which is imposed on data to account, allegedly, for occurrences.

The dialectic makes a master principle of the idea of contradiction. All phenomena in nature and society are presumed to stand inherently, naturally, continuously in conflictual relations.[18] That is *basic* to the dialectic. Differences in nature, ideas, and behavior exist, of course, but

15. R. N. Carew Hunt, *Theory and Practice of Communism*, Macmillan, New York, 1957, p. 20.

16. Engels, quoted by H. B. Mayo in *Introduction to Marxist Theory*, Oxford University Press, New York, 1960, p. 47.

17. Engels, quoted by V. Venable, *Human Nature: The Marxian View*, World Publishing Co., New York, 1966, p. 39.

18. For example, note the following comment of Marx: "In our days everything seems pregnant with its contrary. Machinery, gifted with the wonderful power of shorten-

the insistence on a lock-step, triadic confrontation and resolution of such differences in a dialectical manner is a matter of sheer conjecture. The dialectical process is not a vehicle of inquiry for juxtaposing hypotheses and observed evidence to determine correspondence between theory and fact. Rather, it is a mechanism which is accepted a priori and unilaterally applied to order events in a manner which appears to serve the preconceived purposes of the user.

Second, the dialectic approach to inquiry is a monistic—single cause—route. It appears as one version of the "nothing-else-but" view. Marxists insist on a kind of reductionism. That is, observable change can all be reduced to a singular analytical account. All change, all behavior, all history, and all nature are to be accounted for by dialectical analysis of inherent contradiction. This is not a credible position.

Third, dialecticism tends to become a kind of dogma in the minds of many Marxists. Once fashioned, the dialectic is not regarded thereafter as a provisional product of the evolving epistemology of reflective inquiry; there appears to be no serious *further* concern with inquiry into the principles of inquiry that might threaten the inclusiveness and relevance of the dialectic. The dialectic becomes an article of faith as far removed from criticism as any other absolute.[19] As a consequence, its pertinence is questionable.

Finally, the dialectical model of inquiry leads to what Thorstein Veblen called a "final term"—a teleologically defined end. That is, the spiral-like sequence of thesis, antithesis, and synthesis supposedly yields "progression," "improvement," or greater "truth." Dialectical analysis connotes unfolding maturations; it implies inherent purpose and design beyond discretionary control and has a predeterministic flavor. Its application to history generates the "law of motion" of society which culminates, willy-nilly, in communism. Dialecticism does not *contain* a social-value principle; it implies the need for one, as Marxists are prone to make moral judgments utilizing criteria. But dialecticism is not an inquiry tool with which one can identify or appraise criteria of judgment.

ing and fructifying human labour, we behold starving and overworking it. The newfangled sources of wealth, by some strange weird spell, are turned into sources of want. The victories of art seem bought by the loss of character. At the same pace that mankind masters nature, man seems to become enslaved to other men or to his own infamy. Even the pure light of science seems unable to shine but on the dark background of ignorance. . . . This antagonism between modern industry and science on the one hand, modern misery and dissolution on the other hand; this antagonism between the productive powers, and the social relations of our epoch is a fact, palpable, overwhelming, and not to be controverted." Karl Marx, "Speech at the Anniversary of the *People's Paper*," in Marx & Engels, *Selected Works*, Vol. I, op. cit., pp. 359-60.

19. This observation would not apply to some latterday neo-Marxists or Marxist Humanists. See, e.g., "Radical Paradigms in Economics," *Review of Radical Political Economics*, Vol. III, No. 2, July, 1971.

Fascism

Inquiry for the latterday fascists tends primarily to be an affirmation of an adamant spiritualistic or mystic intuitionism (Italian fascism) or of feelings or instincts (German fascism). Fascists in quest of "knowledge" find both common sense and science of some use but insufficient. Through recourse to Hegelian idealism or primitive mysticism—sentimental feelings or "thought" freed from ties to experience—fascists add to common sense and science to determine what is "known." Fascists abandon tests of logical consistency and evidential demonstrability in what is asserted to be true.

Instead, knowledge ascription is a function of the status and power of leaders. What matters is not what is said (or on what facts or assumptions it rests), but who says it. Uses of idealism, primitive Darwinism, spiritualism, intuitionism, and mysticism are but sentimental trappings to cloak the otherwise naked fact that truth is determined by authoritarian assertion.

It can come as no surprise, then, that a fascist political economy built on and given "credence" by claims to "special" knowledge of leaders would be characterized by the acquisition and retention of totalitarian political control and by the conversion of the economy into a hierarchical, corporatist order in which production and distribution are intended to serve the messianic mission of the elite leadership of the state.

The characterization of fascism as a "retreat from reason" (Lancelot Hogben) is proper. Fascism means action governed by sentiment and duty in the service of fascist ends. Inquiry is converted into propagandistic apologetics; education, into indoctrination; reflection, into discriminatory mysticism. No other ism-ideology is so completely devoid of reasoned credibility.

If the circumstances spawning contemporary revolutionary unrest are to be approached productively and constructively, a model of social, political, and economic inquiry markedly different from the foregoing unacceptable positions must be employed. We seek, then, a provisional formulation on which to ground a normative theory of political economy.

IV. NATURE OF SOCIAL INQUIRY

Social inquiry, we affirmed above, is initiated to remove doubt about existing patterns of thinking and acting. In brief, social inquiry is undertaken to assist with the continuing task of resolving social problems.

Thus the object of this inquiry is and must be the existential social process, including prominently the ideas and institutions governing the determination and administration of public policy and the resolution of conflict (politics) and the production and distribution of real income (economics).

This universe of interest for social inquiry posits an existential world of reality involving both person-person and person-thing relations. Social inquiry is addressed mainly to the former. This existential world is materialistic, but people, with their cognitive and reflective capacities, are a part of this existential universe even as is the physical nonhuman environment. People are in constant interaction with this social process of which they are a part. An individual is no external observer; he or she is a participant-observer employing his or her developing reflective and evaluative capacities on the phenomena sensory perception discloses. The "natural order" is not "out there" in a simplistic sense, discrete, apart from human beings, observed by human beings. As Hannah Arendt reminds us, men and women themselves are engaged in creating, in some measure, the existential universe with which they are in constant interaction, the universe which, therefore, conditions their own emergence and development. Says she,

> In addition to the conditions under which life is given to man on earth, and partly out of them, men constantly create their own, self-made conditions, which, their human origin and their variability notwithstanding, possess the same conditioning power as natural things. Whatever touches or enters into a sustained relationship with human life immediately assumes the character of a condition of human existence. This is why men, no matter what they do, are always conditioned beings. Whatever enters the human world of its own accord or is drawn into it by human effort becomes a part of the human condition.[20]

The invocation of social inquiry, the setting in deliberate motion of these perceptive, cognitive, reflective, and evaluative capacities seeking removal of doubt, is directed to a quest for that which threatens the reasoned quality and continuity of the social process, that is, that which has become normatively problematic. Thus the basic purpose of social inquiry is to explore the existential reality of real human problems. Purposive inquiry is value-laden.

Social inquiry, so conceived, produces explanation drawn in cause-effect terms, in means-consequences terms, in terms which permit one to ask: "If this, then will this follow?" "What circumstances caused this to happen?" "How do you account for the fact that . . .?" "What will the consequences of their actions be?" These are queries requesting causal accounting. If a major tax increase is introduced, then will the rise in the price level be slowed? Since eighteen-year-olds have been given the franchise, has more effective political participation by the young resulted? If economic competition between blacks and whites for jobs were reduced through expanded public employment, then would urban race relations improve? If abortion were legalized in all fifty states, would the national rate of population growth be reduced or reversed?

20. Hannah Arendt, *The Human Condition*, University of Chicago Press, Chicago, 1959, p. 9.

Inquiry, when successful, provides some measure of capacity to explain and predict the course of events; and, with understanding and judgment, a degree of control may be or become possible. Control does not, of course, follow from explanation (we can for the most part explain the movement of stars, but we cannot control them); but the capacity to account for and to anticipate accurately may permit control. As an illustration, the tax cut of 1964, a policy application of the "new economics," did, as expected, contribute significantly to an increase in the gross national product, an increase in the rate of economic growth, and to a modest reduction in unemployment. (Would comparable action produce similar results again?) But were there other consequences which were not wholly foreseen? What, for example, were the costs in increased environmental pollution resulting from this increased growth? In the early 1970s, President Nixon's Phase I, II, III, and IV direct controls did slow the rate of inflation for a time, especially Phase II. But the basic causes of inflation were not well understood nor responded to. Thus new questions are posed; new problems may indeed be created.

But the basic inquiry concern of seeking to account in causal terms is continuous. If understanding is achieved, prediction is possible, and the potential for control results; then the queries shift to those having to do with *who* exercises control, for what purposes, with what consequences, and with what avenues for revision of consequences. The possibility of control invites its use. Assuring its use on rationally normative grounds with consequences known and accepted is no idle concern nor small task. Hazards of misuse notwithstanding, the community, rightly, in its more sober moments, will support inquiry because of its recognition of the need for new knowledge for problem-solving purposes.

Social inquiry is a process of truth-seeking in which there is no "final term," no ultimate conclusion after which further inquiry is not needed or contemplated. On the contrary, inquiry begins for an individual with the emergence of doubt; continues through the formulation and consideration of the probable causes of doubt; and culminates, provisionally, in the selection of the explanation or account which most adequately and completely discloses the causal elements, the means-consequence connections, involved. Hypotheses—preliminary, temporarily conjectural, plausible notions of causal connections—are formed as the vehicles of explanation. They serve as conceptual tools to guide the inquiry process. The formulation of hypothetical explanations is generally considered to be the most creative aspect of inquiry. Certainly none is more important.

The function of hypotheses in guiding inquiry receives extensive treatment in John Dewey's analysis of the inquiry process. At one point he observes,

The history of science, as an exemplification of the method of inquiry, shows that the verifiability (as positivism understands it) of hypotheses is not nearly as important as is their directive power. As a broad statement, no important scientific hypothesis has ever been verified in the form in which it was originally presented nor without very considerable revisions and modifications. The justification of such hypotheses has lain in their power to direct new orders of experimental observation and to open up new problems and new fields of subject-matter. In doing these things, they have not only provided new facts but have often radically altered what were previously taken to be facts.[21]

In passing it is important to observe that the posing of hypotheses, though critical and creative, may also be somewhat hazardous. In the analysis of some problem areas, the formulation of hypotheses which are thought significantly to imperil established power centers in the culture may lead those threatened (or who believe themselves to be threatened) to take measures to suppress such inquiries. Although in the nature of the cases, unquestionable proof would be most difficult to establish, there is good reason to believe that, for example, the investigators of the extent of monopoly in the sulphur industry,[22] the conditions of bracero field labor in California,[23] and the influence of the China Lobby on United States foreign policy in the Far East,[24] respectively have experienced or witnessed vigorous resistance to or suppression of their work, its publication, and/or its distribution.

Social inquiry is a process in a related sense. The operational activity of scholarly inquiry requires that the investigator constantly moves conceptually between the formulated hypothetical account and the evidences which it purports to explain. In this process of relating theory and fact, neither has any prior standing of pre-eminence or priority. In contrast, empiricism is deferential to inductive inference; rationalism is deferential to deductive inference. We suggest that each procedure is an integral part of the kind of thinking which leads to reliable knowledge (see figure 2-1).

Theory tells one which facts to gather and how to arrange them for analysis. Facts are mute; they do *not* speak for themselves. When facts are disclosed which a theory cannot accommodate, then the theory must be revised if it is to continue to be relevant as an explanation. To take an obvious example, the traditional affirmation (theory) that a capitalistic economy automatically generates full employment and distributes income through the market in equitable shares did not fit the facts of the Great Depression in England and America. Lord Keynes formulated

21. John Dewey, *Logic: The Theory of Inquiry*, Henry Holt, New York, 1938, p. 519.
22. Robert H. Montgomery, *The Brimstone Game*, Vanguard Press, New York, 1940.
23. Henry Anderson, *A Harvest of Loneliness*, Citizens for Farm Labor, Berkeley, 1964.
24. Ross Koen, *The China Lobby*, Macmillan Co., New York, 1960. New edition: Harper & Row, New York, 1974. See also, Judith Coburn, "Asian Scholars and Government," in Edward Friedman and Mark Selden (eds.), *America's Asia: Dissenting Essays on Asian-American Relations*, Random House/Vintage, New York, 1971, p. 105n.

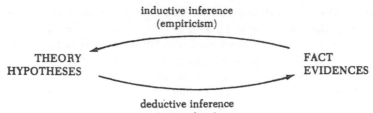

inductive inference
(empiricism)

THEORY   FACT
HYPOTHESES   EVIDENCES

deductive inference
(rationalism)

Search for reliable knowledge requires
both inductive and deductive procedures.

Figure 2-1   Relating Theory and Fact

a new "General Theory" which explained the probabilities under capitalism of an underemployment equilibrium, and Lady Rhys Williams and others moved beyond the narrow assumptions underlying the orthodox analysis of income distribution to anticipate minimum income guarantees. [25]

Thus, what are commonly called inductive and deductive methods (and factual and theoretical material) are *both* required for inquiry. It is helpful to think of the inquirer as continuously engaged in reviewing hypothetical accounts to determine the one (or more likely the combination of two or more) which most completely and simply explains the phenomena under study. Indeed, he or she must continuously make choices of what is relevant, what is pertinent, and which, finally, of competing accounts is the "better." Inquiry is then a process of successive efforts (choices) at more precise and more definitive formulations of explanatory theories which are logically consistent and evidentially grounded. For example, recall the last "who-done-it" you saw or read. Note the successive consideration and rejection of those who might have been responsible for the crime, as the quest for the "guilty party" proceeds. The respective "leads" are, in this context, hypotheses. At the end, you were presented with the evidence *plus* the explanation which *proves* that the "little old lady in tennis shoes" was the guilty one. Regrettably, of course, most inquiry is neither so simple, nor so fictional.

V.   OUTCOMES OF INQUIRY

What are the outcomes of social inquiry? Perhaps Gregor would say "truth ascription"; Dewey often used the expression "warranted assertibility" [26] to denote the fruits of inquiry. We join Dewey in the conten-

25. John Maynard Keynes, *The General Theory of Employment Interest and Money*, Harcourt, Brace & Co., New York, 1936; Lady Rhys Williams, *Something To Look Forward To*. MacDonald and Co., London, 1943.
26. John Dewey, *Logic: The Theory of Inquiry*, Henry Holt and Co., New York, 1938, p. 7 & passim.

tion that the outcome of social inquiry of the kind discussed here is tentative truth. It offers justification on which to assert that such-and-such is, given the evidence, an adequate account in causal terms. The bacterial theory of disease, Keynes' theory of income and employment, the theory of environmental conditioning (culture concept), the theory of biological evolution, are tentative truths. Such truths are sufficiently firmly established to be incorporated into subsequent inquiry; but they are not so firmly set as to be beyond further consideration and modification or even abandonment should subsequent inquiry so require.

In a related sense, the outcome of inquiry is an explanation which exhibits *over time* its continuing capacity to explain and predict in causal terms. Successful inquiry permits the placement of an item in a cause-effect sequence of which it is determined to be a part. There is no reliable knowledge unrelated or unhooked to other knowledge. Truth and continuity are virtually synonyms in this sense.

Such a view, of course, is all very disturbing to anyone who has hung his ego, his intellect, or his career on one or another alleged eternal verity: the law of supply and demand, the law of motion of society, the biological inferiority of non-Caucasians, or the ability of technology to solve all ecology problems.

Successful inquiry permits the provisional removal of doubt. In virtually all cases, it will have generated other doubts, raised other questions, which the investigator comes to see as significant. Indeed, his or her own sense of pertinence will no doubt have undergone revision.

Again, inquiry is a continuing process; it generates a knowledge continuum. The aggregation of all such outcomes of inquiry constitutes the fund of reliable knowledge upon which the human community draws continuously in quest of insight and guidance. Because of the character of the inquiry processes themselves, this knowledge continuum has a kind of self-generative and self-corrective quality. In the process of combining conceptual tools, of generating new hypotheses based on existing knowledge, the adequacy of individual components of that fund is checked anew and, if necessary, revised or recast. The knowledge continuum grows at a seemingly exponential rate (see figure 2-2).

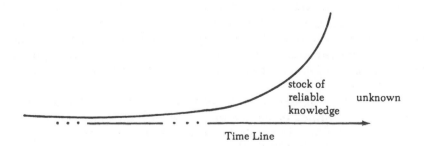

Figure 2-2   Exponential Growth in Knowledge Continuum

We share, then, a common, a communal stock of knowledge. No nation, race, or group has a monopoly either on the generation of knowledge or upon its use. Indeed, without shared insight and inference, that fund of knowledge can neither be sustained nor augmented. All new knowledge consists of new arrangements or combinations of existing items of knowledge. All efforts at censorship, all efforts to hold elements of knowledge secret by denying the opportunity for creating new combinations, abort the inquiry process at its most vulnerable point. No teleological (implying final causes), metaphysical (beyond experience), or occult forces need be called upon to explain such knowledge. Neither divine revelation, august authority, mystic intuition, nor common old horse sense offers an alternative source of reliable knowledge to and for the community. Except, of course, for the human complement itself, the totality of this fund of knowledge constitutes the human community's most basic and precious resource.

Clearly, we are now able to see why it is that social inquiry continuously undermines established· belief and behavior. Deliberate inquiry of the kind described *is* an assault on the mythologies, the simple solutions, the half-truths, the folk wisdom, the eternal verities, the intuited certainties, and the ism-ideologies which men and women have evolved to cover over their gaping areas of ignorance. As the areas of the known expand, so also necessarily do the areas of the unknown, because the act of acquiring knowledge discloses new areas of ignorance to which inquiry may be directed. Intractable problems, the incidences of which cannot be avoided, must be faced. That is why there is, and will continue to be, revolutionary unrest and demands for substantial social and economic change. Serious and extensive inquiry into the several aspects of the "conventional wisdom," East and West, North and South, is mandatory.

Neither doubt nor problems would arise if all that constitutes the status quo here and abroad in belief and behavior were manifestly satisfactory. If there were no serious aberrations in the economic process (inflation *and* unemployment), no "imbecile institutions" in the political process (electoral college, excessive classification of information), no impediments to the growth of discretionary dignity, no denial of access of minorities and women to an adequate education in order "to preserve quality education," no threat to the continuity of human life from air and water pollution; then inquiry would be less urgent, perhaps. Inquiry is needed and is threatening because it *does* raise questions about the wisdom and propriety of doing and thinking as we have become accustomed.

Finally, the scope of social inquiry, so conceived, obviously cannot rationally be confined or limited to market phenomena, economic class struggles, or militant racial or national aggrandizement. Inquiry purposely directed to problem solving must have its perimeters set (and reset) to include the actual determinants of the problems under study. As the quest for "conjugate correspondence"[27] between theory and fact proceeds and guiding hypotheses are fashioned and revised, the scope of inquiry will be modified as is required to disclose the actual existential determinants involved. The perimeters for inquiry *cannot* logically be set a priori and retained inviolate without making the inquiry sterile or trivial or both.

Neither can the scope of inquiry be limited to positivistic matters solely. Increasingly apparent is the recognition that inquiry must extend to include normative as well as positive elements. Not only must the fact-theory dichotomy be abandoned as corruptive and misleading in inquiry, so also must the positive-normative dichotomy be abandoned. That is, inquiry must extend to include "what ought" as well as "what is." The perception of a problem requires the application of value theory—of normative analysis. The nature and warrantability of that perception must also be included in inquiry. Otherwise, social inquiry may quickly degenerate into irrelevancy or apologia. We return to these vital normative concerns below.

An equally significant and troublesome area of underlying assumptions, in addition to views on knowledge and reality, is the social inquirer's view of human nature. Here, too, may be found a striking contrast between beliefs of yesterday's isms and that of a normative and evolutionary theory of political economy. Attention is next directed, then, to people as conditioned beings.

27. John Dewey, *Logic: The Theory of Inquiry*, Henry Holt and Co., New York, 1938, p. 491.

Chapter 3

HUMAN NATURE AND CONDUCT

Those who argue that social and moral reform is impossible on the ground that the Old Adam of human nature remains forever the same, attribute . . . to native activities the permanence and inertia that in truth belongs only to acquired customs.

JOHN DEWEY*

. . . the conditions of human existence—life itself, natality and mortality, worldliness, plurality, and the earth—can never "explain" what we are or answer the question of who we are for the simple reason that they never condition us absolutely.

HANNAH ARENDT**

*John Dewey, *Human Nature and Conduct*, Modern Library, Random House, New York, 1930, p. 109.
**Hannah Arendt, *The Human Condition*, University of Chicago, Chicago, 1958, p. 11.

Every student has heard many times one or more of the following kinds of glib, cliché-like comments: "Everybody has his price." "Africans are incapable of self-government." "'Negras' prefer to live with their own kind." "Lots of poor women have kids just to stay on welfare." What all of these comments have in common is the fact that they reflect the use (perhaps unconscious use) of assumptions about people, their motivations, their nature, and their potential or lack of it. They reflect also, respectively, views held about areas of current revolutionary unrest.

More generally, it is virtually impossible for social, political, or economic problems to be perceived or analyzed, nor remedial policy to be formed without affirming, implicitly or explicitly, views about human nature. In the present day of mounting pressures for substantial, even radical, social and economic change, protagonists on all sides have been exchanging charges and countercharges using a verbal currency containing frequently unflattering contentions about motivation, ancestry, inherent worth, or mental capacity of persons with whom they differ. A few years ago, police officers were "fascist pigs," long-haired youths were "degenerate hippies," governmental critics were "effete snobs," Democrats were "pointy-headed liberals," and businessmen were "filthy profiteers." More recently, conservationists became "eco-freaks" and presidential advisors were seen as "neanderthal types."

One of several purposes in writing this book was to contribute as much as possible to the needed abandonment of language and constructs which "put down" others on the basis of categorical stereotypes, denigrating their status and worth as people. Accordingly, we now examine some underlying assumptions about people and their natures.

I.   CLICHES AND STEREOTYPES

Look again to the areas of revolutionary unrest:

Consider the productivity revolution. People say, "You can't do anything about poverty; the poor are congenitally lazy, shiftless, and unwilling to work even if they had a chance." Others used to say, "The Russians will never have an industrial economy; their people are incapable of learning to develop and apply technology to industry and agriculture." Or again, "It is human nature to get as much as you can for as little as you can."

Consider the participatory revolution. People say, "We should not have given the political franchise to the eighteen-year-olds; they are too immature to use it wisely." Similar allegations, of course, were made earlier about the propertyless, blacks, and females. Others say, "Democracy is impossible; people naturally require a leader to control their emotional and irrational impulses." Or again, "Agitation and marching in the streets merely reflect the innate anarchistic tendencies of the young."

Consider the racial and sexual revolutions. People say, "Everybody knows that blacks have great athletic and sexual prowess." "Obviously, in crises, women are less analytical and more emotional than men." Others say, "The oriental mind is different; Asians don't value human life as we do." Or again, "Show me one major or significant contribution to the arts and sciences or to civilization made by a black, brown, or red man!"

Consider the ecological crisis. People say, "You will never control population. The poor have most of the babies because they have nothing else to do." Others say, "You will not get the environment cleaned up until somebody figures out a way to make a bunch of money out of it." Or again, "People care only about themselves; they don't give a damn about somebody else's having to drink bad water or being able to see the air he or she breathes."

In every case, the contentions articulated in these four areas rest upon assumptions about people and their nature. In the following analysis we explore some of these views.

There is no pretense here to delve deeply into psychological analysis as such. Rather, the purpose is to bring out a view of human beings and their nature which is, we think, generally compatible with much modern psychology and to contrast it with the underlying assumptions of human nature in the ism-ideologies. Taken up first are ideological assumptions about people.

II.   ISMS AND PSYCHOLOGICAL CREEDS

Because, as the foregoing suggests, assumptions about human nature permeate and undergird all inquiry in political economy, the ism-ideologists' psychological creeds are of special significance. The ism-ideologies' respective claims to pertinence hang in part on the adequacy of their views of human nature.

Capitalism

In the ideology of capitalism, the core view of people is clear and consistently applied. It is the belief that people, when they are acting rationally and naturally, seek consistently to maximize their satisfaction, directly as consumers or indirectly as profit seekers. The profit motive, so-called, is nothing more than a contention that individuals will seek to maximize their money income in order to be able to maximize their satisfaction. This construct is at bottom hedonistic and utilitarian.

This psychological creed of orthodoxy, as viewed by Harry Girvetz, consists of four tenets or articles: egoism (hedonism), intellectualism (rationalism), quietism, and atomism. [1] Egoism is the contention that

---

1. Harry K. Girvetz, *The Evolution of Liberalism*, Collier Books, New York, 1963, Chapters 1 & 2.

people are self-seeking, self-serving, pleasure-pursuing organisms. Emergent from the Hobbes, Locke, and Bentham tradition, the principle of hedonism is central. "Nature," says Bentham, "has placed mankind under the governance of two sovereign masters, pain and pleasure."[2] Although in twentieth-century mainstream orthodoxy terms like *hedonism* and *hedonistic calculus* have for the most part been abandoned, maximizing utility is still regarded as the major motivation of behavior in political economy.

Intellectualism is the contention that people are rational beings. Men and women are uniquely endowed with the capacity to take stock, to weigh alternatives, to calculate satisfactions, and to seek congruity with the naturalistic universe. If the quest for pleasure is the initiating element, reason operates to direct the quest. "Self-love is cool; self-interest is enlightened; reason is at the controls."[3] The *meaning* of rationality for the orthodox is the maximization of utility and the minimization of disutility.

Quietism affirms that not only is a person egoistic or rationalistic; one is also fundamentally inactive or passive. People are naturally quiescent; they must be prodded or baited into activity. As in the older stimulus-response analysis, quietism affirms that people must be enticed to participate, to work, to take action. The normal state is one of stable equilibrium; unless disturbed, that state is retained. The attribution to people of inherent indolence and laziness rests on this assumption.

Atomism, finally, is the contention that individuals are discrete, homogeneous, *a*social beings. Society consists of atomistic individuals; it is an aggregation, not a community. The individual is original and given; society is an arrangement of convenience; participation does not affect one's nature. "Men . . . in a state of society, are still men; their actions and passions are obedient to the laws of individual human nature."[4] The capitalist deference to individualism rests in part on this premise.

Perhaps no one has characterized the orthodox view of human nature with greater wit, acidity, and clarity than Thorstein Veblen. In a celebrated passage, he says,

> . . . the human material is conceived in hedonistic terms . . . in terms of a passive and substantially inert and immutably given human nature. . . . The hedonistic conception of man is that of a lightning calculator of pleasure and pains, who oscillates like a homogeneous globule of desire of happiness under the impulse of stimuli that shift him about the area, but leave him intact. He has neither antecedent nor consequent. He is isolated,

2. Quoted in Eli Halevy, *The Rise of Philosophic Radicalism*, Beacon Press, Boston, 1955, p. 26.
3. Harry Girvetz, *The Evolution of Liberalism*, op. cit., p. 35.
4. John Stuart Mill, quoted by Harry Girvetz, *The Evolution of Liberalism*, op. cit., p. 43.

definitive, human datum, in stable equilibrium except for the buffets of the impinging forces that displace him in one direction or another.[5]

The capitalist psychological creed is now archaic and of doubtful pertinence for inquiry. The tenet of egoism (hedonism) is truistic and tautological. To contend that *all* economic behavior is in pursuit of utility maximization is to deprive the principle of any explanatory power whatsoever. No individual act is separable from any other. One is saying only that people are motivated—a truism. To assume at the outset (utility maximization) what inquiry is to explain (human behavior) is to offer a tautology; circular reasoning deprives it of meaning.

The tenet of intellectualism (rationalism) forces the narrowing of the meaning of rationality to maximizing utility and thus into conformity with the egoistic tenet. As we noted above, rationality has a broader meaning— the *general* perception of means-consequence relations. To act otherwise than to maximize profits is to act irrationally? Hardly. Human motivation is much more complex, including that in economic realms, than that allowed for by orthodoxy. The profit motive is an acquired motivation where it occurs at all. To characterize other motivations as irrational or nonrational is inadmissible.

The tenet of quietism is patently false. A person is by nature active, not passive. People are participating organisms. People are in constant interaction with the environment, transforming it and being transformed by it. People are not inert. There is no stable equilibrium for the living.

The tenet of atomism is also patently false. People are products of culture; they are social beings. Since the development of the culture concept over the last century, no credibility can be given to atomism. People do not have original or given tastes; these are acquired in the context of culture. Life is developmental, evolutionary, and social; it is not rigid, static, and individual. The capitalist psychological creed diverts attention from the substantive question of motivations—their character and their consequences.

Marxism

The Marxists see human nature differently. They reject utility maximization (via Bentham) because it is not a historically grounded premise and because of its deference to English bourgeois traits. It is time and culture bound.

In contrast, Marx and Engels, employing dialectical materialism, argue that a person, in both the biological and the cultural sense, is an organism in the process of becoming, of being transformed. A person is a producer and a product of a *particular* kind of environmental conditioning. People create their own natures through *labor*. Human

5. Thorstein Veblen, *The Place of Science*, Russell & Russell, New York, 1961, p. 73.

nature changes over time in consequence of the activity of labor in the context of its use. And the activity of labor and the context of its use are set in and by the successive modes of production and exchange, from primitive communism through feudalism to capitalism. A new order, socialism, followed by communism, will create "new men" (and women) because these Marxist ism epochs will exhibit markedly different settings for the conduct of labor.

Men and women must labor to live. People, by *producing* their material means of life and experience, distinguish themselves from other life forms. "The animal merely *uses* external nature, and brings about changes in it simply by his presence; man by his changes makes it serve his ends, *masters* it." [6] People create their own nature by engaging in productive labor. Within the constraints imposed by Marx's "law of motion" (theory of history), they have a volitional role.

But since the character of labor engaged in is set by the mode of production and exchange, and since conflict is inherent in the mode itself, it is class membership that defines labor roles. [7] Accordingly, it is economic class that defines human nature.

> It is classes which . . . determine in considerable measure the character of the natural environment into which an individual is born. It is classes which set the pattern of his social environment. It is classes which, by assigning him a specific role in the division of labour, determine the manner in which he will deal with that environment. It is classes which, in their revolutionary struggles, overthrow productive systems, transform ownership relations, establish new classes, new divisions of labour, and thus *change* human nature. Thus . . . one may say with perfect faithfulness to the full meaning of historical materialism, that it is classes which have *made* human nature. [8]

Hence, for Marxists, it is the character of a person's employment, one's work experience, as defined for him or her by the economic class structure, which is fundamentally determinant of human nature in the social or cultural sense. Alienation of the workers from their product, their peers, their communities, and themselves is a product of class determination of human nature. Only movement toward socialism and

6. Engels, quoted by Vernon Venable, *Human Nature: The Marxian View*, Meridian Books/World Publishing Co., New York, 1966, p. 69.
7. Conflict within the mode is between the "forces of production" and the "relations of production." "Forces" include materials on which to work, tools with which to work, laborers with skills, and institutions to correlate behavior in use of tools and materials. "Relations" are old institutions of the "forces." In the capitalist epoch, "relations" are mostly private-property institutions. The proletariat as a class is exclusively identified with the "forces of production"; the bourgeoisie as a class is exclusively identified with the "relations of production."
8. Vernon Venable, *Human Nature: The Marxian View*, op. cit., p. 120.

communism can end alienation by removing the class-based division of labor of which alienation is a consequence.

In brief assessment, we can concur in the Marxian emphasis on malleability and evolutionary development of the human organism in general, upon the affirmation of human volition insofar as they allow for it, and in their descriptive commentary on the phenomena of alienation.

But we must reject their reductionism, which overemphasizes class identification and occupational connections as the primary conditioners of human nature. Not all influences, conditioners, are reducible to the economic connection. Scores of other significant kinds of experience and interaction also are involved. Operational conditioners may well include patriotic, tribal, or group loyalties; age, sex, or status considerations; racial, cultural, or lingual traditions; religious commitments or convictions; psychological influences; divergent child-rearing patterns; as well as or in lieu of the impact of occupational conditioners. The myopic focus on class influence, moreover, blanks out inquiry into other sorts of connections between culture and personality, culture and behavior, and culture and attitudes.

Disclaimers notwithstanding, the *range* of volition or choice allowed by Marxists in changing conditions to change human nature is comparatively small. In their view, human decisions can change the pace or rate of change; they cannot modify its course or direction. The "law of motion of society" delimits how much people can decide.

Finally, the Marxist theory of human nature contains an implicit normative principle which clearly elevates the role, labor, and class of the proletariat as superior to that of the bourgeoisie. The proletariat are the "good guys"; the bourgeoisie are the "bad guys." Here, class membership is taken as a sufficient index of human worth. [9] This amounts to a discriminatory, reductionistic stereotyping and cliché-dismissal as destructive in its universe of applications as racism and sexism are elsewhere.

Fascism

The ideology of fascism turns an innocent kid's game of "King of the Mountain"—in which the object is to scramble to the top of a mound and fend off all challengers—into an often manic, consuming life struggle of horrendous import for individuals and society. The fascist view of human nature posits an organism in ceaseless struggle in which one's own emergence and elevation is contingent upon the submergence, subjection, or subjugation of others.

9. An example of the use of class membership as an index of worth is reported by Ross H. Munro, "China's Despised and Suffering Sub-Class," *San Francisco Chronicle*, Oct. 21, 1977, p. 12.

The measures or tests for determining who remains "King of the Mountain" vary some among ideologists of fascism. Expressly and overtly, the customary tests have to do with race, ethnicity, sex, and/or national origin. Implicitly, and in a sense, ultimately, the test is more pragmatic: The capacity (military power, police power, intrigue, coercion, public lies, etc.) to stay on top of the mound is a sufficient index of merit. The fact of attainment of power becomes a sufficient justification for its exercise. Life for the fascists is an unending, no-quarter-given, struggle. Accepting this as fact, fascists determine on discriminatory grounds who is really worthy of surviving in the struggle and on what terms.

The fascists offer an essentially static view of human nature. Basically, people have a "spiritual existence," the character of which is determined by their identification on grounds of race, ethnicity, sex, or national origin and by their placement in a hierarchical ordering which identifies their significance with that of the state and especially with its leaders. We are offered a model of a person as an action-inclined, sentimentally committed, duty-observing, and politically submerged organism. Placement and worth are genetically defined on discriminatory grounds. Fascism affirms "the fertilizing, beneficient [sic] and unassailable inequality of men." [10]

At the hands of German fascists, human nature, in addition, becomes a matter of environmental and racial determinism. For class struggle, fascists substitute race struggle. Exploiting a primitive Darwinism, fascists elevate struggle to an overriding principle. "All life is bound up in three theses: Struggle is the father of all things, virtue lies in blood, leadership is primary and decisive." [11] Hitler therewith affirms the essence of fascism.

Fascists thus assert that the natural, given, and therefore the expected prime mover of people is coercive force. Apply it vigorously or submit to its being applied. People are at your throat or at your feet. "The fundamental motif through all the centuries has been the principle that force and power are the determining factors. All development is struggle. Only force rules. Force is the first law." [12] The "human condition" is therefore one of domination or submission sustained by repression. Life is an eternal struggle, so conceived.

Fascists disparage rationality and reason except in the service of a leader-led context of human relations. Fascism fosters nonreason and antireason, nonrational and irrational attributes, and the abandonment

---

10. B. Mussolini, "Doctrine of Fascism," in University of Colorado Philosophy Department, *Readings on Fascism and National Socialism*, Swallow, Chicago, (no date), p. 17.

11. A. Hitler, quoted in Carl Cohen (ed.), *Communism, Fascism & Democracy*, Random House, New York, 1962, p. 409.

12. Ibid., p. 406.

of any kind of self-conscious autonomy of will, purpose, meaning, or value save that offered by the leader.

Contrary to the fascists, however, reason-based reflection is manifest in all cultures. Nowhere is it confined to an elitist minority. People can be coerced and conditioned to become submissive, to "love their chains," but that is an imposed condition, not a given of human nature. No society can function, no economy can produce and distribute real income, where *un*reason is characteristic.

The fascists insist that people need little or no volition. One's function in life is to obey, to do one's duty, to conform, to observe fascist law and order. But only by thinking for themselves have people ever succeeded in rewriting the rules of the game in a manner to restore the polity or economy to effectual functioning.

The deference to race as the primary determinant of human capacity and potential has been thoroughly discredited in the last half century. The contention that superficially observable physical traits or characteristics, and/or genetically traceable "blood lines" in a racist taxonomy, have comprehensive and definitive influence on thoughts and actions of persons is palpable nonsense.

Similarly, the attribution on spiritualistic and intuitive grounds of a particular efficacy to persons of a specified national origin is also suspect. National traits and attitudes are acquired as a matter of experiential conditioning; they are not innate and given.

Neither evidence nor analysis will sustain the fascist contentions and conjectures regarding human nature. We are left with another variant of an essentially rigid, static, and inadequately grounded view of human nature. Such is untenable.

The ideological views discussed above are unduly narrow in vision, are fragmentary, or are patently mistaken. They grossly understate and sometimes distort the human capacity for reasoned and humane development. They are everywhere obstructive of serious and pervasive efforts at problem solving. Reference to these views here is not merely intended to pose the question of their relevance, but of whether or not such views materially contribute to the many crises being faced.

Needed, then, is a view of persons which is grounded in the evidences of the developmental and evolutionary character of human life; a view which caters to and encourages the expansion of one's capacity for discretionary dignity—the sense of self-worth which comes from having a determinant voice over one's own life and life style; a view which, because it is nondiscriminatory, tends to reduce rather than heighten tendencies to violent conflict.

III.   AN OVERVIEW

A person is "a many spendored thing."

As a physical organism, he or she has evolved characteristically human qualities and capacities including a comparatively large brain, erect stature, opposable thumbs, binocular vision, and a versatile larynx. Presumably, men and women have some basic drives (urges, impulses) relating to hunger, sex, ego-identity, affection, and the like, but the manner of response to such drives is, apparently, entirely culturally determined.

As a thinking organism, he or she is the only theory-building animal. An individual is conscious of self. An individual has the developmental potential for reflection, cognition, rationality, evaluation, and judgment.

As a social organism, a person is both a conditioner of culture and is conditioned by the culture, inescapably so. A person evolves and matures only in a culture, only in a context of interaction with other persons. In a very literal sense, the human organism develops in consequence of taking on the language, the habits of thinking, and the habits of acting which are specified as proper by the culture. A person becomes "socialized"—in the anthropological sense—as he or she is indoctrinated into the mores and folkways of the group. But these same habits of mind and habits of action do, on occasion, come under examination. They are, after all, the fruits of initiative behavior in an earlier day. Hence, as every individual finds himself or herself conforming to the settled conventions of the society, he or she nevertheless is potentially a nonconformist whenever he or she seeks to review and revise any of the cultural "givens." An individual participating as a member of a community is obviously a culture-building animal. Within culturally defined limits—and the limits themselves are subject to progressive redetermination—an individual is a free agent; that is, he or she has *discretion*.

By implication, among one's most distinctively human traits is one's reflective capacity, one's latent potential to perceive and to communicate symbolically regarding means-consequence relations in one's experience. All human organisms—black or white, tall or short, men or women, "primitive" or "advanced"—are in this sense reflective. This capacity we take to be the basic and continuing meaning of *rationality*. If by *education* is meant the development of reflective capacities, all people, in principle, are educable.

We do not presume that the developmental potential is identical for all human beings, nor, for that matter, for all human groups. On present evidence the distribution of potential appears as wide *within* groups identified by age, ethnicity, race, nationality, color, sex, etc., as it is between or among such groups. Even if subsequent inquiry did unexpectedly demonstrate intergroup differentials in potential, such differentials or differences would not become creditable criteria in the designation of human worth. Differences *need* not become the bases for discriminatory treatment or status.

While we do not deny that heredity may play some role in determining reflective potential (the nature-nurture debates continue), we do not concur in the presumption of a *genetic* transmission of culturally acquired habits of mind and patterns of behavior.

Cultural transmission, however, is another matter. In the words of E. H. Carr,

> The essence of man as a rational being is that he develops his potential capacities by accumulating the experience of past generations. Modern Man is said to have no larger a brain, and no greater innate capacity of thought, than his ancestor 5,000 years ago. But the effectiveness of his thinking has been multiplied many times by learning and incorporating in his experience the experience of the intervening generations. The transmission of acquired characteristics, which is rejected by biologists, is the very foundation of social progress. History is progress through the transmission of acquired skills [broadly conceived, we assume] from one generation to another.[13]

The significance of the foregoing for present purposes must be apparent. Capacity for participation in effectual problem solving does not hinge on matters of "maximization of satisfaction," on class conditioning as such, nor on race, sex, national origin, or original nature. The old saw about not changing human nature (in the behavior and attitude sense) is revealed as an especially unhelpful bit of folklore which has no visible evidential support. A person is a product of his or her culture; a person is a builder of culture. The more developed the reservoirs of knowledge and experience upon which to draw, the more effective participant-builder of culture a person can become. Discretion is wider; choice is expanded; insight is deepened; judgment is made more mature. In consequence, limitations on imaginative approaches to problem solving will not be found as deficiencies in "human nature" nor in "racial destinies." Such limitations will, rather, be found in the cultural and attitudinal resistances to the development, communication, and utilization of reliable knowledge in conceiving and recasting the structural arrangements which organize our common lives. They will be found also in the simple physical, emotional, spatial, and temporal limitations of the human organism itself.

IV.   CULTURE AND PERSONALITY

So much for an overview. But our frequently affirmed contention that a person is both product and producer of culture and, hence, in some

13. E. H. Carr, *What is History?*, Alfred Knopf, New York, 1962, pp. 150-51.

sense responsible for determining his or her own nature and the quality of his or her own life requires some additional comment. A normative theory of political economy must be based on a view of human nature more warrantable and more pertinent than the models offered by the capitalists, the communists, and the fascists. To this quest we now turn.

The central contention here is that the particular attitudes, motivations, beliefs, and behaviors which human beings manifest are largely determined by the character of their interaction, conformist and nonconformist, with the intellectual, cultural, social, and physical environmental matrix to which they are exposed and from which they emerge. People acquire such personality traits as submissiveness or aggressiveness, empathy or disdain, indifference or ambition, acquisitiveness or generosity, cooperativeness or competitiveness, in the socialization processes in which they are involved. The extent to which these environmental interactions and processes (as aspects of the cultural matrix) are amenable to directed change, is the extent to which the human agent at large, as the producer of culture, is able to fashion his or her own being, identity, and personality. To that degree he or she may become a contributor to and manipulator of the conditions which produce various beliefs and behaviors, attitudes and motivations.

As mentioned above, we do not enter the ancient and modern heredity vs. environment debates; we presume that some physical differences among individuals and groups may, through public evidential inquiry, be traced to genetic ancestry. But even when observed, they are not a priori an admissible basis for determining worth. Neither are they an admissible basis for proscribing or prescribing avenues of social intercourse. In any case, we do not defer in any sense to a biological determinism as the locus of origin of attitudes, motivations, beliefs, or behaviors, all of which seem dominantly, if not exclusively, a result of environmental conditioning, and such conditioning is in substantial measure potentially responsive to deliberate modification.

If, however, the perspective in vogue (fatalism, nihilism, etc.) does not admit the possibility of directed cultural change through human intervention, any concern with attitudinal or behavioral formation is quite beside the point. Although a significant segment of the counterculture of the young appeared some years ago to have been driven in its frustration and disillusionment to a "do-nothing" perspective, this seems not to be the general view. Abroad, the "revolution of rising expectations" continues, and at home, seemingly, an increasing number of women, young people, blacks, browns, native Americans, students, the poor, and concerned "over-thirties," are turning to "reformmongering"[14] —that is, inducing substantive change in beliefs and behaviors on war, poverty, racism, and the like.

14. Albert O. Hirschman, *Journeys Toward Progress*, Twentieth Century Fund, New York, 1963, part II.

For present purposes, we share the view that the cultural configuration of any society exercises substantial influence on the kind of "human natures" which emerge (1) by specifying the patterns and techniques of child rearing which exist and are operative; (2) by defining the character of educational experience, which modifies or reinforces childhood patterns; and (3) by stipulating the mores, folkways, rules, and regulations of the adult society which significantly impinge upon the individual. Given the limitations of space, for illustrative purposes, we explore a major facet only of the first of these three—namely, the formation in childhood of personality traits.

Most scholars now agree that the human organism's early years have a crucial significance in setting basic personality patterns. Childhood experiences frequently are "key experiences." Attitudes and motivations (acquisitiveness, dominance over others, race hatred, wastefulness, predatoriness) are learned in the socializing processes to which children are exposed. Although personality traits set in childhood may be modified in later years, those set early tend to persist and to establish the patterns of resistance to any changes introduced in later years. Debate continues on the question of whether or not any particular cultural configuration tends to produce a "modal personality structure," "basic personality type," or "national character." But there seems to be little doubt that despite wide international, intracultural and interpersonal differences, similar child-rearing practices *tend* to produce similar personality configurations. [15] An observation of Clyde Kluckhohn is pertinent:

> Every distinct society communicates to the new generation very early in life a standard picture of valued ends and sanctioned means, of behavior appropriate for men and women, young and old, priests and farmers. In one culture the prized type is the sophisticated matron, in another the young warrior, in still another the elderly scholar.
>
> In view of what the psychoanalysts and the child psychologists have taught us about the processes of personality formation, it is not surprising that one or more patterns of personality are more frequent among the French than among the Chinese, among the English upper classes than among the English lower classes. This does not, of course, imply that the personality characteristics of the members of any group are identical. There are deviants in every society and in every social class within a society. Even among those who approximate one of the typical personality structures there is a great range of variation. Theoretically this is to be expected because each individual's genetic constitution is unique. Moreover, no two individuals of the same age, sex, and social position in the same subculture have identical life experiences. The culture itself consists

---

15. See, for example, Milton Singer, "A Survey of Culture and Personality Theory and Research," in Bert Kaplan (ed.), *Studying Personality Cross-Culturally*, Row, Peterson, Evanston, Illinois, 1961, pp. 9-90.

of a set of norms that are varyingly applied and interpreted by each father and mother. Yet we do know from experience that the members of different societies will tend, typically, to handle problems of biological gratification, of adjustment to the physical environment, of adjustment to other persons in ways that have much in common.[16]

In recent years a substantial literature has developed which is concerned with the influence of childhood experience upon personality formation. Inquiries in the fields of anthropology, social and clinical psychology, psychiatry, and psychoanalysis have underscored the significance of the "formative years." Studies have explored such matters as the existence and importance of the Oedipus complex, sibling rivalry, attitudes toward maturing biological processes, identification of basic drives and needs, relations of parents to each other and to their children, tension-creating and tension-relieving conditions, outlets for aggression, cognition patterns and the like.[17] Field studies of anthropologists, psychological testing, personal histories, and psychoanalyses have affirmed the influence which childhood experience has for the patterning of adult attitudes and motivations.[18] Among the major generalizations which these inquiries have produced, none seems more firm than the contention that in a human being's childhood years are established the attitudes, motivations, cognitive capacities, and value orientations which materially condition, some would argue dominate, his or her later life.

Without in any sense intending to be definitive on the matter of personality formation, the main contention can be illustrated by an examination of the influence of differential patterns of parenthood. The impact of "considerate parenthood" (the caption is E.E. Hagen's) on personality formation appears to be markedly different from the impact of indifferent or authoritarian parenthood.

Consider some of the major characteristics exhibited by "considerate parenthood."[19]

16. Clyde Kluckhohn, *Mirror for Man*, Copyright © 1949, McGraw-Hill Book Company, p. 198.

17. An especially helpful bibliography will be found in Singer, "Culture and Personality Theory and Research," Kaplan, op. cit., pp. 69-90. See also, "A Selected Bibliography Bearing on the Mutual Relationship between Anthropology, Psychiatry, and Psychoanalysis," an Appendix to Francis L. K. Ksu (ed.), *Psychological Anthropology*, Schenkman Publishing Co., Cambridge, Massachusetts, 1972, pp. 493-98.

18. See, for example, E. E. Hagen, *On the Theory of Social Change*, The Dorsey Press, Inc., Homewood, Illinois, 1962, pp. 123-61. See also, Abram Kardiner and Associates, *The Psychological Frontiers of Society*, Columbia University Press, New York, 1945.

19. These observations draw upon but are not limited to E. E. Hagen's discussion in his *On the Theory of Social Change*, op. cit., pp. 133-43. No effort is made to employ technical language; the sketch is intended to be suggestive only. See also Alan DeWitt Button, *The Authentic Child*, Random House, New York, 1969.

(a) Considerate parents exhibit love and affection for their offspring in a manner appropriate to the maturity level of the child. Affection is not conditional, fundamentally; it is genuine, consistent, and without demands of reciprocity. Children know that they are valued and desired. Something of this pattern is suggested by Veblen's "instinct" of a "parental bent." The parental bent, says Veblen, "appears to be an unselfish solicitude for the well-being of the incoming generation." [20]

(b) Considerate parents encourage the child's active exploration, under his or her own power, of his or her widening area of consciousness. The quest for awareness is facilitated; questions are answered. The child's "idle curiosity" and wonderment regarding himself or herself, the immediate familial setting, and the larger community are not discouraged; they are stimulated, encouraged, and guided. Parents serve as models of curious and critical awareness.

(c) Considerate parents help the child establish security of expectations. They regard the world generally as understandable and governed by regularities that can be apprehended. They inculcate the cognition that experience can be ordered (or orderly), that expectations can be fulfilled. They help the child to know himself or herself and to trust that knowledge of emerging capacities. They are consistent in their relations with the child; they abstain from capricious and erratic relations with their children. They elicit trust by extending trust.

(d) Considerate parents respect the identity and autonomy of the child organism as a human being whose quest for self-awareness and self-consciousness must not be blighted by either utter disregard or total domination. The child's integrity must be nurtured, identity valued, and dignity as a *person* respected.

(e) Considerate parents stimulate achievement by systems which confer esteem (and may include rewards) related to the scope and character of the performance. They minimize the negative consequences of punishment-oriented relations in favor of successive reinforcement of constructive achievement through recognition. Aspirations to excel in the quest for identity and self-consciousness are stimulated and guided with regard both to the ends sought and the means selected.

(f) Considerate parents seek opportunities to expand and to mature the child's capacity to frame alternatives and to choose among such alternatives. Errors are permitted where apprehension of the relations or mechanisms involved is advanced thereby (and the consequences do not destroy opportunity for further experience in choice-making). But not only is choice made genuine for children, but the dimensions of the choice-making experience are expanded parallel with the child's growing capacity to perceive increasingly complex phenomena. Such parents

20. Thorstein Veblen, *Instinct of Workmanship*, Viking Press, New York, 1946, p. 46.

are mindful of the fact that choices mature more dramatically in the circumstance of having to live with the results which ensue from the choices actually made.

Thus, considerate parenthood helps to establish an environmental matrix in which individuals, in their socialization from birth to adulthood, can become self-reliant rather than self-demeaning; active rather than passive in participation; empathetic rather than indifferent or sadistic; loving and supportive rather than vengeful or callous; cooperative and congenial rather than ruthlessly competitive and suspicious; innovative and creative rather than submissive, conformistic and unimaginative. A society which tends to foster considerate parenthood will, in so doing, contribute to the formation of attitudes and motivations which are conducive to the practice of reformmongering—of problem solving.

Personality patterns established in childhood tend to persist. Although internal frustrations or external situational pressures may lead to personality alteration in later years, such alteration is an adjustment of patterns established in childhood. We intend to posit no psychological determinisms here. We do suggest that attitudes and motivations are in the main acquired and that they are, within limits defined by existing knowledge and within physical and emotional limits of the organism itself, amenable to modification.

In a similar manner, the impact of formal educational experience on the formation of beliefs, behavior, attitudes, and motivations has been and remains a central concern. John Dewey, for one, spent most of his mature years making the case for classrooms which promote creativity, noncoerced growth, and democratic participation by the young in their educational experience. Harold Taylor provides a compelling critique of modern higher education from a similar point of view. [21]

Finally, the impact of the mores, folkways, rules, and regulations of the adult society reworks and reshapes traits set in childhood and modified or reinforced in formal education. In this special case, Marx's insight concerning the impact of the work experience on individuals *may* be found relevant. The character and availability of mass media and their conditioning impact on beliefs and attitudes are also the subject of continuing inquiry and comment, as Marshall McLuhan has demonstrated. [22]

Obviously evident are the multiplicity and the variability of environmental conditioners.

21. Harold Taylor, *Students Without Teachers*, McGraw-Hill, New York, 1969.
22. H. Marshall McLuhan, *The Medium is the Message*, Random House, New York, 1967; H. Marshall McLuhan, *Understanding Media*, McGraw-Hill Book Co., New York, 1964.

V.   CHANGES IN HUMAN NATURE

Perhaps the fact of attitude and motivation alteration and the potentiality for it to be humanistically directed need little documentation to establish their credentials as premises. It may be helpful, nevertheless, to cite material which illustrates and tends to confirm these contentions.

At the outset, we are confronted with the obvious but important fact that cultures are in no case wholly static. Cultural configurations which operate on personality formation must be presumed to be in a state of flux. We would reasonably expect major alterations in culture to be corollated with marked changes in beliefs and attitudes. And such seems to be the case.

Consider the social and economic history of economies that have become industrialized and "modernized." The scientific and industrial revolutions in the West spawned shifts in cognitive perspectives from matters of faith to matters of fact. (Recall Mark Twain's allegoric *Connecticut Yankee*; peruse Veblen's commentary in *Imperial Germany and the Industrial Revolution*.) Value orientations become secular and materialistic. Motivations to work became oriented to commercial and pecuniary considerations. Attitudes toward one's fellow man reflected alienation and estrangement from communal and familial loyalties. Attitudes of deference to clerical authority were eroded. The significance placed upon social position by birth was dissipated. Motivations to individual identity and personal achievement were encouraged. The list could be extended.

The reader can no doubt supply additional and more recent examples of alteration in beliefs, behaviors, attitudes, and motivations. Within recent years attitudes toward infant feeding, planned parenthood, balanced budgets, economic planning, the importance of higher education, wartime allies and wartime enemies, sexual behavior, acceptable hair length and personal attire, the meaning of patriotism, and minority races are undergoing revision. We see some business motivations shift from conquest to respectability and from profit to security of expectations. We see increasing rejection of "materialist" values, of beliefs in the campuses as sanctuaries aloof from the political process, and of income as a measure of social worth. Motivations to elicit divine blessings wither in the face of a secularization of belief and behavior. It is a certainty that beliefs, behaviors, attitudes, and motivations change. It appears highly probable that such change can be directed sufficiently to increase the probability of generating personal traits more conducive to the achievement of needed reforms. Such reforms would consist of measures to reduce the extent and severity of poverty, authoritarianism, racism and sexism, pollution, and war.

Further evidence of the alterability of attitudes and motivations and of the possibilities of directed change[23] of such personality traits is provided in Margaret Mead's anthropological study of the Manus. [24] Ms. Mead had a unique opportunity to study this society both before and after it had had substantial contact with so-called modern cultures. (The interval between field studies was approximately twenty-five years.)

She found that a very large number of the Manus were actively eager to change in a remarkably short time from the old ways to a substantially more "modern" set of attitudes, beliefs, motivations, and behaviors. Elaborate kinship obligations, expectations, and responsibilities were drastically reduced or abandoned; childhood behavior became more imaginative and less merely imitative; adolescent attitudes toward adulthood became less depressed as the oppressive cultural domination over young adults was markedly eased; parental attitudes regarding the role of formal education developed in a fashion to grant significance to schooling as an instrument to train the young in "The New Way"; belief in the capacity of spiritual forces ("Sir Ghost"—the spirit of the most recently deceased male relative) to punish for violation of economic commitments or kinship taboos has been abandoned by all but the oldest members of the society; economic motivation grounded in the threat of spiritual reprisals (not the expectation of power or accumulation of wealth) has been markedly damped or replaced. In brief, deference to spiritual forces has been severely eroded; parenthood patterns have been adjusted to accommodate "The New Way"; and the social structure is much less dominated by authoritarian patterns based upon economic (especially commercial) potency sanctioned by spiritual forces. [25] The significance of the impact of the environmental matrix on personality formation must at this point be evident.

In sum, an individual cannot become an effective participant in the life process generally where childhood training, educational experience, and adult environment depress developmental potentialities:

Where the conditioning environment fails to encourage the development of creative potential, a society will not be capable of developing its own fund of knowledge or of borrowing judiciously from the knowledge and experience of others.

When any change is regarded as a threat to established tradition and authority, change may be violently interdicted.

23. We are aware of the concerns over whether or not "guided change" is manipulative and/or coercive and over its moral admissibility. These issues go beyond the scope of our discussion at this point.

24. The Manus are a people living in the Admiralty Islands in the Southwest Pacific near New Guinea. The area is a United Nations trust territory under Australian administration. See Margaret Mead, *New Lives for Old*, William Morrow and Company, New York, 1956.

25. Ibid., passim.

Where the distinction between productive and unproductive labor relates to hierarchical placement, the working environment will little encourage the flowering of the "instinct of workmanship." [26]

Where the activity of producing goods is demeaned and the inducement to work is coercion, productivity levels will remain low. Where productive energies expended yield capricious, uncertain, and functionally inadequate returns, desire to excel in both quantitative and qualitative terms will be stunted.

Where inquiry is regarded as heresy, it is presumptuous to expect critical reflection regarding economic resource creation, measures to improve political participation, racial and sexual bias and its removal, even-handed law enforcement, and industrial pollution control.

Where individuals conceive of themselves as being without value and significance to others, it is unlikely that they will regard the attentions, ideas, and productive potential of others as of particular importance.

Where the creation of a genuine choice among alternatives threatens the status quo, it is incongruous to think of an unresisted, unruffled transition to society-wide discretionary dignity through the extension of political rights and prerogatives.

The incursion here into the field of culture and personality, as we noted above, is in no sense intended to be more than suggestive and illustrative of the oft repeated remark here that a person is both producer and product of his or her culture. Even so, the previous discussion should suffice to sustain the simple but significant generalizations (1) that a person's "human nature" in the social sense is pliable and flexible, not rigid and fixedly given; (2) that a person has the capacity to reflect in means-consequence terms, is capable of rationality; (3) that people are social animals, that all beliefs and behaviors are acquired and none are innate or original; and (4) that, therefore, a person is indeed educable. Herein lies the optimistic response to the pessimistic posture concerning human nature assumed by the capitalists, communists, and fascists.

Henry Kariel provides a suitable and convenient capstone statement of our essentially normative view of human nature:

> . . . man may be seen as an elusive, incomplete being forever in the process of self-discovery and self-development. He is pre-eminently an innovating creature. In the concise terms of Christian Bay, he "is free to the extent that he has the capacity, the opportunity, and the incentive to

---

26. This "instinct," writes Veblen, "occupies the interest with practical expedients, ways and means, devices and contrivances of efficiency and economy, proficiency, creative work and technological mastery of facts. Much of the functional content of the instinct of workmanship is a proclivity for taking pains . . ." *Instinct of Workmanship*, op. cit., p. 33.

give expression to what is in him and to develop his potentialities." There is no effort here to fill in what he is to be free *for*. He is simply free from those self-mutilating traits that produce the mindless fanatic, enthusiast, or nihilist, that keep him from acknowledging and developing himself. . . .[27]

To which he adds

Man may here be seen as naturally and ideally disposed to make choices, and as being conscious of this disposition. Committing himself to play the roles of his choice, he is, it is true, always in danger of losing his self, giving rise to the question of who, if truth be told, he really is. . . . But however man feels himself to be threatened, he can yet preserve his distinctive identity by recognizing that his dedication to the role he plays is quite deliberate. He is no mere role player, but at core a discriminating being who picks and chooses from available roles. Drawing on his primordial energy, he interprets them, transforms them, and creates new ones. He is a probing, experimenting being, always in motion, attaching and detaching values, inflating and deflating alternatives, unsure of his place in the order of things, skeptical and, above all, aware of his skepticism.[28]

Finally, observes Kariel, this agent-actor-chooser is necessarily an interacting participant:

Remaining equivocal, he is never *wholly* committed to any specific course of public action. Like Melville's Ishmael, he is the participant-observer, implicated in events and yet, in the end, alive and free-floating. But even when sucked down by fate and given no escape, he achieves what autonomy is within his reach. He records, he talks, he establishes connections with the world about him . . . He learns to control his prescribed role in the very process of acting it. However cramped and tortured, he discerns the boundaries of his existence and the amount of improvisation that remains open, testing possibilities . . . He conquers nature . . . by obeying her. . . . He is responsible by his very nature: this is what it *means* to be a person.[29]

Reflect again on the views of men and women associated with areas of revolutionary unrest:

With regard to the productivity revolution: Poverty is *not* inevitable because of congenital indolence.[30] If men and women perceive

27. Henry S. Kariel, *The Promise of Politics*, Prentice-Hall, Englewood Cliffs, New Jersey, 1966, p. 27. (Emphasis deleted.)

28. Ibid., pp. 27-28.

29. Ibid., pp. 28-29.

30. Preliminary reports on field trials of a guaranteed-family-income plan show that the poor are *not* encouraged to become idle and shiftless by publicly provided minimum money income. See Fred J. Cook, "When You Just Give Money to the Poor," *The New York Times Magazine*, May 3, 1970, pp. 23ff. See also, J. A. Pechman & P. M. Timpane (eds.), *Work Incentives and Income Guarantees*, The Brookings Institution, Washington, D.C., 1975.

rationality to mean maximizing profits, it is because that is what they have been taught and conditioned to believe; it is not a matter of original nature. In principle, other and divergent motivations may be taught instead or in addition. One "learns one's instincts" after all.

With regard to the participatory revolution: The nature of people does not make democracy impossible; it has not often enough been tried. Certainly the "cry for a leader" is not innate; it is a product of a particular time and circumstance.

With regard to the racial revolution: Fascist-based and other forms of racism are a fraud. Differences in beliefs, behaviors, and attitudes (and taste in foods, music, etc.) of Jews, blacks, browns, native Americans, orientals, etc. are cultural in origin, not biological. Blacks, Chicanos, Indians, Asians bleed and die, and mourn their dead. Parental love is not a Caucasian monopoly.

With regard to the ecological crisis: No one apparently has yet produced a definitive theory of population; but clearly we are not able to say that population growth must approach the biological maximum. The sexual urge may be innate, but the response thereto is *wholly* culturally patterned. Solutions to the pollution problem, moreover, do not hinge solely or uniquely on making environmental restoration a money-making venture.

In sum, rational reformmongering in the sensitive areas of revolutionary unrest *need* not be retarded by antique notions regarding human nature and conduct frequently derived from the "received systems"—the ism-ideologies. With this realization, hopefully, one more "species" of "underbrush" is cleared away to permit more productive inquiry into the determinants of our particular "time of troubles."

We here conclude consideration of the philosophical underpinnings of a normative and evolutionary theory of political economy. Having attended to the assumptions concerning knowledge, reality, and human nature, we are now in a position to move directly to the presentation of a theory of an evolving, functional economy.

ECONOMY

Chapter 4

THE ECONOMIC PROCESS

... *an evolutionary economics must be the theory of a process of cultural growth as determined by the economic interest, a theory of a cumulative sequence of economic institutions stated in terms of the process itself.*

THORSTEIN VEBLEN*

Because time is fertile with mutations and because there can be no break in continuity, the fact of change and the fiction of freedom to choose are alike inevitable. It is possible, within finite limits, to direct the streams of development; it is impossible, in a world of reality, to fashion an industrial system to a utopian dream.

WALTON H. HAMILTON**

*Thorstein Veblen, *The Place of Science in Modern Civilization*, Russell & Russell, New York, 1961, p. 77.

**From THE POLITICS OF INDUSTRY, by Walton Hamilton. Copyright © 1957 by The Regents of the University of Michigan. Reprinted by permission of Alfred A. Knopf, Inc., p. 160.

Contrary to the design and intent of the ism-ideologies, all economies are always mixed economies. In a literal or puristic sense, there are no capitalist, socialist, communist, or fascist economies. As we shall see, all economies are mixed economies because of the inescapable need to respond to real, genuine problems by reconstituting the mix of institutions, rewriting the working rules, revising the structural fabric of the economy. Probably no pure economy ever existed; certainly no pure economy could survive very long. Problem solving requires structural change, and structural change means mixed economies. Current economies are no exception, of course.

I. ISM ECONOMIES

But ism economies are not mixed economies.

Capitalism

Capitalism exhibits a slate of institutions which includes private property, the profit motive, free markets, classical competition (pure and perfect), and a passive government. Property ownership connotes a legally specified range of choice over the use of an item—to hold, use, sell. Items exchanged are items owned by individuals (human and corporate). The profit motive is a habit of mind which makes the maximization of pecuniary returns the universal motivation for economic behavior. Free markets are exchange arenas where buying and selling occur at the initiative of utility-seeking participants. Markets are "where the action is." Individual participation is aggregated in markets to yield a social result.

Classical competition is the regulatory structure which converts private self-serving activity into a public benefit. Competition denotes an absence of market power—no participant can affect price by his or her own efforts. Competitive markets facilitate purchase and sale activity, which sets market prices. Prices are ratios of exchange. A passive government's main role is to protect property from internal disruption and external threat, to enforce contracts, to engage in needed functions which are not profitable for private enterprise or which yield returns only after a long delay, and to avoid "arbitrary interference" with the normal, natural functioning of market operations.

The foregoing structure, it is thought, will need no revision; the ism can accommodate to problems which arise so long as market prices (product and factor) are flexible and are permitted to seek their own levels without intrusions of government, unions, or other groups. Capitalists see movement away from this *particular* structure as the courting of disaster. This is no mixed economy; this is a natural, self-adjusting, productive, competitive market economy, in their view.

Marxism

The Marxists see a succession of isms from feudalism to capitalism, from capitalism to socialism, and finally to communism. Marxists have no theory of a mixed economy, however. The structural fabric of capitalism is anathema to Marxists. Whatever is bourgeois is inadmissible. Accordingly, specifically rejected is the entire capitalist system. Because of the private ownership of producer goods, that system inevitably generates the capitalists' appropriation of surplus value (labor's product above subsistence appropriated by capitalists), and the exaction of surplus value means exploitation.

The socialist transition economy, therefore, calls for a different *particular* structure. Central are (a) public ownership of all producer goods (factories, mines, mills, farms, machines, tools, inventories) and (b) comprehensive economic planning, in which basic decisions regarding the level, character, and distribution of production are made at the political center. Proposed, then, is a politicized economy in which the dictatorship of the proletariat, a dedicated ruling elite, and its implementary arm, the communist party, operate a civil-service state. Prices are elite-administered; short- and long-term goals are set. The inclusive mission, negatively stated, is to eliminate all vestiges of capitalist structure, belief, attitude, and power. Positively stated, the structural design of socialism is to accelerate the level and growth rate of real income sufficiently to permit movement to the final ism—communism—and to create the new communist men and women who will live within the structure.

Communism will be distinguished structurally by (a) the absence of a political state (productive property will be socialized), (b) the ending of specialization or division of labor and of alienation which results therefrom, (c) the termination of economic classes, (d) the cultivation of artistic and creative endeavors, and (e) economic arrangements which provide for "from each according to ability, to each according to need."

The *particular* structure for each succeeding ism is thus specified. Marxian ideology becomes utopian (Marx's disinterest in proposing "Cookbooks for the future" notwithstanding); there is no post-communism envisioned.

Fascism

Fascism, for some, seems to offer flexibility in economic structure; it appears to offer something of a mixed economy. The fascist regimes in Europe in this century allowed corporate ownership of producer goods, permitted some manipulative use of market allocation, and tolerated, within limits, private economic gain. The *particular* structures under fascism, however, which were rigid, given, and unyielding, were the political institutions of the fascist state, fascist leadership, and the fascist party. The fascist corporatist economy serves the fascist state. The leader reserves the right to issue edicts affecting *any* economic decision at *any* level of inclusiveness in order to secure the consequences he desires. It is an administered economy in which hierarchical ordering characterizes all economic, social, and political arrangements. The mission of the leader for national, racial and ethnic, and personal aggrandizement is the overriding purpose. Nothing is to be permitted to impair that quest.

Accordingly, this fascist economy can adapt to change only as the wisdom or whim or the leader dictates. There is no theory here which abides the modification of economic institutions to serve humane ends-in-view. Democracy is anathema to fascists.

Now with these ism-economy models freshly in mind, continue consideration of their relevance to the problems which are generating revolutionary unrest. The following observations are illustrative and indicative.

The productivity revolution: In an effort to provide adequate real income for everyone, the community faces problems of residual poverty and economic instability. Capitalists call for a maximum deference to the private enterprise sector on both problems. Marxists argue that poverty and instability are inevitable so long as capitalism exists. Fascists would use rearmament to respond to both. Actual problem-solving efforts in developed economies are exploring publicly provided minimum income guarantees, job creation and income transfers to cope with poverty, and a changing blend of monetary, fiscal, and direct economic controls to deal with instability.

The participatory revolution: In an effort to extend participation to people generally, the community faces problems of improving economic performance by making political judgments on economic policy more sensitive and responsive. Capitalists would recommend public policy to enhance "business confidence," not to regulate business. Marxists deny that wide participation is possible under capitalism; reform efforts which merely modify capitalism are abortive; the state is controlled by the propertied class to serve its own interests. Fascists contend that wider participatory control over the economy is both impossible and undesirable. Actual problem-solving efforts in modern economies are addressing wage- and price-restraint mechanisms, tax reform to aid lower-income receivers, and more responsive instruments for national planning.

The racial and sexual revolutions: In an effort to reduce and eventually end discrimination on grounds of race, sex, and color, the community faces problems of providing for meaningful integration of racial minorities and women into the mainstream of the economic process. Capitalists say promoting "equality of opportunity" under competitive market conditions will solve the economic aspects of the problem. Marxists contend that racism and sexism are consequences of retaining the capitalist mode of production. Fascists argue that anti-discrimination efforts will "bastardize" the white race, weaken male supremacy, and destroy a superior culture. Actual problem-solving efforts in the United States are implementing and enforcing Fair-Employment-Practices laws and affirmative-action programs, pressing for the Equal Rights Amendment, ending segregation in housing, and integrating racially imbalanced schools through busing arrangements, and the like.

The ecology crisis: In an effort to forestall the deterioration in the life-support capacities of the environment, the community faces problems of population growth, air and water pollution, and misuse of resources. Capitalists offer no indicators of success or achievement—no principle of economic judgment—save that of aggregate quantitative growth, profit maximization, or satiation of personal utility. Marxists see environmental damage as an outgrowth of "production for profit" by self-serving private enterprise. Fascists tend to be indifferent about environmental deterioration. None of these responses touches the problem directly. Actual problem-solving efforts generally seek to introduce qualitative measures of a tolerable economic life, to press planned parenthood and legalized abortion programs, and to introduce environmental and pollution control measures which override narrow personal and corporate interests.

In the preceding paragraphs, "actual problem-solving efforts" refers generally to an incrementalist approach in which economic options are open and change is possible. If or where elitist controls prevent such efforts, pressures may very well force the relocation of actual political discretion. The forceful relocation, should it occur, indicates the previous absence of democratic instruments.

The foregoing discussion suggests that ism-ideologies are not very relevant to problem solving in political economy. In the following chapters on the economy and polity we present an analysis which we believe is more pertinent to problem solving. If the contention that ism-ideologies are of doubtful relevance seems elemental and commonplace at this point, recall that although most scholars agree that the American economy is a mixed economy, few explain why, and many appear to think that problem solving means moving towards one or another of the ism models. That is, they are quite prepared to argue for the normative use of an ism model—a matter to which we must return below.

"'Begin at the beginning,' the King said, very gravely, [at the trial of Alice] 'and go till you come to the end: then stop.'" We "begin at the

beginning" with some generalities which provide a fresh and fundamental basis for economic inquiry. The approach will be inclusive or
"holistic" [1] in quest of greater relevance.

II. PROVISION OF REAL INCOME

The world has long been and promises to continue to be a place where
people must engage in productive activities to sustain their cultural
existence and to develop what anyone means by civilization. People
seem compelled to employ physical and reflective energies in activities
which result in a conversion of elements in the physical and cultural
environment into the material (and nonmaterial) means of life and
experience. The production and distribution of what economists call real
income—goods and services—is an inclusive and continuing category of
activity which is here termed, "the economic process."

The economic process is a social activity which every people must
perform at all times at some level of effectual performance—even in a
largely unstructured commune. People are associative and participative
in the conduct of their lives. The inquirer must be concerned with
relations among persons as they participate in the activity of providing
goods and services for themselves, their families, and the larger community. Conventional, orthodox economists, for example, who build
upon a Robinson Crusoe analogy [2] are not very helpful because they
fashion an individualistic model which has little congruity or relevance
to the social task of providing real income. Indeed, the motivations and
behaviors attributed to the mythical "isolate" Crusoe could only occur if
Crusoe himself were a product of a fairly well-developed civilization.

How effective people are in carrying on the function of providing
real income depends at bottom on their ability to develop and apply
knowledge to the productive process. As noted in the previous chapter,
the human agent is a tool- and idea-using organism, a theory builder,
and is rational in the respects noted. Human beings can and do perceive
and designate causal connections. Utilizing this, their latent rationality,
people develop an expanding fund of reliable knowledge composed of
verifiable or testable observations of experience. Invention, innovation,
discovery, and borrowing of causal insights contribute to this cumulative expansion of warrantable knowledge.

This accumulation of reliable knowledge is accomplished by the
combination and recombination of tools and ideas. It is a developmental
process. The first automobile was a motorized buggy. New knowledge is
derived by creative and imaginative manipulation of old knowledge. As

1. Allan G. Gruchy, *Modern Economic Thought: The American Contribution*, (1947),
   Augustus M. Kelley, New York, 1967, p. 4 and passim.
2. See, for example, George N. Halm, *Economic Systems* (revised edition), Holt, Rinehart & Winston, New York, 1960, pp. 11ff.

nearly all students know, the Keynesian theory of income and employment, as an example, derives from a partially original recombination of prior orthodox and heterodox formulations about economic instability.

This accumulated fund of reliable knowledge is everywhere the fundamental basis for determining how the economic process shall be carried on and what shall constitute the material and nonmaterial means of life and experience. It is everywhere the basic economic resource. This fund of knowledge defines the range of choice among goods and services which a people share. No people can choose a component of real income which the community does not know how to provide.

Moreover, such knowledge of the arts and sciences applied to the productive process defines the components of the "natural" resource base. Pitchblend and carnotite, for example, were not regarded as economic resources until after the formulation of hypotheses regarding the behavior and properties of radioactivity and the potentiality of nuclear power as an energy source was envisioned. We return to this point below.

Indeed, even the ever-changing pattern of wants, tastes, and preferences, although determined by complex cultural influences of status, proximity, class, income, and the like, is fashioned, nevertheless, within a realm of possibilities defined by advancements in the arts and sciences applied to the productive process. People develop an interest in Beethoven sonatas, Brubeck jazz, folk-rock, or electronic music after the creative act has imaginatively combined musical forms and instrumentation.

The economic process is thus concerned with the employment of warrantable knowledge in providing the real income requisites to civilized existence. But economics is a *normative social* science. Its primary concern is not the development of knowledge about the physical or biological realms. Nor is it concerned directly with the engineering problems of applying science, for example, to industrial production. Rather it is concerned with the development of reliable knowledge about how a human community can be and ought to be organized institutionally to carry on the economic process most effectively. Economics is an inquiry into the person-person relations in providing the material and nonmaterial means of life. Person-thing relations are the necessary bases for the social institutions developed. The economic process is a functionally defined category of human activity. Economics, as a discipline, is a continuing effort at rational analysis of that process.

III.   STRUCTURES AND FUNCTIONS

The economic process is given effect in experience only through institutions. The term *institution* means any prescribed or proscribed pattern of correlated behavior or attitude widely agreed upon among a group of persons organized to carry on some particular purpose.[3] Institutions are the working rules, the codes, the laws, the customary ways which shape and pattern behavior and attitudes in a manner to accomplish some end-in-view or purpose.

Nothing is more conspicuous than the inordinate variability of institutional forms within and among cultures. Anthropologists and others have long catalogued these behavioral forms with great patience and much precision. In the last two centuries the institutions utilized to organize the economic process have ranged widely from fee-simple ownership to equity interests in corporations, from slavery to collective bargaining, from commodity money to demand deposits, from laissez faire to governmental planning, and from artisan entrepreneurship to the corporate "game player." Attitudes, for example, of nationalism, of racial supremacy, of the efficacy of private property or of social ownership, of monogamous marriage, of a singular deity, of military aggrandizement, of labor's right to the whole product of labor, of technological determinism, are also institutional in character.

Crucial for the analysis here is the elemental recognition that all institutional forms, behavioral or attitudinal, are products of the world of experience. Institutions do not originate in heaven, with Mother Nature, or with any other outside-of-experience force. One institution is no more and no less "natural" than any other. People tend to view as natural that which is traditional and therefore familiar. But clearly, institutions of whatever kind are people-made devices for organizing experience and thus, by obvious inference, they are always potentially modifiable by people. The effort to modify structure long sanctioned by tradition is rarely easy; but, however leaden the "cake of custom," people at large do have discretion over the organizational forms which correlate their behavior in the economic, political, and social processes.[4]

That institutions are within the world of human discretion is true despite the fact that behavioral forms and attitudes become habitual in character. Institutions are *constituted* by habits but they are not, of course, *determined* by habits. Once decisions regarding structure are

3. This definition comes from the unpublished writing of J. Fagg Foster, professor of economics, University of Denver. It is similar, but not identical to, a definition provided by Bronislaw Malinowski: "We can define an institution as: a group of people united for the pursuit of a simple or complex activity; always in possession of a material endowment and a technical outfit; organized on a definite legal or customary charter, linguistically formulated in myth, legend, rule, and maxim; and trained or prepared for the carrying out of its task." *The Dynamics of Culture Change*, Yale University, New Haven, 1961, p. 50. Note that this usage is more specific and delimiting than the conventional reference to church, state, marriage, or family as "institutions."

4. But a caveat is needed at this point: No one should treat the introduction of significant adjustments in the fabric of society as a trivial or casual affair. Those engaged in reformmongering that touches the *fundamental* economic and political relations of a society (e.g., matters of political freedom, levels of real income) are assuming an awesome responsibility. The burden of proof is on the advocates of change to demonstrate the probable extent and character of consequences that may fairly be ex-

made, they very quickly pass into settled conventions, into social habits, and seem to later viewers to be constants—even eternal verities. Appearances to the contrary, institutions are not eternal.

Devotees of the institutions of Negro slavery, British imperialism, "manifest destiny" in the United States, Aryan race supremacy, extended families, national sovereignty, economic class rule, the "white man's burden," laissez faire, annually balanced budgets, the gold standard, all believe in the eternal continuity of these respective forms. These devotees are, of course, mistaken. Most of these forms have been abandoned, modified or ignored; in the main, they cease to be operative.

But the demise or abandonment of structure is frequently fraught with violence and bloodshed, as was the case with slavery and as is the case with the demise of racism and colonialism. Massive resistance to changes in institutional controls may bring the equivalent of an American Civil War, lynching parties, a seven-year war in Algeria, an eight-year war in Southeast Asia, an Angolan civil war, an incarceration of a Ghandi, an assassination of a Martin Luther King, Jr., or student or police violence on college campuses. Mechanisms for nonviolent change in structure may also be available.

Institutions are the result of initiative behavior—of conscious, deliberate choice making on the part of people holding and using power to establish structure. While it is true that frequently the specific originators of structures are not recorded and thus are not known to later generations, all structure must originate as conceptions by somebody to organize experience in a certain way or to hold certain attitudes. Habits do not create habits. People create institutions that become habitual.

Confronted with what they regard as real problems, people are prompted to modify, revise, abandon, or replace behaviors and attitudes in an effort to remedy the situation. Are the following assessments credible? Are they fair? In a world of ICBMs, ABMs and MIRVs, an insistence upon unqualified nationalism appears foolhardy in the extreme. In a mass society which is highly interdependent economically,

pected and on that basis to solicit support from those whose lives would be significantly affected by the change. As we note below, it may well be a rational act to oppose change until and unless such demonstrations are persuasive enough to warrant the extension of consent to make the change.

And, of course, experience is a great teacher. Recent disenchantment with some reform efforts from "liberal" and other circles in the areas, e.g., of public housing, welfare relief, tax reform, and urban renewal derives, evidently, from the reformers' failure to take sufficiently into account some kinds of consequences which matter to those whose lives are involved. Public housing may shatter long-standing neighborhood loyalties and accommodations; rules governing welfare relief may contribute to the disintegration of families; tax reform may open more loopholes than it closes; urban renewal may force the poor into even more deprived circumstances. The disenchantment seems to reflect a fundamental defect of some "liberal" reform: that elites know best, that reform means doing to and for somebody, that change means revolution from the top; the result was that no one bothered to make change contingent upon its acceptance by those significantly affected.

the image of an individual worker bargaining on equal terms with a large corporate employer (a migrant farm worker and an "agribusiness"), "freely contracting" regarding conditions of work appears as a bit of unfunny fiction. In an environment of extended and protracted unemployment, the view that the economy will automatically engender forces creating recovery is a remnant of pre-Keynesian fancy. In an economy of prices administered by organized management and organized labor, a singular insistence on the perpetual efficacy of the free competitive price system is naive. In an economy of relative affluence, the continuing deference to constructs of scarcity economics in the face of demonstrated presence of substantial starvation for a minority, is obscene. Behaviors and beliefs observed to be obsolete and obstructive of genuine problem solving are prime candidates for adjustment, abandonment, or replacement.

If institutional structures are not "constants," not eternal verities, nor necessarily continuous, what is? The function, the process, the activity of providing real income is continuous. This social function is inclusive (pan-temporal and pan-cultural) and continuing.

The function of producing food and fiber in agriculture is continuous; the structures of the owner-manager family farm, slavery, public land domain, public provision of agricultural knowledge, corporate farms, and federal subsidy programs are not necessarily continuous (see figure 4-1).

The function of providing continuity in the receipt of money income in highly specialized and interdependent industrial societies is continuous; the structures of old-age pensions, contributory social insurance, grant-in-aid programs for unemployment compensation, "means test" rules for receipt of aid, and family allowances are not necessarily continuous.

The function of developing in the young the ability to think critically and coherently about all areas of their experience is continuous; the structures of current teacher-training programs, colleges serving *in loco parentis*, "multiversities" serving the military-industrial complex through research, authoritarian classrooms, and college admission rules which deny proportional access to women and members of minority groups are not necessarily continuous.

The function of making decisions about what shall be the level, character, and distribution of production is continuous; the structures of collective bargaining, comprehensive economic planning, resale-price-maintenance laws, the achievement of "countervailing power," the creation of "automatic stabilizers" for economic instability are not necessarily continuous. Structures are *replacemental*; functionally defined categories of activity are *developmental*. [5]

5. This distinction comes from the work of J. Fagg Foster, professor of economics, University of Denver.

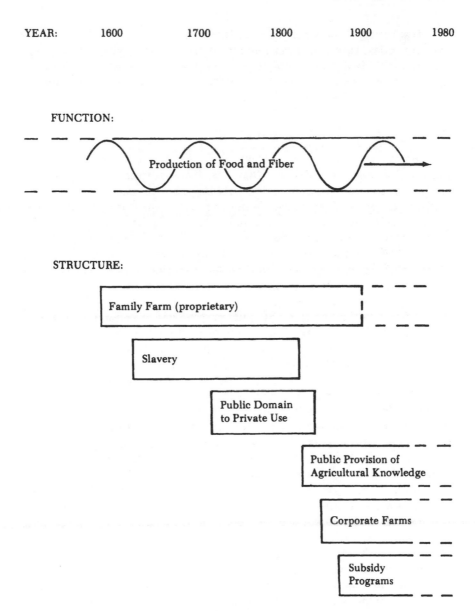

FUNCTION: Continuous and developmental
STRUCTURE: Discontinuous and replacemental

Figure 4-1   Function and Structure (Illustrative Case of Agriculture)

Institutional adjustment means the displacement or replacement of existing codes, rules, or arrangements with new or revised stipulations which order behavior. Functional activities evolve as knowledge is applied to experience; they develop coincident with the community's understanding of its productive options.

IV.   STRUCTURES AND PROBLEMS

In the context of the present discussion, what is the meaning of the phrase, "economic problem"? What does it mean to say that a problem exists? In general, an economic problem may be said to exist when existing institutional structures do not correlate behavior as effectively as rational, reflective utilization of reliable knowledge indicates is possible. People conceive a difference between "what is" and "what ought to be" in these terms. They observe some real impairment in the provision and distribution of real income and sense that the impairment can be removed; they see people denied access to jobs and income on discriminatory grounds and wonder why it is so.[6] Some institutional structures do not perform the function of facilitating the use of rational thought in determining the organizational forms of human behavior and the attitudes which direct or sanction such behavior. The structures have become, rather, vehicles for the exercise or extension of power, or for the maintenance of rank, status, or privilege; mechanisms for "putting down" some in order to elevate others, or for the perpetuation of tradition for its own sake. Such malfunctioning may occur in consequence of the transformation of interests and goals of the participating individuals or because of obsolescence brought on by changes in the arts and sciences applied to the productive process—the knowledge continuum, broadly conceived. A resolution of a problem in this view, therefore, would consist of introducing those changes in institutional structure which would permit restoration of effectual congruity between the state of rational knowledge about how to carry on an economic activity and the correlated behavior patterns and attitudes which incorporate such knowledge into experience. Problem solving always requires institutional change.

Consider the matter of unemployment as a familiar example. Agreement is general that widespread and protracted involuntary unemployment is an economic problem. Certainly we have yet to hear a political candidate campaign on a platform advocating an *increase* in the number of persons without regular and meaningful work. In

---

6. It is true, of course, that problems may sometimes be identified well before any specific solution is perceived. No immediate relief for a genuine hardship may be available. Problems identified and remaining unresolved must be endured. But the conception of a problem as a difference between "what is" and "what ought to be" is not affected. However, solutions must be sought through deliberate inquiry and policy recommendations wherever possible.

societies where a substantial degree of specialization of labor and, therefore, interdependence has developed, continuity in the receipt of a money wage is a critical matter for the average worker. Inability to find or create appropriate employment for large numbers of persons is an economic problem. It has a racial dimension in the United States. Typically, blacks have twice as high an unemployment rate as do whites. [7] Chicanos and native Americans fare little better.

What ought to be is the restoration of a condition in which everyone who wants a job can find one. The problem of unemployment requires for its solution the adjustment of those institutional structures and attitudes which are determined through inquiry to be causally responsible for the condition.

Here, of course, agreement is likely to end. Does unemployment result from a deficiency in aggregate demand or from structural inadequacies or both? Does it result from worker indolence and apathy (a choice of leisure over work), from monopolistic control of industry, from unwarranted intervention of government, from inadequate manpower-training programs, from absence of "fair competition," from discriminatory hiring practices, from automation, or from sun spots? Or does it result from a combination of some of these and others unnamed?

As is apparent, it is the actual analysis of primary causes which is crucial for problem solving. As medical diagnosticians may differ in deciding what are the actual causes of a physical impairment, so economists may differ on the determinants of unemployment. Agreement is general, however, on the need to discover what the determinants in fact are. And while "analyses" of the problem may differ, there is no gainsaying that actual observed poverty from unemployment in the face of certain ability to produce is generally regarded as an economic calamity!

Also apparent here is the fact that efforts to define a problem disclose the value preferences of the definer. The foregoing clearly postulates the end-in-view of full employment. Implicit is the notion that everyone ought to have access to a paying job and that the community ought to employ whatever reliable knowledge it possesses or can secure to accomplish this goal. If, for example, people come to know that an economy organized along quasicapitalist lines will not automatically generate full employment, they may well regard as obsolete those behaviors and attitudes which require that they act as if full employment were automatically secured. If they come to know that

7. The rate of unemployment among black and other nonwhite high-school *graduates* typically is greater than the rate of unemployment among white high-school *dropouts*. In 1974, the percentages were 38.6 for blacks and other nonwhite graduates and 27.7 for white dropouts. See U.S. Department of Labor, Bureau of Labor Statistics, "Table 32, Employment Status of High School Graduates . . . by Sex, Marital Status of Women, and Color, 1959-1974," *Handbook of Labor Statistics, 1975, Reference Edition*, U.S. Government Printing Office, Washington, D.C., 1975, pp. 91-93.

discriminatory hiring practices and inadequate training and education do deny access to meaningful jobs, they are likely to regard as anachronistic attitudes and behaviors which perpetuate such denials.

Conceivably, the "problem" might look very different, say, to a member of an industrial management group. Were he or she to contend that full employment is desirable only so long as management is permitted to secure and retain the largest possible sphere of discretion over its enterprise—to retain inviolate its managerial prerogatives—he or she would be exhibiting a value position different from that alluded to above. Such a person would argue that a problem existed when there was any sort of threat, real or imagined, to the retention of such managerial prerogatives, and that argument will color his or her perspective concerning employment of the work force.

A member of a trade-union organizing committee might contend that full employment is desirable because it will tend to enhance the opportunities of his or her union to organize a body of workers and thus increase the economic power of the union. The labor organizer might regard as a problem any hurdles placed in the path of his or her efforts by organized management or government.

A black community organizer, recognizing well that blacks typically are the last hired and the first fired in times of economic instability, might view full employment as a most desirable condition, because without employment, the aspiration of blacks to gain control over their own lives is most difficult, if not impossible, to achieve. He or she might well view the main problem to be one of discriminatory hiring practices.

But the positions of the industrial manager, the union organizer, or the black leader are not necessarily sufficient or compatible with the more general effort to resolve the problem of involuntary unemployment. Each has an understandable but fragmentary and group-interest-centered perception of the problem. Each defines the problem in a manner reflecting those interests. However meritorious or nonmeritorious these perspectives may be on other grounds, clearly their scope and implications are too narrow to provide access to the economy-wide problem of unemployment. But the normative perspective of each is clearly evident.

In our discussion, we defined the problem of unemployment, in contrast, as the existence of a gap between the current use, or misuse, or inadequate use, of reliable knowledge of the determinants of unemployment generally and the potentially more effective use of such knowledge. Closing the gap between knowledge and practice and restoring a condition of full and nondiscriminatory involvement in the economic process for all represents a solution. Such a solution will normally require the adjustment or modification of those institutional structures which are generating the problem.

Consider now the scope of economic problems—the major problem areas—with which a community must continually contend:

Students are already familiar with the fact that all economic systems, whatever the stage of their development, confront problems in three major areas of the economic process: determining the level, the character, and the distribution of real income. We need only add, for present purposes, the equally elemental recognition that these decision areas continuously involve two sorts of judgment. First, all such decisions, by whomever made, become structural directives to pattern and organize economic functions in particular ways. Policy directives to increase taxes, create a budget surplus, cut interest rates, revamp "success indicators," or introduce a guaranteed annual minimum income, are examples. Second, all such decisions require a response to the query, "Which direction is forward?" That is, a choice of or among institutional structures is always involved, and a criterion of choice defining what ought to be must be employed in choosing among alternatives.

For example, the extraordinary emphasis of a half century and more upon the level of production and its growth is now being joined by an equally insistent query concerning both the cost (consequences) and the character of that growth. Increasing attention in the 1960s and 1970s was focused upon national priorities with the implicit normative concern about the wisdom of pushing an "economy of death" over an "economy of life."[8]

In brief, to determine the level, character, and distribution of production requires (1) that alternatives be framed as policy options, as shifts in prescriptive rules, and (2) that a criterion of choice, a value principle, be employed in choosing among such alternatives or options.

Implicitly, we add a fourth problem area: Who shall exercise political policy-making authority, and on what grounds and to what ends-in-view will it be exercised? The power to decide economic policy has always been among the most potent forms of power. To be able to grant or withhold the means of life to anyone or to any group is a fearsome potency indeed and is well understood by such diverse groups as the White Citizens Councils,[9] the Communist party, brokers of political patronage, corrupt sheriffs, governmental bureaucrats, and

8. Richard J. Barnet, *The Economy of Death*, Atheneum, New York, 1970. Kenneth Boulding, *et. al.*, *National Priorities*, Public Affairs Press, Washington, D.C., 1969.

9. ". . . in 1955 . . . the national NAACP . . . circulated a petition in Yazoo City [Mississippi] advocating integration of the schools. The local Citizens Council was set up then to deal with this problem. . . . The Council went to work to coerce fifty-three of the Negroes who signed the petition to withdraw their names, and the methods used were not very pretty and did little for the dignity and honor of the town. "Give an inch and they take a mile," was the clarion. White employers immediately fired the signers of the petition who worked for them. Those petitioners who rented houses were evicted by their landlords. White grocers refused to sell food to any of them.

power wielders in organized management and organized labor. Because of the obvious potency of economic power, many communities have sought to deny its use to any self-perpetuating fragment or rule-making elite. But obviously, the effort to achieve popular, responsive, and responsible control over economic policy-making power is an un-ending quest.

V.　PROBLEMS AND PRESSURES

"We live," says Barbara Ward, "in the most catastrophically revolu-tionary age that men have ever faced." But this present age is not one, curiously, in which a host of broad *new* problems have suddenly been thrust upon us. Poverty has long been the condition of a very large number of men and women. Efforts to extend political participation have characterized the two hundred-year history of the American experience with self-governance. Repression on racial, sexual, and other trivial grounds dates at least from slavery in a formal sense. Environ-mental indifference and destruction largely describes the nineteenth-century Westward movement in the United States.

The prevailing revolutionary fervor, rather, comes from a growing awareness, on the one hand, of the potentially catastrophic consequences of a failure to meet these problems in their *modern* form in an inter-dependent society and, on the other hand, from an emerging conviction that such consequences need not be fatalistically accepted—these prob-lems can in large measure be resolved. Pressure for change accelerates when small gains in problem solving encourage the belief that much greater gains are possible. The "revolution of rising expectations" occurs only where hope has been kindled or rekindled.

We become intolerant of a six to twelve per cent rate of inflation, of a six to ten per cent rate of involuntary unemployment, and of one-eighth to one-sixth of the population living in poverty in the United States—intolerant because we believe that proper economic manage-ment could reduce instability and poverty.

We become intolerant of a continuing excessive influence of or-ganized economic interest groups (unions, multinationals, professional organizations) upon governmental policy making because we observe their parochial and self-serving gains at the public's expense. We suspect that effective control mechanisms are possible.

We become intolerant of continuing racial and sexual prejudice and discrimination because we know the rising price being paid in

Negro grocers who had signed the petition no longer got any groceries from the whole-sale stores. After several weeks all the names had been withdrawn, and a number of Negroes who had been there all their lives were forced into leaving town altogether." (Willie Morris, "Yazoo . . . notes on survival," *Harpers Magazine*, Vol. 240, No. 1441, June 1970, p. 46. Copyright © 1971 by Willie Morris. Reprinted by permission of Joan Daves.)

economic privation, blighted lives, broken homes, and psychological destruction. We seek policy initiatives to reduce discrimination.

We become intolerant of accelerating environmental deterioration because atmospheric pollution, uncontrolled population growth, and chemical poisoning of water threaten the lives and life-support systems of human and nonhuman support species. We are convinced that better environmental quality can be restored and retained.

Revolutionary pressure and intolerance continue, but the response of the American economy has been judged by many to be inadequate. Ancient maxims concerning tight money and balanced budgets fail to instruct adequately in the management of economic instability. Poverty conditions resist ameliorative measures taken thus far. Racial discrimination in employment ends slowly in spite of Fair-Employment-Practice measures and the like. Some states have revoked their earlier ratification of the Equal Rights Amendment. Substantial inequality of income distribution helps perpetuate de facto segregation in housing. Inflation of the 1970s made the purchase of a new single-family home an option mainly of the upper-income groups. Implementation of desegregation measures in schooling in Northern cities often seems to wax and wane with estimates of available political advantage. Rhetoric on pollution and population control is frequently exemplary; measures to hold polluters effectively to account are in their infancy.

Given such a context, the task here is to attempt to think about the economic process in ways which will permit (or make more likely) responsiveness to revolutionary unrest and the problems engendering it, yet in ways which avoid the infirmaties and/or irrelevancies of the approaches offered by the ism-ideologies.

VI.   DISPOSABLE ADMONITIONS

Finally, it will be helpful to clear away two sorts of simplistic admonitions being advanced by the disenchanted concerning these pressures for economic and social change and the allegedly inadequate response to such pressures.

The first admonition, offered by students and others, is that the existing political economy is so inadequate, corrupt, rotten, unjust, technocratic, militaristic, and discriminatory that it must be destroyed before anything else is done. This wholly negative view does not normally include any substantive notion of what would follow destruction and dismantlement. These nihilists insist, naively we think, that whatever follows such a destruction most certainly would be "better" than what is. A more spectacular "leap of faith" without reason is difficult to imagine.

This nihilistic manifestation of despair ignores one monumental truth, among others, perhaps. That is, that all political economies are necessarily "going concerns" and must remain so. Given only the choice between utter chaos (destruction and dismantlement) and authoritarianism, communities will sensibly choose the latter.

Every economy is now providing the means of life for its people at some level, however inadequate and inequitable by some standards that performance may be. Some economic activities are being carried on effectively. Existing arrangements are functioning to generate and distribute real income. Some of these arrangements (institutions, organizations) *must* display the application of rational, even reflective thinking in means-consequence terms. No economy, not even the fascistic corporate economy, ever operates wholly nonrationally. Elements of non-discriminatory and rational operation account for the "going concern" status, the continuity of the economy, and those elements must be retained if a people are to survive and to have any further choice whatsoever. In despair, one may say; "Stop the world, I want to get off." But that contention is utterly worthless as a response to revolutionary demands for solutions to real problems.

A second admonition, offered especially by revolutionaries (Marxist and others), ignores a related homely truth. Revolutionaries say "throw out the old order, bring in the new," or "wipe the slate clean and start over," meaning thereby to suggest that a new (generally ismatic) comprehensive political economy be introduced to replace one that allegedly exists. We believe this view, also, is utterly without merit.

Revolutionary efforts over the last two centuries appear to indicate that no people can survive a fundamental, in any sense total, reconstitution of economic and political arrangements without literally catastrophic consequences to revolutionary and populace alike. The rivers of blood that flowed in the French Revolution, the Bolshevik Revolution, and the Chinese Revolution attest to the vigor of the revolutionaries and the resistance of traditional orders. No people, seemingly, can be expected, even under heavy coercion, to abandon all significant control patterns that give meaning and predictability to their lives in favor of a comprehensive reordering of their habits and modes of belief and behavior. Piecemeal or fragmentary adjustment of institutional structure is possible, but a thoroughgoing overturn and imposition of a comprehensive wholly new prescriptive order is *not* possible. We do not mean to suggest that a revolutionary relocation of the authority to initiate altered institutional arrangements is doomed to failure. We mean to imply that such discretion, if obtained, cannot in a brief time successfully institute a comprehensive reordering of the myriad structures through which the economy (and polity) functions. [10]

10. It is of interest, for example, that Lenin in 1921, following the trauma and destruction of three years of civil war in the USSR, introduced a very pragmatic New Economic Policy. The NEP was addressed particularly to agriculture; it gave to peasants the right to dispose of their own surpluses (e.g., through sale) and some security in the right to cultivate the land. Restoration of productivity and output in agriculture was of the highest priority. The NEP in agriculture utilized in large

Thus, no knowledgeable student would think seriously of substituting one ism-ideology for another. The Grand Alternatives, yesterday's isms, are not real or genuine alternatives at all. A half-century of agonized concern over whether or not we are headed "down the road to socialism" (or an equivalent) is now understood as a grossly misplaced concern. Leadership, however dedicated, cannot choose a comprehensive system as an alternative to whatever is. Such efforts must fail of their intention.

But acknowledging the actual *un*availability of ism alternatives does not mean that effectual change is impossible or that the matter of choice in deciding "which direction is forward" is but a cruel hoax. As Walton Hamilton puts it,

> If, for us and for others, there can be no choice between systems, it does not follow that there is no need for choice. The great crossroads of destiny are replaced by an endless series of points at which trails meet, intertwine, and go their divergent ways. At a myriad of such points a myriad of individuals make a myriad of decisions. Each of these individuals must determine and must keep on determining for himself which direction is forward. To decision each brings so much knowledge, understanding, and wisdom as he possesses. Persons differ one from another in foresight, in the values they hold, and in the balance they strike between private concern and public interest. The implications of a decision transcend the considerations which have prompted it. In the instance, the act which follows a judgment. may lack significance; in the aggregate, the stream of decisions have a formidable impact upon the economy, the nation, the culture.[11]

In all that follows, then, as a theory of an evolving, functional economy, one overriding contention is everywhere affirmed: The extant economy is one which people over time have chosen to create and which new choices will in turn transform. It is a product of an unending "stream of decisions." The economy was not "out there" waiting to be discovered. It was designed neither by Nature nor by the Almighty; it is no deterministic product of class struggle, race struggle, or technology. It is a discretionary creation of men and women who have (and had) genuine choice. Any existential economy is an eclectic amalgam of a "myriad of decisions." An evolving, functional economy is one over which people in general have discretion. Its resource base, its organizational makeup, its operational codes, the rate and character of its

measure already-understood economic relations. Its character was specified more by the realities of problems faced than by ideologies held. See, E. H. Carr, *The Bolshevik Revolution, 1917-1923*, II, (Macmillan, 1952), Penguin Books, Baltimore, 1966, part IV, chapter 19.

11. From THE POLITICS OF INDUSTRY, by Walton Hamilton. Copyright © 1957 by The Regents of the University of Michigan. Reprinted by permission of Alfred A. Knopf, Inc., p. 165.

institutional change, and its purposes or goals sought and served, are all, in principle, determined by human choice, even though such choice does not and cannot extend to a comprehensive displacement of one "system" with another. Accordingly, it is to this "stream of decisions"— which defines "which direction is forward," which composes and re-composes the structural mix of a political economy, and which deter-mines the degree of responsiveness to demands for extensive, but not comprehensive nor catastrophic, change—that we must turn. Recourse to ism-ideologies tends to abort, pervert, divert, and/or arrest rational reflection upon this "stream of decisions."

As we address this "stream of decisions," recall now the assumptions and postulates on which our analysis will rest:

The following theory of an evolving, functional economy incor-porates the epistemology of rationally formulated, evidentially ground-ed, logically consistent inquiry. It is warrantable inquiry which exploits inductive and deductive inferences and their interdependencies, which purports to explain in means-consequence terms, and which produces tentative truth. The admonition, "do not block the way of inquiry," is respected.

Recall further, that such inquiry is directed to an existential reality of perceived fact, a reality which is inherently processional, and which is itself expanded and transformed by inquiry.

Inquiry is conducted by and directed to men and women who are both products and producers of culture, who perceive means-conse-quence connections and communicate symbolically, who create theory, who are capable of rational, reflective thought, who are in principle educable, and whose "worth" is not at issue. A person's beliefs and behaviors are not predetermined; no one is under teleological controls; no one need merely await his or her fate. Within culturally specified limits which are themselves subject to discretionary revision, a person has genuine discretion. In large measure, people can determine "which direction is forward"; obviously, it is they who provide the "stream of decisions."

Recall finally that the economic process is the object of economic inquiry. The institutional structures of which it is comprised are replace-mental and do change over time. The generalized productive and distributive functions performed are continuous. Problems arise when institutions fail to permit or adequately provide for the use of war-rantable knowledge in performing economic functions.

Problem solving requires adjustment, modification, invention, or abandonment of structure to restore congruity between what is and what ought to be. Clearly therefore, such an approach is necessarily and avowedly normative; the question of value judgments cannot be begged. As will become evident below, value judgments are at the core, not on the periphery, of such problem solving.

It follows, then, that in an evolving, functional economy, unlike all of the ism-ideologies, there is not, and could not be, a slate of particular institutions having some sort of a priori, preferential, or absolutist status. We posit no revered structures to be held inviolate; we affirm the existence of the economic process and the productive functions therein. Here, institutions are dependent variables, not eternal verities.

With these generalities freshly in mind, we can now move on to the particulars of this outline of a theory of an evolving, functional economy —an economy which is the product of the unending "stream of decisions." We consider the following in turn: (1) resource creation, (2) institutional options, (3) operational mechanisms, and (4) principles of economic change.

Chapter 5

RESOURCE CREATION

Knowledge is truly the mother of all other resources.

ERICH ZIMMERMAN*

". . . we cannot ignore the human agency in history, cannot escape the implication that within limits it is a free agency . . . the problems we face are clearly of man's own making. . . . 'Invention is the mother of necessity.'"

HERBERT J. MULLER**

*Erich Zimmerman, *World Resources and Industries*, (rev. ed.), Harper and Brothers, New York, 1951, p. 10.
**Herbert J. Muller, *The Uses of the Past*, Oxford University Press, New York, 1957, p. 35.

Few will disagree with Erich Zimmerman's contention that "Man's own wisdom is his premier resource—the key resource that unlocks the universe." [1] Resource creation is a consequence of the development of reliable knowledge, especially that of the arts and sciences, and its application to and implementation in human experience through institutional arrangements. Men and women choose to create resources. Basic research (science) and its application to the practical problems of real-income production (technology) are thus fundamentally determinant of the resource base for an evolving, functional economy. In a literal sense, people "create" productive inputs by creating the knowledge that gives resources identity.

However, we do not presume that science and technology *determine* institutional structure. The steam engine does not necessarily give you capitalism. People choose structure; machines, of course, do not autonomously choose. We do agree that changes in science and technology frequently so change the context and determinants of problems that a critical and imaginative reappraisal of customary patterns of belief and behavior becomes mandatory. Structural problems *have* arisen in consequence of automation, nuclear energy, and computers. Similarly, resource creation may very well create conditions which will require institutional change. Here is one more reason why all economies are always mixed economies.

For this discussion, three areas of resource creation merit brief and separate comment: human resources, "natural" resources, and monetary resources including capital funds.

I.   HUMAN RESOURCES

The human agent is, of course, the discretionary and operative element in resource creation and hence is the strategic variable in an evolving, functional economy. The numbers of such agents, their attitudes and motivations, and their skills and capabilities determine the effectiveness of this variable in furthering the growth and wide distribution of real income. Thus, in the context here, it is reasonable to think of human agents as being engaged in creating of themselves productive, participative, and initiative resources.

In what sense may it be said that one can create of oneself a "resource"—a productive input? To pose such a question seems to convert an individual into a mere "means" without reference to that attribution of latent dignity which characterizes the Western liberal view of human beings. Men and women, it is said, should themselves be the end; not a means to other ends.

---

1. Erich Zimmerman, *World Resources and Industries*, (rev. ed.), Harper and Brothers, New York, 1951, p. 7.

But no demeaning connotations are implied. On the contrary, creation of human resources implies here an expansion and maturation of the individual's discretionary capacity and role—his or her distinctively human attribute to make rational choices—in the economy and the society. The human organism is a human *agent!* Growth in reliable knowledge and its implementation in experience—"organized intelligence"—gives promise of rendering the human agent itself, through participation in the conjoint determination of social restraints, subject to his or her own direction and his or her own control. As we discuss at greater length below, freedom and discretionary dignity derive from a condition in which restraints are self-imposed through knowledgeable choice. Thus we argue that the human agent can in large measure secure control over the determinants and conditions which define his or her role as a productive input, as a resource.

Three facets of human resource creation which are potentially amenable to discretionary manipulation or modification in a humane and constructive manner are the following: the growth or decline in numbers of people (hence also of the labor force); attitudes and motivations of persons; functional skills and capabilities of individuals. Consider each briefly:

(1) With reference to numbers, it now appears possible to create (within certain psychological and physiological limits) whatever size population a society decides is optimum. No one denies, of course, that what is technically possible may not be socially, morally, or institutionally desirable or immediately feasible. But the variety of biological and technical means available both to achieve birth control and to increase probabilities of conception have materially widened the range of choice regarding population control. No elaborate defense seems necessary for the assertion that, given the now available technical means, *institutional* conditions and practices, in the main, determine population growth rates.

Institutional patterns which tend to be associated with increasing levels of population and rising birth rates include early marriage, religious opposition to birth control, public sanction for large families, rural mores, low status of women, and the like. Falling death rates result from the extension of public health and sanitation measures, improved medical care for mothers and infants, control of endemic and epidemic diseases, and raising of nutritional levels.

Conversely, certain institutional conditions and practices, which are wholly or partially amenable to discretionary change, tend to decrease levels of population. Birth rates typically fall with late marriages, effective dissemination of birth control information and materials, removal of religious and traditional taboos regarding family planning, urbanization, improved status for women, rising rates of economic growth and personal income, social and legal support for abortions, and the like. The contributions of warfare, malnutrition, genocide, and disease to a rising death rate need no elaboration. [2] While it may often be true that emotionally subtle and culturally complex variables operate in a particular society to increase or decrease the population level, we are not therefore entitled to defer to fate or non-experiential forces in lieu of an approach incorporating rational analysis and discretionary control.

Wherever a leadership of a society regards its existing rate of population growth to be too high and therefore problematic (for example, where the birth rate substantially exceeds the death rate so that the "net reproduction rate" is high relative to the economic growth rate), experimentation with institutional devices to control the rate of population growth will contribute to the evolution of a mixed system indigenously unique to the society concerned. The route from what is to what ought to be to solve the problem may well be marked by such institutional way stations as the establishment of birth-control centers, publicly sponsored economic-growth-inducing expedients, programs to urbanize the labor force, guarantees of equal status and pay for women, legalization of abortion (an effective control instrument in Japan after World War II), public information programs, and the like. And the choices of what shall be used to accomplish the task must be both technologically feasible and institutionally acceptable if effective change is to be realized. [3]

The simple fact is that every sane human organism is potentially capable of some significant social and economic involvement. The question of how many human beings can be functionally integrated into the social and economic process is primarily a matter of the society's ability, through institutional innovation, to develop in individuals pertinent attitudes, motivations, skills, and capabilities and to create meaningful economic connections for them. This requires that the institutional mix through which the labor force is created and put to productive work must be flexible and adaptive to encompass more effectual educational and training programs and to assure a national policy of full employment.

(2) The inculcation of attitudes and the acquisition of motivations which are conducive to full and productive involvement of people in the economic process are amenable to discretionary control. As we observed in the materials above on human nature, *all* attitudes and motivations acquire definition and shape in consequence of the interaction of the organism and his or her cultural context. People shape that context: we learn our "instincts." E. E. Hagen, among others, has examined child-rearing practices to determine what prompts the appearance of persons

2. A still useful summary of factors affecting population levels appears in W. Arthur Lewis, *The Theory of Economic Growth*, Richard D. Irwin, Inc., Homewood, Illinois, 1955, pp. 304-19.

3. Recent Indian experience with population control measures is reviewed in "Babies' Revenge," *The Economist*, January 7-13, 1978, p. 58.

who have incentives, are goal oriented, or are interested in problem solving.[4] Attitudes toward work—to seek out or to avoid, attitudes toward sharing the product of work—acquisitive or generous, attitudes toward the meaning of work—trivial or significant, are all learned. Motivations to coerce others, to embellish one's person, to maximize pecuniary returns or profits, to become a status (or sex) symbol, to press for personal, group, or national aggrandizement, are all learned.

An evolving, functional economy, able to respond effectively to problems generating revolutionary unrest, must provide for continual reflective examination of attitudes and motivations, must make normative judgments to determine which should be encouraged and which discouraged, and must organize institutionally in schools and elsewhere to implement such judgments. We suggest that attitudes and motivations which contribute to a productive economy humanely and democratically organized should be encouraged.

(3) Finally, the skills and capabilities which individuals bring to the economic process are obviously amenable to discretionary social and economic policy. No elaboration is needed to detail educational, professional, and technical schools which function to teach people to think rationally and coherently and to equip persons with skills from typing to brain surgery. But an evolving, functional economy must assure that such programs are comprehensively available and that they function to encourage and facilitate the development of such latent capacities, talents, and creativity as individuals possess or can develop. Clearly, as we have often seen, denial of jobs on grounds of color, sex, or race is intolerable. So also are educational systems which penalize imagination, which impose conformistic, subservient, or demeaning self-images, or which destroy curiosity or deny or abort inquiry. In our view, every individual should have the encouragement and the opportunity to develop his or her constructive potentialities as far as his or her intellect and energies will permit. Nonabusive institutional means are available to encourage the formation and utilization of skills and capabilities which a modern economy requires, as democratic systems repeatedly demonstrate, if imperfectly. Presumably only those who feel threatened, like the neofascists, would oppose maximal educational and intellectual achievement for all without regard to differences of, for example, race, sex, color, creed, origin, or age.

II.   NATURAL RESOURCES

The title here momentarily perpetuates a common error by implying that the raw-material inputs for the productive process have a kind of original status in nature without reference to people or culture. References to "natural endowment" of resources, the "law of diminishing

4. Hagen, *On the Theory of Social Change*, op. cit., passim.

returns" in agriculture, the "niggardliness of Nature," the "diminishing supply of resources," and the alleged uneven or unequal dispersion of "natural" resources among peoples and nations appear to incorporate an essentially static image of the resource base in which the stock of resources seems fixedly given. Resources are presumed to be provided on a once-and-for-all basis.

In one sense, of course, this position is credible. In a global and timeless sense, there is only one earth's crust. There are, for example, large yet ultimately finite amounts of fossil-fuel sources. The atmospheric blanket surrounding the earth is on present knowledge a precious "given."

In another, particularly economic, sense this position is not credible:

"Nothing could be further from the truth," argues Zimmerman, than the view that resources are "something static" and "fixed." "Resources," he contends, "are living phenomena, expanding and contracting in response to human effort and behavior. They thrive under rational harmonious treatment. They shrivel in war and strife. To a large extent, they are man's own creation."[5]

Resources expand and contract, are "living phenomena," because they are defined and redefined by the cultural development of knowledge. Resources are functional and operational in an evolving context of productive activity.

> Knowledge is truly the mother of all other resources. To be sure, not even omniscience can create matter or energy out of nothing. Nor can any science, no matter how skillful and advanced, ever restore to human use the energy once locked up in coal, oil, or gas, but spent. The difference between neolithic man, who roamed the earth in misery and fear, and man today, who lives in relative comfort and security, is knowledge— knowledge of petroleum and natural gas, of sulfur and helium, of chemistry and physics, the countless wonders of modern science—and the marvelous apparatus of cultural improvements [institutional arrangements] which knowledge has devised and built for its own application. Freedom and wisdom, the fruits of knowledge, are the fountainhead of resources.

> Seen in this light, the concept of resources is purely functional, inseparable from human wants and human capabilities.[6]

If the term *technology* is given a somewhat more inclusive meaning than its familiar reference to machinery and equipment, it is convenient and helpful to regard the material resource base for any economy as being defined by technology.

> All the material resources . . . whether natural or man made, are the fruits of technology. Technology, in fact, can be thought of as the primary resource; without it all other resources would be economically nonexistent.

5. Zimmerman, op. cit., p. 7.
6. Ibid., p. 10.

This is clearly true of industrial and commercial facilities and of improved agricultural land. But it is also true of coal and oil, of iron ore, and of all the raw materials we obtain from the earth, the forests and the oceans. These are potential resources; they become actual resources only as technology makes it possible to extract them and convert them into useful products.[7]

Or again,

. . . natural resources do not explain the economic level of any society. On the contrary, what the natural resources of any society are conceived to be is determined by the technology of that society.[8]

The view here is not that all things are possible. It is, rather, that advancements in the arts and sciences applied as technology of industry and agriculture constantly expand human discretion regarding the availability of productive inputs; in this sense, the advancements define the range of possible production. Typically, we do not run out of resources. A resource is generally defined *out* of the resource base by advancing technology before supplies are exhausted (flint beds), or new sources of supply are created as utilization increases (petroleum). We would not expect the Sahara to become a major producer of wheat, nor is Duluth destined to become a banana port. There are limits to what can be accomplished in the utilization of science and technology in the creation of physical resources for industry and agriculture. Choice is not infinite, but a rapidly advancing technology has the effect of rapidly stretching the range of choice over inputs. What is here disputed is the half-truth that the resource base is given, that it constitutes a kind of original stock, which, once depleted, can never be overcome or compensated for.

That the frequently frenzied quest for new resources has generated environmental destruction and pollution needs no extensive comment here. Strip-mine plundering in Appalachia for coal, the smearing of seas and coasts with crude petroleum, watershed erosion and devastation by overzealous timber cutting, agricultural chemical pollution of watercourses, exhaustion of soils from overuse, and more, provide substantial evidence of some persons' studied indifference to the environmental consequences of continuing "preemption, exploitation, [and] progress."[9]

There are institutional reasons, but not definitive technological reasons, why sustained-yield timber cutting is not the customary practice, why research efforts to find alternative energy sources for fossil

7. J. F. Dewhurst and Associates (eds.), *America's Needs and Resources: A New Survey*, Twentieth Century Fund, New York, 1955, p. 834.

8. C. E. Ayres, *The Industrial Society*, Houghton Mifflin, Boston, 1952, p. 85.

9. Vernon Louis Parrington, *Main Currents in American Thought*, Vol. III, Harcourt, Brace & Company, New York, 1927/1930, p. 7 ff.

fuels have been grossly underfunded, why polluting chemicals continue to be used in agriculture. The fact of steel availability does not compel its use for the manufacture of 400-horsepower automobile engines. The fact that a supersonic transport *can* be built is not a persuasive argument for the use of resources for its construction and high-altitude-polluting use. In recent years, many of the young in particular have been incensed by a kind of institutionalized "technological compulsionism." If an A-bomb or H-bomb can be built, many scientists have felt compelled to insist that it ought to be built. [10] Proceeding from an ethically relative base (actually, a value void), they frequently have appeared indifferent to the character of the probable use of the new technology being developed. This posture of amorality has been viewed by many as fraudulent; the position is one in fact of denigration of human worth, of inhumane disregard for human life and welfare. Such appearances and allegations may not be definitive, but the burden of proof would seem to be on those who continue to foster the amoral expansion of technological knowledge which has catastrophic potentialities.

But if, for example, the world's energy needs are to be supplied otherwise than through fossil fuels (e.g., solar or thermal or fusion sources); if dependencies on mineral ores and timber supplies are to be significantly reduced; if biodegradable cleansers, containers, and paper products are to be produced; that is, if environmental destruction is to be slowed and finally halted; it will be done in good part through new advances in the arts and sciences applied (technologically) to these troublesome aspects of the productive process. The *dependency* of resources on knowledge is only underscored. What is required are institutional controls grounded in warrantable and credible value theory which redirect the character of the use of knowledge.

III.   MONETARY RESOURCES

"Knowledge is the mother of all other resources," we affirmed above, joining Zimmerman. Can this be the case for financial resources as well as human and "natural" resources? The answer, we suggest, is yes. An evolving, functional economy can generate and apply reliable knowledge of money forms, money functions, and monetary management in pursuit of humanistic goals. Money, too, is a discretionary resource.

There remains, evidently, a substantial folklore and some mysticism concerning money and its social management. Banks sometimes appear architecturally designed to generate awe and wonder. Bankers by recent (but not ancient) custom are accorded deferential esteem because of their presumed knowledge of the intricacies of credit creation and, by

10. A scientist close to the H-bomb project years ago told me that one major motivation for its creation was simply to see whether or not it could be done; the designers wanted to see the "big bang."

extension, of economic activity generally. Their opinions on economic trends and events are sought and reported in the mass media. Awe and deference imply significance. Money does matter; monetary management is important; the creation and control of money and credit (including the banker's role) is a continuing and vital concern to any modern economy. But, awe and deference notwithstanding, the interests and views of the banking community and those of the larger community may not always converge; it is a matter of demonstration and performance rather than hero worship.

It is common to regard availability of money as the determining constraint on what can be done economically. Someone proposes to build a plant or a home, or a community proposes to reduce pollution or feed the hungry, and the cry is raised, "Where is the money coming from?"

For individuals or firms, access to money and/or credit *is* often a determining constraint on what can be done economically. For an economy, the critical constraints more generally are matters of resource availability, productive capacity, manpower levels and skills, and the like. Normally, an evolving, functional economy can find effective ways of providing money and credit for what its real productive capacity permits it to produce. What are constraints for the individual may not be constraints for the economy, as the "fallacy of composition" reminds us. (The fallacy consists of the assumption that what is true for the part is on that account alone also true for the whole.) An economy can build institutions to create forms and control levels of money and credit as required to facilitate the exchange aspects of the economic process generally.

Review some familiar truths:

Money is an institutional invention of ancient vintage; its form is specified by convention, custom, or overt legal act. Normally it is defined with reference to its functions. Money is a medium of exchange, a unit of account, and a store of purchasing power. Its appearance as a medium of exchange several thousand years ago marked the recognition of the significance of exchange for human well-being and the complexity and ineffectualness of direct barter transfers of goods for goods. For anything to serve as a medium of exchange, as money, it must be acceptable to the parties (e.g., in payment of debt); it must be commonly recognized as spendable for goods or services. In modern economies, that acceptability derives generally from legal designation, from a sovereign, solvent government declaring that a particular item, thing, or ledger entry is money. To assure the acceptability and integrity of money, governments must maintain a monopoly over its form and its creation.

The unit-of-account function of money permits one item, money, to serve as an exchange surrogate for all others. The availability of a common unit of account—dollar, pound, peso, franc—permits the formulation of ratios of exchange of money for goods and services—money prices. The significance or value of money, then, is a consequence of its acceptability and exchange-surrogate roles.

The third function for money is customarily identified as a store of value, of purchasing power. The acquisition of money provides, immediately or later, the power to purchase, to command other goods and services in exchange, to exercise discretion. Through purchase from a willing seller, money normally can be promptly converted into nearly any other asset form; through sale to a willing buyer, most items can be converted into money. Money is the most liquid of all assets.

Note that these money functions—medium of exchange, unit of account, and store of purchasing power—are roles which facilitate the production and distribution of real income. Money, as such, is then hardly "the root of all evil." This ancient normative judgment has to do rather with the character of its acquisition and the manner of its use by individuals. All modern economies use money to fulfill these three necessary functions. Because of its crucial role in the facilitation of exchange and the production of real income, the manipulation of the creation of money and credit sometimes becomes a powerful means by which "economic royalists" attempt to exercise discretion over the behavior of others and therewith institute and enforce patterns that tend to sustain their identity as an elite fragment of the larger community. Control of credit creation is important economic power. For a Jacksonian democrat in the 1830s that was the evil to be feared; for a participatory democrat currently it remains a genuine concern.

Money forms, as most are aware, vary over time and place. Rocks, slaves, cattle, wampum, precious metals, printed notes, cigarettes, leger-entry demand deposits (checking accounts), and magnetic tape entries have served or are serving as money forms. Modern economies have moved beyond commodity moneys (gold and silver). The purchasing power of money is not a function of what is "backing it up" (e.g., gold), but of the integrity and wisdom of its management by governmental agencies. A contemporary arch-villain would be dealing in, and appealing to, folklore were he mistakenly to presume that the destruction of the U.S. gold stock in Fort Knox would bring the economy to its knees. A systematic destruction of steel mills or energy sources, on the other hand, doubtless would reduce productive capacity and real-income levels catastrophically.

While gold, a commodity money form, is of little actual significance in domestic monetary management, it retains some symbolic significance internationally. Settlements in international trade do formally exhibit a gold-exchange system, but payments are rarely made in gold. Generally, international trade is facilitated by complex mechanisms of credit creation and debt retirement established on bilateral and multilateral bases and through the assistance of the World Bank and the International Monetary Fund.

In the United States, about three-fourths of the money supply consists of demand deposits; the rest is coins and currency. A variety of "near moneys" also exist—time deposits, savings and loan accounts, and the like—but for present purposes these need not be pursued. The creation of coin and currency is a virtual automatic discretionary response of the U.S. Treasury and the Federal Reserve System (the Fed) to meet the public's demand for cash as reflected at commercial banks. The creation of demand deposits is a more complex matter. But the discretionary roles can be identified.

Commercial banks have direct and continuing, yet limited, discretion over credit creation. Each commercial bank may on its own initiative extend interest-bearing loans to individuals for, for example, purchase of consumer durables and to firms for payrolls, inventory purchase, plant improvements, and the like. Commercial banks may lend from their own resources up to limits set by law and the Fed. Approved loans appear as new demand deposits against which the borrower who received the loan draws checks. As these loans are drawn down by checks written by the borrower, those who receive payment by these checks deposit these new receipts to *their* checking accounts as new demand deposits at (usually) other banks. The extension of the loan by the commercial bank leads to multiple increases of demand deposits in other banks and in the system generally as new deposits created are spent, deposited, and respent in the economy. *Aggregate* demand deposits increase; the money supply is increased, but within limits.

Commercial banks, we said, have direct and continuing discretion, but others also have a decision role. Obviously, a bank can lend only if there are willing borrowers. If few firms and individuals seek loans, little deposit creation can occur.

In addition, the decision role of the Fed itself, though less direct, is central and in most respects, governing. The area of discretion exercised by the Fed is, of course, set by Congress. The Fed exercises constraints over commercial-bank lending power through its influence upon member banks' reserve accounts. The law requires that a portion (usually less than a fifth) of all demand deposits received by commercial banks must be set off in a reserve account at the Federal Reserve Bank. The Fed through various actions can affect the size of the reserve account of member commercial banks and the ratio of reserves to deposits and thus affect the ability of commercial banks to make loans and generate deposits.

The Fed can expand commercial-bank lending power (deposit creation) (1) by open-market purchases of governmental securities from commercial banks, thus adding to reserves, (2) by lowering the bank rate of interest charged by the Fed on loans to commercial banks, thus encouraging additions to reserve accounts, and (3) by lowering the minimum-reserve requirement, which converts required reserves into free or excess reserves, augmenting lending ability.

The Fed can reduce commercial bank lending power (deposit shrinkage) (1) by open-market sales to such banks of government securities to be paid for out of reserve accounts, (2) by raising the bank rate of interest, discouraging borrowing by commercial banks from the Fed to add to their reserve accounts, and (3) by raising the minimum ratio of reserves to demand deposits which commercial banks are required by law to observe.

The Fed's control appears to be more effective on the dampening, or money-supply reduction, side than on the expansion side. On the former, action by the Fed alone can shrink the money supply and reduce economic activity by reducing availability of bank credit. For expansion to occur, the Fed must provide enabling policy (free reserves), some commercial banks must concur, and enough individuals and firms must seek loans at commercial banks. Discretion is dispersed.

Even so, the Fed, through these and other direct and indirect measures, achieves substantial, but not total, control over the money supply as demand deposits.[11] The supply of money is determined as a product of discretionary acts of the U.S. Treasury, the Fed, commercial banks, and private firms and individuals. But the role of the Fed is paramount. Its somewhat novel structure is discussed below in another section.[12]

In sum, the mechanisms (institutions) of money and credit creation and management are such that, under suitable guidance, a modern evolving, functional economy can ordinarily arrange to finance whatever its resources, trained manpower, and cultural climate will permit. Money need not be the tail that wags the economy dog. Monetary mismanagement (or nonmanagement) can of course wreak havoc upon an economy, a contention to which many an economy can bear witness.

Obviously, if all parties with monetary discretion combine to generate a rate of increase in the money and credit supply substantially greater than the rate of increase in real goods and services, inflation pressures will appear. Conversely, if all parties with discretion, especially the Fed, decide to substantially reduce the availability of money and credit, deflationary pressures will appear. Many scholars therefore consider monetary policy *a* major, but not necessarily *the* major, determinant of economic stability.

But for us, the central recognition is that money and credit are discretionary resources and, therefore, that those who exercise control over monetary resources can, in principle, be held accountable; mone-

11. John G. Ranlett, *Money & Banking* (3rd ed.), John Wiley & Sons, New York, 1977, pp. 200-10.
12. Chapter 6, part II(e).

tary authorities can be required to comply with socially and publicly determined purposes. Some accountability is, of course, now being achieved; no doubt it could be improved.

The foregoing, in part, runs counter to an important article of the orthodox faith—of the capitalist creed. That article is the saving theory of capital formation. That theory holds, broadly, that additions to capital plant—investment—can be financed only out of prior voluntary savings as the source of capital funds. Money stock is given and neutral. The supply of and demand for savings is thought to determine the level of investment. [13] Investment is dependent upon prior savings. Although we cannot here hope to examine in detail the savings-investment analysis of modern macroeconomics, three observations are in order.

First, the discretionary expansion of bank credit through the banking system provides one source of investment funds that is not uniquely tied to prior voluntary savings. Thus, voluntary savings may be one way of funding investment purchase, but not the only way nor necessarily a preferred way in a modern economy.

Second, the existence of inequality of income distribution is sometimes defended on grounds that without the wealthy classes, who have incomes in excess of what they can spend on consumption, there would be no savings, hence no investment, hence no economic growth. Not so, says Keynes. ". . . the growth of wealth, so far from being dependent on the abstinence of the rich, as is commonly supposed, is more likely to be impeded by it." [14] We are not, he argues, "dependent on the savings of the rich out of their superfluity" to provide for the "growth of capital." [15] An ancient and major reason for retaining high income inequality loses some of its credibility.

Third, again following Keynes, the arguments urging high rates of interest as a "sufficient inducement to save" at all points below full employment are found wanting. Orthodox economists assumed full employment and regarded decisions to save as sensitive (elastic) to market changes in interest rates. High interest rates would, it was thought, increase the supply of savings and, with sufficient demand, increase investment. However, below full employment, a *low* rather than a high rate of interest stimulates investment spending in the Keynesian model. On maximizing assumptions, the purchase of existing debt instead of the purchase of new plant and equipment is made less attractive with low interest rates, and borrowing for investment purchase

---

13. A more modern orthodox version, the loanable funds theory, adds some monetary aspects to the savings analysis. Keynes' interest theory relates the preferences for liquidity and the supply of money. See Ranlett, *Money & Banking* (2nd ed.), 1969, op. cit., Chapter 14.

14. John M. Keynes, *The General Theory of Employment Interest and Money*, Harcourt Brace, New York, 1936, p. 373.

15. Ibid., p. 372.

is made more attractive. A low interest-rate structure is therefore generally recommended to stimulate investment spending if the economy has significant unemployment and if price inflation can be contained.

Finally, then, when one is asked how the financial resources will be provided to fund capital plant and equipment expansion, the answer in general, is clear: expansion will be financed out of money and credit creation somewhere in the economy by government and private institutions. No modern economy need starve its way to plenty through heavy-handed abstention from consumption to get savings, to get investment, to get economic growth. In principle, investment occurs necessarily at the *expense* of consumption *only* under the unlikely condition of full employment of labor and full utilization of productive capacity and relevant technology. But this condition almost never exists in fact. Exacting a "surplus" from subsistence or below-subsistence incomes to generate investment funds is a travesty. The wretched of the earth pay a large price for economic unwisdom. Although in development efforts consumption and investment generally seem to move together for reasons Keynes helped to explain, suppression of consumption is often regarded as the grim reality and condition of development.

Keynes' emphasis was upon raising income and employment. For him saving is dependent and derivative; it is not necessarily anterior, determinant, and strategic.[16] But this lesson of Keynesian economics evidently is not yet fully accepted.

Obviously, the preceding paragraphs contain no general theory of capital formation. Their inclusion is intended to open a way through some conventional, partially ideological, almost folkloric notions that still sometimes undergird and divert policy considerations. A more adequate theory[17] is beyond the scope of this work, but its formulation would seem to require that account be taken of the following observations:

(1) In real terms, there are opportunity costs; the cost of using resources for one purpose (war goods) is the opportunity foregone to use them for another purpose (peace goods).

(2) Finite limits exist on how much physical capital can be formed. Technology, resource availability, skilled manpower, environmental considerations, site availability (to mention only a few considerations) may well delimit the number and form of options that can realistically be considered.

(3) Those who have discretion over money and credit creation do, in deciding who gets access to financial means, decide what real invest-

---

16. Ibid., p. 375.

17. In this connection see Louis J. Junker, "Capital Accumulation, Savings-Centered Theory and Economic Development," *Journal of Economic Issues*, Vol. I, Nos. 1 & 2, June, 1967, pp. 25-43.

ment shall occur and where material resources will be utilized. These people are credit "rationers," but the supply remains discretionary.

(4) Part of the exercise of discretion over money and credit will be accomplished by manipulation of rates of interest as well as through control of funds.

(5) Economic development is a function of a shifting interplay among a variety of interdependent determinants, including the intensity and character of motivation, the degree of "leadenness" in the "cake of custom," availability of credible leadership, availability of relevant knowledge and technology, availability of educable and skilled manpower, and domestic and external real and monetary capital formation, among others.

In sum, then, money and credit resources *are* important as noted. People do have, or can acquire, discretion over money stocks, over credit creation, over most interest rates, and therefore over capital formation. The latter is a necessary, but not sufficient, condition for the general expansion of real income. But, to mix metaphors, the hands that rock the monetary cradle are visible and in principle controllable; they need not rule the world or an economy.

Chapter 6

INSTITUTIONAL OPTIONS

As a creature of growth, as a tangled affair of multiple authorship, our national economy presents no symmetrical design. It can be given no simple name, it can be blessed by no term of description which is not refuted by an array of fact.

WALTON H. HAMILTON*

[The identity of] any economy, by whatever name it may be called . . . is to be found in its operations as a going concern. Its character is fixed by the detail of concrete arrangements, always fluid, which make it up.

WALTON H. HAMILTON**

*From THE POLITICS OF INDUSTRY, by Walton Hamilton, p. 162. Copyright © 1957 by The Regents of the University of Michigan. Reprinted by permission of Alfred A. Knopf, Inc.

**Ibid., p. 164.

The resource base of an evolving, functional economy, we have suggested, is in large measure a product of the growth of knowledge and technology and the exercise of genuine choice. Similarly, and even more evidently, is the institutional mix of any political economy a consequence of people's discretion. The structural options available are coextensive with people's ability to think rationally and critically about their own economic condition. Institutions, too, are grounded in the growing, cumulative knowledge fund.

A fundamental deficiency of the ism-ideologies is that each of their proffered economies takes a *particular* structural mix as given, as finished and final, and then excludes it from inquiry and appraisal. The structural mix of an evolving, functional economy, in contrast, must be under constant critical scrutiny. At all times some of the economy's institutional elements will necessarily be in the process of being revised, renewed, or abandoned. "Which direction is forward" must constantly be determined anew. Presumably, that is the import of Jefferson's remark about the wisdom of a substantial change in structure every generation or so. How and why this is the case requires some exposition and illustration.

Present-day students are not strangers to the common and necessary condition of living in a collegiate world of overlapping prescriptive and proscriptive canons and arrangements. In attending a college or university students very well may have to accommodate themselves (a) to rules governing on-campus behavior (in the formulation of which they may or may not have had a voice), (b) to curriculum patterns, course and degree requirements, (c) to remnants of family directives and constraints, (d) to national laws concerning military service, (e) to local practices regarding employment and housing options, (f) to peer-group expectations and codes concerning dress, drug use, and sexual behavior, among others.

With minimum exposure to this changing mosaic of institutionalized beliefs and behaviors, students typically pass judgment on such prescriptive and proscriptive rules. Viewed with reference to their contribution to and relevance for the development of the students' capacities for critical and coherent thinking, some rules and practices will appear to have merit; others will seem wrong-headed. Some will seem facilitative and necessary; others will be viewed as redundant, demeaning, silly, or distractive. Some will accordingly be resisted or violated; some will be accepted and made governing; others will become subject to revision, abandonment, and/or replacement. And the construction of judgment along these lines will be a frequent, if not nearly continuous, facet of consciousness for perceptive students.

Present-day citizens are not strangers, either, to the common and necessary condition of living in an economic world of overlapping prescriptive and proscriptive stipulations. As we have repeatedly affirmed, people of necessity live in a mixed economy—an economy of myriad rules, directives, constraints, and patterned belief and behavior. Some are private; some are public. Some are comprehensive; some are more narrow in scope. Indeed, life is impossible without organization, and organization means constraints. But it is also an economy in which institutional components are everywhere the product of initiative behavior directed to some specific purpose or task. On the other hand, advocates of ideology around the world recommend change from existing structure to their own *particular* institutional forms. Each ideology offers an all-purpose slate of economic structures which is, for every society, presumed to be relevant and worthy of adoption. Capitalism, for example, is supposedly "a system for all seasons."

But citizens generally, in an evolving, functional economy, where they have a significant say in the matter, do not accept these ideological offerings in the sense of slavish incorporation or implementation in their experience. People may for various reasons *talk* ideologically; typically, they will not *act* ideologically. As is the case with students, perceptive citizens stand in more or less continuous critique of the economic structures which organize their lives. Wage rates, salary bonuses, trade-union practices, employment alternatives, welfare reforms, price levels, tax changes are the perennial objects of interest and debate; ideological debates concerning public ownership, classic competition, laissez faire governments are of minor concern.

In passing judgment on institutions, existing and proffered, alert citizens in an evolving, functional economy appraise institutions' merits with reference to their pertinence and effectiveness in the rational conduct of important economic activities or functions.

If permitted and encouraged, citizens will participate in the "stream of decisions" which defines economic structure and therewith nonideologically determines "which direction is forward." The outcome inevitably is a structurally mixed economy. If the decisions are indeed rationally and perceptively made, the result is an economy uniquely adept at problem solving.

In evolving, functional economies where advancements in the arts and sciences are being encouraged, the range of available choice among institutional arrangements is steadily widening. Structures are being invented, revised, and/or selected to serve particular ends and purposes. In consequence, the economic process is in the main managed and administered; it is a product of overt decision and action; it is made to function in response to the exercise of considered judgments. It is an economy in which the "working rules"[1] are undergoing deliberate revision.

1. John R. Commons, *The Economics of Collective Action*, The Macmillan Co., New York, 1950, p. 12 and passim.

An understanding of an evolving, functional economy will be enhanced now if we draw on and make specific application of the function-structure distinction introduced above. What are the particular economic functions which must be organized? What are (or have been) the structural options used in carrying out these functions? These questions, respectively, are now our immediate agenda.

I.   ECONOMIC FUNCTIONS

In an evolving, functional economy, the production and distribution of goods and services—the provision of the means of life and experience— requires, obviously, that a variety of economic functions (productive activities) be more or less continuously performed. Such performance is possible only if behavior is patterned, if the functions are organized and given effect through institutional arrangements.

Among the economic functions of such an economy will be found the following:

(a)   industrial production of goods
(b)   provision of basic resources including energy
(c)   production of food and fiber
(d)   design and construction of enclosed space
(e)   creation and control of money and credit
(f)   provision for nondiscriminatory productive participation
(g)   determination of exchange ratios (prices)
(h)   determination of income shares
(i)   production and dissemination of reliable knowledge
(j)   resolution or adjudication of economic conflict
(k)   transport of goods and persons
(l)   communication of word and image
(m) pursuit of overall growth and stability
(n)   provision of medical care
(o)   education of the young and others
(p)   training of the labor force
(q)   protection of environmental quality and ecological balances
(r)   provision for artistic and aesthetic creativity
(s)   provision of recreational opportunities and facilities
(t)   provision of material means for community's defense

Depending on the degree of generality or specificity desired, such a roster of economic functions could no doubt be revised or extended. Because of space limitations, we must confine our illustrative comments concerning structural options to a liberal sampling among these listed functional categories (*a* through *h* will be considered at some length).

II.   ECONOMIC STRUCTURES

To bring into view something of the range of structural options which have been or are being utilized, we draw on materials from the economy of the United States. In citing American examples, we do not mean necessarily to imply that this economy is a paradigmatic "evolving, functional economy" of the kind mentioned above. Neither do we intend here the production of a halo effect or, for that matter, a massive "put down." We are interested in institutional variability and the performance of economic functions to which it is addressed. But with reference both to function and to institutional structure, we too cannot avoid passing judgment. Indeed, the process of selection compels the application of criteria of pertinence; in choosing for relevance, we must perforce take sides. *All purposive inquiry is inherently and fundamentally normative*, academic folklore notwithstanding.

In reviewing examples of how the American economy gives institutional effect to these specific functions, the reader may wish to ask himself or herself whether or not the structures cited appear to contribute to or permit the resolution of problems spawning revolutionary demands for substantial economic and social change. Do the structures tend to provide for augmented growth and more equitable distribution of income? Do they enhance participative and democratic determination of national economic policies? Do they promote nondiscriminatory and meaningful involvement in the economy? Do they assure protection for environmental quality? Do they facilitate a rational consideration of national priorities? The posing of such questions reflects a normative concern. The structural options discussed are not likely to be found wholly consistent with that concern. But the examples chosen are reflective of the evolution of institutional forms. Most are not derived from ideological recommendations. Presumably, all were initially introduced to cope with or respond to an economic problem as conceived by someone.

In the cursory examination of structural options here, note how the older ism-ideology distinctions of public enterprise vs. private enterprise, monopoly vs. competition, command vs. market, compulsion vs. volition, and of bourgeoisie vs. proletariat tend to constrict perception or become passé under the continuing confrontation of genuine problems and the assault of reflective inquiry and inventiveness on those structures and processes deemed problematic. Increasingly obscure are mutually exclusive distinctions between private and public sectors. A diagram developed by Robert Dahl and Charles Lindblom some years ago is still a useful example of the variety of institutional forms which do not "fit" the ism models (see figure 6-1).

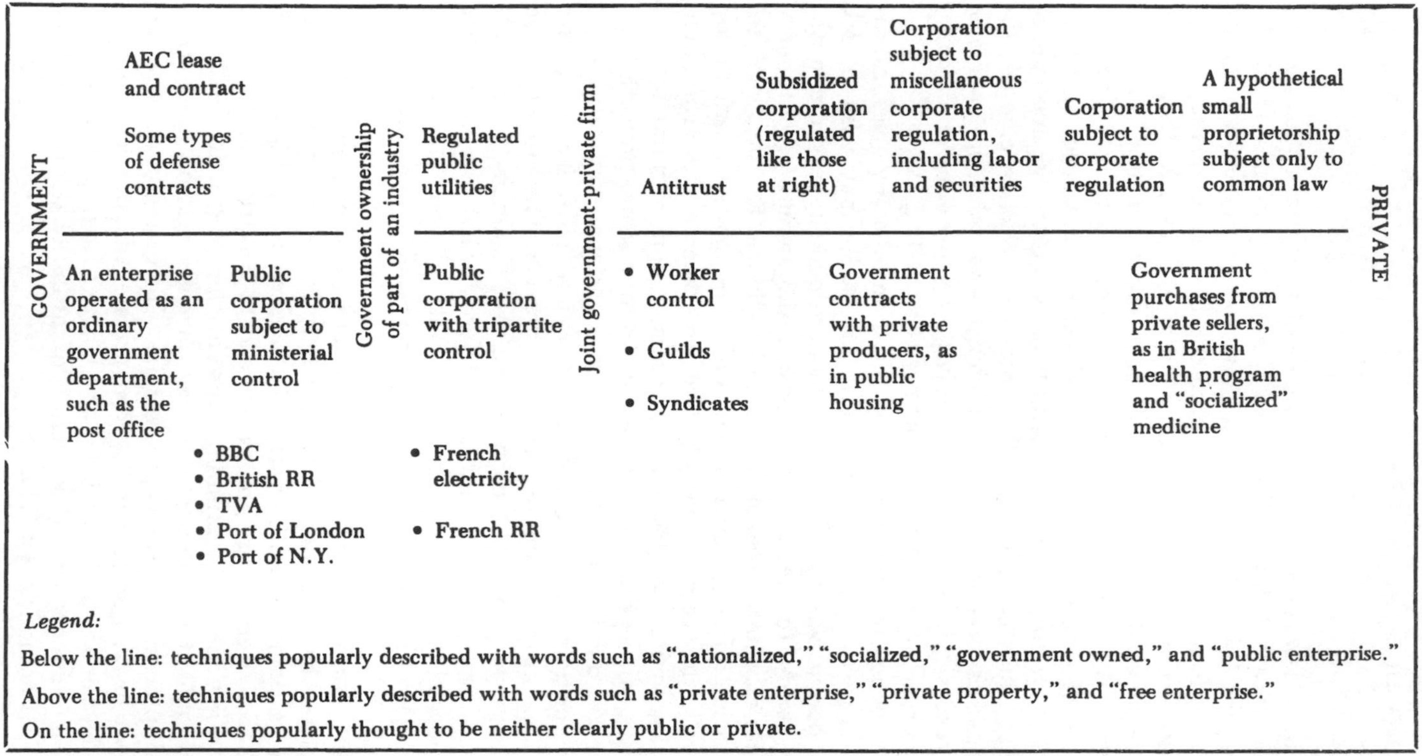

PRIVATE

GOVERNMENT

AEC lease and contract

Some types of defense contracts

An enterprise operated as an ordinary government department, such as the post office

Public corporation subject to ministerial control
- BBC
- British RR
- TVA
- Port of London
- Port of N.Y.

Government ownership of part of an industry

Regulated public utilities

Public corporation with tripartite control
- French electricity
- French RR

Joint government-private firm

Subsidized corporation (regulated like those at right)

Government contracts with private producers, as in public housing
- Worker control
- Guilds
- Syndicates

Antitrust

Corporation subject to miscellaneous corporate regulation, including labor and securities

Corporation subject to corporate regulation

Government purchases from private sellers, as in British health program and "socialized" medicine

A hypothetical small proprietorship subject only to common law

Figure 6-1[2] A Continuum Showing Some of the Choices Between Government Ownership and Private Enterprise

Legend:

Below the line: techniques popularly described with words such as "nationalized," "socialized," "government owned," and "public enterprise."

Above the line: techniques popularly described with words such as "private enterprise," "private property," and "free enterprise."

On the line: techniques popularly thought to be neither clearly public or private.

2. Robert A. Dahl and Charles E. Lindblom, *Politics, Economics, and Welfare*, p. 10. Copyright © 1953 by Harper & Row, Publishers, Inc. By permission of the publisher.

(a) Industrial Production of Goods

As nearly everyone knows, the modern corporation has become the dominant organizational form for industrial production in the United States. In its present form, the modern corporation is itself an evolved product of several hundred years of institutional tinkering and experimentation. In the process, the meaning and structure of private enterprise and private ownership have been transformed; an impressive instrument of obtaining and retaining economic power has been fashioned; and a potentially "efficient" vehicle for the direction and coordination of productive activity has emerged.

As most students know, the attractiveness of the modern corporation derives from its legal-entity status, the limited liability accorded investors, its potential longevity (immortality), its capacity to fragment equity interests and increase its access to loanable funds, and the provision of certain tax advantages not available in other forms.

In addition, the corporate form typically affords the corporate decision maker an opportunity (thought it is not always exercised) to interpose the corporation as a legal personality between himself or herself and those who are influenced by his or her decisions (see figure 6-2). By acting for and in the name of the corporation, he or she is able, if it is desired, to obtain a measure of insulation and anonymity in the exercise of economic power. For some this is no doubt a major attraction, potentially irresponsible though it may be.

Finally, as noted, the modern industrial corporation proves to be an effective instrument through which to marshall and utilize economic power. Characteristically it is organized internally on an authority-responsibility model—the conventional pyramid—with authoritative decisions made by executives at the top and flowing down through the organization. Compliance and responsibility flow from subordinates upward. Typically there is little or no pretense to the provision of "participatory democracy," however benevolent and public spirited the executives may be. But even this bastion of inviolate managerial prerogatives seems now to be coming under serious scrutiny. [3]

Even so, the modern corporation comes out of no ideological handbook—capitalist, communist, or fascist. Some surface appearances to the contrary, it is not in design a fascist structure, although the fascists are prepared to modify and redirect corporate structures to their own purposes.

Modern industrial corporations are integrated economic bureaucracies which have achieved and largely retain the status of "private" industrial governments (having significant capacity to compel or forbid

---

3. For example, Seymour Melman, "Industrial Efficiency under Managerial versus Cooperative Decision-Making," *Review of Radical Political Economics*, Vol. 2, No. 1, Spring, 1970, pp. 9-34.

PROPRIETARY ENTERPRISE

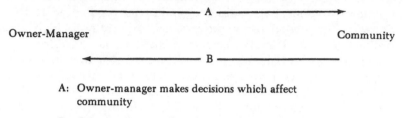

A: Owner-manager makes decisions which affect community

B: Community reacts directly upon decision maker

CORPORATE ENTERPRISE

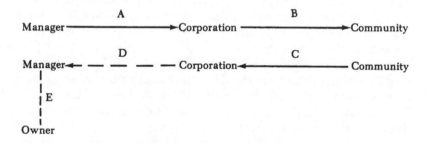

A: Manager makes decision in name of corporation

B: Decision affects community

C: Community reacts to corporate decision

D: Manager-decision maker feels impact of decision only indirectly

E: Separation of ownership and managerial control

IMPLICATION

Corporate form affords manager an opportunity to interpose the corporation (a legal entity) between himself or herself and those who are affected by the decision.

Figure 6-2   Corporate Decision Making

economic behavior). [4] These private industrial governments have used or are using such devices as the following, among others, to secure and retain economic power:

(1) cartel agreements which set noncompetitive prices, stipulate the form and timing of technological innovations, and divide markets into monopolistic preserves (duPont, Alcoa?);

(2) holding-company organization which permits the pyramiding of control through the device of creating corporations for the express purpose of holding controlling equity interest in one or more other corporations (Insull empire, Kaiser Industries, AT&T);

(3) price-leadership practices which, through overt or covert arrangements, permit the dominant firm in an industry to serve as a de facto price setter for the entire industry (General Motors, U.S. Steel?);

(4) corporate mergers which create multiproduct conglomerate enterprises and provide evidently for some dispersion of risk (Ling-Temco-Vought, Litton Industries, Firestone);

(5) patent control and licensing agreements which empower holders of patented knowledge (legally recognized private property in ideas) to control who uses new technology and on what terms (United Shoe Machinery, Hartford Glass, IBM);

(6) tying agreements which permit large manufacturers to require that jobbers or distributors of their products, as a condition of getting major products, also sell their minor products, and/or adhere to a fixed-selling-price policy (Standard Oil of California and Standard Stations);

(7) interlocking directorates which permit individuals to serve concurrently as members of governing boards of directors of a number of corporations (industrial and financial), thus concentrating the influence and control of such individuals;

(8) trade associations of producers of comparable products or services which provide for fuller communication on price and production policies among members and which assist in the marshalling of political opposition to public policies deemed undesirable (National Association of Manufacturers, Iron and Steel Institute).

Some of these practices have over the years been subjected to modification or control by courts, legislatures, and regulatory bodies. However, such constraints in the aggregate seem not to have seriously eroded the pervasive power of these private industrial governments.

The foregoing techniques for gaining control have been and/or are being used, evidently, to control supply sources, eliminate or control competitive rivalry, pool managerial talent, secure tax breaks, participate more effectively in contract negotiations, protect the intraindustry position of the firm, regulate or manipulate prices, protect market value of investments, improve dividend prospects, gain better access to credit

4. Walton Hamilton, THE POLITICS OF INDUSTRY, op. cit., passim.

sources, mount contra-trade union power, diversify risk, foster improvement in quality of product, control product design, enhance capacity for political influence, gain access to or protect research findings and research staff, prevent infringement on conventional marketing area, regulate the introduction of new products and technology, among others.

All such devices and others unnamed, obviously, are volitional. They are institutional measures to secure, extend, or retain discretion over some significant facets of the productive process. They all reflect the exercise of human choice; each of these devices for obtaining power and all rationale offered in its defense were consciously developed by "corporate stewards" (executives), their lawyers, spokesmen, or their academic apologists. In Galbraith's view, corporate power is sustained, revised, and extended by technical specialist teams—the technostructure —who have come into de facto control of the largest corporations. [5] Such choices are fallible; they are properly objects of inquiry and appraisal.

We pose the question: does the exercise of power in these listed ways serve a defensible, nonideological principle of the public interest? Sometimes yes; sometimes no. We cannot presume a definitive answer, but what of the auto industry's tardiness in the introduction of long-known safety features on American automobiles[6] and its lobbying opposition to strong emission-control standards?[7] Is it important that in 1967 there was only one black man with an authorized auto dealership in the United States?[8] What of the food and pharmaceutical industries' introduction of food additives and drugs which sometimes are inadequately tested, are physically harmful, or are worthless for the purpose intended?[9] And what of the long-term studied resistance of consumer-goods industries to product safety, full-knowledge labeling, and the elimination of deceptive packaging?[10] And when is an industrial firm culpable in the production of military hardware? Was the protest a few years ago against the production of napalm by Dow Chemical warranted?

Are those who exercise discretion over corporate policy as an economic elite of technical experts, corporate managers, executives, and directors somehow entitled to their status and role? What is the warrant? The modern corporation which confers this power is an institutional innovation. Its adaptability to serve power ends is extensive, as we have seen. How does the community at large assure itself that such

5. Galbraith, *Economics and the Public Interest*, op. cit., pp. 81-145.

6. Ralph Nader, *Unsafe at Any Speed*, Grossman Publishers, New York, 1965.

7. "Pollution Ruling Jars Car Makers," *The Sacramento Bee*, September 9, 1970, p. A 11.

8. "Black Dealer Woes," *The Wall Street Journal*, September 8, 1970, p. 1.

9. John Grant Fuller, *200,000,000 Guinea Pigs*, Putnam, New York, 1972.

10. Ralph Nadar, *Beware*, Law-Arts Publishing Co., New York, 1971.

discretion is used in the community's behalf? To date, commission regulation, antitrust litigation, countervailing power, and the "noblesse oblige" of the corporate stewards have all been inadequate to the task. To the question of accountability and democratization of economic power, we return below.

Structural changes under consideration: Some would eliminate the facade of "privateness" from the large industrial corporation and require the full disclosure of its operations, including its unit costs. Others would introduce selective controls over specific areas of corporate discretion, for example, prices, character and amount of investment spending, etc. Others would utilize public ownership in limited areas of private default. [11] Hope springs eternal for yet others (especially those of the orthodox school) who believe in more rigorous antitrust enforcement to legislate competitive behavior. Ralph Nader wants to revive the idea of federal chartering of corporations, require full disclosure of corporations' operations, and perfect accountability mechanisms for corporate decision makers. [12] Still others have suggested "yard-stick" public enterprise in otherwise "private" industries; some want governments to buy equity interests (controlling?) in large corporations, etc.

(b) Provision of Basic Resources Including Energy

In major urban areas, electricity is usually generated by privately owned, monopolistic public utility corporations whose rates and service are subjected to control by independent regulatory commissions (an institutional invention of the late nineteenth century) representing the public. Many agree that over the years those supposedly doing the regulating have themselves become subservient to or are largely under the control of the regulated industries. [13] In rural areas, the Rural Electrification Administration (a federal government agency) has helped finance the creation of a large number of cooperative electrical systems. In the Tennessee Valley, expansion of public electrical enterprise (TVA), which lowered previously prevailing rates by about 50 per cent, led to a substantial expansion of so-called private enterprise. [14]

The oligopolistic petroleum industry prior to 1969 apparently had an administered supply structure (production quota system) covering most major firms, fields, and states under the de facto aegis of the

11. Galbraith, *Economics and the Public Purpose*, op. cit., pp. 274-85.
12. Eileen Shanahan, "Reformer: Urging Business Change," (Ralph Nader interview), *The New York Times*, January 24, 1971, pp. F1 & F9. This view is now expanded in Ralph Nader, Mark Green & Joel Seligman, *Taming the Giant Corporation*, W. W. Norton & Co., New York, 1976.
13. For example: George J. Stigler, ". . . as a rule regulation is acquired by the industry and is designed and operated primarily for its benefit." *Bell Journal of Economics and Management Science*, Vol. II, No. 1, Spring, 1971, p. 3.
14. Clair Wilcox, *Public Policies Toward Business* (4th ed.), Richard D. Irwin, Homewood, Illinois, 1971, p. 519.

federal government (Bureau of Mines) and the Texas Railroad Commission.[15] ". . . the companies wholly owned the oil they produced in almost every country around the world and could determine levels of production, prices, exports, and investments."[16] Since 1969, their position has changed dramatically. The major companies have become minority owners in producing areas. In October 1973, the consortium of governments of oil-producing countries (OPEC) began unilaterally setting prices and production levels. Domestically, the industry's ancient tax haven of depletion allowances was, in 1974, eliminated for major producers but retained for independents. The retention or removal of federal price controls on crude oil, gasoline, and natural gas remains (as of this writing) a source of agitated debate in and out of Congress. Those recalling the "energy crisis" of 1973-1974 with the accompanying administered supply, administered prices, and administered profits will have little trouble acknowledging, however, that the oil industry still constitutes a private industrial government with substantial economic power.[17]

In the soft-coal industry, cartelization of the mines (market sharing and price administration) occurred in the late 1930s under governmental auspices (Guffy Act); the effort was abandoned in the early 1940s. More recently, substantial private regulation (price, wage, and market administration) of the industry was being accomplished by the United Mine Workers' Union through its wage and manpower agreements with management. Technological overhaul of mining operations, including long-term manpower reductions (displacement), were negotiated on condition of providing higher wages for workers remaining in the industry.[18]

The development of atomic energy began, for reasons of cost and security, as a governmental monopoly. Controlled by a presidentially appointed commission (AEC), the atomic energy industry was a prime example of public ownership and control coupled to dominantly private operation. Through an elaborate system of contracts most AEC production was provided by large corporations (often on a cost-plus basis) and much AEC research was provided by universities. Ideologically grounded efforts to increase the role and control of private oligopolistic firms in the production and distribution of atomic power have been commonplace over the last several years.[19]

15. A. Shonfield, *Modern Capitalism*, Oxford, New York, 1965, p. 439.

16. William D. Smith, "The Oil Industry—Caught in a Tug-of-War," *The New York Times*, July 7, 1974, Sec. 3, pp. 1. Copyright © 1974 The New York Times Company. Reprinted by permission.

17. John M. Blair, *The Control of Oil*, Pantheon Books, New York, 1976.

18. M. Fainsod, L. Gordon, & J. C. Palamountain, Jr., *Government and the American Economy*, W. W. Norton, New York, 1959, pp. 629-38.

19. Ibid., pp. 680-702.

Structural changes under consideration: Proposals exist to invigorate or to modify the regulatory commissions to restore and extend their power and interest in regulating industry on behalf of the public. [20] A breakup of the largest oil firms (divesture) is again being urged. [21] Private suppliers of power would no doubt like a larger slice of the atomic-energy development programs. Private petroleum companies are moving to secure control of alternative energy sources. [22]

(c) Production of Food and Fiber

Orthodox capitalist economists are inclined to point to the agricultural sector as a major remaining example of classically competitive markets (so many buyers and sellers that no one can control price). The capitalist sees the almost daily price fluctuations for major commodities (wheat, corn, cattle, hogs) as a continuing manifestation of the invisible hand of market pricing and resource allocation, which must indicate a largely free private enterprise sector of farmers. Regrettably, perhaps, the foregoing is at best but a part of the picture; it may not even be the major part. Actually, the structural mix in agriculture is an interesting and instructive amalgam of institutional constraints and options.

In the agri-businesses, the "factories in the field" of California's Central Valley (and elsewhere), the corporate farm is commonplace, with its attendant acquisition of economic (and political) power. Cooperative enterprises have found favor as producer-controlled marketing agencies and as instruments of collective purchase of farm machinery and equipment. Federal programs to manipulate agricultural supply to support prices in an attempt to provide parity incomes to farmers of major crops date back nearly half a century. Ingenious have been the devices (soil banks, acreage diversion programs, etc.) to provide continuing and handsome subsidies to mainly the upper third (ranked by value of farm-product sales) of food and fiber producers. [23] Such subsidies in the early 1970s were running approximately $4.5 billion per year. [24] Shortly thereafter, subsidies and production constraints were reduced because of the move toward full production to meet mounting world-wide demands for food.

20. Warren J. Samuels & Harry M. Trebing, *A Critique of Administrative Regulation of Public Utilities*, Michigan State University, East Lansing, 1972.

21. Robert Sherrill, "Breaking Up Big Oil," *The New York Times Magazine*, October 3, 1976, pp. 15 ff.

22. E.g., William D. Smith, "The Oil Industry—Caught in a Tug-of-War," *The New York Times*, op. cit., pp. 1 & 5. Also, U.S. Congress, Senate Committee on Energy and Natural Resources, Subcommittee on Energy Research and Development, *Petroleum Industry Involvement in Alternative Sources of Energy*, U.S. Government Printing Office, Washington, D.C., 1977.

23. *The American Almanac For 1974* (The Statistical Abstract of the U.S.), Grosset & Dunlap, Inc., New York, pp. 587 & 596.

24. Executive Office of the President, Bureau of the Budget, *The Budget in Brief, Fiscal Year 1971*, Government Printing Office, Washington, D.C., 1970, p. 36.

Differently constituted supply-control measures are used for some specialty crops in quest of administered prices and incomes. For example, the state government of California participates as supervisor to assure that only the tonnage of fresh peaches agreed on by the growers and packers (at a negotiated price per ton) is actually canned in the factories. A state inspection system assures that "excess" tonnage is dumped.

The publicly provided flow of reliable knowledge and technique from research centers (e.g., land-grant universities) to food and fiber producers through county agents, university extension services, and governmental publications is a large-scale subsidized support program which also dates back to early in this century.

Innumerable governmental programs over the years have sought to assure the availability (and low cost) of credit to farmers for land and supply purchases.

Thus, ostensibly free-enterprise agriculture has been for many decades, and remains, the eager recipient of an impressive array of publicly provided benefits, subsidies, and controls. The *consequences* of unbridled classic competition—low prices generating low incomes, excessive production, no control over markets—are intolerable in agriculture. Perhaps we should look again, and skeptically, at this normative use of the competitive model.

Finally, agriculture seems destined for some administered wage setting. Institutions of collective bargaining are slowly being extended to agricultural labor following the long and bitter table-grape and lettuce boycott battles waged by Cesar Chavez and the farm workers. Interestingly, the federal government, which in the Wagner Act and elsewhere provided for and encouraged the establishment of good-faith collective bargaining procedures for industrial workers, in this instance appeared for a time to side with the grape growers in the boycott dispute. The Department of Defense, by dramatically accelerating its purchase and shipment of table grapes to United States troops in Southeast Asia, eased some of the economic sting of the boycott. [25] The government's role is not necessarily consistent or predictable.

Organizational efforts of farm workers in the 1970s were plagued with a bitter jurisdictional dispute between Chavez's United Farm Workers and the Teamsters. The latter, evidently with the aid of the growers, made heavy inroads on the number of contracts negotiated by the UFW. An agreement in 1977 divided jurisdictions and resolved the dispute. New legislation in California (1975) established an Agricultural Labor Relations Board which now supervises agency elections and aids in the development of collective bargaining in agriculture.

25. *El Macriado*, Vol. III, No. 7, July 15, 1969, p. 4. Regarding the Pentagon's purchase of lettuce, see *El Macriado*, Vol. IV, No. 13, January 15, 1971.

Structural changes under consideration: Legislative proposals have been made to eliminate all subsidies, or alternately to put dollar limits on the amount of subsidy payments going to any one farmer or agri-business. Others have suggested that greater public support be given to the bottom two-thirds (ranked by income) of the farmers, who historically have received a very small piece of the subsidy pie. Some would extend income-maintenance legislation to farm workers. A few would drop all acreage and production controls, and let the market mechanism eliminate all who become, as a consequence, marginal producers.

(d) Design and Construction of Enclosed Space

The organization of the task of providing buildings and homes in which people work and live also shows both the now commonplace complexity of the economic fabric and its mainly nonideological character.

The design and engineering work occurs in private professional firms, in public and private colleges and universities, in public agencies at local, state, and federal levels. Public and private building is accomplished mainly by contract arrangements with construction corporations. What can be built is in part determined in urban areas by local zoning codes. Such codes can sometimes be manipulated or circumvented by local power groups.

Substantial assistance to the purchasers of residences has been provided by the mortgage-loan guarantees of the Federal Housing Administration and the Veterans Administration. The funds themselves come mostly from private lending firms whose operations are subjected to some statutory controls. Interest rates on guaranteed loans are administered as matters of public policy. Private home owners gain an important subsidy in income-tax deductions on mortgage interest paid.

The funding of construction of public works (schools, libraries, hospitals, post offices, etc.) has never been *off* the agenda of major governments. Grants-in-aid and loans for construction are frequently made to governments, higher education institutions, and private corporations for a variety of authorized purposes and with many types of "strings" attached.

Legislatures and the courts have become involved in the question of whether or not the transfer of residential property may be denied to willing buyers on racial and color grounds. Therewith lies also, in effect, the question of the continuance of racially segregated schooling. Although the institution of "restrictive covenants" is no longer an enforceable constraint in the courts, the prejudice-based denial of access to housing in some areas continues. It is curious to find some who proclaim most loudly the virtues of private ownership (and of "unlimited discretion" to dispose of their property as they will) among those who would deny on race and color grounds the right of others (who are financially able) to buy, hold, and use private property (residences) in areas of *their* choice. One has "freedom" to sell to whomever he chooses; the other is denied the "freedom" to buy. Is that the freedom provided by "the American Way"?

Structural changes under consideration: Since the rediscovery of poverty in the ghettos and barrios, a large number of proposals for changing the prescriptive rules to improve poor people's housing have been forthcoming. Rent subsidies have been proposed; a few such programs have been introduced. Consideration is being given to measures to improve access of minorities and the poor to mortgage credit. In some areas conservationists are seeking to forestall the manipulation of zoning codes which will serve land-speculation interests. Elsewhere zoning laws are being revised to reflect renewed interest in environmental quality. But despite heroic efforts in some quarters, the level and character of urban planning appears not to have been equal to the task placed upon it. Perhaps in few other places in the economy is a substantial rethinking and overhaul of institutional arrangements more desperately needed. Moreover, no proposals appear yet to have surfaced which are large enough in scope to give promise of a substantial improvement in the housing conditions for the third to a half of Americans who appear to remain ill-housed based on contemporary standards of health and decency.

(e) Creation and Control of Money and Credit

In few areas does the American experience demonstrate greater institutional hybridity. That an evolving, functional economy requires a national policy and structure on the creation and control of money and credit has in general been well enough understood since the reports of Alexander Hamilton to the Congress in the 1790s. With President Jackson's veto of the Second National Bank in 1832, the United States was left without a formal national banking system until the creation of the Federal Reserve System in 1913.

This central banking system is a remarkable admixture; its character reflects the somewhat ambivalent attitudes toward banking which developed out of nineteenth-century experience. Created by an act of Congress, the Federal Reserve System (hereafter, the Fed) is owned "privately" by the member banks of the system. Its directors are appointed by the federal executive branch; its range of discretion over money and credit is specified by Congress. But its exercise of that discretion within the range prescribed is largely on its own volition; the Fed has a significant amount of autonomy of operation within rather broad limits set by Congress. It appears reasonable to assert that such discretion is exercised along lines which leaders in the banking community (mainly private) believe to be in their interest and in the public interest.

The Federal Reserve System functions, as most students are aware, as the economy's central banking system and is the federal government's monetary agent generally. But the power and ability of the Fed to control demand-deposit money (some 75 per cent of total money supply) hinges on its policy options, which affect the reserve-account position of member banks. As was noted above, the manipulation of bank rates, open-market purchases and sales of government securities, and the adjustment of the minimum ratio of reserves to deposits permits the Fed, with the participation of member banks and others, to tighten or loosen money and credit. Thus the Fed is a curious blend of so-called public and private elements and arrangements. Clearly it emerges from no ideologist's roster of idealized institutions.

Structural changes under consideration: Criticism of the way the Fed has used its largely autonomous power to manipulate (administer) money supplies and interest rates has led some (notably Representative Wright Patman of Texas) to recommend sweeping changes in the Federal Reserve System. Not excluded is serious consideration of the abandonment of the Fed in favor of a simple nationalized central bank. Others (especially Milton Friedman, et al.) would retain the structure, but drastically narrow the Fed's discretionary powers to make independent judgments on monetary policy. Under current practice, the main instrument through which the Fed is held to account appears to be its leaders' annual (or oftener) "command" appearance before committees of Congress concerned with economic and monetary policy. The necessity to appear, explain, and justify actions previously taken and contemplated provides a significant means, though not a very powerful one, of impinging upon the Fed's decision-making processes. But since monetary policy is indeed too important to leave to bankers, especially where it bears importantly on the level of income and employment, we can expect continuing efforts to assure the responsiveness and responsibility of the Fed to, at least, a congressional conception of the public interest.

(f) Provision for Nondiscriminatory Productive Participation

The American Dream in the more popular literature has long included the concept of a fair chance, of equal opportunity, and of a system where family position, wealth, and ethnic and national origin counted less than the individual's own abilities. "What can you do?"[26]—not

---

26. Perhaps it should be noted here, as a caution, that "What can you do?" has also no doubt at times become a discriminatory application of a meritocracy principle in which human worth is judged according to some hierarchical ordering of occupations (jobs vs. positions!). The American Dream seems to have been more of a commitment to participate—tritely, "to put the shoulder to the wheel"—than to grade people by work status.

"Where did you come from?" or "Who is your father?"—was thought to be a more typical question posed by employers to would-be employees.

That the cold world of reality did not correspond very well with the dream of open economic access needs little elaboration here. The virtual genocide practiced by some against the native American, the long-term and passionate institutional and ideological defenses of slavery, the job discrimination against successive waves of urban emigrants, the emigrant exclusion laws, the many devices by which women were excluded from professional training and executive positions, the demeaning treatment of "coolie" railroad labor and predominantly Mexican farm labor, the postslavery economic subjugation of blacks, the exploitation of child labor—all subverted the American Dream. It was not a free-market mechanism, neither an accident, nor fate that produced the stultifying stereotypes of Pullman sleeping-car porters being black, of policemen being Irish, of Japanese being gardeners, of women being secretaries and teachers, of Jews being entertainers and professionals, of Portuguese being fishermen, and of Italians being vegetable merchants. People who are denied access on grounds of race, sex, or ancestry to some or most occupations will be compelled to find economic connections in whatever minimal areas are left open to them by prevailing mores and power centers. The elemental plausibility and retention of the stereotypes derive from that fact.

Even so, Americans have retained the ideal of fair chance, of equal opportunity. It was a concept of fair chance which presumed classically competitive conditions—conditions where everyone started even and where pecuniary judgments were determinant.[27] The dream was the rags-to-riches, Horatio Alger, model. Much of the structural change intended to extend economic opportunity and end economic discrimination retains this infirmity (the presumption of classically competitive conditions), based at bottom on deference to ideology. That is, society's task is, for example, to equip its members with skills and knowledge to struggle and succeed in competition against others in the unfettered labor markets. Then it follows that one should defer to market judgments of who should have what kinds of jobs.

Perhaps one relieving virtue of the American experience in this area is that after decade upon decade of "benign neglect" of the fact that neither the overt use of hiring power by private and public agencies nor the alleged free-market mechanism was functioning well to end discrimination in economic connections, structural change began to be introduced to reduce such prejudicial treatment of people. In consequence, the employment of women and children came under the protection of federal laws and supportive court decisions. Massive denials on grounds of race and color finally led to the adoption and

27. We return to this matter below in chapter 16.

implementation of Fair-Employment-Practice laws and regulations. In the armed forces, overt formal discriminatory treatment was ended de jure, even though de facto racism apparently continues in some areas.

A study prepared by the Council of Economic Advisors some years ago attempted to measure the economic costs attributable directly to racial discrimination in employment. [28] The price tag (for those who think mainly in dollar signs) on such discrimination ran nearly to $20 billion per year in 1962 prices. Presumably this study and others added evidential support to arguments of those seeking national measures to end economic discrimination.

Access to jobs has been enhanced also by the widening of access to higher education through Educational Opportunity Programs, tuition waivers, reserved entrance allotments, individually determined entrance requirements, and the like. Elsewhere some progress has been made in rewriting the rules to provide equal pay for equal work (e.g., for men *and* women in public education), ending unwarranted preferential treatment.

Structural changes under consideration and already made: As noted above, the Equal Rights Amendment, proposing equality for women, is before the states for ratification. The National Organization for Women and others are seeking an end to "male chauvinism" in a wide range of social, political, and economic areas. The federal government is implementing an affirmative action program to end discrimination in public employment and in institutions accepting federal grants. Conscientious efforts are being made to end stereotyping of ethnic and minority-group occupations in public-school textbooks and in television advertising. Some officials of large corporations (e.g., Pacific Telephone) who have become genuinely concerned about their social responsibilities are beginning to initiate job-training programs directed uniquely to members of the community who have been victimized by social, educational, and employment discrimination. State and local governments in some sections are expanding nondiscriminatory employment opportunities.

(g) *Determination of Exchange Ratios (Prices)*

Those who accept the conventional wisdom of orthodoxy have always insisted that all modern economies must have a price system. Many a scholarly journal article and popular tract on the virtues of capitalism have discussed the nature and necessity of "the price system." [29] With the assertion of the need for *a* price system or systems there is no quarrel.

28. Executive Office of the President, Council of Economic Advisors, "Economic Costs of Racial Discrimination in Employment," (mimeographed), September 25, 1962.

29. A widely reprinted article of this kind—which has been called a "minor classic in economics"—appeared shortly after World War II. The article is R. A. Radford, "The Economic Organization of a P.O.W. Camp," *Economics*, Vol. 12, 1945.

But the authors of these articles go further. In their judgment, one particular price system is superior beyond all others. That system is the allegedly autonomous, self-adjusting, naturalistic, free price system of a capitalist economy. Indeed, as many students are well aware, "economic theory" is frequently taken to mean "price theory." The study of movements toward or departures from competitive equilibrium prices has been a central focus of inquiry in mainstream economics.

Most economists have long since abandoned the contention that free-market pricing under pure and perfect competition describes comprehensively an existential economy or even a major economic sector within an economy. But economists have been and are still exploring price phenomena under a variety of market forms and structures and over differing time periods. The study of pricing under conditions of monopolistic competition, oligopoly, duopoly, as well as under pure competition and pure monopoly, is commonplace. The exploration of short-run and long-run adjustments is routine. But this inquiry at its core proceeds as an examination of the extent and character of *departures* from the normative ideal of pure and perfect competition. Noncompetitive prices may well be recognized as typical in many areas, but the normative merit of the competitive model is not considered; it is assumed. Protestations that the competitive norm is merely an analytical abstraction which is not meant to describe reality miss the point. At issue is the *character* of the abstraction, not the *need* for abstraction. All inquiry, of course, does require selectivity of some elements for study to the exclusion of other elements. Those elements chosen for emphasis by capitalist economists are market phenomena operative in an economy uniquely comprised of capitalist institutions. The classically competitive model has become a normative, Platonic ideal—always to be sought but never fully achieved.

In consequence, deference to the orthodox perspective narrows the range of choice of analytic models to one—a free competitive price system—and converts it into a criterion of judgment by which to test or measure actual market performance. The *proper* price system is the abstract ideal. The closest approximation of market behavior and operation thereto is what is meant by economic efficiency. Departures from the competitive norm are wrong to the degree that they depart. With this conceptual frame, any other normative model of pricing is inadmissible on its face.

That this mode of inquiry is constrictive and delimiting is apparent. A different pricing perspective is desirable; a more inclusive theory of price is on the agenda for inquiry. Observation of actual behavior is a useful place to begin. Before considering some examples of how the price-setting function is actually performed in the American economy, note the following:

Prices are exchange ratios; they stipulate the terms of exchange throughout any post-barter economy. As prescriptions governing behavior, they function as institutions. Folklore or theory notwithstanding, prices are set by people, directly or indirectly. Prices are administered; they are the product of human discretion. Most are set directly as an exercise of economic power by a relative few; a few are set indirectly in consequence of decisions of an aggregated many. People, operating in markets of varying scope and composition, functioning in planning bodies of various kinds, and subjected to various pressures and conditions, set prices.

Prices set in institutional settings where capitalist institutions exist and operate as orthodoxy prescribes may still be thought of as market-determined prices. In the modern world, such cases are rare. Prices set in organized markets for grain, stock shares, or debt instruments *may* at times approximate free competitive-market pricing. Prices set in institutional settings otherwise constituted are administered prices. By far, the overwhelming bulk of prices actually paid are to a greater or lesser degree administered by those who have acquired pricing power.

Of course, no price setter's discretion is infinite. He or she (or they) may indeed have to take some or much cognizance of demand conditions, of cost factors, of behavior of other firms, of government policies. But even though the extent of pricing power varies, some power to affect prices is held by virtually all sellers and by many buyers; zero market power is an anomaly. Economics, as with history, should be taken straight without chasers of fancy (to borrow, and modify, a line from H. J. Muller).[30] People administer prices; they prescribe behavior when they determine exchange ratios; when they change prices, they are engaged in institutional adjustment. They are modifying previously established prescriptive relations which set the terms of exchange of goods or services for money.

The relevant questions have never been, Are there prices? Are they necessary? Are some prices natural and others arbitrary? How far does this price deviate from the normal price? Rather, we might now want to ask, Who set these prices and on what grounds? How and why were prices set at this level? What are the consequences of pricing judgments? Do such consequences tend to support or impair an expanding, equitable, nondiscriminatory flow of real income? (The latter query may also be asked of an institutional change elsewhere in the economy.) Seen in this light, the normative theory of price of capitalistic orthodoxy is at least incomplete; in some areas it borders on the irrelevant. At best it

30. Herbert J. Muller, *The Uses of the Past*, New American Library, New York, 1954, p. 37.

becomes a rarely seen special case in those unique circumstances where the structures assumed in classical competition are found to exist.

As John Kenneth Galbraith remarks,

> We are profoundly conditioned by the theology of the market. Consequently, nothing seems good or normal that does not accord with the requirements of the market. A price that is fixed by the seller to a singular degree does not seem good. Accordingly, it requires a major act of will to think of price-fixing as both normal and having economic function. In fact, it is normal in all advanced industrial societies.[31]

However, special case or not, so long as the facade of free-market pricing can be maintained, so long will price administrators be able to disclaim any significant responsibility for their exercise of economic power in price setting. "Perhaps the oldest and certainly the wisest strategy for the exercise of power is to deny that it is possessed."[32] Price administrators can deny that they have autonomous or quasiautonomous judgment; the market allegedly dictates to *them*. In consequence, the deference to orthodoxy has long impaired the community's capacity to hold wielders of price-setting power adequately to account. Slumlords, auto manufacturers and dealers, appliance makers and sellers, medical doctors, auto mechanics, college trustees, drug makers are all engaged in price setting. They wield economic power. Only with great difficulty are their pricing judgments held to public scrutiny and judgment.

Consider the American experience. The function of determining exchange ratios, of exercising control over price, is an ongoing prerogative of private industrial governments, of public governments, and of imaginative structural combinations of each. We offer some examples of each.

Administered pricing in America's "private" corporate industry has been a prominent object of inquiry at least since the economic convulsions of the Great Depression.[33] It has been a fact of corporate economic life even longer.

31. Galbraith, *The New Industrial State*, op. cit., p. 190.
32. Galbraith, *Economics and the Public Purpose*, op. cit., p. 5.
33. See, for example, Gardiner C. Means, "The Reality of Administered Prices," (1935) in his *The Corporate Revolution in America*, Crowell-Collier Press, New York, 1962, pp. 77-96. Also, G. C. Means, *Administrative Inflation and Public Policy*, Anderson Kramer Associates, Washington, D.C., 1959; and G. C. Means, "The Problems and Prospects of Collective Capitalism," *Journal of Economic Issues*, Vol. III, No. 1, March 1969, pp. 18-31. In addition, see Walter Adams and Robert F. Lanzillotti, "The Reality of Administered Prices," in United States Senate, Committee on the Judiciary, Subcommittee on Antitrust and Monopoly, *Administered Prices: A Compendium on Public Policy*, Government Printing Office, Washington, D.C., 1963, pp. 5-21. The latter document includes divergent views as well.

Says Gardiner C. Means,

An administered price has been defined as a price which is set, usually by a seller, and held constant for a period of time and a series of transactions. Such a price does not imply the existence of monopoly or of collusion. However, it can occur only where a particular market is dominated by one or relatively few sellers (or buyers). It is the normal method of selling in most markets today. Its significance, in contrast to the classical market price, rests, first, on the fact that it lies entirely outside traditional economic theory and, second, that where the area of discretion in price administration is large, administered prices produce economic results and problems of economic policy quite different from those dealt with by traditional theory.[34]

Research done by A.D.H. Kaplan, Joel B. Dirlam, and Robert F. Lanzillotti suggests that virtually all large-scale corporations apparently have established mechanisms and assigned responsibilities for determining prices, have formulated pricing policies, and have adopted (formally or informally) criteria to apply in setting prices, that is, chosen goals which pricing policy is designed to achieve.[35] The pricing mechanisms, the pricing policies, and the goals sought obviously vary widely among enterprises. The Kaplan-Dirlam-Lanzillotti study identifies and analyzes five such pricing objectives: (1) "Pricing to Achieve a Target Return on Investment," (2) "Stabilization of Price and Margin," (3) "Pricing to Maintain or Improve Market Position," (4) "Pricing to Meet or Follow Competition," and (5) "Pricing Related to Product Differentiation."[36] It is apparent that all of these are directed, in whole or in part, to protecting and, if possible, extending the life and sphere of the corporation and the discretionary economic powers of its decision makers.

The same inquiry examines variations in administered-pricing practice in the following industrial areas: steel, aluminum, meats, automobiles, consumer appliances, industrial electrical equipment, farm machinery, gasoline, cellophane and nylon, organic chemicals, and industrial gases.[37]

For present purposes the foregoing may be taken as a representative sample of private industrial governments. We presume, therefore, that administered pricing is typical of large-scale corporate enterprise; that is, substantial pricing power exists and is used.[38]

34. G. C. Means, *Administrative Inflation and Public Policy*, ibid., p. 4.

35. A.D.H. Kaplan, Joel B. Dirlam, & Robert F. Lanzillotti, *Pricing in Big Business*, The Brookings Institution, Washington, D.C., 1958, chapter 2.

36. Ibid.

37. Ibid., chapter 1.

38. The contention is sustained by other research, of course. Among the first to provide extensive monographic materials on corporate pricing were Walton Hamilton and

Administered pricing is also accomplished by and in public governments. At the national level, comprehensive price setting occurred in World War II (Office of Price Administration)[39] and during the Korean conflict (Office of Price Stabilization). Price setting on specific public goods and services is regularly pursued (for example, postal rates and prices on government documents). At the state and local levels, prices are administered by boards of trustees or regents on tuition and fees in public higher education, by port authorities on berthage, by highway commissions as tolls on super highways, and by housing authorities on public rental housing. State legislatures set minimum prices through resale-price-maintenance laws (fair-trade laws) and maximum prices (interest rates) on small loans.

Finally, administered pricing is accomplished frequently through joint involvement of private economic power groups and agencies of public government. An old but still pertinent example is the National Recovery Act (1933-1935), in which the president and Congress encouraged private industry to use existing trade associations (or newly created ones) to draw up "codes of fair competition," price lists, to which all participants would be expected to adhere. This price fixing was called "industrial self-government"; it was intended to speed recovery by forestalling unfair or "cutthroat" competition, that is, competition in terms of price. Although the NRA was invalidated by the Supreme Court in 1935 and that system of price setting under government aegis formally ended, other mechanisms (e.g., basing-point systems) for administering prices were and still are being utilized, as was noted above.

A more recent "joint venture" in pricing of industrial commodities is found in the integrated and interdependent relationships between the defense industries, the Pentagon, and Congress—what some are now calling the military-industrial complex. Over the last third of the century, as military appropriations have taken generally a heavy share of the national budget, we have witnessed a succession of new terms which identify or relate to these joint pricing activities—*cost-plus contracting, noncompetitive bidding* on contracts, *cost overruns.* [40] By what-

others, *Price and Price Policies*, McGraw-Hill, New York, 1938. See also, Alfred R. Oxenfeldt, *Industrial Pricing and Market Practices*, Prentice-Hall Inc., New York, 1951. More recently note Gardiner C. Means, *Pricing Power and the Public Interest*, Harpers, New York, 1962; also, John M. Blair, *Economic Concentration: Structure, Behavior and Public Policy*, Harcourt Brace Jovanovich, New York, 1972. Also, U.S. Congress, Senate Committee on the Judiciary, Subcommittee on Antitrust and Monopoly, *Administered Prices* (Hearings, 26 volumes), U.S. Government Printing Office, Washington, D.C., 1957.

39. See John Kenneth Galbraith, *A Theory of Price Control*, Harvard University Press, Cambridge, Massachusetts, 1952.

40. Richard J. Barnet, *The Economy of Death*, op. cit.; John Kenneth Galbraith, *How to Control the Military*, Doubleday, Garden City, New York, 1969; John J. Clark, *The New Economics of National Defense*, Random House, New York, 1966.

ever names, the reference is to a segment of the system at large in which economic power is joined overtly to political and military power; as a consequence, the choice and pricing of war goods is administered by the strategically placed few who have acquired discretionary power. Barnet calls such men the "National Security Managers."[41] How is the price of an ABM installation determined or that of a C5A jet transport, or a prototype supersonic airplane? It is a negotiated product of deliberations of the interested parties to the contracts—the industries concerned and the Department of Defense. After the deliberations, Congress may become a party. Administered pricing is the rule; apparently there are no significant exceptions.

Other instances of "joint-venture" administered pricing could, of course, be cited. From the commodity buyer's point of view, the imposition of excise taxes and duties on imports in different ways amounts to conjoint price administration. Public licensing of those providing professional and personal services (psychologists, barbers, etc.) may result in de facto public involvement in price setting, if only indirectly. Public provision of medical and hospital care through such programs as Medicare typically involves agencies of government in conjoint public-private administration of prices paid. The list could be extended.

In sum, in examining structural options through which the function of determining exchange ratios is accomplished, we have been driven out of the simplistic comfort of the "market mentality." Galbraith *is* right; it does require "a major act of will to think of price fixing as both normal and having economic function." But only with such an "act of will" can we escape from the "theology of the market" and begin to formulate a theory of price which *is* compatible and relevant to an evolving, functional economy. In the process we will discover that there is more than one price system; indeed, available structural options include a choice among pricing mechanisms.

Recent experience is instructive. Given the fact of extensive private-industrial-government (corporate) control of prices and given a long-term tendency for such administered prices to rise, most recent proposals for structural change regarding price and price systems involve efforts to control inflationary consequences of private pricing judgments. Under the Johnson administration, wage and price guideposts were established to provide a standard which private corporate price makers could use to determine "allowable" increases. "Jawboning" (public verbal persuasion) was the major enforcing instrument. Success was modest, but not insignificant.[42]

41. Barnet, ibid., pp. 86 ff.
42. John Sheahan, *The Wage-Price Guideposts*, Brookings Institution, Washington, D.C., 1967, p. 196.

The Nixon administration initially abandoned the wage and price guidepost structure as of no value. After two more years of steadily rising prices, however, there was a partial return to jawboning and informal guidelines. Then the Nixon administration introduced direct controls over wages and prices (Phases I, II, III, and IV) in the early 1970s, but ideological reluctance, sometimes indifferent administration, and less than total coverage produced only modest success. [43]

Structural change under consideration: With some moderation in the rate of inflation in the late 1970s, little structural change appears under consideration. The popular conditioned aversion to "controls in peacetime" makes members of Congress and others wary of initiating changes for partial or general regulation of prices. Presumably, Congress would again vote standby authority for the executive to control prices if inflation were again to become "double digit." Some scholars believe that inflation will never really subside until the general public recognizes that private price administration is primarily responsible for price-level increases and that public regulation is introduced to provide continuing control over such price judgments. [44] To the extent that these scholars are correct, selective direct controls on most strategically significant industrial and commodity prices are likely to be found in the near future on the national policy agenda if serious inflation remains a problem.

(h) Determination of Income Shares

Because a price paid by one represents a part of an income share to another, the connection between this section and the preceding one is necessarily close. Students generally are aware of this circular flow of income found in all exchange economies. Our concern here is with the structural options through which income shares have been, are being, and might in the future be made available. Are there viable, effective, and equitable institutions for the distribution of income (money and real)?

The significance of this activity in an evolving, functional economy, of course, can hardly be overemphasized. So interdependent have modern economies become that virtually everyone is dependent on the flow of money income to provide his or her only access to the stream of real goods and services. Dollars of income are admission tickets to the real income required to sustain and enrich life. The size of these money incomes and the continuity of their receipt are necessarily critical concerns for nearly everyone. A marked reduction, an outright denial, or even an extended break in the provision of income may well lead to

43. Philip Shabecoff, "Former Price Czar: 'It was Frightening'," *The Sacramento Bee*, April 21, 1974, p. C7.

44. Gardiner C. Means, et al., *The Roots of Inflation*, Burt Franklin & Co., Inc., New York, 1975. See also, "Wage and Price Controls—Pro & Con," *Congressional Digest*, October, 1970.

economic and physical disaster for those affected, as "The Other Americans"—the 20 to 30 million living in poverty, who get too small and infrequent a share, can attest. Indeed, malnutrition or starvation is a fact of life and death for a sizeable segment in the United States. In the late 1960s, a reasonable estimate was that some 10 million Americans were malnourished from poverty,[45] and there is little evidence that substantial improvement has been made since then.[46]

The choice of institutional structures through which to arrange the sharing of money and real income is as urgent and compelling as any other economic choice a people are called upon to make. One does not have to be an economic determinist to recognize that maldistribution of income has been and remains a major contributor to the continuing revolutionary unrest domestically and internationally. Pervasive poverty amidst actual or potential plenty is a nearly universal concern. Few accept the notion that poverty is inevitable; its reduction, and if possible its elimination, are on most national agendas. The emerging recognition that it is possible through social and political action to raise levels of real income is a potent source of activist ferment, and properly so.

A person, who no doubt was a humorist and social critic, once characterized income shares as consisting of "earnin's, findin's, and stealin's."[47] He or she was reflecting the convention of the day, no doubt, that the former was normatively meritorious, but the latter two (although everywhere present) were clearly not reputable. That distinction between "earned" and "unearned" income permeates, more, it plagues, most discussions of structural options and institutional change in the distribution of income. We shall, for a time, pass by a discussion of the normative aspects as such—the questions of merit and justice—to return to it more conveniently in a later chapter. But we will not be able to avoid the three categories, because in a somewhat modified form they are reflected in ideological attitudes concerning both existing and prospective structural mechanisms for distributing income.

Orthodox theorists, for example, sometimes draw a distinction between functional and personal distribution of income. Functional distribution is ᵕ.at provided by the operations of a classically competitive labor market and is explained by the theory of marginal productivity.[48] The markets are believed to provide shares for all participants equal to the market value of the actual productive contribution they make. Such shares are *earned*. The competitive labor market is a soulless taskmaster

45. Citizens' Board of Inquiry into Hunger and Malnutrition in the United States, *Hunger, U.S.A.*, New Community Press, Washington, D.C., 1968. See also, Nick Katz, *Let Them Eat Promises*, Doubleday Anchor, New York, 1969.

46. Nearly twenty-six million Americans were below the official poverty level in 1975. "Big Increase in 'Officially' Poor," *San Francisco Chronicle*, July 14, 1977, p. 9.

47. Regrettably, I have been unable to identify the author of this trilogy.

48. On the relevance of marginal productivity theory see Lester C. Thurow, *Generating Inequality: Mechanisms of Distribution in the U.S. Economy*, Basic Books, Inc., New York, 1975.

which rewards only the worthy and only in proportion to their worth as measured in and by the market. Where market power of individuals is zero (under perfect competition), income shares are determined allegedly by markets, not by the discretionary acts of persons.

Personal income, the amounts actually received by persons, on the other hand, may well include functional (earned) income, but it also includes "findin's" or "stealin's"—that is, income from inheritance, property, or other nonfunctional or nonmarket sources. Shares over or in lieu of "functional" earnings *are* determined by discretionary acts.

Ideologically, the orthodox have always come down hard for earnin's (due to the Puritan ethic?) over findin's and stealin's. Folklore insists that men and women, if they are able, *ought* to work and earn their income share. Indolence is an economic sin.

Marx would agree. "He who does not work, neither shall he eat." The labor of the proletariat is eulogized. But Marx would argue that their share is shorted under a capitalist economy. In the analysis of surplus value, he insists that part of the "earnings" of the industrial workers is siphoned off as surplus value (difference between laborer's product and laborer's cost) by the capitalist to sustain his overriding class position (stealin's). Capitalists do not *earn* surplus value; they, in consequence of ownership, *appropriate* surplus value. The share going to this class (the bourgeoisie) is extracted from workers and constitutes exploitation. Given the class structure of society, such exploitation is, in the Marxian view, inevitable and therefore nondiscretionary, unless the entire system is overturned.

Fascists at bottom don't worry much over marginal products or surplus value. If might makes right, income shares under fascism are a matter of exploit and imposition of superior will. Findin's or stealin's income may be; earnin's it is not. Income shares are distributed at the discretion of the ruling fragment or its leader in a manner to help secure that level of support which will make its ambitious expansionary schemes possible. Shares are distributed on denigrating criteria. Those whom fascists put down as scapegoats (non-Aryans) may be denied access to income shares in whole or in part. Those its chooses to advance (party members) may be accorded a seat at the table of relative affluence. Income shares are largely a discretionary exercise of those who hold political and economic power.

But as models of income distribution, these ism-ideologies offer precious few structural options. After one reviews the conjectural justice of free-market factor pricing, the conjectural class exploitation of Marxist dialecticism, and the racist, sexist, and raw power allocation of the fascists, the real world of determining shares seems far removed indeed, and it is. Existential options are cut mainly of other cloth.

As with prices, *income shares are administered.* Allocations of money income to individuals and institutions are determined by persons who have discretion over such matters. Again here, those who actually make such decisions have varying degrees or amounts of such decision-making authority. They frequently must acknowledge and perhaps even respond to a variety of events, conditions, decisions, laws, prices, and directives initiated by others. They may have to share discretion with a few or many others. But share determination (wages, salaries, rents, interest, profits) is a discretionary process. It need not be carried on competitively or exploitively.

Consider some of the structural arrangements through which distributive judgments are made: [49]

The wages and salaries of something approaching a quarter of the employees in American corporate enterprises are set in consequence of conjoint labor-management collective bargaining deliberations undertaken under the aegis of enabling congressional legislation. As noted above, farm workers, finally, are gaining access to this income-share-determining structure. The quest for agreed compromise may have its limitations as a normative premise, but there is little dispute about the fact that collective bargaining publicly *locates* discretion over wages and salaries and provides *a* means of resolving conflict over distributive shares.

The wages and salaries of all public employees are administered by agencies of the public governments (state personnel boards, legislatures, boards of regents, Congress, civil-service commissions, city councils and the like). Under conditions of national emergency, national direct controls have been used (World War II, Korea, Nixon's Phases) comprehensively to regulate changes (mainly to arrest increases) in existing levels of income shares. National legislation for more than a generation has been setting minimum wages (and maximum hours) for workers engaged by firms operating in interstate commerce.

To those who dance only to the beat of the capitalist drummer and who, while granting most of the foregoing, insist that the income shares of most of the rest of the labor force are determined in conventional supply-and-demand fashion, we say, check again. The requisite conditions for unfettered market pricing of income shares simply do not exist. Such conditions include worker mobility, worker availability on an incremental-unit basis, full worker knowledge of labor market, homogeneity of labor offered, and infinite divisibility of labor units. Factor market [50] "imperfections," existential departures from these conditions, are legion.

With reference to the supply side of labor markets, for example, mobility conditions are thwarted by nonpecuniary incentives and

---

49. In the interest of brevity, the following discussion does not include reference to the institutional arrangements stipulating income shares as dividends, interest, inheritance, and the like.

50. In conventional, orthodox economics, the factors of production are land, labor, capital, and management. A factor market, then, is where these productive inputs are exchanged for income shares of rent, wages, interest, and profit.

"noneconomic" concerns over schooling, neighborhoods, and climates; organization of workers into bargaining units makes their availability on an incremental-unit basis for supply-curve purposes difficult to conceive; perfect knowledge conditions are aborted by simple ignorance and the unwillingness to explore alternative positions; homogeneity conditions are negated by the accelerating increase in skill levels and the multiplication of job categories; divisibility conditions are submerged in the increasing "lumpiness" of factor combinations. [51]

On the demand side, the schedules of alternative offers to hire (demand curves) are subverted by perpetuation of customary wage levels (e.g., interregional wage differentials), by the processes of collective bargaining which make demand contingent upon the nature of the bargain struck in negotiations, and by the impact of external conditions and controls such as the rate of growth in aggregate demand, tax levels and their character, potential governmental interest in the concentration of economic power, and the like. The conclusion, then, is that the actual conditions, the imperfections, are so much at variance with competitive supply-and-demand functions in the labor factor markets that one simply cannot assume that the *market* does in fact determine the work-earnings linkages and therewith income shares. [52]

In the so-called private sector, factor prices and thus income shares are determined in mainly private (nongovernmental) repositories of economic power. In some places, the power has been extensive and one-sided (Southern textile mills, corporate agriculture); in others, the power is narrow, restricted, and mainly one-sided (proprietary firms, personal services). Normally, only specific inquiry into a particular industry, area, or firm will permit identification of the locus of discretion and the manner of its use.

Finally, income shares are composed of, or augmented by, an extensive array of transfer payments (defined by the orthodox as income received for which no productive service is performed) to individuals and institutions. Although there may be dispute about the inclusion of some of the following as transfer payments, none can deny either the variety or significance of such payments. The structural options heretofore generated to distribute income directly or indirectly as transfer payments include:

—grants for dependent children
—grants to the blind and handicapped
—old-age assistance programs
—unemployment compensation

51. This phrase refers to the proportionate and specific combinations of factors—persons, machines, and other inputs—specified by the nature of the task and the relevant technology. A "lump" of inputs might involve (say) four workers, two machines, one room in a plant, and one supervisor. Internal variations of components of the "lump" would not add to productivity or efficiency.

52. On imperfections, see Thurow, *Generating Inequality*, op. cit., pp. 211 ff.

—social security (in part)
—Medicare (in part)
—subsidized housing
—food stamps
—school lunch programs
—G. I. Bill (tuition, books, maintenance)
—tax-avoidance loopholes
—stock dividends
—bad debts
—charity medicine
—charity legal aid
—interest on government bonds
—soil-bank payments
—depletion allowances
—appreciation of property values
—inventory valuation windfalls
—inheritance
—scholarships
—accelerated-depreciation allowances
—investment tax credits
—personal gifts

It is clearly evident that the receipt of transfer payments, directly or indirectly, is not the exclusive privilege of any one class, group, or income-level segment.

Structural changes under consideration: Obviously, every currently proposed change in tax rates and tax structure in effect is a proposal to alter the patterns of "after-tax" income receipt. As many are aware, a substantial effort is being made to develop and expand collective-bargaining-type mechanisms in public employment at all levels. Interestingly, the negotiations center not alone on income shares going to the public employees, but also on the income and services going to recipients of public services (social workers and their welfare clients, nurses and their patients, teachers and their students).

A major policy shift to provide some kind of guaranteed annual minimal income for all persons was under extensive review a few years ago. Proposals included elaborate family-allowance programs, negative-income-tax schemes, and other measures to assure that no individual or family would be left in utter privation or destitution. [53] Substantial bi-partisan support was evident, but ideological anxiety over the possibility of "somebody gettin' somethin' for nothin'" seemed to plague all such discussions.

53. See, for example, James Tobin, "Raising the Incomes of the Poor," in Kermit Gordon (ed.), *Agenda for the Nation*, Doubleday, New York, 1968, pp. 77-116. Also, Otto Eckstein (ed.), *Studies in the Economics of Income Maintenance*, Brookings Institute, Washington, D.C., 1967.

Ideological opposition, of course, is not necessarily directed to all "unearned income" (findin's and stealin's) and subsidies; it frequently is focused upon a moderately augmented transfer going to the poor, who politically are among the least powerful.

Finally, the rapidly rising administered prices for hospital and medical care are forcing consideration again of various proposals for a national health-insurance program. The very poor get an insufficient measure of charity medicine. The very rich can pay for all the care they think they need. Those in the expansive middle-income brackets are often *un*able financially to secure the care which on medical grounds is deemed advisable. Experience with fragmentary programs in the United States (Medicare) and with nearly comprehensive medical programs abroad (United Kingdom) suggest that a comprehensive national health plan for the United States is medically, technically, and institutionally feasible.

Alienation, embittered frustration, and revolutionary unrest will certainly continue until such measures as a guaranteed annual minimum income and a comprehensive health-care plan are adopted as a demonstration that established centers of power can respond with viable institutional changes to real human need. But even these adjustments will not touch the more basic concern for much less inequality in income distribution.

Enough has been said, hopefully, to demonstrate without equivocation that in a society where any significant measure of freedom exists, institutional invention and experimentation is routine and commonplace. When problems arise, solutions are sought as institutional change. The sparse structural options recommended by yesterday's isms simply are not often relevant. In the nature of the case, no "slates" of structure conceived a priori, that is, without reference to the existential determinants of real problems, could be relevant, except by accident. Only through open-ended, nonideological inquiry can problems be identified and creative solutions as institutional adjustments be sought. Again the admonition, "Do not block the way of inquiry." "Which direction is forward" can then rationally be ascertained—over and over again.

Perhaps a cautionary note should now be added. In determining direction "over and over again," the foregoing discussion has properly focused on incremental changes, on piecemeal adjustments of existing institutional forms. This incrementalist approach does *not*, however, preclude a consideration of a more fundamental kind of departure which would invoke the necessity of thinking in more general terms about the most basic goals and purposes of the society. Especially at major moments of crisis and decision (e.g., in 1933 in formulating domestic economic policy to cope with the Great Depression; in 1945 in formulating policy to cope with the post-World War II world), it may indeed be necessary to rethink overall priorities and their implementation. For reasons explored below, the implementation will necessarily be incrementalistic, however. At such crisis junctures, the normative use of ism-ideology models has often been urged. By now we are aware that isms do not in fact define direction. Neither do they provide operators' manuals for political economies.

Chapter 7

OPERATIONAL MECHANISMS

It is certainly possible to plan ourselves into serfdom; it is also possible to plan ourselves into freedom. . . . The result just depends on what sort of instruments we use and how much sense we show in using them.

BARBARA WOOTTON*

I have a theory of power; that if it's going to be responsible, it has to be insecure . . .

RALPH NADER**

*Barbara Wootton, *The New Leader*, August 24, 1946, pp. 8-9. Reprinted with permission from *The New Leader*, August 24, 1946. Copyright © The American Labor Conference on International Affairs, Inc.

**Ralph Nader. Quoted by Eileen Shanahan, "Reformer: Urging Business Change," *The New York Times*, January 24, 1971, p. F9. © 1971 The New York Times Company. Reprinted by permission.

To those, particularly among the young, who are alienated and sometimes depressed by the seemingly glacial slowness with which genuine reform is accomplished, we would offer a word of optimism. It is possible, we believe, not only to *create*, but to *operate* an evolving, functional economy in a manner which provides at once for the continuing resolution of real problems and for, as a necessary corollary, the growing discretionary control of people over their own lives and economic well-being.

Revolutionary unrest, the pressures for genuine substantive reform and reconstitution of the political economy, continues unabated. Ideas which are understood to be true and to be relevant have a fearsome potency indeed. So long as people live and think, such ideas will constitute a force subversive of social myth and elitist power. The operation of an evolving, functional economy is a consequence of informed will, commitment, and responsive and responsible social action.

In the preceding sections, we have explained that in principle the provision of resources (physical, human, financial) on which an evolving, functional economy must draw is a product of the exercise of the human agent's own discretionary capacities. We create the resource base. Similarly, we have suggested that the range of institutional options which have been and may be used to organize economic activity and to provide institutional implementation to a variety of continuing and necessary economic functions is also a product of the human agent's discretion. The rosters of institutions of yesterday's isms are conspicuous in the paucity of options provided and the infrequency of their actual use.

The operational maxims of the ism-ideologies fare little better. The simplistic operational code of capitalism defers to consumer sovereignty in classically competitive markets to determine the level, character, and distribution of real income. The simplistic operational code of Marxian socialism defers to the central planner's sovereignty of the dictatorship of the proletariat to determine economic decisions. The operational code of Marxian communism awaits definitive formulation. The simplistic operational code of fascism defers to the manipulative control of a coercively sustained political elite. Clearly, for the operational code of an evolving, functional economy, we must look elsewhere.

I.   DISCRETIONARY MECHANISMS

In one sense, what is sought and required here is an operational maxim which is also simplistic. As resources are discretionary, as institutional structures are discretionary, so also must operational mechanisms be discretionary. An evolving, functional economy is one which operates to give those who receive the incidence of economic policy discretion over that policy. Although a more extended comment on popular determination of public policy appears below, what is sought operationally is economic democracy. Capitalist folklore notwithstanding, the existential operation of an *imperfectly* competitive market system does not provide economic democracy. For that matter, neither does a perfectly competitive market system, given wide inequality of income distribution.

The needed operational mechanisms must in general be of a kind (1) which provides for the generation of and access to information (reliable knowledge) about how well existing institutional structures are providing for effective performance of economic functions; (2) which provides efficient ways for those significantly affected by economic policy to exercise discretion over such policy; (3) which prohibits the denial of discretionary participation to anyone on trivial or prejudicial grounds; (4) which assures that consequences of policy judgments are the subject of competent and continuing inquiry and that the results are fully communicated to the many who hold discretion.

In considering how such participatory economic democracy can become a reality, we must remind ourselves that, in an exchange economy, levels of money income are an important determinant of the amount of economic discretion held. Some kinds of effective choice making obviously are contingent upon the size of income and the fixed charges or claims on that income. It would appear that widespread and excessive inequality of income is incompatible with the operation of a popularly controlled discretionary economy. In addition, for an indefinite future, it seems likely that discretionary prerogatives will also necessarily depend in part on the kind and character of position held. Precisely *identical* areas of discretion based on economic position seem no more feasible than *identical* incomes. But denial of access to economic position on discriminatory grounds is a constriction on participatory economic policy making for which there is no persuasive defense.

Finally, in proposing an operational motif for an evolving, functional economy which places discretion over policy with those significantly affected by that policy, we do not presume that a plebiscite will be conducted (say) three times daily to determine policy. We are talking about basic, ultimate discretion over economic policies—policies which define structure and delimit operations—being held by the community at large. Individual men and women elected (or appointed) to positions of discretionary power will no doubt make the actual decisions. But in a democratic evolving, functional economy, mechanisms must exist to hold such decision makers to account, to assure that they are responsive and responsible to the popular will. And that task, for ideological reasons and otherwise, is an *unending* quest.

To stimulate reflection on some operational devices and approaches that might function to provide and sustain popular control of an evolving, functional economy, we examine briefly (1) registry mechanisms for making economic choices, (2) mechanisms which introduce a measure of coherence and coordination in economic operations, and (3) mechanisms which help to hold decision makers to account for their judgments. Glibly, the concern is one of determining where and how to "lean on the system" in an effort to assure its operation for human and humane purposes.

II.   REGISTRY OF CHOICES

There are at least four main areas of choice in and through which individuals and families may participate in economic decisions. They are market involvement, job involvement, organization involvement, and political involvement (see figure 7-1).

First, individuals, in the purchase of goods and services, can, under some circumstances (as the capitalists say), by their market behavior (buying or not buying) reward or punish producers and distributors on grounds of price, quality, availability of goods, politics of firm, hiring practices, integrity of enterprise, or whatever. But the *range* of choice available to an individual buyer will be effectively circumscribed by the amount of his or her available disposable income (or access to credit), the number and variety of choices provided by producers and distributors, the knowledge held of other options, and the amount of time that can be devoted to the exercise of market choices.

Sellers presumably must respond to the extent and character of effective demand for goods and services, but they effectively manipulate that demand themselves through advertising, their impact on income distribution, and their quasipolitical intraindustry and interindustry involvements.

Concurrent Areas of Choice

Discretionary Roles in Economic Decisions

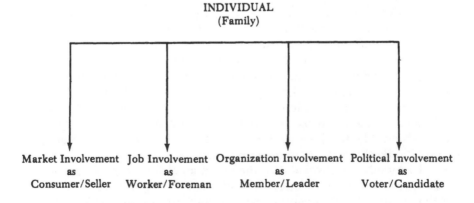

INDIVIDUAL
(Family)

Market Involvement	Job Involvement	Organization Involvement	Political Involvement
as	as	as	as
Consumer/Seller	Worker/Foreman	Member/Leader	Voter/Candidate

Figure 7-1   Registry of Choices

Thus, the effective range of buying power available to a welfare mother with dependent children, to an itinerant farm worker, to a by-the-day domestic worker, to a married student couple in slumlord-owned off-campus housing, or to an aged couple on Social Security may be negligible. The effective range of buying power available to a legislator in the "pocket" of lobbyists, a medical doctor, a middle-level corporate executive, or an entrepreneurial professor may be comparatively extensive indeed.

The effectiveness, therefore, of the consumer markets as a registry of choice varies widely with income, knowledge, and time available to buyers and with the options provided by, and the market manipulative power of, sellers. There is wide dispute concerning the potency of such individual market choices in determining economic policy. However that may be, there can be little doubt that more equitable income distribution, provision of more reliable information concerning products, the elimination of false and deceptive advertising, and careful public scrutiny of demand creation would significantly improve the choice-registry function of individual market behavior.

A second avenue for registering economic judgments is through discretionary involvement in decisions made on the job, in regular employment connections. Although there is a considerable practice of denying to employees any significant role in determining and administering policy in business firms and governmental agencies, the potentialities for effective participation should not idly be dismissed. Much, perhaps most, economic organization appears to be patterned on the authority-responsibility model, in which decisions are made by those in authority at the top (who have the "responsibility") and are followed as "orders" presumably by those "below." But this overstates what is and aborts what might be.

All, or nearly all, productive behavior is cooperative, as countless commentators have affirmed. And cooperative behavior, if it is to succeed at anything more than a perfunctory level, requires the consent and tacit or explicit commitment or involvement of the participants. Folklore notwithstanding, one would expect the degree of authoritarian economic control achieved to be *inversely* proportional to economic productivity. The more complete and meticulous the control of subordinates, the *lower* one would expect the volume and quality of economic performance to be in the shop, the foundry, the office, the classroom, or even the board room. Concentration camps aside, there would always seem to be room for some measure of discretionary involvement. Men and women are not automatons; all have judgmental capacities reflecting their experience and their running critique of the economic undertaking. Authoritarian control denies these judgmental capacities to the organization. Whether utilized or not, such capacities are valuable sources of insight and potential reform.

Whether or not formal mechanisms exist to provide for discretionary participation of course is very important; making economic choice effective at work is obviously easier with such supportive structure than without. But even without formal participatory structure, opportunities for informal critique of working rules, firm directives, organizational goals, public posture, and overall economic performance appear repeatedly. Informal leadership appears; working rules are appraised; subtle and not-so-subtle measures secure shifts in working rules and organizational goals. Gross ignorance of this fact has lead to slowdowns, strikes, and sabotage. Effective choice is being exercised in fact. It might well be expanded.

The folklore which equates authoritarian control with economic efficiency tends to narrow or negate this avenue of choice and hence is cause for concern. But the flaw is in the folklore, not in the wisdom of encouraging continuing discretionary involvement of people in determining the conditions and purposes to which their economic lives are committed.

A third registry mechanism potentially available is the exercise of judgment on economic policy as a participating member of an organized economic interest group. In principle, individuals should have the continuing right to participate in deliberations on proposed economic policies and actions of the organization(s) to which their economic connection grants access. Further, individuals have the obligation to assist where necessary or desirable in the implementation of those policies.

At first hearing, the foregoing may sound naive and pretentious. "Everybody knows" that economic interest groups such as labor unions, professional associations, and trade associations all have their respective special privileges or vested interests to push or protect. "Everybody knows," without ever having heard of Michels' "iron law of oligarchy," [1] that such organizations are typically under the control of self-perpetuating and self-serving elites. "Everybody knows" that such organizations exist primarily to serve their own economic interests under the rubric that what is good for them is good for the country. "Everybody knows" that such groups gain their ends-in-view by skillfully playing the game of brokerage politics in which backs are reciprocally scratched and legislators and votes are bought and sold under and over the counter.

How is it conceivable, then, that such instruments of private economic power could serve as a registry of choices which could on any occasion serve the public interest? In our haste to *describe* an economy in which brokerage of economic interests appears commonplace, even epidemic, we tend, it appears, to presume the "natural law" status of

1. Roberto Michels, *Political Parties: A Sociological Study of the Oligarchical Tendencies of Modern Democracy*, (1915), (trans. by Eden and Cedar Paul), Free Press, Glencoe, Illinois, 1949.

the "iron law of oligarchy" and the inevitability that the desires and goals of an economic interest group will be contrary to public well-being.

With reference to the American cultural experience, for example, there is a mores-based commitment to the *idea* of democratic participation in policy making. Most private economic trade and professional organizations are *pro forma* designed to permit control by the membership. Even corporations are supposed to be governed by the equity interests. Louis Kelso and Mortimer Adler have fabricated a comprehensive model of "popular" economic control based on a greatly expanded distribution of equity share holdings. They call it "People's Capitalism."[2] Some members of Congress, who may or may not have exhibited an interest in the democratization of deliberative procedures of Congress itself, nevertheless professed great concern about the alleged lack of worker control over their own trade unions. With the Landrum-Griffin law (1959) they sought in part to return control of trade unions to the workers themselves. For a century, cooperative enterprises have evangelistically pressed the Rochdale "cardinal principle" of "one man, one vote." Annual balloting (nominations and elections) for officers of professional associations is commonplace. Annual conventions sometimes permit substantive consideration of policy questions.

Our point is an elemental one; effective participation of individuals in the policy-making processes of economic interest groups frequently is possible, even though by default or design the exercise of such discretionary involvement may have become a novelty.

Similarly, there is little to suggest, but nothing to preclude, a convergence or identity between a policy position of an economic interest group and that of the community at large. The identity or its absence, in any case, is a matter of inquiry into the evident consequences and a normative assessment of their merit or tolerability. What is clear, of course, is that mere assertion or conjecture does not establish convergence of public and private interest.

As many readers will recognize, registry of choice through economic interest groups has already been effective in some cases. The Welfare Rights organization has helped to dramatize the gross inequities, the demeaning characteristics, and the often inadequate support levels of the existing amalgam of welfare programs. Younger, more militant professionals have organized "radical caucuses" in the professional organizations and threatened to gain control, displacing old-guard elites in the process. A few trade unions appear to have made some efforts to end racism in employment, improve or end ghetto and barrio deprivation, and the like. Social workers, teachers, professors, public employees, members of the clergy, among others have on occasion provided for discretionary involvement of their members in formulating and

2. Louis O. Kelso and Mortimer J. Adler, *The Capitalist Manifesto*, Random House, New York, 1958.

implementing actions to recast or revise inhibitive or discriminatory economic policy which comes within their respective purviews.

A cautionary note is needed here, however. Left standing by itself, the preceding paragraph may be read as "Go join a pressure group." Such an interpretation would reduce the more inclusive concern here to one of enshrining a pluristic model of political participation.

But the matter is more complex. It is not necessarily easy to "go join a presure group." Moving from an unorganized to an organized status is often difficult; sometimes it is impossible. Interest groups operate as miniature private governments, often delimiting memberships and usually exercising some powers within the universe of their interests. There is little applicable public law that ensures access and involvement. The group may have a legitimacy, be formally authorized, and be delegated authority. Following delegation, public government normally abdicates further responsibility. The actual operation and control of the group may be under a self-perpetuating fragment or elite that has mainly parochial interests and little concern to bring outsiders in. We must realistically expect, then, that major fresh policy initiatives will be required before significant numbers of the thirty to forty per cent or more people in the U.S. who are outsiders will be able to exercise their options for interest-group participation. Such initiatives will doubtless include the development of some rules governing the delegation of power and its exercise. [3]

In any case, interest-group involvement, even where successful, cannot stand alone; at best it can be a useful part of a more general effort to expand discretionary involvement.

Fourth and finally, there are, of course, opportunities for registering choice on economic questions by involvement in the political process at large. Holders of political office do repeatedly make economic judgments. Although we return to this matter below, it is worth mentioning here that rare indeed is the occasion where political candidates for the same office do *not* reflect significantly or even fundamentally different views on major economic questions—welfare reforms, poverty programs, stabilization policies, environmental restoration, consumer protection, and the like. The tendency to dismiss party nominees as nothing more than "Tweedledee and Tweedledum" appears to spring in part from a simple ignorance of the nature and consequences of contemplated economic proposals. Whether a presidential candidate is inclined to take the economic policy advice of a Milton Friedman, a Walter Heller, a Paul Samuelson, a Paul Sweezy, a Paul McCracken, a Herbert Stein, an Alan Greenspan, a Lawrence Klein, or a John K. Galbraith is of more than passing interest! Jobs, income, welfare, and perhaps even "domestic tranquility" hang in good measure on the

3. On this and related matters see Theodore Lowi, *The End of Liberalism*, W. W. Norton, New York, 1969.

quality and sophistication of such advice. In brief, as a community at large, we need, directly or indirectly through the political process, to choose our economic experts with great care. Genuine choice customarily is possible; its more extensive and informed use is much to be desired.

III. OPERATIONAL COORDINATION

Where, in an evolving, functional economy in which "a myriad of decisions" must continuously be made, are the operational mechanisms which introduce coordination and coherence in economic behavior and processes? Where in an evolving, functional economy is there a counterpart for the alleged order-inducing role of the automatic, mechanistic, competitive market of the capitalists or the central-planning authorities of the Marxists or the socialists, or the unidirectional coercive control exercised by a militantly constituted political elite of the fascists? How in an economy subject to discretionary control of people generally can order be achieved and sustained?

A fragmentary glimpse of what is actually occurring in major economies provides an initial response to these questions. Coherence and coordination are now being accomplished in ways not adequately explained by the zero-planning model of capitalists, the central-planning (but divergent) models of the Marxists and the fascists.

There is no great mystery here. In all major economies most coordination of economic activity is accomplished by conventional habits, traditional institutional prescriptions, and the arrangements, contracts, and agreements worked out over previous months, years, and even decades to order behavior. *All economies are mainly traditional economies.* Even in rapidly growing systems, we presume, at least ninety-nine per cent of economic activity consists of doing today what the working rules, the contractual agreements, the habits of marketing, the conventions of consumption specified as yesterday's behavior. All organized economies are and must be habit ridden. Institutions become habitual. Habits conserve what is. Order and coherence are provided in the degree to which habit and convention are followed.

As consumers we buy largely on habitual patterns of acquired taste; as workers we labor as accountants, machinists, drivers, lecturers, or politicians mainly in the accustomed patterns previously worked out. As manufacturers we supply a mix of products which habitual techniques and buyers' practice will permit, using mainly a mix of labor and materials from conventional supply sources. Economies are going concerns; they operate on habit-based expectations, experience-grounded predictions, and enforceable promises. Thus, recourse to traditional economic behavior provides *most* coordination and coherence— but not all.

People as discretionary agents and as astute observers of the consequences of economic undertakings perceive problems arising with some of these habitual and conventional patterns. When particular customs and conventions break down, when to continue to base behavior on them would result in an observable contravention or impairment in the flow and distribution of real income, that is, when economic problems surface, how then is order, coherence, and coordination achieved in an evolving, functional economy?

The answer is through *democratic economic planning*. It appears inescapable that such planning for order and coherence in an evolving, functional economy will be conducted in both the public and the private realm and at varying levels of inclusiveness. But the central issue concerns the locus and use of economic discretion to induce change in *existing* patterns of coordination and coherence *because* they have become problematic.

Given a democratically organized polity, economic planning must be undertaken at a level of inclusiveness coextensive with the determinants of the problems being considered. [4] This suggests that coherence and coordination in the decision-making processes concerning changes in the aggregate level of employment and income, the overall pattern of income distribution, the determination of basic decisions on resource use (military vs. civilian, investment goods vs. consumer goods, domestic vs. foreign aid), general or selective wage and price controls, the control of money and credit, and the like, must be provided for in the public realm at the national level. And we are, of course, already accustomed to treating fiscal policy, debt policy, monetary policy, transfer-share policy, direct-controls policy, national-priorities policy, and subsidies policy mainly at that national level.

On the other hand, there may very well be a universe of private-industrial-government planning (firms and unions) in which private repositories of economic power may exist and function to initiate changes in conventional practices and procedures. Subject to some constraints and accountability, such repositories of private discretion may be expected to make decisions altering the patterns of coordination and coherence in such areas as resource utilization, demand management, product research and development, manpower recruitment and utilization, and pricing policies, among others. [5]

But much economic planning will more generally occur in conjoint public-private institutions in which discretion will be shared, but not necessarily equally. Normally public government retains its basic sovereignty and hegemony—it can define the character and duration of sharing. Existing and potential examples of such conjoint economic-planning approaches include regulatory commissions, military-procure-

---

4. We return to this and related matters in chapter 13, part IV.
5. In this connection, see Galbraith, *Economics and the Public Purpose*, op. cit., part III.

ment arrangements, the "grants economy" (Kenneth Boulding's caption for a plethora of grants-in-aid arrangements), collective bargaining under the aegis of governmental policy, use of tax powers as a constraint or subsidy instrument, public-works-construction arrangements, "indicative planning" (French type of cooperative governmental and industrial determination of major production targets), wage-price guidepost stipulations and negotiations.

Even so, wherever the planning decisions are made and whatever the public-private mix of participating parties, all such decisions to alter existing coordinating patterns are a product of a trial-and-error process. That is, when problems in the production and distribution of real income are encountered in an evolving, functioning economy, inquiry is induced. Analysis is offered; causal explanation is provided. Predictions of probable consequences are appraised for all relevant alternatives. A choice among options is made; structural shifts are recommended. Power repositories (public and private) implement policies; trial runs or pilot programs may be started. Consequences are observed and assessed. Further shifts in structure are suggested if the adjustment fails in important respects.

The basic and continuing questions *are not:* Shall there be planning? Won't planning destroy freedom? Doesn't planning mean authoritarianism? Instead, we pose questions of the following kind: Who is doing the planning? For what purposes is planning being undertaken? Are such purposes compatible with the public interest? What are the predictable consequences of the planning decisions being made? Can the planners be held accountable to the community at large?

The last question requires more extensive elaboration.

IV. HOLDING PLANNERS TO ACCOUNT

There are no easy answers to the questions of how in an evolving, functional economy those who make economic decisions can be held responsive and responsible for their judgments. Many mechanisms have been tried; a few have been wholly or partially successful (see figure 7-2). But as we noted above, in the nature of the case, the quest is unending.

Some aspects of the American economic experience are germane and instructive at this point. Look first to some efforts in the public regulation of private corporate businesses.[6] The regulation of private monopolistic corporations through designedly independent regulatory commissions began at the national level in 1887 with the Interstate

6. For an overview of the problem together with suggestions for structural change see the following: Corwin D. Edwards, "Policy toward Big Business: What Lessons after Forty Years?" *Journal of Economic Issues*, Vol. IX, No. 2, June, 1975, pp. 343-63; Joseph F. Brodley, "Industrial Deconcentration and Legal Feasibility: The Efficiencies Defense," ibid., pp. 365-80; Warren J. Samuels, "The Industrial Reorganization Bill: The Burden of the Future," ibid., pp. 381-94; Ralph Nader, Mark Green and Joel Seligman, *Taming the Giant Corporation*, op. cit.

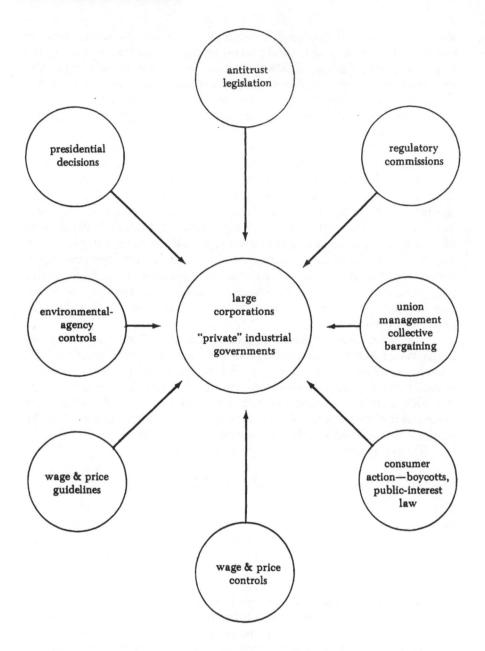

Examples of historic and current instruments used to seek public control over, or to exert public influence upon, private economic-planning decisions in the industrial sector.

Figure 7-2   Holding "Private" Planners to Account

Commerce Act, as is commonly known. After nearly a century, regulatory-commission control over prices charged and the quality of service or product provided suffers from at least two major infirmities: The regulatory agencies sometimes suffer from a hardening of their bureaucratic arteries, from political manipulation, and from inadequate staffing and budgets. More importantly, gradually some commissions appear to have come under the more or less complete control of the industries they are supposed to regulate. [7] There seems to be little doubt that the commission-control approach has been an essentially conservative approach to the social control of private economic power. [8]

The experience with antitrust legislation and enforcement appears to exhibit no startling or continuing successes either. This effort to "regulate competition" began, of course, with the Sherman Act of 1890; it is derived from orthodox theory and ideology. The intended antitrust policy is one of "makin' little ones out of big ones" in the pursuit of the multiplicity-of-firms condition approaching classically competitive markets. That such an application of ideological precepts would be difficult, if not impossible existentially, must have been understood from the outset, but belief in ism-ideology dies hard. In any case, the normative use of the competitive ideal has been attempted again and again in quest of the closest approximation of zero market power which the prevailing technologies, the corporate revolution, judicial opinion, and community sensibilities would permit. Of course, that approximation has not been very close at all. Antitrust prosecution has neither terminated nor dramatically reduced or restrained private industrial government. That *more* irresponsible and unaccountable abuses of economic power might have occurred in the absence of the prosecutors' "cop-on-the-beat" presence is not disputed; neither can it be proved. Threat of antitrust litigation with its attendant expense, energy drain, political repercussions, and adverse publicity may indeed continue to operate as a moderate deterrent, but nowhere apparently is there a serious analytic demonstration of its adequacy or sufficiency. Given the inapplicability of the basic theory behind antitrust litigation, larger staffs and higher budgets would not suffice to salvage this means to accountability, regrettably.

Not everybody shares that pessimistic view, of course. The interest in a significantly reformed regulatory-commission control [9] and in

---

7. This phenomenon has been recognized for at least the last third of a century. See Horace M. Grey, "The Passing of the Public Utility Concept," in American Economic Association Committee, *Readings in the Social Control of Industry*, The Blakiston Co., Philadelphia, 1947, pp. 280-303, for an early example.

8. That the regulatory commission approach was understood to be a conservative response from the beginning is suggested by Gabriel Kolko in *The Triumph of Conservatism*, Quadrangle Books, Chicago, 1967.

9. See, e.g., Paul W. MacAvoy (ed.), *The Crisis of the Regulatory Commission*, W. W. Norton, New York, 1970.

invigorated antitrust investigation, litigation, and enforcement[10] has not wholly disappeared. Such efforts have the virtue of a comprehensive approach, but one must presume that were reform and invigoration really viable options, such changes would long since have been introduced. Existing and entrenched political and economic power in governmental agencies (including Congress) and in the industrial sectors seems able to forestall significant changes in the public-utility and antitrust approaches.

A third and different approach was offered in the early 1950s by John Kenneth Galbraith. [11] In Galbraith's view, classic competition was, of course, inapplicable to the corporate world, but fortunately another kind of autogenesis was at work. The accretion and aggregation of private economic power would automatically spawn its own countervailing power group. For example, the appearance of concentrated economic power by corporate managers would generate the emergence of organized labor to offset and restrain such management power. Similarly, corporations selling, for example, farm machinery and using oligopolistic powers to set price, will stimulate the appearance of farm-machinery buyers with oligopsony power organized through coops and the like. Some balancing off or equilibration of aggregated private power was a natural consequence, and the public interest would be reflected in the compromises struck.

While this approach may have had some limited descriptive use, it was rather more of an apologia for doing little. It foundered on the absence of convincing evidence of the appearance of countervailing power, especially without governmental help, and on the impropriety of assuming that the *fact* of compromise, despite some waste, would somehow *constitute* the public interest. [12]

Efforts to hold private industrial government to account through the injection and exercise of the power and stature of the presidency has been too infrequent and inconclusive to constitute a general approach. John F. Kennedy did, of course, face down the steel industry in a confrontation over general steel-price increases in the early 1960s, but even

10. See, e.g., Edwin Mansfield (ed.), *Monopoly Power and Economic Performance*, (3d ed.), W. W. Norton, New York, 1974, part III. Also, Sylvester E. Berki (ed.), *Antitrust Policy Economics and Law*, D. C. Heath, New York, 1966; Mark J. Green, *The Closed Enterprise System*, (Ralph Nader Study Group Report on Antitrust Enforcement), Grossman, New York, 1972; Willard F. Mueller, "Antitrust in a Planned Economy: An Anachronism or an Essential Complement?" *Journal of Economic Issues*, Vol. IX, No. 2, June, 1975, pp. 159-79; and Mark Green, "A Reform Era for Antitrust," *The New York Times*, March 27, 1977, pp. F1 & 6.

11. John Kenneth Galbraith, *American Capitalism, The Concept of Countervailing Power*, Houghton Mifflin, Boston, 1952. Galbraith has long since moved beyond this position. See his *Economics and the Public Purpose*, op. cit.

12. In this connection see, Bernard D. Nossiter, *The Mythmakers: An Essay on Power and Wealth*, Houghton Mifflin, Boston, 1964, pp. 106-35.

though the prices were initially rolled back, the price paid in business confidence in the presidency was high, and selective, steel-price increases about a year later largely negated the initial rollback. [13] The later increases were not resisted.

Public control of private industrial government is not needed if one accedes to the views of a group of self-styled corporate "trustees" or stewards—corporate executives who affirm their responsibilities to the social order as wielders of economic power. ". . . ownership carries social obligations, and . . . a manager is a trustee not only for the owner, but for society as a whole." [14] He fulfills this obligation, allegedly, by conducting "the affairs of the enterprise in such a way as to maintain an *equitable and working balance* among the claims of the various directly interested groups—stockholders, employees, customers, and the public at large." [15] Such executives are "part of a group that enjoys power only so long as it does not abuse it." [16] There is no *problem* of accountability; the corporate stewards may be expected to adjudicate these rival claims more knowledgeably and skillfully than could the community or an agency of the community (government). But as a superficial canvass will disclose, the ownership concern with dividends has indeed a prior and superior claim on the corporate stewards' "objective" dispensations. But more importantly, of course, here is an ill-concealed appeal for elitist determination of economic policy, on grounds of expert and superior knowledge and skill, within the power universe of the corporate "trustee"-manager. He is accountable mainly to his directors and perhaps to the equity interests; the rest is window dressing. Economic planning in this guise installs essentially undemocratic patterns of policy making, claims to efficiency and objectivity notwithstanding. [17]

Moreover, efforts to hold segments or sections of the public government and its economic decision makers to account have been dramatically less than impressive. Those making national monetary policy operate at the end of a long tether indeed. The Federal Reserve Board (the Fed) has largely autonomous power to "create conditions of ease in the money market" or to depress the money and credit supply and to raise interest rates. Public scrutiny and scolding through congressional committees seems to be a not-too-effective control instrument indeed. Of

13. Ibid., pp. 17-23.
14. Editors of Fortune Magazine with collaboration of Russell W. Davenport, *U.S.A.: The Permanent Revolution*, Prentice-Hall, New York, 1951, p. 88.
15. Frank Abrams, Chairman of Standard Oil of New Jersey, quoted in ibid., p. 80.
16. Ibid., p. 80.
17. Another form of elitist apologia for the corporate power system is discussed by Rick Tilman, "Apology and Ambiguity: Adolf Berle on Corporate Power," *Journal of Economic Issues*, Vol. VIII, No. 1, March, 1974, pp. 111-26.

more importance is the executive branch's pressure on the FRB chairman. That the Fed may frequently act wisely is not at issue; its accountability is. [18]

The economic planning of fiscal policy fares little better. In the formulation of spending policy, constituent interests of economic interest groups, pork-barrel subsidies for home-district voters, or ideological hangups over the proper role of government in the economy often make sensible fiscal management of the economy difficult. In the formation of tax policy (and in consideration of tax "reform" measures), account must be taken of the apparent fact that the Internal Revenue Code often appears to be a reasonably fair indication—in its distribution of loopholes, exemptions, and deductions—of the loci of private economic power. The problem of accountability is further complicated by the seniority and committee systems through which congressional minorities have extensive power to block or substantially alter fiscal policy and economic-reform legislatio.

Finally, the comparative autonomy of the president in the conduct of foreign policy permits the generation of policy and the undertaking of military commitments abroad which place direct and substantial burdens upon the economy. Anyone recalling the rise and fall of United States involvement in Southeast Asia in the 1960s and 1970s and its attendant impact on the domestic economy needs no further elaboration. [19]

In sum, the American economy seems not yet to have evolved an adequate and continuing set of structures through which to hold economic planners to account. [20] But perhaps there is also experience which suggests alternative approaches. Is this not also an area in which institutional invention is both possible and probable? Look again to the areas where, in an evolving, functional economy, choice can be registered and made determinant

Consider again the market behavior of consumers. We have already noted the obvious option of the individual to buy or not buy. But consumer power can go further.

There are a few instances, perhaps atypical or even trivial, where on a national scale buyers' refusal to buy a commodity has led to its withdrawal and a probable loss to the seller. Ford's Edsel is a sometimes

18. Arthur M. Okun, *The Political Economy of Prosperity*, W. W. Norton, New York, 1970, p. 81.

19. Ibid., pp. 62-99. See also, U.S. Congress, Joint Economic Committee, *Economic Effects of Vietnam Spending*, Washington, D.C., Government Printing Office, 1967; U.S. Congress, Joint Economic Committee, *Economics of Military Procurement*, Washington, D.C., Government Printing Office, 1968; U.S. Congress, Joint Economic Committee, *The Military Budget and National Economic Priorities*, Washington, D.C., Government Printing Office, 1969; U.S. Congress, Joint Economic Committee, *Changing National Priorities*, Washington, D.C., Government Printing Office, 1970.

20. Ralph Nader (ed.), *The Consumer and Corporate Accountability*, Harcourt Brace Jovanovich, New York, 1973.

cited example.[21] Another was the apparent failure of designers and manufacturers to force "midi-length" dresses on the female buyers in the early 1970s. But generally, single-commodity boycotts have little effect. Efforts in the mid-1970s to organize against high meat prices and, later, coffee prices generally failed. The impact of such price increases is not likely to be thought significant enough to prompt a change in buying habits and social-action initiatives.

Of greater significance, and perhaps more successful (as noted previously), was the nationwide boycott on the purchase of table grapes initiated by Cesar Chavez and the Farm Workers Organizing Committee to mount pressure on the organized growers to bargain with organized farm workers. A subsequent effort at a lettuce boycott to press the FWOC case in a jurisdictional struggle with the Teamsters and the growers appears to have been less successful.

Also of significance are the examples of community-level consumer boycotts. In several areas of the American South, blacks have organized successful boycotts against white merchants and the white power structure in order to press their demands for an end to segregated schooling, for an end to the illegal use of police power, for the opportunity to exercise their voting rights, and/or for equal justice before the law. In some large college and university communities, students have succeeded in organizing rent strikes in protest against what they believe to be excessive prices for rental housing and indifferent physical maintenance of the residential units. In addition, peaceful picketing and other demonstration techniques have seemingly helped to secure changes in discriminatory hiring practices against blacks, chicanos, and women. Many have attempted the organization of national buyers' boycotts against firms making war goods, but evidently none has been particularly successful.

Although historically at the national level efforts to organize consumer boycotts as a device to hold economic decision makers to account (for their judgments on the character, quality, and price of goods offered) have not been dramatically successful except in isolated instances, the approach need not be abandoned. Given currently available organizing and communicative techniques, the consumer-boycott approach may yet become a more viable instrument for holding decision makers to account where other instruments did not or cannot work. But no one should underestimate the difficulties of initiating and sustaining such an effort.

Operational mechanisms for holding decision makers to account on the job need little elaboration here. A century-long struggle for recognition and bargaining rights of trade unions has, with the assistance of enabling legislation, generally succeeded in providing a check on

21. Galbraith suggests that it is exceptional. See his *New Industrial State*, op. cit., p. 206n.

managerial economic planning concerning wages and working conditions in those industries now organized by the unions. But even this approach is still avant garde in the textile mills of the American Southeast, in agriculture, and in public employment.

For decades, statutory prescriptions concerning worker welfare have fixed responsibility directly upon some classes of employers, as in the case of workmen's compensation laws. Conceivably similar assignments of responsibility could be considered with reference to firms' annual employment levels and wage payments. Some corporations are beginning to explore the feasibility of increasing substantially the degree of participatory involvement provided for their employees. [22] Given the participatory revolution now underway, such exploration must be expected to continue and expand.

If for the moment we consider students in higher education as being "on the job," clearly there are a large number of experiments under way in which students are finding new means of holding academic planners to account. By seeking and gaining de facto (and de jure) participatory rights in the governance of colleges, students are exercising significant, occasionally decisive, influence on policy which directly affects their lives. Students properly are helping faculties and administrations to fulfill their educational obligations. Says Harold Taylor,

> . . . it is . . . the obligation of the college to find ways in which the seriousness of choosing can become part of the student's psychic development. Without the confrontation with choice, there is little opportunity for the student to learn to know himself and what it is he wants from his education and his life. If within the context of his education his choices are eliminated in what he will choose to study, how he will learn to study it, and how he will choose to live, he is unlikely to find either motivation for what he does or a full intellectual character of his own. [23]

Accordingly, in some institutions of higher learning, students now sit with full voting and deliberative rights in academic senates and academic departments. Students are now participating in decisions concerning the acquisition, retention, tenure, and promotion of faculty members; the reform of curriculums; the allocation of budgets; and the like. There has been pressure to place students (and faculty) on governing boards of colleges and universities.

But the matter does not end there. A striking and promising approach to holding powerful private economic planners to account is reflected (1) in the activities of "public-interest law firms," which have

---

22. James MacGregor, "The Honor System," *The Wall Street Journal*, May 22, 1970, pp. 1 & 12. Also, Michael Poole, *Workers' Participation in Industry*, Routledge & Kegan Paul, London, 1975; Gerry Hunnis, G. David Garson, and John Case (eds.), *Workers' Control*, Random House, New York, 1973.

23. Harold Taylor, *Students Without Teachers*, op. cit., p. 217.

been organized to represent the public interest (through, e.g., class-action suits) in more effective regulation of private corporate behavior; [24] (2) in the work of Ralph Nader and his associates in their representation of the consumer interest in auto safety, pure foods, and the like; [25] and (3) in the programs of such groups as the California Rural Legal Assistance organization, which sought to assure the rural poor of de facto equity before the law (and agri-business) with regard especially to their working and living conditions. [26]

Interestingly, the potency of these three approaches is indicated in part by the vigor of the opposition appearing against them. The public-interest law firms were threatened by adverse Internal Revenue Service rulings which would have denied the deductability of contributions made in their support (their life blood). Ralph Nader won a law-suit against General Motors evidently for the latter's intimidative har-rassment and invasion of his privacy. [27] A governor of California sought continuously to use his influence to dry up the meager flow of federal funds which was sustaining the California Rural Legal Assis-tance program. [28]

In addition, citizen groups, old (Sierra Club) and new (Friends of the Earth), are developing new and expanding old approaches to hold economic planners who pollute or despoil the environment to account. Aggressive lobbying before hearing bodies and legislative committees, injunctive court action, even physical confrontation, are being used to compel public attention to the consequences of decisions being made and to interdict and modify such decisions.

Recent proposals in still another area were directed to improving policy and increasing decision-maker accountability in national econ-omic planning for full employment and economic growth. This fresh approach to national planning was introduced in legislation by Senators Hubert Humphrey and Jacob Javits in the Senate in May 1975. The bill was the Balanced Growth and Economic Planning Act of 1975 and was offered as an extensive amendment to the Employment Act of 1946. [29]

24. Gordon Harrison & Sanford M. Jaffe, *The Public Interest Law Firm*, Ford Founda-tion, New York, 1973. For comment on the shift from procedural victories to concern with the substantive decisions themselves, see Carlyle W. Hall, Jr., "In the Public Interest," *The Center Magazine*, Center for the Study of Democratic Institutions, Santa Barbara, California, January/February, 1977, pp. 29-32.

25. See, e.g., Julius Duscha, "Stop! In the Public Interest," *The New York Times Mag-azine*, March 21, 1971, pp. 4ff.

26. An episode in this effort is reported by Ridgway M. Hall, Jr., "Last Minute Rescue for Legal Aid," *The New Republic*, November 21, 1970, pp. 13-15.

27. Thomas Whiteside, *The Investigation of Ralph Nader*, Arbor House, New York, 1972.

28. Ridgway M. Hall, Jr., loc. cit. See also, Peter Barnes, "Reagan Versus the Poverty Lawyers," *The New Republic*, January 23, 1971, pp. 15-17.

29. U.S. Congress, Senate, *Balanced Growth and Economic Planning Act of 1975*, (S.B. 1795), 94th Congress, 1st Session, 1975.

The new legislation would have established an Economic Planning Board in the executive office of the president. The new board would have responsibility for

> anticipating the Nation's economic needs, measuring available national economic resources, assuring an adequate supply of industrial raw materials and energy, outlining economic goals, and in the light of long-range economic trends and opportunities, for developing a proposed Balanced Economic Growth Plan, and recommending policies to achieve the objectives of the plan.[30]

Provision was made in the bill for wide participation of interested persons and groups in the development and revision of plans. The bill also provided for congressional review of each Balanced Growth Economic Plan and for congressional approval or disapproval by concurrent resolution. The energy crisis, high inflation, and high unemployment of the 1970s prompted this major effort to institute effective economic-planning machinery at the national level.

A subsequent bill, the Balanced Economic Growth Act (introduced by Congressman Bolling in October 1975), proposed to tie a more simplified long-term planning function to measures for the achievement of full employment. Under this bill the Council of Economic Advisors (with additional support) would take on the long-term planning role, and the community, through its government, would assure that every person who desired a job would have one as a matter of right in the private sector or in the public sector.[31]

Finally, recourse to the political process itself remains a major route to hold economic planners to account in all sectors of the economy (public and private). Since this argument is developed at some length in a later chapter, it will suffice here to reiterate that most of those elected to public office at the state and national levels are de facto economic planners. Directly as they participate in the formulation of (say) tax and expenditure policies and indirectly as they set the terms and scope for the exercise of private economic power, those we elect into office become determiners of the level, character, and distribution of real product. By the more effective democratizing of the political process, they, too, can be held to account.

Surely little elaboration is needed. No president in a third of a century has repudiated the Employment Act of 1946. Each has favored publicly using the full powers of the federal government "to promote

---

30. Ibid., p. 3.
31. U.S. Congress, House of Representatives, *Balanced Growth and Full Employment Bill of 1975*, (H.B. 10373), 94th Congress, 1st Session, 1975.

maximum employment, production, and purchasing power."[32] Few economists would denigrate the inquiry and policy-recommending functions provided by the Joint Economic Committee (members of Congress and staff) in its examination of problems of poverty, stabilization, budgeting, and other economies. With the public sector itself accounting for nearly a third of the total product and with extensive influence on the remaining two-thirds, no member of Congress can avoid acting contra-laissez faire, campaign rhetoric notwithstanding.

No perceptive citizen will deny that his access to the flow of real income is significantly, at times dramatically, affected by decisions emanating from the White House, the House and Senate chambers, the Supreme Court, and his own state house. But that citizen also knows that "eternal vigilance" and continuing political activism are required if public and private economic planners are to be held accountable for their economic judgments.

32. U.S. Congress, Joint Economic Committee, *Twentieth Anniversary of the Employment Act of 1946: An Economic Symposium*, U.S. Government Printing Office, Washington, D.C., 1966. The Joint Economic Committee began in 1976 publishing studies under the general title, *Achieving the Goals of the Employment Act of 1946—Thirtieth Anniversary Review*.

Chapter 8

PRINCIPLES OF ECONOMIC CHANGE

The history of the human race is that of a perpetual opposition of these forces, the dynamic force of technology continually making for change, and the static force of ceremony—status, mores, and legendary belief—opposing change. Most of the time and in most parts of the world status has prevailed . . .

CLARENCE AYRES*

All the societies that have survived have done so, obviously, because in spite of their crippling fantasies they have been technologically viable. This power of intelligent co-operation still remains; indeed, it is more potent by far than ever before, as indeed it must be, since the tools we now manipulate in concert are more complicated and more potent than ever before. . . . Our task is to devise efficient organizational expedients and instrumentalities to do better . . .

CLARENCE E. AYRES**

*Clarence E. Ayres, *The Theory of Economic Progress*, University of North Carolina Press, Chapel Hill, 1944, p. 176.

**Clarence E. Ayres, "The Theory of Institutional Adjustment," in Carey C. Thompson (ed.), *Institutional Adjustment*, University of Texas Press, Austin, Texas, 1967, p. 16.

How simple our response to revolutionary unrest could be if any one of the single-minded concepts of social and economic change advanced in yesterday's isms were indeed pertinent to our age and our problems.

At the outset, let us remind ourselves of what, in general, these ideological concepts of change are:

The theory of change for capitalists contemplates an episodic shift from what is unnatural and not capitalist to that which is natural and capitalist. Movement toward the free-enterprise, free-competition, minimum-government economy is what is meant by progress. No post-capitalist experience is envisioned. Atomistic, automatic, unfettered markets distinguished by continuous flexible pricing will permit the capitalist system to adapt to all externally originating change.

The theory of change for the Marxists is a stages-of-history model in which successive modes of production and exchange (substructure) impose their dominion on the other aspects of the culture (super-structure of government, law, family, religion, etc.). The genesis of change is found in the dialectically conflictual elements of the mode of production. This conflict is reflected in the class conflict in each of the successive modes between those who own and do not work and those who work and do not own. The direction of change through the several stages (feudalism, capitalism, socialism, communism) is given; volitional and organized men and women can accelerate or retard the pace, however. It is unlikely that the respective stages of this "law of motion of society." can be skipped or by-passed.

The theory of change for fascists is the great-man theory. All history is the "lengthening shadow of great men," who, as necessary, coercively impose their wills on the larger society and shape and pattern events to their own whims and desires. Fascism, as with other isms, is a final form; there is no theory which contemplates a postfascist order. Explore now the implications:

To those agitating about the productivity revolution and the un-relieved real-income gap between minimal physical need (to say nothing of health and decency standards) and existing economic performance, we would have an ism-ideology answer: As capitalists, we could say that starvation, poverty, and malnutrition can be removed by creating unfettered markets for those willing and able to offer marketable skills. End impairments of markets: end poverty. As Marxists, we could say that poverty is a necessary consequence of a capitalist mode of production and the attendant class-based exploitation. End capitalism: end poverty. As fascists, we could say that poverty for the racially and nationally superior can be ended by coercive seizure from the racially and nationally inferior. But spiritual and national aggrandizement supplant in significance any mundane interest in material well-being. Make war: ignore poverty.

To those agitating about the participatory revolution and the de facto absence of governance by consent, we would have an ism-ideology answer: As capitalists, we would argue that market participation creates economic democracy. Government protects capitalistic institutions once they emerge. More capitalism: more participation. As Marxists, we would argue that meaningful participation in a capitalist world consists of accelerating class conflict and hastening the demise of capitalism. After the proletarian revolution, a dictatorship of and for (but not by) the proletariat rules. End capitalism: increase participation. As fascists, we would argue that there are only the leaders and the led. Followers need no discretionary participation. They need direction. Great men direct change. More obedience to authority: no need for participation.

To those agitating about the racial and sexual revolution and the continued use of race, color, sex, and ethnic origin as criteria of human worth, we would have an ism-ideology answer: To the capitalist, a singular episodic shift from unnatural to natural economic institutions would indirectly end economic discrimination. Free markets are color-blind. With a cash nexus and market mentality the only relevant color (in the U.S.) is green (as in currency). Increase capitalism: reduce racism and sexism. To the Marxist, racism and sexism are a residue of private ownership (including private ownership of people, i.e., slavery). Racism and sexism are tied to class and class struggle. End capitalism: end racism and sexism. To the fascist, racism and sexism are not problems; they are virtues. Fascists celebrate racial, sexual, ethnic, and national differences. Cultural growth and change are products of racially superior male people. Life is an eternal struggle for survival; only the superior survive. Increase fascism: increase racism and sexism.

To those agitating about the ecological crisis and environmental despoilation, we can infer ism-ideological answers: To the capitalists, a singular shift to more unfettered markets would permit profit-motivated enterprises to make a business out of cleaning up the environment. (Technically, the "externalities" of microanalysis become an object of inquiry and capitalist pursuit.) Capitalism can respond best to any economic need. Unleash capitalist incentive and institutions: reduce pollution. To the Marxists, a stages-theory shift from a capitalist to a Marxian-socialist mode alone can end bourgeois self-serving, profit-accumulating, class concerns in favor of proletariat concerns. Only the mode shift and proletarian class supremacy can deliver on environmental restoration. End capitalism: end pollution. To the fascists, force alone (in the hands of great leaders) moves people and generates economic and social change. If pollution is a threat to fascist aggrandizement and aggressive ambitions, simple fiat, appropriately directed and coercively enforced, will suffice. Increase fascism: control pollution.

I.   GENERAL CHARACTERISTICS

But as we have noted above, the ism-ideologies' single-minded recipes for social and economic change either are in fact irrelevant to these areas of contemporary revolutionary unrest or they are positively contributive to the problems. Where may we then turn? In responding to the pressure for extensive social and economic change, how can we determine which direction is forward? Where is there an alternative to the natural-order-based maximizing of capitalists, the law-of-motion class struggle of the Marxists, and the mystic potency of great men of the fascists?

A part of the answer is already evident in what has been argued above. A number of characteristics of an alternative theory of social and economic change may now be summarized:

(a) Economic and social change is in large part discretionary. Men and women, in the main, make their own history. Change is not predetermined by some teleological force or phenomenon. Neither is change a consequence of fate or a mere dance of atoms. All structure is a product of human creation; all structural change is a consequence of human choice. The economic order is amenable to reasoned control; there need be no deference to impersonal market forces, to class struggle, to activistic sentimentalism, or to aggressive racism.

(b) Social and economic change *consists* of a revamping of habits of mind and habits of behavior, of institutional forms, of prescriptions and proscriptions, of working rules, all of which organize activity in the performance of functions. In consequence, an acceptable theory of social and economic change must be a theory explaining institutional initiation, adjustment, modification, or abandonment.

(c) Since the reality of life is with process, social and economic change must be viewed processionally. Structural change is a matter of a constantly evolving, necessarily fragmentary, transformation of ordering arrangements; it is not and cannot be a matter of piecemeal or comprehensive episodic shifts (as with capitalism and fascism). An economic order is cumulatively developmental; it is not conflictually displacemental (as with Marxism). This process does not terminate so long as life continues. There is no structurally definable "place" (capitalism, communism, fascism, socialism) which, once attained, will not thereafter require further change and adjustment. All of yesterday's isms are utopian in this sense and therefore are devoid of relevance for the resolution of real problems facing real people.

II.   DYNAMIC ELEMENT

The core of an alternative theory of social and economic change is now in view.

The dynamic element which continuously operates to erode confidence in existing structures is the human being's capacity to think reflectively and critically, to perceive means-consequence connections, and to formulate theories incorporating such reflections. A person's own developmental capacity to produce and disseminate reliable knowledge and to relate it, to apply it, to incorporate it in his or her experience generates a continuing challenge to received doctrines, to traditional habits of mind and behavior, to unquestioned faith in ism-ideologies. The expanding fund of knowledge is both a product of such reflection and a source feeding such reflection. "Let us admit the case of the conservative," says John Dewey; "if we once start thinking, no one can guarantee the outcome, except that many objects, ends and institutions will be surely doomed."[1]

Men and women are question-posers; they ask "Why?" In that role, they are subversive, potentially, of every (or any) existential rule, convention, habit, institution, statute, decree, canon, custom, or code. In asking "why," people subject "what is" (belief and behavior) to critical scrutiny; they think. And in consequence of the thinking, "what ought" is formulated. A person's developmental capacity to perceive a difference between "what is" and "what ought" makes of him or her a purposive agent—a problem solver. Effort is directed to the reordering of some facet of the life process.

The dynamic in social and economic change is thus men and women themselves. Veblen would say that the initiating elements are "idle curiosity"—a proclivity which, as Allan Gruchy describes it, "drives men to inquire into the nature of things, to work out explanations of the world's events"[2]—and the "instinct of workmanship"—a proclivity which "occupies the interest with practical expedients, ways and means, devices and contrivances of efficiency and economy, proficiency, creative work and technological mastery of facts."[3] For Veblen, these are common human propensities which, whether innate or acquired, are directed or guided by intellect and channeled by culture. For us, Veblen helps affirm the genesis of change in the reflective curiosity of people and its rational application to their evolving experience.

III. RETARDING ELEMENT

But social and economic change are also, of course, resisted. People's proclivities, innate or acquired, to retain habits of mind and habits of

1. John Dewey, *Characters and Events*, Henry Holt and Co., New York, 1929, Vol. I, p. 1.
2. Allan G. Gruchy, *Modern Economic Thought: The American Contribution*, Prentice-Hall, New York, 1947, p. 65.
3. Thorstein Veblen, *The Instinct of Workmanship*, Viking Press, New York, 1946, p. 33.

behavior which confer status, permit retention of power, provide self-identity and the like, operate to arrest change. How so?

Institutions, we have said, are constituted by habits. They prescribe and proscribe behavior and attitudes. They are created to serve various purposes and functions. They correlate, organize, and order behavior. One kind of purpose or function performed, usually that which led to the institution's creation, is to provide a means to apply reliable knowledge to the performance of those continuing economic (or political or social) functions which the community has come to identify as important. We listed in chapter 6 a number of such economic functions which are essential to the continuity of the life process. Included were the industrial production of goods; provision for nondiscriminatory productive participation; transport of goods, ideas and persons; the production of food and fiber; and the determination of income shares, among others. When or to the extent that an institution is providing for the use of warrantable knowledge in the effective performance of one or more of these continuing functions, it may be said to be operating instrumentally—that is, to be engaged in the performance of an *instrumental function*.[4] The portion of total attention and energy devoted to this *kind* of activity will, of course, vary widely among institutions.

But institutions also characteristically perform a different *kind* of function *as well*. Structural arrangements may be created (more likely, diverted from their original purpose) and retained for the purposes (a) of hierarchical ranking of persons, defining their relative place and status; (b) of conferring esteem and privilege on an elite segment of the community; (c) of establishing and coercively sustaining discretion by the few over the many; (d) of destroying levels of mutual trust, integrity, and confidence, on which alone cooperative and productive work depend; (e) of inhibiting or destroying the rights and opportunities of people to gain and use skills and knowledge; (f) of sustaining or protecting the self-image and self-identity of individuals in the institution without regard to the impact on or consequences for others; (g) of perpetuating customs and traditions of deference to authority; and (h) of protecting the power and continuity of the structure *as such* without any necessary regard to its instrumental effectiveness,[5] among others.

Institutions committed to purposes such as these function typically to inhibit or impair efforts at institutional modification or adjustment.

4. John Kenneth Galbraith uses *instrumental function* to mean almost the reverse of that intended here, i.e., to serve "the goals of those who have power in the system." *Economics and the Public Interest*, op. cit., p. 7. Compare the usage here also with that of Adolphy Lowe, *On Economic Knowledge*, Harper and Row, New York, 1965.

5. "Erasmus speaks of the self-preservative function of institutionalized dogma as the 'Law of Degeneracy.' As summarized by Salomon, this law refers to '. . . the thesis that all social institutions, including religious institutions, are driven by their desire to survive into programs of self-entrenchment and self-aggrandizement in the course of which their original faiths and ideals are perverted and abandoned.'" Milton Rokeach, *The Open and Closed Mind*, Basic Books, Inc., New York, 1960, pp. 68-69.

In brief, we can now call this an *invidious function*[6] (Clarence Ayres would call it a *ceremonial function.*)[7] of institutions in contrast to the *instrumental function* noted above.

The continuing and central task in social and economic change of the institutional fabric is one of *increasing* the degree and magnitude of *instrumental* performance and *decreasing* the degree and magnitude of *invidious* performance.[8]

Here is a preliminary way of perceiving a difference between "what is" and "what ought to be." Here, potentially, is a way of determining "which direction is forward." Here is a provisional way of defining the nature of politico-economic problems. Here is a part of the explanation for the contention that the solution of social problems requires institutional change, adjustment, or abandonment.

IV.   EXAMPLES AND APPLICATIONS

Some examples may help to clarify the distinction. Return briefly to the four areas of revolutionary unrest.

Regarding the productivity revolution: Opinion polls show repeatedly the community's unease with the whole design, structure, and consequences of the existing institutions providing welfare. Politicians seek instant accolades for "dumping" on the recipients for their alleged fecundity, their alleged inability to handle money, their alleged success in "avoiding useful work." Most readers have heard colorful tales of welfare frauds, welfare cheats, free-riders, freeloaders, and the like. The structure may well be faulty, but wherein lies the fault?

Welfare institutions are designedly intended to provide some meager and continuous income for those who do not have or could not have economic connections sufficient to meet their minimal real-income needs. Presumably that is the instrumental function. Thus vast programs to provide assistance for dependent children, the blind, and others have been developed. Also presumably, our economic and financial capacity and productivity is such as to cast no doubt on the ability of the system to generate enough money and real income to meet these needs.

6. The word *invidious* is used extensively by Thorstein Veblen. For him, *invidious* is a "term used in a technical sense as describing a comparison of persons with a view to rating and grading them in respect of relative worth or value—in an aesthetic or moral sense—and so awarding and defining the relative degrees of complacency with which they may legitimately be contemplated by themselves and by others. An invidious comparison is a process of valuation of persons in respect of worth." *The Theory of the Leisure Class*, Modern Library, New York, 1934, p. 34.)

7. The distinction drawn here between instrumental and invidious functions is in part derivative from a distinction Clarence Ayres makes between technology and ceremoniality. See his *The Theory of Economic Progress*, op. cit., chapters 6 & 8 especially.

8. An excellent amplification of this point is developed by Paul Dale Bush (professor of economics, California State University, Fresno, California) in a paper entitled "A Veblen-Ayres Model of Institutional Change" presented at the meetings of the Western Economic Association in Anaheim, California, June 21, 1977.

But the welfare undertaking is plagued by other activities and purposes which seem clearly to be ceremonial or invidious in their impact if not in their intent. Forcing male heads of families to leave their homes in order for the dependent children to qualify for aid is a familiar example of an invidious prescription in the welfare package. So also is the role sometimes imposed on social workers to become part-time sleuths and law enforcers. So also is the failure to adjust support levels promptly with changes in the cost of living. So also is the effort to deny food stamps to persons because they live in communes or have long hair. So also are administrative arrangements and regulations which demean recipients and destroy their sense of their own worth. So also are meticulous qualification requirements which deny aid altogether to perhaps half of those actually living in privation.

Regarding the participatory revolution: Consider the Community Action Programs of the U.S. federal poverty programs of the mid-1960s. [9] Enabling legislation called for "maximum feasible participation" by "the poor in the programs that will affect their lives." [10] The instrumental function being served was to provide for more extensive participation of the poor in the community-level economic planning needed to improve the level and quality of life in the ghettos and the barrios. "Local community action programs are central to the war on poverty. . . . The individual community decides how best to attack poverty in its midst. Initiative and direction must come from the community itself." [11] The instrumental function was to bring greater meaning and amelioration to the lives of the poor by placing significant but not necessarily controlling discretionary planning authority in the hands of representatives of the poor themselves.

In some one thousand such community-action organizations, this authority was commonly used to question existing policy and to propose changes. As questioning developed, as agitation for change began, as proposals for restructuring local institutions and regulations developed; those holding existing power over the lives of these people (city halls, slumlords, boards of education, county planning boards, etc.) began to resist these efforts. Political feedback to Congress intensified to the point where, for these and other reasons, in the legislative changes introduced in 1967, Community Action Programs were mandated a diminished role, and political authority started to flow back to more traditional centers. "Maximum feasible participation" proved to be "infeasible"

9. See James L. Sundquist (ed.), *On Fighting Poverty*, Basic Books, New York, 1969. Also, Joseph A. Kershaw, *Government Against Poverty*, Markham Publishing Co., Chicago, 1970.

10. Reprinted with permission of Daniel Bell and Virginia Held from *The Public Interest*, No. 11, Summer 1969, p. 149. Copyright © 1969 by National Affairs, Inc.

11. Ibid.

mainly, but not wholly, because of the threat to established structures and the status and power positions of public officials. As Daniel Moynihan puts it:

> At the risk of oversimplification, it might be said that the CAP's most closely controlled by City Hall were disappointing, and that the ones most antagonistic were destroyed. There was a large area in between, but it tended to receive little attention. For the most militant agencies, something like a four-stage sequence seems to have been followed. First, a period of organizing, with much publicity and great expectations everywhere. Second, the beginning of operations, with the onset of conflict between the agency and local government institutions, with even greater publicity. Third, a period of counterattack from local government, not infrequently accompanied by conflict and difficulties, including accounting troubles, within the agency itself. Fourth, victory for the established institutions, or at best, stalemate, accompanied by bitterness and charges of betrayal. Whatever else had occurred, the quest for community had failed.[12]

Some professed to see in the legislation establishing the CAPS "a mandate for federal assistance in the effort to create political organizations for the poor."[13] The resistance is understandable. It took federal legislation in the Wagner Act to give industrial workers more control over their own lives by affirming and enforcing the right to bargain collectively. Even when new institutions are formed to initiate community planning, if judgments become mainly concerned with retention of power per se and, by extension, with the retention of rules, regulations, and programs generated by such established power centers, little energy and attention can be devoted to the noninvidious purposes of such new institutions. In consequence, another batch of promises for substantive reform is breached with attendant rage and frustration. Debate continues on what was and what might have been.

Regarding the racial and sexual revolutions: Consider the impact and import of racial discrimination in public education. So central has this concern been in the public's attention since the 1954 desegregation decision of the Supreme Court, little detail is required.

Most will acknowledge that among the major instrumental functions of public education is the creation and maintenance of a learning environment in which all children can develop their rational, cognitive, affective, creative, aesthetic, and communicative capacities as far as our understanding of the acquisition of these capacities and our resources

12. Daniel P. Moynihan, *Maximum Feasible Misunderstanding*, Free Press, New York, 1970, p. 131. Copyright © 1970, 1969 by The Free Press. A Division of The Macmillan Company.

13. Ibid.

will permit. Such an environment should be imaginatively creative, continuously supportive, academically interesting, encouraging of participation, and stimulative of feelings of self-worth. To succeed, the environment must not be punitive, repressive, ego-destructive, emotionally dislocative, demeaning, spontaneity-dampening, or authoritarian. That a large number of public and private schools manage to focus heavily on these instrumental functions is readily granted. The systems include a large number of dedicated, even heroic, instructors who, often with inadequate support and excessive numbers of students, still are able to create excitement over the development of the mind and the acquisition of skills.

Yet in some systems we continue to endure, as we have for decades, arrangements in education which sanction or tolerate the invidious use of race and sex (and national or ethnic origin) to deny or abort access to these instrumental functions of education. The "separate-but-equal" doctrine, which established parallel (but in fact unequal) educational systems for blacks and whites in much of the South was, of course, invidiously grounded. The textbook writers who for a century have written romantically and expansively about the American West and the "courageous" whites who "conquered" the "primitive" Indians, writers who picture family life as that of WASP middle-class America with very limited and demeaning or trivial roles for women, writers who depict blacks and chicanos in menial occupational roles inculcate and perpetuate a racially and sexually invidious view of people's worth. "Institutional racism" continues in public schools where the "track system" directs blacks and chicanos into academically inferior classes (causing intraschool segregation), where counseling systems discourage upward-mobility aspirations of minority students, and where racial and ethnic prejudice of teachers impinges adversely upon their instructional methods and grading practices. Access to desegregated educational opportunity continues to be impaired by an invidiously grounded unwillingness of communities to abide either de facto integrated neighborhoods or the busing of children, and an unwillingness to provide adequate financial support (bond issues, tax overrides, etc.) for public schooling in the core cities of America.

Regarding the ecological crisis: A major difficulty in retaining (and restoring) a habitable environment with breathable air, potable water, and protection of interdependent life cycles (including human beings') from destruction is that there have been precious few institutional arrangements directed to environmental and ecological protection. In the main, only *after* substantial environmental havoc has been produced (or threatens) through wanton timber cutting, oil spillage, mining of agricultural land, overgrazing, strip mining, radioactive-waste leakage, bulldozing for freeways, internal-combustion-engine pollution, or agricultural-chemical poisoning, are prescriptions and proscriptions introduced. Conservation efforts date from the turn of this century. The recognition of an ecological crisis dates from the mid-1960s only.

Some examples: The instrumental functions of the Atomic Energy Commission included the meticulous regulation of the peaceful energy-generating use of atomic fission. This role was offset and impaired in part by the AEC's apparent institutional reluctance to promote and require adequate inquiry into safety margins on nuclear reactors and radioactive-waste disposal by private corporations and other interested parties. In consequence, in the opinion of many, a monumental threat, potentially catastrophic, confronts the larger community.[14] Private and public producers of atomic power must, if necessary, become willing to forego criteria of profitability, market expansion, interindustry market power, bureaucratic continuities, and status of firms and directors in determining judgments on plant creation, plant location, safe plant operation and safe atomic-waste disposal.

The decision to construct a nearly 800-mile "hot oil" pipeline across Alaska from the northern slopes to a southern accessible port appears to be another instance of a triumph of pecuniary and nationalistic criteria over ecological values. Oil companies spent over $1 billion in developing these Arctic oil fields. The Interior Department report on the matter contended that "development of the petroleum reserves on the North Slope of Alaska is essential to the strength, growth and security of the United States."[15] This same report also acknowledged that the

> Impact of the proposed action would extend to many facets of the existing Alaskan environment. Environmental impact on fish and wildlife resources would include some local loss of wilderness . . . disturbance of wildlife and alteration of some fish and wildlife habitat. . . . Many effects would be temporary . . . but others would persist, including those following possible oil pollution accidents which might involve the pipeline route itself and oceanic areas.[16]

The Interior Department and the state of Alaska attempted to supervise the operation to "reduce foreseeable environmental costs to acceptable levels.[17]

But what are "acceptable levels" of hazard to the environment? And what of the secondary environmental effects resulting from an

14. See, e.g., Ralph E. Lapp, "The Nuclear Power Controversy—Safety," *The New Republic*, January 23, 1971, pp. 18-21; Reprinted in Ralph E. Lapp, *A Citizen's Guide to Nuclear Power*, op. cit. Also see Dennis Farney, "Atomic-Age Trash," *The Wall Street Journal*, January 25, 1971, pp. 1 and 10.

15. "The Pipeline," *The New Republic*, January 31, 1971, p. 9.

16. Quoted in Ibid.

17. Ibid. See also, Thomas M. Brown, "That Unstoppable Pipeline," *The New York Times Magazine*, October 14, 1973, pp. 35 and 88-108.

inadequately planned and controlled "opening-up" of the heart of the Alaskan wilderness? The American community hardly needs yet another rerun of the penchant of some for preemption, exploitation, plundering, and spoilation of its wilderness areas. The Alaskan heartland is the last remaining large wilderness area in the United States.

What needs over and over to be restated is that although human discretion (technologically, institutionally) is very wide and growing, it is not infinite. In the nature of the case it can never be. The ability to know and the power to act are circumscribed by physical, reflective, and behavioral limitations of people. Not all consequences of *mistaken* judgments are reversible! On some questions we must be *right* the *first* time; there is no going back; no saying "sorry about that." The destruction of oceanic life, the poisoning of our atmospheric blanket, the release of large volumes of radioactive particles in war or by accident, the massive erosion of topsoils and the life forms dependent thereon would all appear to fall in this irreversibility category. [18] The instrumental function in ecological efforts is, of course, to sustain life and that on which it depends. Invidious functions in agencies and enterprises threaten that continuity, whether the functions are exhibited by an oil company, a corps of engineers, a land developer, a state highway commission or the Congress.

To reiterate: Breakdowns, dislocations, interruptions, impairments, or disjunctions in the operation of political and economic institutions constitute *problems*. Such problems are resolved (where resolution has intelligible and communicable meaning) by the adjustment or modification of institutional arrangements to increase the instrumental functioning and/or to decrease the invidious functioning of such institutions. Social inquiry (including political and economic inquiry) must, then, be directed to the institutional fabric, the problems generated therein by, for example, deference to status, power, or privilege and to the formulation of alternative structures which enhance instrumental performance at the expense of such ceremonial or invidious performances. Thus, all social and economic change requires discretionary control over and adjustment of institutional structure which has become problematic. As we have alleged above and explain more fully below, such discretionary control ought to be democratically grounded.

V.   LIMITING CONDITIONS

But affirming the need for social change as institutional adjustment and understanding the anatomy of a social problem will not suffice. A word

18. On the question of irreversibility, an interesting and disturbing analysis has been developed by Nicholas Georgescu-Roegen. See Nicholas Wade, "Nicholas Georgescu-Roegen: Entropy the Measure of Economic Man," *Science*, Vol. 190, October 31, 1975, pp. 447-50; also Nicholas Georgescu-Roegen, *The Entropy Law and the Economic Process*, Harvard University, Cambridge, Massachusetts, 1971.

about some limiting conditions which impinge on such social and economic change is also required. Three such limiting conditions are considered here: [19]

(1) The availability of warrantable knowledge poses one limitation. Our knowledge of a social or economic problem or process is, of course, never complete. Always people must judge on imperfect understanding and inadequate evidence. But the growth of reliable knowledge which renders some structures observably obsolete also is, of course, the primary source drawn on in framing alternative institutional forms. What is attempted as social change is limited, then, by the level and sophistication of our knowledge of means-consequence relationships. No one can hope to predict all relevant consequences, but inquiry should extend as far as wit, time, and energy will permit. For example, much of the economic growth of the United States, industrial and agricultural, occurred without sufficient attention to the environmental and ecological hazards being created. Once the implications of such consequences are known, a community cannot thereafter unknow them. They become new evidence of which account must be taken. So a community learns and applies its learning to judgments made subsequently. Elemental? Of course. The point is offered as a cautionary note to those possessing power who are prone to ignore evidence, the community's level of understanding, and the existential facts of problematic situations.

(2) The ability of a people to understand and accept the change being introduced is also a limiting condition on institutional change. Institutions are constituted of social habits. To change institutions requires that those whose behavior (and attitudes) will be changed by the adjustment be fully appraised of what is contemplated, be able to see themselves functioning normally and effectively in their altered or new behaviorial role, and on that basis be prepared to accept and/or participate in the change and to alter behavior and attitude patterns accordingly. [20]

This perhaps is why "revolutions from above" typically fail in their intention to rewrite living and working rules. Only "evolutions from below" can succeed. Those whose behavior is to be revised must themselves understand the need for it, concur with it, and participate in it. Otherwise nothing substantive changes; the canons, codes, customs, and conventions remain largely as before.

19. The position here developed is adapted from a formulation by Professor J. Fagg Foster, in "The Theory of Institutional Adjustment," (mimeographed) University of Denver, (no date), and "The Fundamental Principles of Economics," (mimeographed) University of Denver, 1972. A modified version of these principles appears in my article, "A Social Value Theory in Neoinstitutional Economics," *Journal of Economic Issues*, Vol. XI, No. 4, December, 1977, pp. 823-46.

20. S. Herbert Frankel provides a useful additional insight: "The fact is that change has been resisted in Africa and is still resisted there, as it is the world over, not because of outworn tradition, or ceremonials as Ayres [Clarence E.] called them, but because

The greater the degree of success in involving people in the identification of what is for them problematic, in the framing of alternatives as to what is to be done, and in implementing the proposals for reconstituting structure which will organize their lives, the more effective and lasting is the change. Since the common people bear the effect of change finally and most potently, they are less likely to be deferential to invidiously or ceremonially warranted defenses of what is. People are educable; they will wish to see instrumental functions performed. They are aware of whose real income is impaired with economic instability, whose sons die on battlefields, whose children are denied educational access and adequate medical care, and whose jobs are denied on invidious grounds. There are no guarantees, of course, but social and economic change will generally be more effective and less invidious where those who receive the incidence of policy have a voice in determining that policy. It is for this reason, ideology notwithstanding, that economic planning must be democratically controlled in fact if it is to be effective.

(3) A third limiting condition is a simple one. It has to do with the degree and timing of contemplated structural change. Any proposed abandonment of invidious or ceremonial activities of persons in institutions (to increase the effectiveness of the institution in performing its instrumental functions) must do the least possible violence to other instrumental functions of that or other institutions. Adjustment must be "minimally dislocative."

For example, if, in a college, the grading system is punitive and observably is impairing the development of reflective capabilities of students, the modification of that prescription should be undertaken in a manner which does not disrupt or impair other educational activities (e.g., effective instruction) which are still thought to be functionally useful in the instrumental sense.

As we noted above in another connection, no people can be expected to recast the whole (or even a major part) of their behavioral or attitudinal patterns in a very short time. Especially is this true if point #2 above is ignored. In effecting social and economic change a people cannot stop and start over, cannot wipe the slate clean and begin all over again. All social change must be piecemeal. As the Fabian Socialists say, it must be "step by step." Anyone who has visited or lived in a "foreign land" or who has been inducted into the armed forces knows what is meant by *cultural shock*. A largely new pattern of behavioral forms, expectations, and attitudes is encountered. Only

better alternative modes of action were not, or were not observed to be available, or did not prove, or were not expected or thought likely to prove more successful." (S. Herbert Frankel, "Ayres and the Roots of Economic Progress," in William Breit and William Patton Culbertson, Jr. (eds.), *Science and Ceremony: The Institutional Economics of C. E. Ayres*, University of Texas Press, Austin, 1976, p. 67.)

with difficulty and over time can a successful adjustment to such changes be made. [21]

Even so, the foregoing should not be read as an argument against extensive and fundamental change. If (but only if) these three limiting conditions are in fact met, extensive structural change can be made more rapidly than one might otherwise suppose. Habits of mind and habits of behavior (Veblen's "patterns of use and wont") of course *do* change. Consider for a moment the impact of the Keynesian and post-Keynesian contributions on our attitudes toward balanced budgets, the meaning of full employment, and the economic role of government. Consider the alterations of behavior involved in the use of federal tax, expenditure, and debt policy in the macromanagement of the economy. Consider also the "agonizing reappraisal" of American foreign policy in the late 1960s and the early 1970s. Consider the intellectual and emotional flailing about as the community seeks seriously to address the questions of welfare reform. Consider the import of enterprises seeking to be "equal opportunity employers" and of trade unions advocating nondiscriminatory membership.

The community often appears to be developing a changed attitude toward change. Does the community seek less often to arrest change and to preserve what is on invidious grounds? Does it seek more often for opportunity to use participatory involvement, including genuine discretion to affect the course, extent, and timing of economic and social change? Assessments will differ.

But again the caveat: Change for the sake of change is no gain. The burden is on the agitator to demonstrate the merit and viability of proposals for change. Novelty may be entertaining, but it is hardly a *reason* for modifying accepted patterns and expectations which organize experience. The *reason* for making changes in structure is to increase people's control over their own lives through the discovery of more instrumental solutions to economic and political problems.

In sum, an evolving, functional economy is a discretionary economy; it must accord the community at large fundamental and continuing control over resource creation, over the structural mix, over operational mechanisms, and over the processes of institutional adjustment. No ism-ideology is sufficiently comprehensive, sufficiently relevant, sufficiently flexible, sufficiently well grounded in the historic evidences of the human condition, sufficiently attuned to problem

---

21. An interesting, if inconclusive, exercise would be to ask which of these three limiting conditions appear to have been violated in some major historical attempts at comprehensive (nationwide) adjustments which subsequently had to be abandoned. For example, did the Chinese Great Leap Forward in the 1960s overlook numbers one and three of the above? Did the introduction of the Weimar Republic in Germany in the early 1920s err in regard to number two? To what would one credit the failure of Prohibition in the U.S. in the late 1920s and early 1930s? Etc.

solving, or sufficiently applicable to vital issues to claim our reflective or effective allegiance. Of course, it is a fact that people believe in yesterday's isms. But as paradigms of political economies, as models on which and from which to frame social and public policy, such beliefs are fatally defective. In addition, they are in plain fact inapplicable.

We have explained that an evolving, functional economy must be discretionary; we have proposed to place that discretion ultimately with the community at large. But the reasons for that placement have, for the most part, been asserted; they have not here been developed. Accordingly, we now turn to an examination of the political process and to the fashioning of a theory of a participatory, democratic polity to parallel the foregoing theory of an evolving, functional economy.

POLITY

Chapter 9

THE POLITICAL PROCESS

Life is perpetuated only by renewal. If conditions do not permit renewal to take place continuously it will take place explosively. The cost of revolutions must be charged up to those who have taken for their aim arrest of custom instead of its readjustment . . . who having power refuse to use it for ameliorations.

JOHN DEWEY*

. . . no man or limited set of men is wise enough or good enough to rule others without their consent . . . all those who are affected by social institutions must have a share in producing and managing them. . . . The keynote of democracy . . . [is] the necessity for the participation of every mature human being in formation of the values that regulate the living of men together.

JOHN DEWEY**

*John Dewey, *Human Nature and Conduct*, Modern Library/Random House, New York, 1930, pp. 167-68.
**John Dewey, *Problems of Men*, Philosophical Library, New York, 1946, p. 58.

As interdependent fellow-travelers on this troubled planet, we face two monumental ironies in this "most catastrophically revolutionary age." Since "life is perpetuated only by renewal," we must understand the nature of these ironies and act on that understanding as discretionary human agents if renewal is to be made possible.

On the one hand, devotees of the Grand Alternatives—yesterday's ism-ideologies—see themselves as avant-garde determiners of "which direction is forward." They purport to offer genuine options in response to revolutionary unrest. Capitalists say, "We alone can offer freedom and affluence." Communists say, "Capitalism is doomed; we are the wave of the future." Fascists say, "We offer the only alternative to communism or chaos." But nearly everywhere the "opaque facts" of existential experience with real problems render these "options" and "alternatives" inapplicable.

On the other hand, advocates of a non-ism, nondoctrinaire, non-invidious democratic alternative, who characteristically eschew revolutionary pretense or posture, are actually offering the *most relevant*, the *most genuinely revolutionary* options and alternatives available. The democratic contention that "those who receive the incidence of policy ought themselves to have discretion over such policy" is a fundamentally revolutionary dictum. It constitutes a continuing threat to all models and forms of elitist rule and invidious warrant; it is everywhere a potential assault on the status quo. In comparison, the change-inducing, reformmongering potential of the ism-ideologies is miniscule.

But for such a contention to become persuasive or carry conviction, it will be necessary briefly to examine the political facets of ism-ideologies, provide a restatement of some fundamental principles of political phenomena, and reformulate a theory of participatory democracy. Turn now to the first of these topics.

I.   ISMS AND POLITIES

Curiously, no one of the major ism-ideologies offers a comprehensive theory of political behavior, although each purports to provide a general belief system to guide social conduct. In widely divergent ways, each ideology is incomplete; in some respects each is also mistaken.

Capitalism

The political content of orthodox capitalism originates with and is delimited by a long-conditioned predisposition to assert a dualism of the economy and the polity—of the private sector and the public sector. We are witness to the ideological use of a contemporary counterpart of the medieval "doctrine of two swords."[1] That doctrine divided society into

---

1. See George H. Sabine, A *History of Political Theory*, Henry Holt, New York, 1937, p. 194.

discrete realms of spiritual or religious interests and institutions, and temporal or secular interests and institutions. The counterpart distinction is between the economy, consisting of a free-market system and involving pecuniary interests and utility maximization, and the polity, consisting of governmental institutions and involving power interests and compulsions to intrude on private enterprise. Dual controls exist: market forces govern economic affairs; power forces govern political affairs. The continuing threat is the encroachment of the power forces on the market forces. According to the orthodox capitalist, these are separate jurisdictions which interact, but the identities and prerogatives of each must remain inviolate.

Over the years, this basic dualism has taken a variety of forms: For Adam Smith, the distinction is between "natural liberty" and "systems of preference or of restraint."[2] For Friedrich A. Hayek, the distinction is between "competitive coordination" vs. "conscious social control"—that is, freedom under competition vs. tyranny under planning.[3] Milton Friedman provides a more recent and rigid version:

> Fundamentally, there are only two ways of co-ordinating the economic activities of millions. One is central direction involving the use of coercion—the technique of the army and of the modern totalitarian state. The other is voluntary co-operation of individuals—the technique of the market place. . . . A working model of a society organized through voluntary exchange is a *free private enterprise exchange economy* . . . competitive capitalism.[4]

Finally, scholars of comparative economic systems employ the distinction between the "market mechanism" vs. the "command principle."[5]

The point of this resume is that those of capitalist persuasion *begin* inquiry using a version of this dualism as an organizing premise. Implicit, moreover, is the normative preference for "natural liberty," "competitive coordination," "voluntary co-operation," and "market systems" over "systems . . . of restraint," "conscious social control," "central coercive direction," and the "command principle." The orthodox admit the need for government, but fear it. Accordingly, the public sector, insofar as is possible, is to be kept small, quiescent, and supportive of the private sector.

2. Adam Smith, *The Wealth of Nations*, Random House/Modern Library, New York, 1937, p. 651.

3. F. A. Hayek, *The Road to Serfdom*, University of Chicago Press, Chicago, 1944, pp. 35-36.

4. Milton Friedman, *Capitalism and Freedom*, University of Chicago Press, Chicago, 1962, p. 13. (Emphasis in original.)

5. E.g., Gregory Grossman, *Economic Systems*, Prentice-Hall, Englewood Cliffs, New Jersey, 1967, pp. 13-15; Jan S. Prybyla, *Comparative Economic Systems*, Appleton-Century-Crofts, New York, 1969, passim.

Thus, the proper functions of the government are those Smith advocated—defense against external enemies, protection of persons and property domestically, administration of justice including enforcement of contracts, and the construction of public works and the performance of public functions which would not be profitable enough for private firms to undertake.[6] Nineteenth- and twentieth-century scholars have advocated some expansion of functions to include regulation of monopoly, subsidy to businesses, etc., but always with reluctance. Government intrusion is to be feared.[7] The threat mundanely is of higher taxes, of limits on freedom of business action, of enmeshing red tape, of perversion of market forces, and of outright authoritarianism.

Fears of government could be moderated if its power were legally and carefully delineated and constrained.[8] Accordingly, the orthodox have long advocated a constitutional republic in which the threat of power is reduced through the division of powers or fragmentation of functions among, in the U.S., three branches (legislative, executive, judicial) and the duplication of powers among units (bicameralism, federalism) to permit a balance of power and countervailing checks.

Discretion on economic matters will reside with consumers who are sovereign as they make choices in competitive markets. On political matters historically, suffrage for male property owners was largely unquestioned. Extension of the franchise to others without a comparable economic "stake in society" remained a worry. Genuine choice for those formally enfranchised is to be assured.

Finally, although it cannot be developed extensively here, brief mention must be made of some of the commonalities between the foregoing ideological frame and contemporary political pluralism.[9] What the political pluralists—the group theorists—are advocating seems to be a more extensive application in politics of basic constructs of orthodox theory and ideology. The pluralists also assume the *primacy* of men's desires and interests; this assumption is the counterpart of the capitalists' deference to given wants and tastes. Accordingly, political behavior is, and must be, merely the pursuit of these interests within political institutions. Political institutions operate to compromise, balance off, or adjudicate conflicts among and between interests of individuals and groups even as competitive markets serve to balance rival desires. A legislator is a broker of interests. Legislative institutions are brokerage houses. The commercial analogy is appropriate. It follows, then, that there can be no concept of the public interest beyond the

---

6. Smith, *Wealth of Nations*, op. cit., p. 651.
7. Girvetz, *Evolution of Liberalism*, op. cit., chapter 4.
8. Ibid., chapter 5.
9. For an excellent and fuller account, see John C. Livingston and Robert G. Thompson, *The Consent of the Governed*, (3rd ed.), The Macmillan Co., New York, 1971, pp. 103-51.

reduction of conflict, the balancing of claims, the equating of private interests. Similarly, before Keynes, market equilibrium defined the public's economic interest. Pluralism is a model of ethical relativism exhibiting a social-value void comparable to that of orthodox economic analysis.

In brief critique, the dualistic view of the polity and the economy is anachronistic and mistaken. The assumptions of conceptual and behavioral divorcement reflect the eighteenth- and nineteenth-century time- and culture-bound English experience. The delimited functions of government are no guide to political conduct or policy. The experience of quasidemocratic societies, evidently without exception, is to modify and extend agendas as problems confronted require. The constitutional constraints on political power are instructive. Foreclosing the acquisition of autocratic political power is commendable, of course; putting baffles and barriers in the way of democratic control of power is not. Pluralistic formulations—from the political "realists"—reflect the abandonment of efforts to think constructively about normative matters. However, we are compelled as a community to apply conceptions of the public interest. From where will they come if not from reasoned assessments of political experience? The ethical sterility, and therefore inapplicability, of pluralistic balance forces those seeking reasoned guidance for public judgment into other more relevant and promising areas.

Marxism

The political content of Marxism was and remains underdeveloped. Ironically, although Marx was among the most active, pungent, and astute political observers and commentators of the mid-nineteenth century, he and Engels did not formulate a coherent and inclusive theory of the political process.

With the formulation of an economic interpretation of history, Marxists appeared to regard political activity and institutions as a mere reflection of more basic economic forces and pressures. Since the core of the economic interpretation is the substantive role played by the mode of production and exchange, political matters are reflective of conflictual relations within the mode—conflict between economic classes.

Engels' analysis of the origin of the state places it coextensive with the appearance of economic classes. The state emerges to adjudicate conflicting claims of economic classes—propertied vs. nonpropertied. The state comes under control of the ruling class and is used to serve and protect their interests. Historically the state has had no other function.

Because the Marxist historical law stipulates a succession of modes, of ism systems, and because the displacement of one mode with another results from dialectical conflict, Marxists see political behavior as class *agitation*—favoring or opposing class interests, aiding and abetting class conflict. They do not appear to have a theory of political *participation* or political *action* apart from class membership and class struggle.

Marxism, accordingly, exhibits the following reductionistic characterizations:

Under capitalism, governmental institutions, including military and police organs, are used primarily to protect and extend the economic hegemony of the bourgeoisie. Private ownership of productive means is protected; the exaction and accumulation of surplus value by the capitalists from the workers is assured; the underlying population becomes increasingly alienated. Government is an instrument for waging class warfare.

Under socialism, achieved as a necessary consequence of a necessarily victorious proletarian revolution, government will come under the aegis of an elite cadre of party leaders serving as the "vanguard of the proletariat." This literal "dictatorship of the proletariat"—Lenin's "democratic centralism"—converts government into an instrument for the fulfillment of revolutionary aspirations. This Marxist government, seeking legitimacy under a Rousseauean "general will" theory of democracy, uses its power to obliterate all remnants of bourgeois culture, attitudes, and institutions. But at no time is the right to rule subjected to a genuine public test. An effort is launched to create a community of "new men." The authoritarian character of the socialist-epoch government is admitted by Marxists and defended as essential to prevent counterrevolutionary efforts by residual elements of the capitalist class.

Under communism, the state withers away; the role for organized government dissipates. Marxists believe that if the socialist transition state can raise sufficiently the level of real output *and* create people with new Marxist attitudes and behaviors, there will be no need for governmental institutions with powers of mandamus and injunction.

In sum, Marxists see government under capitalism as an instrument of class oppression, government under socialism as necessarily authoritarian, and government under communism as unnecessary.

Missing from this ideological political frame is an understanding of, or commitment to, democracy. In spite of some early observations of Marx which tend to support the democratic view, the bulk of the Marxian literature appears to denigrate democratic politics as superficial and inattentive to the basic economic-class conflicts of which all politics, in their view, are an expression. Normally, Marxists seem unable to abide democracy.

Even more troublesome, perhaps, is the seeming inability of Marxists to recognize the continuing necessity of rationally ordering the process of determining and administering public policy (discussed below as the political function). They have no inclusive theory of the political process, nor can they provide a frame on which one might be developed.

Fascism

The political content of fascism need not detain us long. Fascism, as most are aware, is primarily a political ideology. It vigorously affirms the necessity and virtues of totalitarian and authoritarian rule. In this century, fascist politics has become a world-wide opprobrious characterization; it epitomizes the most despised mode of rule making on the current scene. Consideration of a few elements of this ideology will, even so, be helpful.

Fascists regard the state as a separate entity, "the highest spiritual entity in the political world." [10] It is an organic entity; it is an existential reality; it is a repository of comprehensive sovereignty, fascists claim. The state is supreme; its power is total. "All is in the State and for the State: nothing outside the State, nothing against the State." [11]

Fascist leaders identify with the organic state and insist that their behavior is committed to the preservation, protection, extension, and service of the state. Accordingly, fascist ideology elevates the principles of hero worship and personality cults to surround emergent leaders with the desired mystic potency and ceremonial trappings. Leaders who proclaim their identities with the state need such worship and cultism in order to secure a sufficient measure of spiritualistic submergence and submission to sustain their elitist rule. The hero-leader becomes the visible surrogate symbol for the mystic, organic state. Party, policies, and postures are directed to the creation and enhancement of the identification of leader and state.

Fascists regard democracy as impossible. Following Thomas Carlyle and Roberto Michels, among others, they regard as inevitable the locating of actual political power in the hands of a minority—an elite segment. ". . . society will always organize itself in the shape of a pyramid, with an elite or aristocracy occupying strategic positions at the apex, supported by the majority of the population at the base." [12] For fascists, democracy normally is an illusion; history, they claim, is on their side; they see no long-term successful democratic experiments.

Moreover, in their view, it is fortunate that such is the case, since democracy must mean rule by the incompetent. "Most people are either too stupid or indisposed to occupy themselves with political concerns." [13] Fascism "proclaims that the great mass of citizens is not a suitable advocate of social interests for the reason that the capacity to ignore

10. Mario Palmieri, quoted in Cohen, *Communism, Fascism & Democracy*, op. cit., p. 378.

11. Ibid., p. 379.

12. Vilfredo Pareto, quoted by A. James Gregor, *The Ideology of Fascism*, Free Press, New York, 1969, p. 40.

13. A. James Gregor on Roberto Michels, ibid., p. 86.

individual private interests in favor of the higher demands of society and of history is a very rare gift and the privilege of the chosen few." [14]

But the fascists have their problems. Concepts of an organic state are conjectural and nondemonstrable. Perhaps "thinking makes it so"? Democracy, of course, is not impossible. Viable democracies exist in a variety of sizes. There is no inherent reason that democracies cannot succeed. The belief in heroes probably should not be carried into adulthood.

Democracy is not undesirable. On the contrary, the following chapters are intended to explain why it is potentially the most efficient, humane, and stable of all modes of organizing the political process.

II. POLITICAL LEGITIMACY

From one vantage point, all four of the separately identified areas of revolutionary unrest—productivity revolution, participatory revolution, racial and sexual revolutions, and the ecological crisis—are but facets or expressions of a common democratic quest. That quest is for discretionary dignity.

The search is for that dignity which derives from (1) making a meaningful contribution to and having an adequate share of the flow of real income; (2) having a genuine voice in determining the rules under which one lives; (3) living noninvidiously in a *community* of "ungraded men"; and (4) having active involvement in environmental restoration and protection. The search is for genuine and expanding choice. Choice confers dignity. This quest for discretionary dignity, we suggest, is a truly revolutionary quest.

A government which affirms and implements dignity-generating conditions can claim the loyalty and support of its citizens. A political process that provides for discretionary dignity for its citizens will be regarded as morally approvable and legitimate. We can now better understand why, as we observed at the outset of this study, government by consent of the governed is now "on the banner" of nearly every major nation state—East or West, North or South. Lip service is paid to democratic rule—"People's Democracies," "Peoples' Capitalisms"—because all regimes are in search of legitimacy.

As John Livingston and Robert Thompson observe,

> The question of legitimacy . . . is the question of whether a political system is regarded by its citizens as entitled to make a moral claim on their loyalty and obedience. . . . The fundamental political problem is always that of seeking to support the structure of political power with the voluntary support of those who are governed . . .

14. Alfredo Rocco in University of Colorado Philosophy Department, *Readings on Fascism and National Socialism*, Swallow Press, Chicago, 1952, p. 37.

Before any political regime can be considered stable, the exercise of power in that regime must be judged to be legitimate by the majority of those over whom it is exercised, so that their participation in its processes and their acquiescence in the execution of its laws are a matter of willing obligation, not of brute force or the threat of force. A substantial portion, at least, of those who are ruled must obey not out of fear but because they feel they ought to. This is what we mean by a legitimate government; those subject to its commands regard them as bearing the stamp of rightful authority rather than sheer power. Often, the claim to legitimacy is neither rational nor consistent, but it is always an effort to create a psychological and moral sense of obligation as the basis for the citizen's obedience to law and his loyalty to the regime.[15]

The ism-ideologies are advanced by their protagonists as "explicit models . . . which seek to translate political power into legitimate authority." They are offered to the anxious but unwary as preferred mechanisms with which to translate "power into authority," to make "the exercise of power nonarbitrary," and to assure that the exercise of power is made "subservient to justice, reason and morality."[16]

But is discretionary dignity really obtainable through the application of the ism-ideologies to experience? We contend that it is not. Ideologists' aspirations to legitimacy and pertinency to problem solving notwithstanding, ism models are different—fundamentally different— from democratic models. Ism models, we suggest, do not provide competent guidance for contemporary political activism. Indeed, conceptually, ism political models have very little common content with democratic models; in part they are incompatible. To argue that democratic theory and practice are genuinely revolutionary (in the sense of fundamental, nonviolent change) and that ism theory and practice is in this sense contrarevolutionary, conservative, change-resisting, and nonlegitimate is to swim against the tidal flows of the folklore. Some general comments on the political process and structure should help us to avoid succumbing to the icy waters of ideological contention.

III.   DETERMINATION OF PUBLIC POLICY

Above, we speak of the need to find a more inclusive perspective from which to view political economy. In that context, we identify an inclusive and continuing *economic* function in the social process as "the production and distribution of real income" and point out that all

15. John C. Livingston and Robert G. Thompson, *The Consent of the Governed*, (3rd ed.), Macmillan, New York, 1971, pp. 19-20. Copyright © 1971, The Macmillan Company.
16. Ibid., p. 20. See also John H. Schaar, "Legitimacy in the Modern State," in Philip Green and Sanford Levinson (eds.), *Power and Community: Dissenting Essays in Political Science*, Random House/Vintage, New York, 1970, pp. 276-327.

societies at all times must assure that this activity is carried on at a level which is tolerable to those involved. Economic institutions organize behavior to provide "the material means of life and experience."

In an exactly parallel fashion, we can now identify "the determination and administration of public and social policy" as an inclusive and continuing *political* function in the social process which all societies at all times must somehow implement. The political process is comprised of those activities and procedures through which decisions affecting the community at large are made. Political judgments establish the structures which organize, pattern, and give meaning to our lives. Thus the use of political discretion operates to stipulate (prescribe and proscribe) the laws, codes, rules, statutes, decrees, and regulations which order our relations with each other. Political activity is more inclusive and exhibits a more determining role or character than other forms of social activity. We have already noted in some detail how political processes are used to establish and modify economic institutions. As additional examples, repeatedly decisions are required to develop organized ways of educating the young, of defining tolerable ways of achieving recognition, of specifying the conditions of work, and of determining group purposes and priorities.

People live only in groups; they are communal animals. Group life compels association. Associative behavior must be organized. Organized control devices—institutions—must be adopted; canons of proper and improper conduct must be determined; acceptable patterns of relationships among persons must be delineated. Such adoption, determination, delineation as a decision-making process *is the political process* of determining and administering public and social policy.

In the words of Sheldon S. Wolin,

> The system of political institutions in a given society represents an arrangement of power and authority. At some point within the system, certain institutions are recognized as having the authority to make decisions applicable to the whole community. The exercise of this function naturally attracts the attention of groups and individuals who feel that their interests and purposes will be affected by the decisions taken. When this awareness takes the form of action directed towards political institutions, the activities become "political" and a part of political nature. The initiative may originate with the institutions themselves, or rather with the men who operate them.[17]

The "main point," continues Wolin, "lies in the 'relating' function performed by political institutions."

> Through the decisions taken and enforced by public officials, scattered activities are brought together, endowed with a new coherence, and their

17. Sheldon S. Wolin, *Politics and Vision*, Little, Brown and Co., Boston, 1960, pp. 6-7.

future course shaped according to "public" considerations . . . political arrangements provide a setting wherein the activities of individuals and groups are connected spatially and temporally.[18]

In this context, then, the "political order" is seen as "a common order created to deal with those concerns in which all of the members of society have some interest."[19]

So viewed, the political process is more inclusive than what ordinarily comes to mind as governmental activity. Politics, of course, includes much that occurs in government but is not limited to that realm of structure. The determination and administration of public policy is also sometimes observable in the activities, for example, of corporations (when they administer prices), organized churches (when they interdict some kinds of inquiry in parochial schools), trade unions (when they set the conditions of bargaining), and college communities (when they determine access to and the content of higher education).

One narrowing of the idea of the political function as the decision-making process on communal questions is also required, however. We must distinguish between what is public and what is nonpublic.[20] The distinction is a matter of scope and consequences. As stated, the political process is concerned with questions "in which all of the members of society have some interest," with public and social policy matters. But not all associative behavior is necessarily political. Family relations, simple friendships, sports and games, religious worship, *may* well be so confined in their scope and so devoid of social significance as to be almost wholly apolitical or nonpolitical. Associative behavior becomes a public and therefore political matter when the consequences which ensue extend beyond the members of the group themselves and impinge on the lives of others in some significant manner (see figure 9-1). Thus, the extent and character of conjoint action of people in groups determines whether or not such actions become a public matter and a political question. John Dewey puts the point this way:

> The characteristic of the public as a state springs from the fact that all modes of associative behavior may have extensive and enduring consequences which involve others beyond those directly engaged in them. When these consequences are in turn realized in thought and sentiment, recognition of them reacts to remake the conditions out of which they arose. Consequences have to be taken care of, looked out for. This supervision and regulation cannot be effected by the primary groupings themselves. For the essence of the consequences which call a public into being is

18. Ibid., p. 7.
19. Ibid., p. 9.
20. A different and provocative analysis of "The Public and the Private Realm," is provided by Hannah Arendt, *The Human Condition*, University of Chicago, Chicago, 1958, pp. 22-78.

A PRIVATE MATTER

Consequences circumscribed: no significant impact on others.

A PUBLIC MATTER

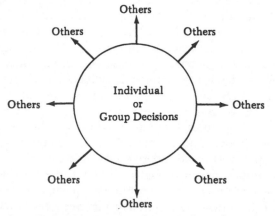

Widening circle of significant consequences: they extend to others who require review of decisions and accountability of decision-makers.

Figure 9-1 Private and Public Questions

the fact that they expand beyond those directly engaged in producing them. Consequently special agencies and measures must be formed if they are to be attended to; or else some existing group must take on new functions . . .

. . . when a family connection, a church, a trade union, a business corporation, or an educational institution conducts itself so as to affect large numbers outside of itself, those who are affected form a public which endeavors to act through suitable structures, and thus to organize itself for oversight and regulation.[21]

21. John Dewey. Reprinted from pp. 27-29 from THE PUBLIC AND ITS PROBLEMS, © 1954 by Mrs. John Dewey by permission of the Swallow Press, Inc., Chicago.

When such consequences of group behavior impinge on others, of course, differences will arise concerning the propriety of what is occurring and what ought to be done. The determination of public policy as a process of changing the working rules will necessarily generate some conflict. Some will support; some will oppose. Accordingly, political processes must not only provide for the group decision-making process itself on public questions; it must also provide for the tolerably non-destructive resolution of conflict arising therewith. Indeed, some scholars see this as a major political characteristic. John Livingston and Robert Thompson suggest that

> In the broadest sense, a situation may be said to be political when it contains individuals and groups with incompatible and conflicting interests, desires, or values. Political processes are those procedures used to resolve such conflicts. When political conflict occurs, it is impossible that all those with claims will be treated equally in the resolution of their differences. Any conceivable solution of differences will favor some individuals or groups over others. For this reason, politics is always concerned with power, with the exercise of discretion over the behavior of others, and with the ability to shape common policies and decisions binding on others in accordance with one's own desires. . . . Wherever there is conflict, there is politics.[22]

Politics may always be "concerned with power," but, as Livingston and Thompson elsewhere make clear, the study of politics is not merely an inquiry into power relations. To take the dictum, as others have done, that politics is a study of who gets what, when, and where seems to suggest that power and its use and abuse exhaust our interests. The focus on power—"the exercise of discretion over the behavior of others" —may connote to the unwary the idea that the political process necessarily consists of "shoving other people around," of the few exercising their will over the many. Such may well be involved on some occasions, but it is not all that is involved. There are occasions where people in groups exercise jointly their discretion over structural forms which organize their behavior. When the consequences widen, those significantly and newly touched must be brought into the decision-making process. Power then is held conjointly, and the restraints instituted are self-imposed; discretion is democratized.

IV. STRUCTURE AND FUNCTION

In any event, the determination and administration of public and social policy (which will include the resolution of conflict) is a processional

22. John C. Livingston and Robert G. Thompson, *The Consent of the Governed* (2nd ed.), Macmillan, New York, 1966, p. 4. See also, Sheldon S. Wolin, *Politics and Vision*, op. cit., p. 11.

concept. Again here, as with the economy, a distinction must be drawn between function and structure. The decision-making process on public matters is a functional category of activity; it is *developmental*. The institutional structures through which it is given effect vary from culture to culture and within a culture over time. Institutions are *replacemental*. All existing polities at all times are necessarily mixed polities. All characteristically are also evolving and changing; all exhibit movement and reconstitution. Neither people nor their institutional progeny are immortal, desires notwithstanding. "Life is perpetuated only by renewal."

Accordingly, it is a serious mistake to *identify* the political process as such with any *particular* political structure. The process continues; the structure changes. For example, the United States Constitution, which specifies the fundamental structure and functions of the oldest continuous national government in existence survives because the community at large continues to accept its provisions as the basic ordering principles of our political lives and because the judicial system provides sufficient elasticity and variability through interpretation to permit the adaptation of the Constitutional structure to new issues and problems.

In the taxonomy of governments, the differences in governmental structures are, of course, crucial whether drawn conceptually from Aristotle's famous roster or from other sources. Parliamentary systems, unitary systems, oligarchic systems, representative systems, plutocratic systems, tripartite systems, democratic systems, check-and-balance systems, authoritarian systems, monarchial systems, totalitarian systems, patriarchal systems, and matriarchal systems are each and all model complexes of political institutions. Obviously, they incorporate and represent widely differing ways of organizing the decision-making processes on public issues.

Structural particulars of the United States would include judicial review, initiative and referendum, secret ballots, "one-man, one-vote" rulings, advice and consent of Congress, congressional seniority rules on committee chairmanships, district gerrymandering, political parties, executive privilege, black caucuses, media-image campaigns, mass demonstrations and congressional hearings. Custom-ridden, tradition-burdened, change-resisting though they may be; rigid and unreflective though their defenders be; even so, each institution was the product of an earlier exercise of discretion. All are amenable to modification, adjustment, or abandonment. No political institutions predate discretionary men and women. All references to presocietal social contracts, to natural-order-based institutions, and to "revealed origin" of political institutions are at best sheer conjecture; at worst, they become mystic defenses of systems of oppression. Slavery, private property, and male chauvinism are not natural institutions; neither God nor Nature ordained the U.S. Constitution, the Supreme Court or states' rights.

In political processes as in economic processes, there is no denying the glory of consciousness; it is the awareness that the human being is a social animal and a discretionary agent. People choose political institutions and therewith determine how well or poorly the determination and administration of public and social policy are handled.

Accordingly, here too, we readily acknowledge that we are consciously and deliberately offering an essentially normative analysis of the political process. The *choice* of political institutions and an evaluation of their performance *necessarily* involves the application of criteria of choice, of standards of judgment, of principles of social value. These criteria themselves must also become the object of inquiry; we undertake an analysis of that subject in the final section of this work.

V.   POLITICAL INTERDEPENDENCE

Some years ago, John H. Schaar, reflecting upon the turmoil of the day, affirmed the significance of political interdependence in a particularly telling and moving way. Speaking of attitudes toward the alienated, he says,

> . . . he who veils fear and envy as patriotism, and hides contempt under the slogans of tolerance, or openly urges ferocity against the young and the radical, sins against life and the future. We are members one of another. The established, the respectable, and the frightened of this land appear on the edge of an utterly nihilistic war against the future—war against their own young, who *are* the future; and war against the black and the poor, who once were creators of wealth, but who now are seen only as expensive and dangerous nuisances. This war must be prevented, for we are members one of another.[23]

Students will no doubt differ on whether or not the "war against the future"—in particular the young—was "prevented," has been "wound down," or was provisionally ended coincident with the withdrawal of U.S. armed forces from Southeast Asia. There will be differences also regarding the current attitudes and actions of the "established, the respectable, and the frightened" toward the "radicals" and the "blacks and the poor." Few would dispute that the poor and the blacks (among others) have been bearing a disproportionate share of the destructive impact of public policy which allows simultaneous high unemployment and high inflation—"stagflation." Is this a "war against the future"? Again, views will differ.

What Schaar's observations illustrate for our purposes, however, is the fact of political interdependence. Whether the major constellations of political protagonists remain as Schaar describes them or not is a

23. John H. Schaar, "Legitimacy in the Modern State," in Philip Green and Sanford Levinson (eds.), *Power and Community: Dissenting Essays in Political Science*, Vintage, New York, 1970, p. 282.

crucial matter to those directly affected as well as to the larger community. But when Schaar reasserts that "we are members one of another," he is giving currency to an ancient dictum with major continuing significance. That dictum specifies the need for political *community*. Watergate and the aftermath of political apathy and massive distrust of politicians and political institutions threatened the continuity of political community.

What seems to be required is a quantum leap in understanding of the real issues at stake and a marked stiffening of commitment and will in the daily employment of that understanding. We hope what follows will contribute modestly to each. For indeed, "we are members one of another," and the political interdependency connoted means precisely that we *do* share a common destiny. There literally is "no place to hide." Internacine conflict, intergenerational conflict, intergroup conflict, international conflict are, with modern verbal and physical weaponry, intolerably hazardous. Only the ill-informed and the insensitive presume that "things will come out all right," that there has been no erosion of political community. We proceed on the assumption that a continuing political problem is upon us, that it is a real and basic dilemma, that we do not necessarily have multiple chances to try again if we fail. But we do profoundly believe that it is in general terms resolvable. Participatory democracy is, we think, the necessary vehicle of resolution. We suggest in what follows that it is both desirable and possible.

The political dilemma of which Professor Schaar writes—the threat of those who would wage "war against the future" and against the young, who are the future—is manifested in areas of revolutionary unrest.

The productivity revolution implies that men and women are not compelled to live at each other's expense in real-income terms. To cripple one segment by perpetuating its poverty is to cripple all other segments of a community, because they too are necessarily interdependent participants. Those, for example, who vehemently resist an adequate annual-income guarantee are, perhaps unknowingly, making "war against the future." They evidently are unaware of the income and employment effects of increased spending. They are unaware of productivity effects of increased skill levels and motivation. In other words, they are unaware of the attained levels of economic interdependence. They are, moreover, imposing, directly or indirectly, a condition of human degradation on others without being mindful of the *self*-degrading consequences which accompany such action. We are indeed "members one of another." A theory of participatory democracy must be pertinent to this concern.

The participatory revolution, perhaps most obviously, is a counterthrust to those who would make "war on the future." As this chapter, we trust, will demonstrate, the cry from the ghettos and the barrios, from the campuses and the communes, from the disenfranchised and the disenchanted, from poor nations and poor neighborhoods is to have a significant say about the conditions that govern one's own life and that of one's family and community, that is, to *participate* in the formation of decisions which organize and give pattern and meaning to experience at work and at leisure. Here, as elsewhere, it is abundantly evident that we share a common destiny.

Elitist power wielders impair the responsiveness of the political process. The Establishment, however defined and perceived, seeks to perpetuate the Establishment. Political interdependence is ignored. Participatory involvement is misdirected or denied by routine mass-media support of incumbents, by reapportionment compromises which preserve officeholders rather than maximize voter power, by nomination procedures which deter the able from becoming candidates, and by mechanisms and rules of public funding of political campaigns which advantage incumbents over other candidates.

The foregoing is not intended to imply that the participatory revolution makes no use of parties or other organizations of political activity. Parties and other organizations help to convert unorganized opinion into informed opinion through an educative process. Neither does the foregoing discussion provide a halo effect for people generally nor a eulogy for the fact of participation without reference to the purposes of such participation. It is rather addressed to elites who succeed in gaining control over parties and other political machinery to serve their own ends-in-view. The fact of interdependence is important; the enhancement of participation is important. But the necessity to judge the character of political behavior remains; we cannot evade the normative question.

A participatory revolution must wage a vigorous campaign in support of the future. The widening circle of serious consequences which spread from particular political judgments makes it absolutely necessary that wielders of power be held responsive and responsible for the judgments made. The phenomenon of "going into the streets" is not normally a first effort to invite attention to real political grievances; it is rather an often desperate, near-final effort to make very visible concern over the denial of participatory involvement on a major issue like peace, food prices, or unemployment. We are indeed interdependent with one another, and most demonstrations are an effort to communicate widely a recognition of that interdependency and to press for some sense of shared action and communal concern for the threatening consequences of political judgments. A theory of participatory democracy must come to terms with political accountability.

The racial and sexual revolutions, too, reveal vividly the effort to thwart those who threaten the future. Perhaps the issue is most poignantly seen in the differing approaches of some black leaders to the quest for noninvidious participation in the society. Some, in bitterness borne of hearing empty rhetoric, of witnessing job discrimination, and of observing unenforced equality-inducing legislation, have turned to separatist, segregative, and insulative proposals to divide blacks and whites. Others, recognizing and experiencing the bitterness, nevertheless recognize the fact of interdependence, and press for integration in schools, neighborhoods, and at work.

The separatists, in despair of integration, would make a virtue of rejection and seek community, identity, and a sense of self-worth within a smaller, racially identified, geographically distinct area, sector, or region. The integrationists, sensing that smaller communities are not likely to be viable, that intricate economic integration has made racial integration mandatory, seek imaginatively to find ways to lean on the system legally in order to end de facto and de jure segregation through voter registration, black caucuses, political-party involvement, and the like.

Indicative in a small way of the more widespread recognition of racial interdependence are the increasingly negative reactions to *tokenism*. Integration is not, obviously, realized when a black secretary is hired as a receptionist, a black dean is employed in a university, or when an ethnic studies center is added to a multiversity. Indeed, with reference to the studies center, a measure of achieved integration would be the absence of the need for one, or minimally, a center in which white students were heavily enrolled in black-history courses and the like. A theory of participatory democracy should help to make racial and sexual revolutions passé.

The ecological crisis has brought the drift of the "war against the future" into nearly everyone's awareness. The evidences are everywhere suggesting that we really are in danger of pushing pollution beyond our capacity to purify and of ravaging the known resources more rapidly than science and technology can define new resources.

Faced with a mounting demand for energy and the political, economic, and environmental problems of supply, efforts are being made to develop power from nonfossil sources (fusion, solar), but significant displacement of fossil fuels is evidently some years off. The interim expansion of nuclear-fission power plants poses a serious radiation hazard in the minds of some competent observers, industry assurances of safety notwithstanding.

Faced with the probable disappearance of coast redwoods (outside parks) within one generation, people have accelerated efforts to increase the acreage spared from the clear-cutting chain saws. Faced with auto-exhaust-generated massive air pollution, engineering urgencies in Detroit have shifted somewhat from annual stylistic body changes to smog-free combustion in engines. Faced with the recognition that ecological recovery of natural life forms on Alaska's North Slope is very much slower than in more southerly areas, oil companies exploring and drilling on the North Slope have begun actions to minimize disturbance.

Faced with the possible destruction of life forms in the oceans of the world also within one generation, some companies have begun efforts to reduce the oil spillage, the dumping of chemicals into the sea, and to protect some endangered marine life, including whales. But in the absence of enforceable national and international controls, the hazards, the pollution, the spoilage, and the contamination are likely to continue.

Despite some gains in awareness, we have yet fully to recognize that biological life, too, is an interdependent affair. We perforce must share a common environment. Life forms and life chains must be sustained; human life is an integral part of the whole. [24] Where making "war on the future" means making war on the environment, humankind evidently exhibits a death wish. No longer can we speak of "conquering nature"; the heyday of that myopia is long since gone.

A theory of participatory democracy will have relevance for people who recognize the need for changing the attitudes of pre-emption and exploitation and for altering or abandoning practices of environmental rape and short-run maximization of pecuniary gains. It is these people who, in becoming political activists, are effectively engaged in environmental restoration.

In sum, all of these areas of revolutionary unrest come into focus wholly or partially as manifestations of a continuing political problem. Jointly and separately they represent that which threatens "the established, the respectable, and the frightened of this land"—those who would wage "an utterly nihilistic war against the future."

That political dilemma, we repeat, can in large measure be resolved, we think, using a theory of participatory democracy as a conceptual vehicle of resolution. We must expand our understanding of the character and potential of this analytical vehicle.

24. In an article explaining the successful battle to block the continued construction of a massive jetport just north of the Everglades in Florida, Philip Wylie vigorously articulates the interdependency principle: "Man's great illusion continues. Nature cannot be conquered or controlled by man, as men believe, because man is not in charge of it and never will be. Who is in charge of wind and rain, of green plants and photosynthesis, or birds, insects, the seven seas? Nobody. Nature is in charge, exclusively and forever. The Everglades offer a textbook illustration of what mankind has not yet begun to face that is true:

"Nobody owns anything, and all anyone has is the use of his presumed possessions.

"That is the ecological law. It is true for Communists as for capitalists, for disadvantaged peoples as for the affluent and industrial societies. And it is absolute.

"We do not own the Everglades or any part of that strange land, even if we have a deed to it. We are allowed its use. All we do own is what our individual skins contain. To save them we must save whatever chains of life are essential to our own . . .

"If all the ecologists could pool all they know and add all the data from every science, they would be unable to say what life forms and life systems are essential for man's survival. We know too little about the intricate, living understructure supporting our species to risk losing any wild living form, weed or pest or predator, lest one break in the planetary, life-sustaining system be fatal." (Philip Wylie, "Against All Odds, the Birds Have Won," *The New York Times*, Section XX, February 1, 1970, p. 11. © 1970, The New York Times Company. Reprinted by permission.)

Advocates of a non-ism, nondoctrinaire, noninvidious democratic alternative, we said above, are actually offering the most relevant, the most genuinely revolutionary options and alternatives available. We have arrived at a point where such a contention needs explication. Reflect again on the irony of "democracy" being paraded as a symbol and rendered invisible in substance, of being revered in theory but denied in practice. Virtually every adult reading these lines has had the experience in a trade union, church, club, or office of being told that democratic participation is fine in principle but is inappropriate here for this or that reason. ("Pay your dues and shut up, if you want to keep your job." "Oh, we never question the minister's judgment." "Membership is limited to Caucasian males; sorry about that." "I'm paid to manage this place; you're paid to do what I tell you!") Full discretionary participation is denied because some are, it is said, too old, too irresponsible, too inexperienced, too low in rank, too poor, too black, too dumb, too foreign, too feminine, or whatever. And such denial of d'scretionary involvement means a substantial discrediting of person, a destruction of dignity, for those subjected to it.

The democratic idea is revolutionary; it is a live and fearsome threat to all repositories of political power and authority which ground their legitimacy in invidiously used distinctions. The dignity conferred by democratic participation affirms the worth of people; it implies that their lives too can make a difference. The present levels of revolutionary unrest will not, in our judgment, abate or disappear until participatory democracy moves from an idea of promise to a more commonplace description of practice. If that is to occur, our understanding of a theory of participatory democracy as an alternative to the political postures and admonitions of the ism-ideologies must be expanded appreciably. To that task we now turn.

Chapter 10

PARTICIPATORY DEMOCRACY

Every government degenerates when trusted to the rulers of the people alone.
The people themselves therefore are its only depositories. . . . The influence
over government must be shared among all the people.

THOMAS JEFFERSON*

. . . democracy is belief in the ability of human experience to generate the aims
and methods by which further experience will grow in ordered richness. . . .
Since the process of experience is capable of being educative, faith in democracy
is all one with faith in experience and education.

JOHN DEWEY**

---

*Thomas Jefferson, *Notes on Virginia*. Quoted by Harry K. Girvetz, *Democracy and Elitism*, Charles Scribner's Sons, New York, 1967, p. 110.

**John Dewey, "Creative Democracy—The Task Before Us," in Carl Cohen (ed.), *Communism, Fascism and Democracy: The Theoretical Foundations*, Random House, New York, 1962, pp. 688-89.

The democratic idea, we have observed, is indeed revolutionary. We have suggested that the idea is pertinent to our age and to our problems. But perhaps nowhere in the analysis of political economy is there greater confusion than over the meaning and possibility of democracy. We are told on many sides that participatory democracy is impossible, that it is undesirable, that it is utopian, that it is idealistic, and that it is a naive pursuit. In this and the following chapters, we seek to clarify the meaning of participatory democracy, affirm and demonstrate its relevance, explain its operation, and note the obligations it imposes on those who are participants. We suspect that democracy is an idea whose time, at last, has come.

But the case must be made; affirmation will not suffice. Again, we must, so to speak, back off and find an inclusive and basic vantage point and attempt to bring political inquiry to bear on political reality.

I.   INDIVIDUALS AND THE STATE

We identified above an inclusive and continuing political function everywhere common to human culture—the determination and administration of social and public policy. Social life compels conjoint public-policy formation, and all human life is social.

The diversity of political forms and structures among constituted groups is at least as broad and change-exhibiting as that of any other dimension of organized life—family or economy. All polities are mixed polities. All represent embodied authority. All profess legitimacy. All are vehicles through which the one, the few, or the many prescribe and proscribe most of the basic institutional arrangements which organize the life process. Included are systems of property control and use, codes delimiting criminal behavior and punishment, specification of distributive shares of income, acceptable practices in rearing the young, mechanisms for resolving or minimizing conflict, specification of the terms of exchange, and the like.

Government as a term and a category, then, refers to the aggregate of institutional structures which organizes the process of determining and administering public and social policy. Government is structure through which structures (including political institutions themselves) are determined. Governments consist of an array of arrangements through which publics are identified and/or created, through which conjoint public decisions are made, and with which determined policy alters the patterned fabric of our ordinary lives. Participating individuals determine the array of arrangements.

So perceived, there is no need for deference to concepts of a social-contract state (John Locke), a general-will state (N. Lenin) or an organic state (G. Gentile). The alleged discreteness and autonomy of the state may be abandoned; the distinction between state and government may be abandoned; the tension-breeding dichotomies of government vs. the individual and of the public vs. the private may be abandoned.

A theory of participatory democracy requires the dropping of the concept of the state and a revision of the concept of government. Governments, as institutional structure, perform functions which provide for the creation and re-creation of a political *community*. The core significance of governments is not so much their power to direct and constrain—their powers of mandamus and injunction—although that is real and significant; rather, it is their instrumental and facilitative capacity to provide the community with a common vehicle for public-policy formation and implementation. No other social institutions occupy this ground so prominently; none has this as its *raison d'etre*. The political function is in fact inclusive and continuing; it is inclusive of those aspects of the economic process which involve decision making directed to matters of public policies and their implementation.

The significance of the departure which participatory democracy makes from yesterday's isms is evident in the markedly different conception it incorporates of the relation between an individual and the state (and government) (see figure 10-1).

In capitalism, there is a denigration of the state and a eulogization of the hedonistic individual (that "homogeneous globule of desire"). Everywhere it is the individual (or corporate "person") vs. the state, private vs. the public.

	DENIGRATED	EXTOLLED
CAPITALISM	state and government	hedonistic individual
MARXISM		
on capitalism	capitalist state serving bourgeoisie	proletarian class
on socialism	nonconforming individual	dictatorship of proletariat
on communism	state and government	classless society
FASCISM	discretionary individual	organic state and leader
DEMOCRACY	organic state but not government	discretionary individual

Figure 10-1   Individuals and the State

In Marx's analysis of capitalism and communism, there is denigration of the state and eulogization of an economic class (the proletariat), and ultimately of a nonalienated "new man." In Marx's socialism, there is denigration of the nonconforming individual and eulogization of the socialist state (the dictatorship of the proletariat).

In fascism, there is denigration of the individual and manic aggrandizement of the organic state. The state is all.

In participatory democracy, there is no denigration of the individual; neither is there eulogization of the state in any form. There is denigration of the separate-entity, organic state, but not of government. The government is to be an instrument; the state is not to be the master. Extolled is the discretionary individual as a participant in creating community.

II. POLITICAL FUNCTIONS

With the foregoing in mind, it is now possible to delineate some of the more particular functions which a government will undertake where a theory of participatory democracy supplies the rationale and legitimacy. Put differently, the following is a roster of specific and continuing political functions which are instrumental to public choice making characterized as participatory democracy:

(a) continuing provision for noninvidious political participation

(b) creation and renewal of mechanisms to assure genuine political choice

(c) continuation and extension of participatory procedural guarantees (freedom of belief, speech, press, assembly, and petition)

(d) creation and retention of a responsive and responsible representative body to deliberate upon and determine public policy

(e) creation and retention of a responsive and responsible executive agency to implement and administer public policy

(f) provision of full and free flow of information to community on performance of governmental persons and agencies at all levels

(g) administration of prompt, even-handed, nonpunitive, noncapricious justice to law violators

(h) maintenance of civil order without violation of civil rights and civil liberties

(i) resolution or adjudication of political conflict

In addition, there are some distinctively economic functions performed by government which merit inclusion here. (There is a necessary overlap with some of the productive activities delineated for an evolving, functional economy above.)[1] They include the following:

(a) stabilization of the aggregate economy with regard to income, employment, and prices

1. See in this connection, Richard A. Musgrave and Peggy B. Musgrave, *Public Finance in Theory and Practice*, McGraw-Hill Book Co., Inc., 1973, pp. 3-22.

(b)   distribution and redistribution of money income via taxes and transfers

(c)   provision of public goods and services

(d)   resource creation, utilization, and conservation

(e)   regulation and control of private centers of economic power

Examples of structures through which many of these economic activities are provided in the American political economy have been provided in previous chapters. Illustrations of structures which organize the more distinctively political functions are considered in due course below.

What is important to recognize here is that these statements of functions *constitute an agenda for government* under the theoretical aegis of participatory democracy. Recall J. M. Keynes' petition to his fellow political economists:

> Perhaps the chief task of Economists at this hour is to distinguish afresh the *Agenda* of Government from the Non-Agenda; and the companion task of Politics is to devise forms of Government within a Democracy which shall be capable of accomplishing the Agenda.[2]

Now it is of the very essence of participatory democracy that the "Agenda of Government" be "distinguished afresh" frequently. That is, the functional tasks (and therefore the structural institutions which implement functional tasks) must be subjected routinely and profoundly to critical review and scrutiny. The members of the community must repeatedly ask of each other, "Is this activity or task one that ought to be performed by government?" If so, what structural changes, revision of prescriptive arrangements, are required for that activity or task effectively to be performed? As successive national administrations have come openly or reluctantly to understand, the agenda is not *given*; it is not static, rigid, or frozen—ideological predelictions notwithstanding. The government is to be used; agendas must be newly drawn. The character of that agenda is the principal area of contention in political debate.

Perhaps the quickest access to the details of a major agenda, for example, is the annual federal budget for the national government. Not only does minimal scrutiny reveal the funded categories of activity; in addition the magnitudes of funds requested (more accurately, appropriated) under each head glibly, if crudely, indicate the degree of

2. John Maynard Keynes, *The End of Laissez Faire*, Hogarth Press, London, 1926, pp. 40-41. Perhaps, in fairness, we should add the passage which appears below the one quoted: "The most important *Agenda* of the State relate not to those activities which private individuals are already fulfilling, but to those functions which fall outside the sphere of the individual, to those decisions which are made by *no one* if the State does not make them. The important thing for Government is not to do things which individuals are doing already, and to do them a little better or worse; but to do those things which at present are not done at all." (Ibid., pp. 46-47.)

significance attached to each head by those making policy in the public's name. Journalists, especially, have a field day when the budget is released by comparing amounts spent for cancer research, for example, to that spent for space shuttles or the amount spent in defense of civil liberties compared to that spent in an effort to maintain civil order.

A theory of participatory democracy differs from each and all of yesterday's isms in the respect that the isms tend to freeze the public agenda and the distinction between the public and the private sector. A democratic polity keeps the agenda perpetually thawed. Moreover, a democratic community not only keeps its options comparatively open, but also recognizes that it has itself the capacity and the will to *create* options, to "distinguish afresh" its agenda, to find new ways of responding to its recognition of communal interdependence.

Men and women living in community organize the process of reaching communal judgments in institutions (government). Governments exercise hegemony in a context in which common judgments constitute *self-imposed* restraints. Governments become instruments for the creation and implementation of conjoint decisions made by publics as they are formed, become aware of their identity, formulate options, choose among alternatives, and implement their judgments. *The general constraint is that those who receive the incidence of policy must have and retain discretion over that policy.* This manifestly is an interactive process consisting at all stages of deliberation and social action. Common, noninvidious participation must be accessible to all. Each must have his or her opportunity to know what occurs, to voice his or her views, to seek to persuade others, to join with others in, for example, balloting and/or petitioning, to stand for leadership roles, and otherwise to exercise his or her capacities as a participating agent-actor, as a participant-observer, as a democrat.

In communities which carry out the political function via participatory democracy, then, actor-agent men and women create and re-create the government and its agendas as their cognitive and reflective scrutiny of existential fact and their concern for the retention of procedural guarantees for continuing control over their own lives suggest. Such involvement and participation provides discretionary dignity.

III. LOCUS OF DISCRETION

Democracy, as an idea, we have noted, has won the world. Leaders in all nonfascist systems seem to decorate their pronouncements with the plumage of democratic verbal finery. They recognize that democracy is a "plus" word, that people associate "goodness," "acceptability," and "legitimacy" with the term. As with "freedom" and "competition," it connotes a desired condition. The reason seems clear. World-wide, people see in democracy, evidently, the possibility of self-determination of policy and an opportunity to reduce the levels of anguish and desperation resulting from the repression, oppression, and aggression pursued by self-serving elites or fragments of the community bent on retaining or extending their status and power.

Whether or not this anguish and desperation will in fact be reduced depends in part on whether or not the idea of democracy can be rescued from its ism-ideological, public-relations, and manipulative uses and restored to its role as a revolutionary political concept. Here we make such an attempt.

The essential idea of democracy is not difficult to identify. The core meaning is that the ruled are also the rulers; that those who receive the incidence of decisions shall *themselves* have discretion over such decisions. Democracy means the popular determination of public and social policy; the locus of discretion resides permanently—in the long run and in the short run—with the whole community. In a phrase given currency by Lincoln, and memorized by nearly every American schoolchild, it is government *of, by, and for* the people. In language now familiar here, democracy means that no one shall be denied on invidious grounds the right and opportunity to participate in the creation and re-creation of his or her community. A democratic order is a community of largely "ungraded men," in which, for example, rank, wealth, sex, race, ethnicity, origin, or class may not be used to confer rule-making discretion upon some fragment of the community.

Democracy incorporates the idea that "we are members one of another." It includes recognition of interdependence and community. It affirms that the test of legitimacy in rule making is the consent of the governed (see figure 10-2).

Democratic Systems	*Undemocratic Systems*
Discretion Resides with Whole Community	Discretion Resides with Fragment of Community

IMPLICATIONS:

• Governance by consent of governed	• Governance without consent of governed
• Rulers and ruled are same people	• Rulers and ruled are different people
• Government of, by, and for people	• Government of (?), for (?), but not by people
• Popular determination of policy	• Elitist determination of policy
• Restraints are self-imposed	• Restraints imposed from top down
• Noninvidious participation	• Invidious denial of participation
• Egalitarian community	• Hierarchical community
• Leaders accountable	• Leaders not accountable
• Power held is insecure	• Power is coercively secured and held
• Educability of people assumed	• Elites said to possess superior wisdom

Figure 10-2   Locus of Discretion

John Dewey, the pre-eminent American philosopher of democracy, provides succinct language to distinguish the democratic form from others:

> The keynote of democracy as a way of life may be expressed . . . as the necessity for the participation of every mature human being in formation of the values that regulate the living of men together.[3]

And further:

> Democratic political forms . . . rest back upon the idea that no man or limited set of men is wise enough or good enough to rule others without their consent; the positive meaning of this statement is that all those who are affected by social institutions must have a share in producing and managing them. The two facts that each one is influenced in what he does and enjoys and in what he becomes by the institutions under which he lives, and that therefore he shall have, in a democracy, a voice in shaping them, are the passive and active sides of the same fact.[4]

If our rescue of the idea of democracy is to be completed, however, the term and the concept must normally be stripped of its modifiers and qualifiers and be left unadorned, undraped, and resplendent in its simplicity, beauty, and elegance—as in sculpture with the Greek's Three Graces and Michelangelo's David. Clearly, any modifier or qualifier which subverts the historic core meaning must be stripped away. Consider briefly some examples:

Pluralistic democracy means brokerage and compromise of differences among competing, mainly economic, interest groups. Discretion resides with the more powerful of these groups, not with the community generally.

Conservative democracy means the creation of constitutional barriers and baffles to the exercise of popular will. Popular judgments must be screened to assure that they represent no serious threat to the propertied elite. Discretion resides with those who control the constitutional forms, not with the community generally.

Plebiscitary democracy has as its main purpose the provision of a voting vehicle through which a people may "demonstrate and proclaim" its support for an elite who control the political economy. The power of the authority figure is not in question; he is in no sense vulnerable to the outcome of the voting. Discretion resides with the authoritarian elite and especially its leader, not with the community generally.

Democratic centralism is Lenin's caption for the dictatorship of the proletariat. The communist party elite is the self-styled vanguard of the proletariat offering a government *of* and *for* the proletariat, but not *by*

---

3. John Dewey, "The Democratic Form," in Joseph Ratner (ed.), *Intelligence in the Modern World: John Dewey's Philosophy*, Modern Library, New York, 1939, p. 400.
4. Ibid., p. 401.

the proletariat or the whole people. Discretion resides with the party elite, not with the community generally.

Peoples' democracies (or "people's democratic dictatorship"—Mao Tse Tung) are variants of Marxist elitism. Presuming to embody the will of the people as defined by the party and its elitist leadership, peoples' democracies deny choice over basic structure and social policy to the larger community. Discretion resides with the party cadre, not with the community generally.

Because, perhaps, of this tendency of elitist groups to mask their power wielding in democratic rhetoric, we and others have thought it necessary to make secure the core meaning of democracy by adding the modifier, *participatory*—hence, "participatory democracy." Strictly speaking this modifier is not needed except as a counter to distinguish the central idea from elitist use and abuse. To protect the term, so to speak, from this subversive usage, we here will continue to use the modifier *participatory* in spite of its recognized redundancy.

Although it may be surprising to some, this conception of democracy as a political process providing for noninvidious, uncoerced discretion by a people over its own institutions and life styles was quite adequately captured in *The Port Huron Statement* of the Students for a Democratic Society in the early 1960s. Ignore for the present at least the more recent public contentiousness over the SDS and explore the content of their initial position. Evidently Tom Hayden was the principal author:

> We would replace power rooted in possession, privilege, or circumstance by power and uniqueness rooted in love, reflectiveness, reason, and creativity. As a *social system* we seek the establishment of a democracy of individual participation, governed by two central aims: that the individual share in those social decisions determining the quality and direction of his life; that society be organized to encourage independence in men [we assume they mean to include women] and provide the media for their common participation.
>
> In a participatory democracy, the political life would be based in several root principles:
>
> that decision-making of basic social consequence be carried on by public groupings;
>
> that politics be seen positively, as the art of collectively creating an acceptable pattern of social relations;
>
> that politics has the function of bringing people out of isolation and into community, thus being a necessary, though not sufficient, means of finding meaning in personal life;
>
> that the political order should serve to clarify problems in a way instrumental to their solution; it should provide outlets for the expression of personal grievance and aspiration; opposing views should be organized so as to illuminate choices and facilitate the attainment of goals; channels

should be commonly available to relate men to knowledge and to power so that private problems—from bad recreation facilities to personal alienation —are formulated as general issues.[5]

Thus we see the elements of popular control, of overt involvement in decision making, of conjoint participation in the creation of one's own community, and of the relevance of meaningful involvement for problem solving affirmed. Such affirmation can have significance only where political institutions provide for nonelitist, noninvidious participation.

Participatory democracy encompasses a fundamentally different view of people and of the kind of leadership which is pertinent to their lives and well-being. The justification for locating discretion with the whole people rests on the demonstrable contention that people are educable, are capable of effective participation, and are able to judge the adequacy of adjustments made in response to real problems. Their sense of what is just reflects their own experience with justice.

Some remarks of John Dewey will again be instructive. He writes further about the democratic form:

The individuals of the submerged mass may not be very wise. But there is one thing they are wiser about than anybody else can be, and that is where the shoe pinches, the troubles they suffer from.

The foundation of democracy is faith in the capacities of human nature; faith in human intelligence and in the power of pooled and cooperative experience. It is not belief that these things are complete but that if given a show they will grow and be able to generate progressively the knowledge and wisdom needed to guide collective action. Every autocratic and authoritarian scheme of social action rests on a belief that the needed intelligence is confined to a superior few, who because of inherent natural gifts are endowed with the ability and the right to control the conduct of others; laying down principles and rules and directing the ways in which they are carried out . . .[6]

A particular perception of equality underlies belief in the democratic form. Continues Dewey,

Belief in equality is an element of the democratic credo. It is not, however, belief in equality of natural endowments. Those who proclaimed the idea of equality did not suppose they were enunciating a psychological

---

5. Students for a Democratic Society, *The Port Huron Statement*, SDS, Chicago, Illinois, 1966, pp. 7-8.
6. Dewey, "The Democratic Form," in Ratner (ed.), *Intelligence in the Modern World*, op. cit., p. 402.

doctrine, but a legal and political one. All individuals are entitled to equality of treatment by law and in its administration. Each one is affected equally in quality if not in quantity by the institutions under which he lives and has an equal right to express his judgment, although the weight of his judgment may not be equal in amount when it enters into the pooled result to that of others . . .[7]

And further,

While what we call intelligence may be distributed in unequal amounts, it is the democratic faith that it is sufficiently general so that each individual has something to contribute, and the value of each contribution can be assessed only as it enters into the final pooled intelligence constituted by the contributions of all. Every authoritarian scheme, on the contrary, assumes that its value may be assessed by some *prior* principle, if not of family and birth or race and color or possession of material wealth, then by the position and rank a person occupies in the existing social scheme. The democratic faith in equality is the faith that each individual shall have the chance and opportunity to contribute whatever he is capable of contributing and that the value of his contribution be decided by its place and function in the organized total of similar contributions, not on the basis of prior status of any kind whatever.[8]

We suggest that Dewey's affirmation of a democratic faith was and is warranted. Consider whether or not it is the case that in recent years events have overtaken elites and their alleged superior wisdom and insight.

For purposes here of stimulating inquiry, allow the assertion that elitist judgments have repeatedly proven to be seriously flawed or mistaken. (Cautious readers perhaps should treat this assertion, and others to follow, as questions to be explored rather than as settled conclusions to be accepted.) Whether or not majoritarian judgments would have been less flawed or mistaken is of course conjectural. But majoritarian judgments, when they are mistaken, do come "home to roost" promptly on those who made the judgment. The interest of the majority in a timely reconsideration of the problem and continued experimentation with more promising solutions is substantial. Not so with elitist policy formation. The propensity of elites caught in mistaken judgments seems to be to hide or distort the truth, to deny responsibility, to find scapegoats, and/or to exercise control over the media to manipulate verbal and visual symbols to convert "defeats" into "victories."

7. Ibid., p. 403.
8. Ibid., pp. 403-04.

Examples of elitist fallacies will occur to many readers. In the following, we suggest examples of flawed or mistaken judgments in areas of revolutionary unrest. [9] (Again, the wary reader may wish to consider these as hypotheses to be tested or as propositions to be demonstrated. Space limitations do not permit elaboration here.)

In the realm of the productivity revolution, elitist influence upon and control over governmental institutions has for decades forestalled any really substantive overhaul of the tax system, which provides differential tax advantages for the business sector and abundant tax loopholes for the rich. [10] In consequence, the tax system may well be inadequate to support the needs of the public sector—the sector most responsible for creating community. Effective redistribution of income and the elimination of poverty probably must await the end of elitist tax favors. That the larger community is avidly interested in such reforms is illustrated nearly every day in the press and in political campaigns.

Of even greater significance is the gross mismanagement (or non-management) of the national economy in the late 1960s and 1970s. The inability of congressional leaders and President Johnson to effect proper antiinflation policy as the Vietnamese war was accelerated, the inability of President Nixon and his conservative advisors to understand and control inflation except through an administered recession, and the inability of President Ford and his ideologist advisors to prevent "double-digit" inflation concurrently with near "double-digit" unemployment (the worst since the Great Depression) must stand as flawed performances of major proportions, producing a decade and more of economic deprivation and disillusion for those least able to bear them. The early years of President Carter's term of office appeared to reveal no substantial breakthrough in understanding of, or control over, tendencies to "stagflation."

In the realm of the participatory revolution, the elitist and autocratic determination of representation to and control of the 1968 Democratic convention in Chicago led to a near breakdown in the party nominee-selection process. The political support garnered by Eugene McCarthy in 1968 and by George McGovern in 1972 was secured in part by developing substantial interest among the politically alienated outside the regular machinery of the party. The "New Politics" was not a product of traditional party control. Reforms in delegate selection initiated after 1968 were reflected in the conduct of the 1972 convention. Although there has been some abandonment of delegate-quota systems since 1972, clearly the party must remain noninvidiously acces-

9. For additional examples of faultable leadership, see Morton Mintz and Jerry S. Cohen, *Power, Inc.*, Viking Press, New York, 1976.

10. See Philip M. Stern, *The Great Treasury Raid*, New American Library, New York, 1965, and P. M. Stern, *The Rape of the Taxpayer*, Random House, New York, 1973.

sible if it is to survive. Comparable concern seems not to be present among Republican Party leaders.

In the realm of the racial revolution, examine the near century-long elitist paternalism of the Bureau of Indian Affairs in its relations with the remnants of the so-called Indian tribes in the United States. Whatever may have been the bureau's conception of "doing what is good for the Indians," it was to be done *to* and *for* Indians; not generally included was relinquishing discretion *to* the Indians to do for themselves. And in particular, the BIA was not to become a political lever at the disposal of native Americans to protect themselves from further economic exploitation, political exclusion, or cultural disintegration by the more avaricious segments of the Anglo community. [11]

In the realm of the ecology crisis, no detail is needed here to document the massive reluctance of corporate elites to initiate controls and corrections for environmental destruction and pollution. The auto industry's opposition to smog-reducing innovations, the oil industry's resistance to curtailments in off-shore drilling, the lumber industry's defense of clear-cutting of timbered slopes, the chemical industry's reluctance to curtail production of various herbicides and insecticides, and the land developers' massive incursion into farmlands, watershed, and wilderness areas are commonplace examples. In California in 1972, concerned environmentalists were compelled to go the initiative and referendum route to put a strong environmental protection and anti-pollution policy and program before the community generally. A scare campaign, evidently heavily funded by oil companies and others, contributed to its defeat. More recently, Congress, public agencies, and the states appear to have been unduly deferential to the oil industry and private transit industries in the latters' opposition to the development of modern innovative public transit systems. Such public systems, of course, would help reduce the public's dependence on pollution-prone private automobiles. [12] In few areas has fragmentary elitist judgment been so tardy, provincial, profit-oriented, self-serving, and fallible as in the control and elimination of environmental destruction.

As we have repeatedly contended, elites have as their primary concern the perpetuation of their identity and their discretion as elites. Their interest in and assistance with conflict resolution and problem solving in the larger community are secondary and peripheral. Majoritarian judgments in the community at large, though obviously fallible, will, where discretion remains located with the community generally, look to the recasting of institutional structure which has become problematic,

11. See Edgar Cahn (ed.), *Our Brother's Keeper: The Indian in White America*, World Publishing Co., New York, 1969.

12. For comments on newly emerging public transit systems see Gary E. Park, "Calgary/Edmonton," *Mass Transit*, Vol. 5, No. 4, April, 1978, pp. 10-13 ff.

disfunctional, obsolete, elite-preserving, or a threat to the continuity and well-being of the community. The pressures to end poverty, elitism, racism and sexism, and pollution seem mainly to come from anguished segments of the larger community, not from the established public and private power centers. [13]

Implicit here again, of course, is a theory of leadership which departs fundamentally from those associated with the ism-ideologies, in which leaders are identified as wielders of power over other people's lives. The hierarchical structure of an army or bureaucracy which orders the placement of persons with regard to their control over others tends to *identify* leadership with power held and used. Locating power in the hands of the people generally, then, would seem to imply to elitists an absence of leadership or at best the presence of mediocre leaders (i.e., nonelite) in a democratic order. Agonies over rule by the incompetent, the ill-informed, the unwise are then voiced (especially by elitists).

Locating discretion in the community at large, however, does not mean an end to leadership; it means a transformation of the meaning of leadership. Genuine democracies, we suggest, can and do produce fine and able leaders whose influence is not a function of their power to coerce, but of their power to persuade and convince through reasoned verbal and written intercourse. A democratic order makes use of experts, specialists, creative and imaginative policy framers, technicians, and effective communicators, not by giving them power without accountability, but by providing support for the continuing development of their expertise and for wide, unfettered communication of their analyses, assessments, recommendations, and critiques to the larger community. The leaders' roles are mainly instructive, educative, and communicative, not coercive.

Leaders emerge to help articulate the problems and ills of society and to serve as rallying points around which publics can be organized and around which those seeking policy solutions for real problems can coalesce for effective social and political action. Those elected to office are given a contingency grant of representative leadership. Their judgments on behalf of the community are to be appraised as to adequacy and propriety *by* the community. The extension of rule-making authority is conditional and temporary. Accountability is the name of the game. Leaders must remain responsive and responsible to the larger community.

13. This does not deny, of course, that leadership for economic, political, and social reform *sometimes* comes from individuals and groups who are not themselves seriously affected by the problem. For example, in the 1960s, middle- and upper-class youth were heavily involved in voter registration drives among blacks in the south, joining resident black leadership, especially in the churches. On the other hand, leadership for the organization of farm workers, evidently, came largely from the ranks of farm workers themselves.

Thus in a democratic order, the primary functions of leaders is to help frame public-policy options, to explore and communicate probable consequences, and, where authorized, to enact and implement structural change under the continuing aegis of popular control. The demands upon the intellectual and creative capacities of such democratic leaders are of course enormous. Such leaders have no grounds on which to defend their leadership roles and their being singled out to exercise such roles except their demonstrable capacities for assisting the community in *its* task of *self-rule*. Leaders can legitimately lay claim to significance and accompanying status on *no* other grounds. Family lineage, wealth, age, sex, race, national origin, and class identification as such are all irrelevant.

Here, as must now be clear, is where most ism-ideologists founder. Capitalist leadership is identified with the strategic placement and decision-making role of business entrepreneurs. Marxist leadership is identified with the strategic placement and role of the Communist Party leaders acting for the proletariat. Fascist leadership is identified with the strategic placement and role of the leader—*der fuhrer*—and his fawning party functionaries. As Dewey says, all ism-ideologies utilize some a priori index of identification—an index not subject to rejection or substitution by those who are the recipients of policy judgments of elitist leaders.

The locus of discretion must, then, under a democratic order remain with the community at large. Though the community's judgment of leaders and policies is of course fallible, the community stands in the most advantageous place to define and to recognize the fact of fallibility and, possessing discretion, is in a position to correct such fallacies. Locating basic discretion *anywhere else* produces no such impulse or opportunity for policy correction and problem solving.

A "nihilistic war against the future" is not likely to be waged by a *community* against *its own* future. Only where discretion resides not with a fragment, but with the whole community is it politically possible to recognize and respond to the affirmation that "we are members one of another."

Chapter 11

STRUCTURES OF DISCRETION

No idea which we have is more sane, more matter-of-fact, more immediately sensible, than that of self-government. Whether it be in the field of individual or of social activity, men are not recognizable as men unless, in any given situation, they are using their minds to give direction to their behavior.

ALEXANDER MEIKLEJOHN*

We, the People, acting together, either directly or through our representatives, make and administer law. We, the People, acting in groups or separately, are subject to the law. If we could make that double agreement effective, we would have accomplished the American Revolution.

ALEXANDER MEIKLEJOHN**

---

*Alexander Meiklejohn, *Political Freedom*, Harper & Row, New York, 1948, p. 13.
**Ibid., p. 15.

L ocating discretion with the community at large is a necessary but not sufficient condition in the quest for participatory democracy. If a community is to implement the inclusive and continuing function of determining and administering public policy, that function must be organized institutionally; it must be given effect through prescriptions and proscriptions which establish and sustain genuine choices and therewith provide discretionary dignity for all participants.

As with the economy, so also with the polity. The structural fabric which organizes the political process must be the object of continuing scrutiny, inquiry, and adjustment. The mix of instruments through which to effect popular choice making must be modified as is required to extend and inform the choices of actor-agent men and women, whose aggregate judgments determine the structural fabric of society and the values served therewith.

It will now be evident that because a deference to any ism-ideology tends to freeze structure and to establish, to rationalize, and "validate" fragmentary rule by an elite, and because a deference to participatory democracy tends to thaw structure and to erode invidious support for fragmentary rule, democracy and isms are fundamentally different *kinds* of perspectives. There is, as the philosophers say, a missing middle between them. There is virtually no common content. Democracy is not similar to *any* ism. It is no synonym for capitalism; capitalist democracy, socialist democracy, or communist democracy are each contradictory captions. The adjectives distort the meaning of the noun they are intended to modify. Ideologists habitually use the rhetoric of democracy because they are well aware that the idea of democracy has become the test of legitimacy before the world. They seek to gain respectability and credibility by riding into consciousness and conviction on the coattails of the democratic perspective. But that use of language is deceptive. The litmus test for ideologists is a simple one: Ask where, at bottom, will discretion over policy lie. If it is anywhere but with the whole community, democratic pretentions are transparent and false.

Democracy affirms a process of decision making in which all who are significantly touched by policy have the opportunity and needed information to participate, directly and indirectly, in the deliberations which produce or change that policy. Ism-ideologists accept some institutional structure as articles of faith (capitalism and the market mechanism, Marxism and public ownership, fascism and the *fuhrer* rule) which are not only beyond inquiry; they are beyond the reach of the community acting conjointly to transform its own political economy. The admonition, then, is this: take all pronouncements of ism-ideologists affirming their democratic sympathies with much skepticism.

If we are to live as "members one of another" in a community characterized by popular control of policy, the political process, we said, must nonetheless be organized. In the previous chapter we delineated some subsidiary political functions, the structural implementation of which is essential to achieving de facto participatory democracy. As we did with the economy, let us now turn to the American experience for some examples of political structures which serve or thwart the achievement of participatory democracy.

In so doing, we will not comprehensively review the Constitution with its specification of a check-and-balance triadic structure for a republican government and the respective functions set off for each of the three branches and for the federal government at large. We take it as generally agreed that the Constitution itself, apart from the first ten amendments, from the point of view of democratic theory, is basically a conservative document. As *The Federalist Papers* make clear, anything approaching direct or participatory democracy was much to be feared by many of the Founding Fathers. "Democracy—government by the people, or directly responsible to them—was not the object which the framers of the American Constitution had in view, but the very thing which they wished to avoid."[1] Nearly universal suffrage was established not in the Constitution, but by amendments to it. The differing political philosophies of the Declaration of Independence and the Constitution have long been an area of scholarly interest and debate.

For present purposes of illustrating political institutions which contribute to or retard the appearance of participatory democracy, we draw mainly on more recent examples of working rules which organize the political process. Again, the intent here is both illustrative and normative.

I. POLITICAL PARTICIPATION

The central concern here is with the matter of legally enforceable political franchise. The familiar quest for universal suffrage is coincident with the push for participatory democracy.. Here the American de jure record, although agonizingly slow in developing, is nonetheless good. Principally through the device of amendments to the Constitution, the vote has been extended successively to formerly disenfranchised groups.

The Fourteenth Amendment declares as citizens all persons born or naturalized in the United States and affirms the political rights of male citizens over twenty-one years of age.

The Fifteenth Amendment guarantees that neither national nor state government shall deny or abridge the right to vote "on account of race, color, or previous condition of servitude."

The Seventeenth Amendment provides for the popular election of senators.

1. J. Allen Smith. Quoted by Earl Latham (ed.), *The Declaration of Independence and the Constitution*, D. C. Heath, Boston, 1949, p. 31.

The Nineteenth Amendment precludes the federal or state governments from denying or abridging the right to vote "on account of sex."

The Twenty-fourth Amendment says that the right of citizens to vote in national elections "shall not be denied or abridged by the United States or any State by reason of failure to pay a poll tax or other tax."

The Twenty-sixth Amendment extends voting rights to eighteen- to twenty-one-year-old persons. Aspects of the implementation of this amendment were referred to the courts as questions of residency and other matters were raised.

Formal enfranchisement would seem now to approximate universal suffrage. Remaining impediments evidently are not a matter of de jure denial but of de facto discouragement through registration complexities and intimidative local measures governing voting behavior. Efforts are under way to reduce residency periods to qualify as a voter and to introduce a much greater measure of uniformity among the states in residency rules. Only when a de jure right is easily transformed into a de facto vote is the move to participatory democracy supported.

II. GENUINE CHOICE

Political choice for citizens is genuine in a representative democracy when two fundamental conditions are met: First, procedures for selecting candidates (e.g., parties) have produced potential leaders whose views and skills are widely known. Second, voting and other avenues of choice making, when aggregated, actually are determinant, that is, produce results significantly different than would otherwise be obtained. Genuine choice, then, is a function of having credible options and of choice among options making a difference.

The first condition is addressed mainly to party machinery. Party organization exists, as is well known, to organize individuals of similar political persuasion, to identify and promote candidates, to support and communicate creative thinking on issues of political significance, and to solicit support for endorsed candidates and programs. Genuine choice is subverted to the extent that these functions are not adequately carried out.

The second condition is addressed primarily to the principle of majority rule. Majority rule here connotes the necessity for protection of minority rights. [2] The fifty-per-cent-plus-one rule is adopted, not because majorities are necessarily right, of course, but because no alternative embodying minority rule is compatible with participatory democracy. Jefferson's admonition is properly recalled at this point: "The will of the majority is in all cases to prevail," he remarks, but the will of the

2. A considerable literature explores this difficult question. See, e.g., Thomas Landon Thorson, *The Logic of Democracy*, Holt, Rinehart & Winston, New York, 1962, pp. 151-62.

majority "to be rightful must be reasonable."[3] The burden of demonstrating reasonableness is upon the majority. This makes the judgments of the majority an object of scrutiny and debate. We speak of a tyranny of the majority when the rights of minorities fully to utilize the political process to become a majority are denied.

Other procedural rules which have evolved to make political choice genuine include the following: An Australian ballot[4] is intended to provide for uncoerced choice by attempting to assure secrecy in marking and counting ballots. The initiative and referendum process provides a means for the people to legislate directly by providing for the creation of a policy alternative via petition and, if successful, a mandatory vote at a regular election.

Further reforms in nomination and election processes are under consideration. The physical strain and financial drain of some twenty-three state primaries in 1972, and an even larger number in 1976, led many to continue serious consideration of the adoption of a national primary-election instrument. Perennial efforts are made to dump the archaic structure of the Electoral College. But differential estimates of the effects of its abandonment on small and large states have, with other concerns, forestalled action. Formal franchise is not sufficient. Choice must be made genuine. The task of assuring genuine choice is a continuing procedural responsibility.

III.   FIRST-AMENDMENT GUARANTEES

Ironically, the achievement of a participatory democracy in which *substantive* questions of structure and goals are always amenable to review, revision, or abandonment, nevertheless absolutely requires certain *procedural* options and conditions to be present. The latter are, in an instrumental sense, given and constant, but they are not "given" in the a priori, idealistic, beyond-inquiry, or eternal-truth sense. Broadly speaking, most of the procedural givens for participatory democracy are included in the First Amendment to the U.S. Constitution.

That amendment, as most will recall, insists that "Congress shall make no law respecting an establishment of religion, or prohibiting the free exercise thereof; or abridging the freedom of speech, or of the press; or the right of the people peaceably to assemble, and to petition the Government for a redress of grievances." By Supreme Court interpretation of the Fourteenth Amendment, the Bill of Rights is being extended to the states.

3. Quoted in Livingston & Thompson, *The Consent of the Governed*, (3rd ed.), op. cit., p. 88.
4. "An official ballot printed at public expense on which the names of all nominated candidates appear and which is distributed only at the polling place and marked in secret" (*Webster's Third New International Dictionary*).

The significance of these procedural guarantees cannot be over-stated. Without free speech, free press, and free assembly there can be no honest and penetrating deliberative process on substantive questions. Participatory democracy can invoke self-rule only when the exercise of discretion is informed via candid, extensive, threat-free interchange of ideas and information—free speech and press. That interchange is possible only where uncoerced and unmanipulated assembly is possible. Holding incumbent policymakers to account requires voting prerogatives *and* petitioning rights.

Conservative elitists typically want to put limits or constraints on the use of these procedural options on grounds that some speech is dangerous (gives aid and comfort to ideological enemies), that the press must be curbed (through prior censorship), or that assembly must be restrained (illegal and unconstitutional incarceration of persons). Always the few perceive their knowledge and insight to be superior to that of the many and are prepared to abort the First Amendment to enforce that "superiority."

But as the thoughtful will recognize, the only sure way that error is discovered and corrected is for policy and its defense to be continuously made a public affair. The community must routinely know what is being done in its name and allegedly on its behalf by its incumbent leadership. Without First-Amendment procedural guarantees, that discovery and correction is impossible. Quite aside from other considerations, surely the sordid Watergate affair has reaffirmed the significance and role of a free press and the real and continuing threat of official secrecy. Accordingly, it is a cause for grave concern to advocates of participatory democracy when polls of American opinion show faltering support for the First Ten Amendments and when the First Amendment especially is seen as dangerous and threatening.[5] Concern is intensified when an incumbent administration in its politically expedient advocacy of "law and order" seems willing and able to violate rights assured by the First and other amendments. A recent analysis by Richard Harris provides a most sobering argument that the Nixon administration, 1968-1972, through its Justice Department, consciously acted to subvert these guarantees. Says Harris,

> None of these officials [members of the Nixon administration] has acted or spoken in any way that would demonstrate an understanding of how

5. James W. Prothro and Charles M. Grigg, "Fundamental Principles of Democracy: Bases of Agreement and Disagreement," *Journal of Politics*, Vol. 22, Spring 1960, pp. 276-94. Does it follow that such faltering support undermines a belief in the possibility and desirability of participatory democracy? The answer is negative, of course. We have at no point argued the infallibility of popular judgment. Democracy is not inevitable. People can be conditioned to demean their own capacities and sense of self-worth. The "grave concern" voiced does not reflect adversely on people generally, but on the experiences they have had which prompt them to see political freedom as threatening.

fragile a system our democracy is. If they do in fact understand that, then their official actions—in pressing for laws that can now be used to crush civil liberties, in prosecuting leaders of the anti-war movement to still dissent, in harassing the press to end criticism, in invading the privacy of tens of thousands of citizens to catch a handful of crooks, in illegally suppressing protest to show firmness—must be taken as signs that they see the system's weakness as an opportunity, not a peril. The system has survived this long largely because no President before now has used, or allowed to be used in his name, the people's deepest fears to divide them and to turn the majority's tyrannical instincts against his political enemies. No one can say that the President willfully set out to undermine the Constitution that he swore to uphold. But how would the results be different if he had?[6]

Where court interpretation and/or executive enforcement tend to narrow the range or abort the intent of these procedural guarantees (the First Amendment in particular), *whatever* the character of the apologia advanced to justify it, participatory democracy is made increasingly impossible. Elitist power wielding ascends; people's control over their own lives and community recedes; freedom dies. Private institutions like the American Civil Liberties Union may succeed in slowing the trend. They can hardly be expected to reverse an oppressive pattern pursued by any national administration whose political influence and media manipulation beclouds the issues, heightens the fears, compels compliance, and postures as savior to the larger community.

IV. RESPONSIVE LEGISLATIVE BODY

In any community of any appreciable size, face-to-face direct democracy, town-meeting style, is, of course, not physically possible. Structural mechanisms are created, therefore, to provide for the representation of the views and interests of the many through the selection of a representative few to constitute a deliberative body. Wherever there is (or has been) any pretense to democratic rule, such bodies have been created (legislature, congress, assembly, parliament, diet, duma). Students everywhere are generally familiar with the fact and character of such institutional forms. Virtually all are aware that these bodies function through committee structures and plenary sessions, that they may be bicameral or unicameral in form, that specific deliberative and discretionary roles are frequently assigned to particular segments (e.g., in Congress, the House originates money bills, the Senate "advises and consents" on executive appointments), and that their de facto power

6. Richard Harris, "Reflections: The New Justice," *The New Yorker*, March 25, 1972, p. 105.

may be extensive or negligible depending upon constitutional designation and the power realities of other agencies and individuals, especially executive ones.

Accordingly, attention here is confined to brief comments concerning institutional arrangements that have evolved within or are tangential to this general structure. Again the focus is upon the American experience.

How in a participatory democracy is representativeness to be insured? Partly, of course, this quest was realized in the successive extensions of suffrage, as noted. But of nearly equal significance is the prescription which compels a redrawing of congressional districts after each national census. That the redistricting process is sometimes undertaken to produce particular political results (gerrymandering to emperil the reelection of a particular candidate) is no revelation. But the recent structural shift of great moment in this area is the series of one-man-one-vote rulings of the Supreme Court in the 1960s, which directed the reapportionment of state legislatures in a manner to make the electing districts roughly equal in numbers of eligible voters.[7] These Court rulings produced a dramatic increase in the representation of urban voters at the expense of overly represented rural voters in most state legislatures. The significance of the rulings is suggested by the fact that the people of Los Angeles County increased their representation in the California State Senate from one to fifteen in a body consisting of a total of forty senators. Important recasting of legislative agendas has followed this shift in the pattern of representation.

The theory of representation to be employed is still at issue. Some have argued that an elected official is to be merely a vehicle, a transmission instrument, for the views and opinions of his or her constituency. He or she need hold no particular view of his or her own. The representative's task is merely to voice his or her constituents' opinion and to press and bargain for laws incorporating that opinion.

A contrary view, more in accord with the theory of participatory democracy developed here, is that an elected representative's responsiveness and responsibility is to be differently accounted. The person's election must be based on an understanding of his or her views on the issues. As an elected representative, one's responsibility is to engage actively in an educative process involving one's self, one's constituents, and one's legislative colleagues in proposing and debating legislative actions to deal with acknowledged real problems. A political representative in this case must retain his or her own identity, integrity, and views on particular issues. He or she must remain responsive to the views of constituents and inform voters of what is being done, why it is being

---

7. See Livingston and Thompson, *The Consent of the Governed*, (3rd ed.), op. cit., pp. 344-49.

done, and what the expected consequences are. The representative must lay his or her records of deliberative involvement publicly on the line and seek reelection on no other basis. But such a representative is not merely a funnel or a transmission belt. An agent-actor, an elected member of a legislative body must raise and extend the reflective capacities of himself or herself and that of his or her constituents as far as possible. A representative in a participatory democracy is a teacher as well as a deliberator. (Older readers will recall Adlai Stevenson's instructional campaign in 1952 in this connection.[8]) Such a person must periodically be held to account at the ballot box.

The committee structure of legislative bodies also requires brief comment if our understanding of the structuring of the political process is to be extended. All presumably understand that committees are the primary arenas of legislative action; substantive deliberation in plenary sessions is rare. The volume of work in a deliberative body together with its increasing complexity compels some specialization of interest and parceling out of legislative proposals—bills. Committees are a nearly inevitable result of the need for specialization of labor in a deliberative body. So much is commonplace.

What merits comment in this context, however, is the fact that where, and to the extent that (as in the United States Congress), leadership of these respective committees is determined by the institution of seniority alone, the invidious use of longevity-in-office *may* threaten the ability of committees to serve as initiators and assessors of policy proposals. Longevity *may* sometimes correlate positively with functional effectiveness based on familiarity and experience, but that is a matter to be explored, not assumed. The concern is that committee leadership may be unimaginative, conservative, tradition-serving, and status-quo-defending at a time when legislative action on a particular problem is sorely needed. Where this condition exists, the deliberative and decision-making functions of a legislative body are markedly impaired; they may even be arrested on major issues.

Second, where the committee system in force permits one committee (e.g., the Rules Committee) to parcel out bills and thus to determine the character and extent of the work of other committees, formidable power is held without adequate mechanisms for holding such committee power responsible. The possibilities for "wheeling and dealing" are legion under these circumstances. Negation of participatory democracy via an absence of representative accountability is quite possible.

Third, where, and to the extent that, elected represenatives' patterns of behavior may fairly be characterized as the brokerage of rival or

8. See, Walter Johnson (ed.), *The Papers of Adlai E. Stevenson*, Vol. IV, Little Brown, Boston, 1974.

conflicting economic and other interests, the potentiality exists for serious impairment of the deliberative functioning of a legislative body. If legislators see their role primarily as that of mongering concessions among the established power fragments in the community, then the focus of policy consideration will be confined to the interests of these fragments to the exclusion of the interests of the larger community. Or as Veblen might phrase it, to view legislative proposals with an "eye single" on their impact on constituent "vested interests" is to abandon the interests of "ungraded men." The risk is that compromise may be viewed as a principle or a criterion instead of a tactic; the balancing of factional interests may come to be thought of as the meaning of the public interest.

Regrettably, it appears that students have sometimes been taught that such balancing and compromise is the "stuff and substance" of the democratic process. Nothing could be further from the truth. Allowing a legislative body to be converted at times into a brokerage house or a marketplace of interests is to defer to "the third house," the house of the lobbyists. The third house often appears as the aggregate of well-heeled legislative advocates who tend to see the world through the (usually) economic eyes of their employers.

A legislative brokerage house is not a deliberative body; it is not an educational institution. It is more like its namesake—a commercial enterprise—claiming deliberative standing. A legislative body must be both a deliberative and an instructional institution—and more. Brokerage politics tends to foreclose consideration of and judgments concerning public policy except on criteria which are likely to be invidious because the interests of the unorganized, the poor, the disenfranchised are deemed less worthy of concern than those of the organized agricultural, industrial, commercial, and professional groups. We are not likely to see an early end to pressure-group politics and to occasional brokerage-house behavior of representatives. But a considerable gain, if only a beginning, is the recognition that another model of political activity is available. A more warrantable concept of the public interest may yet be formulated.

For that to occur, the more basic relativism and positivism of brokerage politics will, we suspect, have to be abandoned. Political relativism is reflected with the assumption that interests are pluralistic, given, and incommensurable; they are whatever they are. A legislator can balance or compromise or accommodate interests. The query to the lobbyist is simply, "For whom or how many do you speak?"

Political positivism absolves the legislator of moral responsibility. Politics here is amoral. The legislator's role is to reflect and accommodate interests, not to judge interests. There is no concept of the public interest as an "ought to be."

Finally, the effectiveness of a deliberative body in a participatory democracy is enormously enhanced where institutional structure is provided which puts researchers and scholars at the disposal of legislative members. If our characterization of a legislative body as one which prominently has an educational function is accepted, clearly support agencies and individuals to undertake research projects and studies for legislators are very much to be desired.

In the United States at least, a remarkable improvement in this area is evident in the last three or four decades. For example, the establishment of the Joint Economic Committee in Congress by the Employment Act of 1946 has led to the preparation of a number of significant studies of the performance of the American economy on poverty, income distribution, instability, impact of military spending, and the like. Congress is supported in addition by the members' own staffs, the Legislative Reference Service, and the Library of Congress personnel.

At the state level perhaps California has been a leader in this endeavor. Not the least of the legacies left by Jesse Unruh during a decade of leadership in the California legislature in the 1960s was his contribution to the creation of research support agencies for the members of the legislature. It is extremely important that members of the legislature not be utterly and totally dependent upon executive agencies for all of their information on, for example, revenue sources, tax incidence, project funding, and the like. Informed deliberative judgments on the political issues at hand are impossible in the absence of pertinent information generated by competent advisors.

In recent years, there have been serious and sometimes successful efforts constructively to modify legislative processes in some of the areas mentioned above. Party caucuses have in a few key instances forced the removal of some "seniority" committee chairs. The hold of Rules Committees has been eroded. The efforts to reformulate rules for "ethical conduct" in Congress include a concern with the reporting of and constraints upon outside income for legislators, thereby eroding dependence on third-house sources. Congressman John Moss (California) and others have succeeded in reducing somewhat the degree of secrecy in governmental operations and have helped to open deliberative processes, thereby enhancing accountability. From the perspective in this book, such efforts are much to be encouraged.

V.   RESPONSIVE EXECUTIVE AGENCY

A participatory democracy does not live by universal suffrage and a responsive legislature alone. Popularly determined laws—prescriptive rules for organizing community—passed in the name of and for the interest of the community must be administered from the same perspective. A failure to administer or implement laws altogether or a failure to execute rule changes from the democratic perspective will abort or render useless the finest product of the legislator's craft.

Welfare mothers in poverty have seen legislative intent twisted by constrictive eligibility judgments and by callous or vindictive enforcement of antifraud provisions. Organized labor saw collective bargaining rights established in the Wagner Act of 1935, but strikes seemed necessary to secure compliance in many industries, including steel.

Black voters in the South have been denied their legally sanctioned vote by the intimidative demeanor and illegal questioning of registrars of voters. Federal supervision has sometimes been required to ensure compliance. Chicanos, blacks, Asians, and women have all observed on some occasions sluggish enforcement of Fair-Employment-Practice codes and nondiscriminatory housing provisions.

Environmental-protection laws against industrial pollution of streams, against overgrazing and excessive timber cutting in national forest areas, and for constraints on strip mining of coal are sometimes indifferently enforced. President Nixon's assertion of executive power in impounding funds authorized by Congress for, as an example, expenditure on pollution-control installations was at issue in the impeachment deliberations in the House of Representatives.

In sum, a vigorous and powerful executive and his or her executive agency can, by ignoring the legislature, by exercising influence upon the legislature, and/or by selective implementation of legislative decisions, shape the structural fabric of a society nearly as much as the legislative body itself can shape it. Holding the executive and his or her support structure accountable and responsible, then, is of equal importance for participatory democracy to that of holding the deliberative body accountable.

As with legislators, frequent elections of executives for limited terms provides an important measure of accountability, of course. But as the British scholar Harold Laski observed with reference to the presidency on his last trip to the United States (if we recall correctly): "You curious Americans assume that all the great events of history will occur at intervals of four years." Laski's barbed wit was indirectly affirming his preference for a parliamentary system where the executive is drawn from the legislative ranks and where generally the prime minister may be called to account by a confidence vote whenever the issue is important and the chamber is severely divided. The acknowledged difficulties of the Nixon impeachment process led many to seek less traumatic and dislocative means of removing an unsatisfactory U.S. president from office. [9]

---

9. For example, TRB, "Turbulence Ahead," *The New Republic*, July 20, 1974, p. 4.

But our interest in the executive, the office and supporting agencies, goes beyond these legitimate but familiar considerations. What habits of mind and habits of behavior in an executive agency are compatible with, indeed supportive of, participatory democracy?

Perhaps of greatest significance is the perception of the office of the executive (mayor, governor, president) which an incumbent (or candidate) holds. Central is the recognition that an executive officer in a participatory democracy literally and symbolically has the whole community as his or her constituency. Perhaps more than any other political figure, he or she must serve as spokesperson (at times as an advocate) for those who otherwise have little or no political voice.

The considerable power associated with the office is legitimately used only where and to the extent that it facilitates the protection and extension of the community's capacity and opportunity to govern itself. As noted elsewhere, this includes sustaining the procedural givens of the First Amendment. The executive's power of decision must, then, be enabling, instructive, and supportive; it must not be divisive, capricious, or invidiously discriminatory. [10] Some elemental political maxims and admonitions follow from this contention:

(1) Although it is regrettable that it must be mentioned, the pronouncements of the executive must be meticulously truthful. The appearance of a "credibility gap" in the Johnson and Nixon administrations is a measure of the departure from democratic practice. No executive can lie to the public without a massive violation of the minimal conditions for self-rule. A community, where we are indeed "members one of another," can only be sustained on trust, on the presumption of integrity. The absence of integrity in the person or office of the public's executive, therefore, is wholly subversive of trust at the point where it is most critical. [11] The existence of a "credibility gap" is a crypto-fascist condition. As actor-agents we must be able to distinguish early between error of judgment and purposeful deception. Errors can be corrected; deception is anathema to participatory democracy.

(2) The institutionalized habits of belief and behavior which cast the executive in the role primarily of a wielder of control over other

10. The agony that was Watergate, President Nixon's conduct of his office and the behavior of his chosen subordinates after 1968, and especially after 1970, may well be recalled in this connection. On present knowledge, no other president in U.S. history so consciously and consistently amassed and abused executive powers to serve his own passionate quest to retain his office and position. The transcripts of presidential conversations are almost totally devoid of any concern for the public interest; manifest instead is a dominant concern for the retention of political power and the public-relations appearances related thereto. In this connection, see Henry Steele Commager, "The Constitution is Alive and Well," *The New York Times*, August 11, 1974, p. E 17.

11. See, for example, Hannah Arendt, "Lying in Politics," *New York Review of Books*, November 18, 1971, pp. 30 ff. See also, David Wise, *The Politics of Lying*, Random House, New York, 1973.

people's behavior are at least incomplete and at worst also anathema to participatory democracy. This makes power and its retention by the executive the overriding consideration in all major judgments concerning the administration of policy. A necessary corollary of myopic concern with power is concern with status, honor, and respect—more, deference—shown and demanded for the office and person where such power is held. This means that the question of correctness or viability of policy must play second fiddle to the bearing of policy on this power position and the ceremonial deference shown that power. Certainly the primary example of this century in the United States is the behavior of President Nixon in the period from 1969 to 1974 as revealed and reported by the publications of the Select Senate Committee on Presidential Campaign Activities (Senate Watergate Committee), [12] of the Judiciary Committee of the House of Representatives in its impeachment investigations, [13] and of the White House Transcripts of tapes. [14] Abuse of executive powers is copiously disclosed in all of the foregoing. Another glaring example of an apparent absence of this democratic leadership role was the war in Southeast Asia, spawned, engineered and defended by American presidents and their advisors [15] without overt and formal approval of the Congress in the early stages and over the objection of the Congress and the larger community in the later stages. The disease of the "arrogance of power" (Senator Fulbright's phrase) seems to have been exhibited by at least three presidents—John Kennedy, Lyndon Johnson, and Richard Nixon. It would obviously be folly to suggest that they were the first to contract this virus.

(3) The institutionalized habits of mind and behavior which see the executive and his or her office as the representative of a particular fragment of the community is contra-participatory democracy. The executive office in a democracy is not to be something to capture to serve parochial or provincial interests. While it is naive to deny that an incumbent may tend to use his office to cater to the economic, financial, and ideological interests of the critical segment of his perceived constituency, it is difficult to defend this as a legitimate action or a desired trait. It follows, for example, that in making appointments to the Supreme Court, the Federal Reserve Board, regulatory agencies (FCC, FPC, etc.), and elsewhere, the vested interests are not uniquely to be served. The necessary breadth of an elected executive's constituency

12. U.S. Congress, Senate Select Committee on Presidential Campaign Activities, *Presidential Campaign Activities of 1972* (Hearings & Report), op. cit.

13. U.S. Congress, House of Representatives Committee on the Judiciary, Hearings and Report [The Impeachment of Richard M. Nixon], U.S. Government Printing Office, Washington, D.C. 1974.

14. *White House Transcripts*, op. cit.

15. David Halberstam, *The Best and the Brightest*, Random House, New York, 1973. Also, The Senator Gravel edition, *The Pentagon Papers*, Beacon Press, Boston, 1972.

suggests the wisdom that he or she have a paramount concern for the many over the few.

(4) An elected executive, as with an elected representative to a deliberative body, must also function in the role of a teacher. Certainly a major criterion in considering a candidate is whether or not he or she is educable. Can the person learn, and is the person willing and able to use his or her increasing insights and understandings to enhance the community's understanding of its own condition and problems? Some examples come to mind. Dwight Eisenhower's farewell address as president in 1960 contained important insights concerning the rise of and threat from the military-industrial complex. John Kennedy's Yale speech of June 11, 1962, sought to bury some of the orthodox myths of ages past concerning the role of the national government in promoting economic stability. Lyndon Johnson spoke with some eloquence in 1964 about the emerging federal role in extending educational opportunity at all levels and about some new approaches for ending endemic poverty. Richard Nixon ended nearly a quarter-century of national self-imposed ignorance concerning Mainland China by his visit there in 1972 and by his reopening of cultural and economic intercourse. His real, if tardy, dismantlement of the Cold War with the USSR was a major achievement. (Following Nixon's resignation, Gerald Ford succeeded in restoring a measure of public trust in the office of the president, but in his own mind and in fact he was not an innovator.) Jimmy Carter has attempted to instruct the community and the Congress on the need to moderate rising demands for energy and to reduce dependence on oversea sources of oil.

Such cases are commendable as occasions when political leaders sought to move beyond narrow political motives to instruct the community concerning important events and conditions significantly affecting their lives. In most, perhaps all, of these instances (and others also, no doubt) one must presume that the presidents were drawing on extensive advice and counsel from knowledgeable members of their respective administrations. John Kennedy's months-long tutorial in economics under Walter Heller is widely known. Henry Kissinger's role in Richard Nixon's China policy shift and achievement of detente with the USSR appears to have been substantial.

Executive leadership thus assumes a demanding, if exhilarating, dimension. One must be a teacher and learner in addition to other roles and responsibilities. And that activity must occur partly in public view, where critics, friendly and unfriendly, will wish to have their say. The threatening and politically hazardous character of this facet of executive leadership drives some incumbents into relative isolation in order to insulate themselves from such criticism. Press conferences are not held for extended periods. Public speeches and appearances are reduced with remaining ones orchestrated for audiences not likely to raise objections.

But such insulation and isolation are extremely hazardous from the point of view of the participating democrat, because he or she is denied his or her right to know. Breaking or eroding continuous and substantive communication between the electorate and the leadership is a recipe for disaster. Not a little of the unrest of these last few decades derives from this closing of eyes and ears by public officials. A president who watches pro football on television while a large peace demonstration is underway within earshot is incurring considerable political risk.

(5) An elected executive is directly accountable to the community at large. At the national level this poses a special obligation upon the president to protect the community from the intimidative use of power by small but potent segments of the community.

Only the president can assure the retention of civilian control over the military establishment. Several recent presidents have had to reaffirm this Constitutional dictum. Harry Truman was compelled, he thought, to relieve General Douglas MacArthur of his command in the early 1950s. Dwight Eisenhower, evidently, resisted the advice of the Joint Chiefs and others to provide military support to the French in Southeast Asia. More recently, General John P. Lavelle was given an unprecedented demotion upon retirement (in 1972) for conducting unauthorized bombing in North Vietnam, and Jimmy Carter in 1977 found it necessary to "discipline" two generals for their public criticism of foreign-policy positions.

Only the president, in many circumstances, has the resources to hold concentrated corporate power to account. Where the individual wealth of scores of corporations (ATT, GM, USS, etc.) exceeds the wealth of all but the very largest states, and where such wealth confers upon these corporations a significant discretion over economic policy (e.g., price setting), the executive agency of the public must be prepared to review and reverse, if necessary, such private-industrial-government decision making. John Kennedy found it necessary to confront and face down the steel industry on price increases in the early 1960s. Richard Nixon might have used his position more vigorously to control the efforts of ITT to subvert the Chilean government of Salvador Allende in the early 1970s.

Only the president, in most circumstances, has the potential to prevent traditional federal agencies from subverting the intent of Congress by bureaucratic blunting and diverting of legislative directives. All large-scale organizations develop rigidities in which the survival of the institution and the protection of the positions and status of individuals associated therewith typically take precedence over other criteria. This phenomenon, though not peculiar to government (contrary to the folklore), does of course occur there. Accordingly, when congressional action calls for revamping of agencies, redirection of their functions, reconstitution of their organization, or termination of their existence, only the president can directly assure compliance. Even so, some presidents have found it easier, apparently, to create new agencies than to transform or redirect existing ones.

In sum, in a participatory democracy, the symbolic significance of the elected executive official imposes exceedingly heavy burdens upon the person who assumes that responsibility. Not only must much of his or her life be conducted in public; he or she must attempt to exhibit those habits of mind and habits of behavior which are compatible with the assumptions and values of a self-governing community. The special and difficult kind of leadership required is not everywhere understood. Regrettably, elitist remnants of ism-ideological perspectives impair that understanding.

VI. FULL INFORMATION

In addition to the Constitutional procedural guarantees discussed above and the means and mechanisms for holding elected legislative and executive officials accountable, the provision of prescriptive rules and institutional arrangements to assure that full and accurate information is available to the people generally must be very high on the agenda for participatory democracies. The need is evident; the institutional means to provide such information in the United States, though probably adequate, are by no means exemplary.

Scholarly inquiry, writing, teaching, and publication in American higher education, for example, is largely unfettered evidently in the sense of overt political intrusion on what is taught and written. One does occasionally hear complaints from the conservative fringe about economics departments having too many Keynesians or neo-Marxists on the staff. More seriously, instructors are sometimes denied reappointment or tenure apparently because of their political beliefs. [16] Scholarly materials occasionally are suppressed. [17] But the overall level of scholarly and academic freedom seems comparatively high. When attention is directed, however, to research funded or supported by off-campus groups such as private agencies, corporations, or public government bodies, it is clear that those supplying the funds generally influence what *kinds* of inquiry are funded, even where there is no overt effort to bias the inquiries themselves.

In the area of the mass media, as most students are well aware, the picture is one of extraordinarily impressive technical communicative capacities under control essentially of private repositories of power. While broadcast media, for example, strive to retain their autonomy, they appear at times to be vulnerable to political pressure set in motion

16. Soma Golden, "Radical Economists Under Fire," *The New York Times*, February 2, 1975, pp. F1 & 2.
17. Discussed briefly in chapter 2, part IV, above.

by the federal government through the regulatory influence of the Federal Communications Commission and more directly by a variety of actual and threatened constraints. Again, the attacks on the alleged lack of objectivity of the press and broadcast media by the Nixon administration through public utterances of the vice president, and through the prior censorship of the publication of *The Pentagon Papers*, [18] have few, if any, precedents in the American experience. However, no government stands mute in the face of heavy criticism, and the last few national administrations in the United States have reaffirmed that fact.

Finally, we must note that the press of the United States does in fact represent a considerable spread of editorial opinion and political philosophy. The difficulty is that, with the steady reduction of the number of newspapers, any reader in his own area may very well *not* have more than one editorial bias accessible. The number of one-newspaper cities continues to grow. To get more variety or comprehensiveness of coverage, an ordinary citizen is usually compelled to tap many additional publications. Only by moving to nationally distributed publications does one find a reasonably extensive choice. And there the financial costs become prohibitive for many if not most middle- and lower-income families and individuals. The economic costs of producing a national publication operate on the other end to reduce the number and to muffle the more critical perspectives of magazines and journals.

The paperback revolution (publication of books in soft and less expensive covers), by making materials available at more moderate prices, has contributed significantly to the provision of more definitive analyses on our common condition. The dissemination of information in book form continues to get a modest public subsidy on postal rates. With regard to commercial publishing, the overriding concern seems to be, "will it make a buck?" Will the firm recover its costs and more? Pecuniary criteria *may* coincide with the community's right and need to know, but there is no necessary assurance that they will. And while publishers will occasionally publish works which they feel "just ought to be published," with less concern for profitability, obviously the number of such "public-interest" undertakings must, in the nature of the business, be few.

A participatory democracy can only thrive where a full and free flow of information, analyses, policy proposals, and critiques is assured. That result will only come when a people organizes effective institutions specifically to accomplish that task.

VII.   ADMINISTRATION OF JUSTICE

Those who suppose that in a participatory democracy the agreed-upon prescriptive and proscriptive rules are not enforced, that a state of near-

18. The Senator Gravel edition, *The Pentagon Papers*, op. cit.

anarchy results, are mistaken. Alexander Meiklejohn made the point most effectively some years ago: ". . . a free government, established by common consent," he says

> may and often must use force in compelling citizens to obey the laws. Every government, as such, must have external power. It must, in fact, be more powerful than any one of its citizens, than any group of them. Political freedom does not mean freedom from control. It means self-control.[19]

Or again,

> At the bottom of every plan of self-government is a basic agreement, in which all the citizens have joined, that all matters of public policy shall be decided by corporate action, that such decisions shall be equally binding on all citizens, whether they agree with them or not, and that, if need be, they shall, by due legal procedure, be enforced upon anyone who refuses to conform to them. The man who rejects that agreement is not objecting to tyranny or despotism. He is objecting to political freedom. He is not a democrat. He is the anarchist. . . . Self-government is nonsense unless the "self" which governs is able and determined to make its will effective.[20]

The issue, then, in a participatory democracy is not the presence or absence of enforcement of laws popularly determined. They will and must be enforced.

The problem is much more difficult. Critically significant questions which must be faced and answered include the following: (1) What principle of justice should be reflected in the institutions charged with enforcement of laws? Ought the Benthamite principle of equational justice to apply, wherein punishments are neatly graded to fit the varying severity of the crimes? Do we take "an eye for an eye and a tooth for a tooth" and a life for a life? (2) What kinds of errant behavior are *most* threatening to the continuity of a self-governing community? What behaviors are to be defined as criminal acts? Are crimes without victims (e.g., homosexual relations between consenting adults) of equal concern to crimes with victims (armed robbery)? Is public criticism of an incumbent government's war policy a crime? (3) Are the laws and codes even-handedly and noninvidiously enforced? Should the rich as well as the poor serve jail sentences for flagrant traffic violations? Is conviction for murder directly correlated with low income and race?

We cannot presume to respond adequately to such queries here, but a few comments may nevertheless be in order.

In a participatory democracy, in institutions creating and enforcing the laws, the equational theory of justice (an eye for an eye) will not be

19. Alexander Meiklejohn, *Political Freedom*, Harper & Row, New York, 1948, p. 13.
20. Ibid., p. 14.

admitted as the general principle. Such retaliatory measures, the quest to get even, the balancing of punishment and crime, will be seen increasingly as irrelevant to the effort to secure compliance with self-imposed, communally sanctioned restraints. Balancing the scales does not necessarily constitute justice. This intriguing matter will occupy us at some length in the final chapter of this book.

The kinds of errant behavior regarded as criminal will in a participatory democracy continuously remain an object of scrutiny. But some past or current practices (institutional operations) which appear incompatible with a free society include the following: First, the use of the Federal Bureau of Investigation since shortly after World War II as an agency to investigate the political beliefs and behaviors of citizens cannot be condoned. The FBI's pursuit of political activists has habitually gone well beyond ordinary criminal investigation. The FBI has infiltrated activist groups, funded their activities, and manipulated their behavior. Unevaluated information from FBI files has been released to selective individuals. [21]

Second, the domestic surveillance carried out by the Army Intelligence section into the political activities of candidates, officials, and citizens in the late 1960s and early 1970s cannot be condoned. Information compiled on thousands of individuals has been fed into massive data banks. Although public criticism is supposed to have led to the destruction of much of this information, some believe that these records have not been cleared. Accordingly there has been, we assume, a chilling and intimidating effect from these surveillance activities on those who would demonstrate, verbalize, and act on their opposition to existing policy and the manner of its enforcement. [22]

In another area, on the other hand, the administration of justice has been and is being improved by institutional reforms of substantial significance. The recent advent of public-interest law firms, rural-legal-assistance programs, and the like (as mentioned earlier) have begun to correct for a condition in which only those moderately well off financially could afford to secure professional legal assistance to resolve conflicts and conditions arising in their working experience as well as their personal lives. These structural innovations have thus sought to make the administration of justice more even-handed by lowering or removing the financial barrier to the acquisition of legal counsel.

But the elimination of political intimidation in the enforcement of law and the removal of financial barriers to counsel, though important,

21. See, for example, Victor S. Navasky, "Can You Tap This," *The New York Times Magazine*, July 16, 1972, pp. 8ff. Also, Pat Watters and Steve Gillers (eds.), *Investigating the FBI*, Doubleday, New York, 1973.

22. See, U.S. Congress, Senate Committee on the Judiciary, Subcommittee on Constitutional Rights, *Federal Data Banks, Computers and the Bill of Rights* (Hearings), U.S. Government Printing Office, Washington, D.C., 1971.

do not ensure noninvidious and nonpunitive justice. In addition, a participatory democracy must demand that common political obligations of a citizen are not subverted by capricious and selective law enforcement on invidious grounds. Blacks did not see even-handed justice in the raids on Black Panther and Black Muslim headquarters in the late 1960s and 1970s. Students did not see even-handed justice in the long-delayed federal investigative interest in the Kent State shooting of students by members of the National Guard and in the conduct of the police on the streets of Chicago during the Democratic Convention of 1968. Women do not see even-handed justice in male-dominated legislatures taking self-righteous stands in opposing reform of abortion laws. The poor do not see even-handed justice in the indifferent enforcement of fire and sanitation ordinances upon owners of slum housing and in the enforcement of consumer-protection laws. Native Americans do not see even-handed justice in the tardiness of settling their claims against the government for land seizure and in the massive failure to honor treaty obligations. Chicanos do not see even-handed justice in the weak enforcement of laws to prevent exploitation of migrant farm workers and in the tardy implementation of Fair-Employment-Practice laws.

Political repossession of control by the community over its enforcement agencies will not guarantee an end to punitive, capricious, and invidious judgments. Indeed, majorities sometimes act punitively, cappriciously, or invidiously. But such repossession does offer some promise of ending those patterns of law enforcement which cater to the elitist segments—the wealthy, the privileged, the power wielders. If we are indeed "members one of another," there is no escape from the need for institutional adjustment to ensure even-handed administration of prescriptive rules. The creation of community is impossible until a substantial measure of success is achieved in this area.

VIII.   CIVIL ORDER

Where the disintegration of community has proceeded to the point where the political choice becomes in fact one between chaos and order, a people will normally choose order. This is so because order (even authoritarian order) provides, after a fashion, for continuity in the social and political process; chaos does not. And people will not rationally choose to suspend continuity.

Accordingly, where the unrest exhibited in demonstrations in the 1960s and 1970s in the streets and on the campuses seemed to threaten continuity, the cry—especially of white, middle America—for "law and order" had an element of legitimacy about it. It may well be that the fears of people were needlessly heightened by self-serving individuals: the press and broadcast media very likely did, on occasion, exaggerate the magnitude of the threat and distort the thrust of the protests; some of the protesters themselves did evidently seek to maximize television exposure for their own ends. But the point is that tolerable maintenance of civil order *is* an altogether legitimate demand; community is impossible without it. The difficult task, of course, is to maintain civil order in a manner which protects and extends the discretionary involvement of the members of the community, which retains and enhances the civil rights and civil liberties of the community generally. The absence of order, the absence of common acceptance of prescriptive rules even as those rules are being critically reviewed and revamped, means the absence of an *opportunity* for deliberative consideration of needed changes. Demonstrations are (regrettably) sometimes essential to direct attention to social, economic, and political ills, but precious little creative reflection on alternative institutional options or hard-headed analysis of probable consequences of contemplated structural changes can occur in street rallies or mass marches.

The maintenance of civil order, then, is not the peculiar or exclusive interest or concern of an Establishment or a fragmentary political or military elite. Participating democrats must also insist on the maintenance of civil order. But participating democrats, of course, must insist on much more as well.

The "much more" must include at the outset a recognition of those institutional proscriptions in the first ten amendments to the Constitution which protect an individual accused of breaching the peace, of violating order, from arbitrary exercise of coercive police power. A review of these Constitutional guarantees will bring them prominently into view in this context:

The Fourth Amendment protects against "unreasonable searches and seizures."

The Fifth Amendment protects against being held for a capital crime without indictment; against double jeopardy; against being compelled "to be a witness against himself;" against being "deprived of life, liberty or property without due process of law;" and against the taking for public use of private property "without just compensation."

The Sixth Amendment provides the accused in a criminal prosecution with "the right to a speedy and public trial by an impartial jury;" "to be informed of the nature and cause of the accusation; to be confronted with witnesses against him; to have compulsory process for obtaining witnesses in his favor, and to have the assistance of counsel for his defense."

The Seventh Amendment provides for trial by jury "in suits at common law."

The Eighth Amendment provides that "excessive bail shall not be required, nor excessive fines imposed, nor cruel and unusual punishments inflicted."

While presumably nearly everyone is aware that court decisions continue to interpret and even modify the enforceable meaning of the critical passages of these amendments, everyone also knows what the general thrust of these maxims is intended to be: order shall be obtained in a way which does not violate these basic protections for the accused against the accuser, including the state. The fact that in our anxiety and apprehension over crime and demonstrations in the streets, we sometimes tolerate, even demand, violations of these constraints on power, does not negate their pertinence for a participatory democracy.

In dealing with demonstrators seeking redress for real and/or imagined grievances, for example, police officers must not be permitted to usurp the roles of a jury and judge. Police may use only such force as is reasonably required to apprehend an individual appearing to break the law. They may not use more force than is necessary for such apprehension. They may not decide on the spot the guilt or innocence of the individual; they may not administer punishment. Any one or any combination of these latter actions constitutes an *illegal* use of force and violence. Such force and violence are especially disturbing because police officers, one must assume, have training adequate to permit them to make a determination of what may and may not legally be done.

The last two decades have been punctuated by outbreaks of violence in Detroit, Chicago, Berkeley, Washington, D.C., and elsewhere where illegal use of police power has seriously violated the civil rights and liberties of individuals. There are, to be fair, at least an equal number of instances in which police units, in the face of massive and often obscene provocation, have "kept their cool," have held meticulously to their limited roles, and have risked injury to protect rights of demonstration, assembly, and speech. The object is not to point trembling fingers of accusation or to lay on bouquets of praise. It is rather to encourage reflection upon the *way* in which "law and order" are sustained.

The way in which law and order are sustained will be materially improved to the extent to which more effective ties are established between the community and police units. Often the alienation of the police from the community appears as pervasive as that of criminals. A democratic community not only must retain control over its enforcement agencies to prevent abuse of police powers; it must also support the agencies' instrumental role and avoid isolating them from the rest of the community.

Federal and state programs supporting increased education and training for law-enforcement officers evidently are having a salutory effect on the way in which enforcement agencies cope with unrest. However, to view the problem as one of enhancing the punitive coercive capacity of police with advanced weaponry (urban street tanks, stun guns, etc.) is to opt for the fascist bent.

In addition, some dissident groups have also learned that their challenges to civil order, where violence is consciously chosen as a means, are counterproductive to the achievement of their ends. Recourse to violence, whatever the motive, *ends* deliberation; it does not promote it. As Mahatma Ghandi, Martin Luther King, Jr., and Cesar Chavez have argued and shown, the philosophy of nonviolence can be an effective guide to social protest and reformistic behavior. [23]

In sum, civil order is necessary for participatory democracy, but the institutional means of its attainment *must* be compatible with the end-in-view of a free, self-governing community. We cannot long regard ourselves as "members one of another" so long as the illegal use of violence is condoned or recourse to violence to serve invidious ends is permitted.

23. See, for example, Martin Luther King, Jr., *Letter from Birmingham Jail* (pamphlet), American Friends Service Committee, Philadelphia, 1963. The letter also appears in Martin Luther King, Jr., *Why We Can't Wait*, Harper and Row, New York, 1963, 1964, pp. 77-100.

Chapter 12

THE RESOLUTION OF CONFLICT

. . . this [democratic] theory of man and the state postulates no utopian society free from the clash of conflicting interests; not designed to end conflict, it invites the use of governmental power to preserve diversity. Politics and the coercion entailed by political settlements are accepted as indispensable, positive goods, and the political process is supported not as a prelude to ultimate harmony but as intrinsically desirable.

HENRY S. KARIEL*

With the growth of complexity . . . there are too many subordinate groups and organizations that can injure the operation of the whole by the withdrawal of consent and the exercise of an effective veto. Democracy has been the only solution mankind has found to this problem.

HARVEY WHEELER**

*Henry S. Kariel, *The Promise of Politics*, Prentice Hall, Inc., New Jersey, 1966, p. 37.

**Harvey Wheeler, *Democracy in a Revolutionary Era*, Center for the Study of Democratic Institutions, Santa Barbara, California, 1968, p. 74.

Conflict is, and will remain, a part of the human condition. Much human conflict has a political dimension; it is concerned with the character and administration of public policy. The differing conditioning experiences to which people are exposed, the differing value systems to which they have become committed, the divergent purposes to which human energy and intellect are put, the differing perceptions of reality people hold, the differing developmental capacities which people acquire and exhibit make inevitable that some such experiences, value systems, purposes, perceptions, and capacities will be in conflict with others when they are directed to public questions.

A polity cannot long exist in the absence of institutions through which conflicts are registered, transformed, resolved, or rendered impotent. A participatory democracy must provide for the management and resolution of conflict in ways which are not subversive or destructive of the procedural canons which distinguish a participatory democracy as a paradigm of policy formation.

At an earlier point we noted that politics is sometimes thought of as consisting largely of conflict and its management and control. [1] Although we recognize conflict and its resolution as an attribute of politics, we did not and do not *identify* politics with conflict. Conflict is a part, not the whole, of communal policy making.

Conflict management or resolution in a participatory democracy must be undertaken in a manner which is compatible with (1) the retention of full-scale noninvidious participation of actor-agent citizens, and (2) the retention of deliberative processes which capitalize upon the emerging reflective capacities of such citizens.

I.   PRIVATE INTERESTS VS. PUBLIC OBLIGATION

The task of resolving and adjudicating political conflict as a continuing political function has been inadequately dealt with by the ism-ideologists. Their models are not particularly pertinent or helpful to a participatory democrat. They tend to misconceive the dual roles of persons as private beings and as public participatory agent-actors.

> At the heart of political life there is . . . an inescapable tension between interest and duty, between the inclination of the private life and the obligation of the public role. [2]

With the capitalists, the private life of "interests" is supreme. Consumer sovereignty and personal utility maximization reign unchallenged. Conflicts arise due to differing versions of private life or interests, and these conflicts are resolved via the impersonal adjudicatory operations of the marketplace. Balance, compromise, equilibrium of

---

1. See, for example, E. E. Schottschneider, *The Semi-Sovereign People*, Holt, Rinehart & Winston, New York, 1960.

2. Joseph Tussman, *Obligation and the Body Politic*, Oxford University, New York, 1960, p. 18.

pleasure and pain, of utility and disutility, *constitute* resolution of conflict. Capitalists extend this private-world mechanism of balancing interests to encompass the public world of obligation and insist that the principles of market resolution of conflict (balance and compromise) must also apply to the public realm of tribunal deliberations over public policy. A market mentality is exhibited in a kind of "marketplace democracy"[3] as a result. Such is unacceptable to a participatory democrat.

With the Marxists, the ascendency of private interests and their dominion over public obligation is completed with capitalism. Here, reality is conflict; class conflict reflects economic realities. In the socialist stage, remnants of private interests are destroyed; public obligation is defined by the party elite. Conflict is resolved by enforcing obedience to the general will. In the communist stage, class conflict will have disappeared; new communist men and women will show no tension between private interest and public obligation. Private interest will have been deliberately eliminated from people's conditioning experience; public obligation is defined ideologically. Such is unacceptable to a participatory democrat.

With the fascists, conflict is the essence of the life struggle, in which the stronger (racially identified and therefore the more worthy) survive. Private interests are tolerated when no public question or policy is at issue or when no questioning of the leader's monopoly on coercive violence is involved. Conflict resolution means imposing invidiously grounded power against those who dissent. There is no public obligation except for unquestioning obedience to higher authority. No tension develops between private interest and public obligation because the former is everywhere understood to be subservient to the latter and because public obligation in the sense of deliberative and discretionary involvement in public questions is usually forbidden. Such is also unacceptable to a participatory democrat.

In the theory of participatory democracy, in contrast, the primacy of private interests and the market compromise of those interests over public obligation (as in capitalism) must be rejected. In addition, the authoritarian character of public obligation, with the absence of discretionary involvement and accompanying dignity for agent-actor citizens (as in Marxian socialism and fascism), must be rejected.

In the first place, to see compromise or conflict resolution as occurring in the market is to perceive all questions as matters of private interest; "public obligation" is reduced to protecting the market compromise and accommodation of private interests. But, as Tussman says, "governing ourselves is not doing what we want [e.g., satisfying private interests]; it is doing what we think best"[4] (e.g., accepting the public obligation to deliberate with others on the wisdom of public policy).

3. Ibid., pp. 104-21.
4. Ibid., p. 110.

Compromise is a sometime tactic; it is not a principle of conflict resolution. It is devoid of defensible or communicable normative content; it leaves unexamined the use of wants (expressed as private interests) as the standard of public worth.

In the second place, to perceive public obligation as a mere matter of obedience to authority is to deny wholly the possibility of self-rule, of self-imposition of rules, of self-government. Democrats accept the fact of private interests and public obligations; they acknowledge the probability of tension existing between them. Democrats *internalize* the tension between the two and seek that level of awareness and that measure of commitment to community which will prompt the agent-actor citizen where necessary to place his or her public obligation for deliberative participation in self-rule ahead of the satiation of his or her private interests. *Thus, in a participatory democracy, the public obligation is to obey*, not the general will or higher authority in the ideological sense, but *the commitment to involvement in pursuit of the public interest and the observance of democratically determined restraints.*

Participatory democrats proceed on the assumption that, with instructive conditions, a recognition will develop of the often necessary priority of a community and its continuity over transient wants and private interests. Most recognize that interdependence has proceeded to the point where crippled communities produce crippled individuals. Where no such recognition exists or where it cannot be created, democracy is impossible. That recognition is enhanced by experience, which shows that, because of its superior pertinence for problem-solving, democracy is in fact more efficient than other theories and models of the political process. But few have argued that it is inevitable or immortal. Experience suggests that democrats can be cautiously optimistic about resolution of the internal tension between private interest and public obligation, because communities operating democratically have demonstrated such resolution.

II.   CONDITIONS OF CONFLICT RESOLUTION

What is the situation, however, in which conflict develops among individuals and groups with regard to differing views of "what ought to be" or, in a *public* sense, "what one thinks best"? Conflict resolution in this context in a participatory democracy is more difficult. Here, clearly, democracies must evolve modes of operation (institutional mechanisms) which meet several specific conditions:

(1) Conflict must be resolved in ways which minimize destructive consequences on individuals' self-image, their sense of self-worth. Settlements should not demean, destroy dignity, or impair peoples' interest in subsequent participation. The point is not to destroy people or their deliberative capacities; the point is to settle differences with reference to issues and consequences, not to personalities.

(2) Conflict must be resolved in ways which enhance the community's understanding of its own problems. Resolutions should be instructive, educative, and restorative in their impact. Achieved settlements should reduce the probability of future conflict on those questions. If that is impossible, at least such settlements should reduce the dislocative and destructive consequences of the conflicts' reappearance.

(3) Conflict must be resolved in a way, if possible, which extends the options for resolution of subsequent and similar problems, which augments the range of questions subject to deliberative review, and which permits new judgments to be made about the significance and relevance of differences which arise, that is, a way which permits new priorities of public discourse to emerge and to dominate policy consideration.

III. STRUCTURES FOR RESOLVING CONFLICT

The development of an institutional structure to facilitate the resolution and adjudication of political conflict which meets the conditions just cited and which avoids the often undemocratic views of the ism-ideologists is no simple and transient matter. The imagination and creative potential of the most ardent participatory democrat will be sorely taxed. Fortunately, we are not compelled to start from ground zero. Pertinent historical and current experience is available on which to draw. For obvious reasons, we tap the American experience. Our interest is illustrative, not definitive:

First, the electoral process itself can be perhaps the most important vehicle for conflict resolution. In a participatory democracy, elections must be issue oriented; competing proposals for structural change must be offered by parties and candidates; access to media must be assured to all seeking elective office; campaign funding at all levels must become a public obligation to prevent private interests from masquerading as public benefactors; elective positions must be attractive enough to interest the able and the committed; opportunity to organize publics (constituencies) in support of candidates and parties must be assured; elitist control of candidates and parties must be precluded.

That these conditions exist only in part in the United States will be acknowledged by nearly everyone. On the one hand, campaigns have too frequently become personality contests run by advertising agencies; political parties have jousted each other for centrist positions minimizing differences and homogenizing proposals for institutional reform; media access is greater for candidates who will tap their own wealth. Potential character assassination, loss of privacy, and inadequate remuneration discourage potential candidates.

On the other hand, as we noted above, the McCarthy, Wallace, McGovern and Carter campaigns in the late 1960s and 1970s did demonstrate that it is still possible successfully to organize in part outside the regular party machinery. The Democratic Convention in Miami in 1972 demonstrated that traditional control of a party can be broken and a new coalition of publics created. Well over eighty per cent of the delegates had never attended a national political convention before. Quite clearly, the "reforms" introduced and contemplated for the Democratic Party after 1968 were generally intended to enhance participatory democracy as here set off. The rules for 1976, however, represented a partial return to more traditional patterns.

Second, public governments have in this century in the United States created institutional machinery to provide for conflict resolution in the economy. Statutory enactments of laws assuring industrial workers "the right to organize and to bargain collectively through representatives of their own choosing" in 1933 and 1935 were watershed judgments seeking legislative correction of industrial conflict—more, warfare —between organizing labor and organized management. The Labor-Management Relations Act of 1935 (Wagner Act) proscribed certain managerial tactics ("unfair labor practices") used to harass and disempower labor. The Labor-Management Relations Act of 1946 (Taft-Hartley Act) outlawed certain labor practices (e.g., secondary boycott) in order to constrain labor in its dealings with management. Collective bargaining, once authorized and established by this legislation, provides for negotiational resolution of labor-management disagreements, where each side enters negotiations with, and seeks therein to retain, substantive economic power with which to press demands and to counter pressure from the other side (strikes and lockouts, for example).

Even though judgments concerning the propriety of bargains struck must be made *independently* of the fact of reaching agreement, it is nonetheless the case that pounding walnut tables in paneled board rooms by labor and management representatives over contract terms is much to be preferred to pounding workers' heads on picket lines by those maintaining "law and order" on managements' terms. It is important to recall that well over a thousand collective-bargaining contracts are agreed to each year in the United States without serious disruption of lives or the economy.

Where collective bargaining fails to produce settlements, the labor acts permit third-party involvement through mediation and arbitration. Infrequently, when these measures also fail, a reluctant Congress may impose compulsory arbitration (as in the case of the railroads' effort to eliminate the jobs of railway firemen over the objection of the firemen's union), or a president may invite disputants to the Blair House across the street from the White House, where less formal "compulsory arbitration" will be pursued.

That collective-bargaining institutions may be unable to deal with issues the causes of which lie outside the discretion or jurisdiction of organized management and organized labor is commonly recognized. Examples would include conditions of general price inflation or technological displacement of an industry. That collective-bargaining agreements may not be compatible with the public interest (as in the case of "sweetheart contracts") is often acknowledged. However, the concept that compromise permeates the theory of collective bargaining, that it is an ethically relative concept, and that it is therefore normatively unacceptable is much less frequently agreed to.

It appears reasonable to assume that because the creation of existing collective-bargaining machinery occurred only under the aegis and leadership of public government, revisions needed to improve the machinery's conflict-resolving capacities and to move judgments from excessive concern with private interests of the contending parties to a greater concern with public obligations, will also have to await creative initiative from public governments. And the fact that collective-bargaining machinery, even with its admitted inadequacies, has not yet been made generally available to private and public employees at all levels is a measure of the dogged resistance of private and public governments to that modest amount of democratic participatory involvement which such machinery provides.

Third, legislative bodies in a participatory democracy should play a significant role in political-conflict resolution. Here, if anywhere, the distinction between private interests and public obligations, between deference to wants and reference to oughts, should be in view for all to see and to mark well. Here, if anywhere, the distinction between compromise as a principle and compromise as a tactic should also be evident.

The legislative role in political-conflict resolution arises from the legislature's nearly unique opportunity and responsibility to determine the form and timing of conflictual issues brought forward for consideration. Legislators, on their own and through the committees on which they serve, determine in large measure:

(1) which conflictual issues will be taken up for consideration (Shall the legislative agenda include consideration of an agency to conduct long-term national economic planning? Shall the Pentagon budget be cut by a quarter?);

(2) the scope and breadth of the conflictual issue to be considered (Shall tax reform deal with a handful of loopholes or with the inequities and infirmities of the federal tax structure at large?);

(3) the sorting out and aligning of interest blocs concerned with the conflictual issue (Who will favor; who will oppose? In a consideration, e.g., of a reduction in the military budget, will not segments of the armed forces, the pertinent parts of the armament industry, and the trade unions affected all seek to protect their particular programs from curtailment or cancellation?);

(4) the timing and scheduling of deliberation on conflictual issues in committees and on the floor of legislative bodies (Will not those who set the agendas of committee work, who schedule the hearings, who

compose the legislative calendars in fact decide whether and how particular issues will be considered?);

(5) the number and form of structural options which are to be given serious consideration. (In the conflict over poverty-relief measures, shall the negative income tax, the family-allowance plan, and others all be taken up? What attention, if any, shall be given to recommendations of the executive branch?);

(6) the choice among available options which could be enacted (In extending health care, shall the Kennedy plan, the AMA plan, the Nixon administration plan, or another be adopted?).

In sum, the legislative process is designedly a vehicle for political-conflict resolution. Indeed, a deliberative body can, in the absence of an executive veto, generally prescribe the terms of settlement of political conflict. Whether a legislature functions successfully in that role depends upon the ability of legislators to distinguish between private interest and public obligation. Conflict is resolved, at bottom, only by resolving the problems which set it in motion. Problem solving means serving the public interest noninvidiously; it means restoring effective, functional involvement through institutional adjustment. It does not mean catering to or balancing off private interests. A legislator's acceptance of his or her public obligation "is not doing what we want; it is doing what we think best." Where deliberative processes exhibit this public obligation, those who lose in a conflict only lose their claims to set the terms of settlement on *that* conflictual issue. They do not lose their standing as participants nor their rights to reframe their questions and purposes and to press them in new guise again. Affirmation of private interest, however, is no defense against public obligation. Only by pursuing the latter can "the war against the future" be ended and a meaningful community of "ungraded men" be created and sustained.

Fourth, and finally, in the American scheme of government, some contribution to the resolution of political conflict is made by the formal judicial system. To be sure, most of the attention of the adversary court system is devoted to resolving civil conflicts and to adjudicating criminal cases among and between the state, individual persons (warm blooded) and corporate "persons" (cold blooded). But the involvement of the judicial branch in the political process does occur, especially at the level of the Supreme Court.

Whether or not the Supreme Court should have *any* such involvement in a participatory democracy is a crucial matter. Clearly, in the American experience, the Supreme Court's role has been so significant as the ultimate authority in determining Constitutional questions, and its status in consequence has been so high, that few would consider curtailing its power or recommending its abandonment despite its anomalous position as an elitist institution.

In blunt fact, of course, the Supreme Court is a largely undemocratic institution. The capacity of the community at large routinely to hold the Court accountable is virtually nonexistent. John Roche is probably correct when he contends that the Supreme Court

> is a Platonic graft on the democratic process—a group of wise men insulated from the people . . . acting as institutional chaperones to insure that the sovereign populace and its elected representatives do not act unwisely.[5]

There is little doubt that the black-robed nine are seen by many as modern counterparts of philosopher kings. Conservatives and liberals separately damn the Court for decisions of which they disapprove, but (as President Roosevelt found out in the late 1930s) proposals for substantive changes in the structure or role of the Supreme Court are often met with derision and vigorous opposition. To that extent, the American community has been conditioned to regard the Court and its power as a part of their most basic vision of the American system. To that extent we cherish an undemocratic institution.

Given the Court's supremacy and its consequent authority to review legislative and executive decisions on Constitutional grounds, what contribution, good or ill, does it make to the settlement of political conflict? Three facets of the Court's operations merit comment here:

(1) The Court sometimes performs an oracular function.[6] There may indeed be some virtue in having an institution one of the purposes of which is to provide for philosophical, moral, and/or ideological articulation of issues before the community. In such articulation, assumptions may be set off, reasons given, conclusions drawn, and consequences predicted. This essentially educative role exposes the bases for and the implications of political conflict over issues. That contribution can be important.

From the participatory democrat's point of view, however, the oracular posture is presumptuous. The implementation of these philosophical, moral, and/or ideological views in judicial decisions produces consequences. If those consequences "sour"—are unfortunate, discriminatory, or mistaken—there is little recourse to those responsible. That the Court has been in error on many crucial issues is illustrated—with the aid of hindsight—by the fact that the Warren Court of the 1960s in its support of civil rights was in large part reversing discriminatory judgments made by earlier courts, such as the "separate but equal doctrine."[7] Other examples of errors in judgment: the Court's recourse to a laissez-faire ideology in deciding economic questions in the 1930s and its approval of the forceable relocation of Japanese in California in 1942.

(2) The Court sometimes performs a settlement function. Societies do need institutional arrangements which provisionally settle matters in

5. Quoted by Livingston and Thompson, *The Consent of the Governed*, (3rd ed.), op. cit., p. 461.

6. Ibid., pp. 464-72.

7. Ibid., p. 472.

conflict in the sense of rendering decisions which are then more or less immediately accepted as putting an end to *that* dispute. In principle, there is no particular reason why such decisive judgment might not reside with a legislative chamber. But in the American system, where brokerage politics can keep some conflicts from being aired at all and can delay decisions indefinitely, the Court operates as an institution of "final" settlement. Buck-passing *may* end; obfuscation *may* be circumvented; untoward delay *may* be overcome.

But the Supreme Court judges are political men also. Their decisions to hear cases or not, to schedule their hearings early or late in the term, to deal with a conflict as a Constitutional question or not are made with an eye on the political community. Finley Peter Dunne's Mr. Dooley suggests that the Supreme Court "follows the 'lection returns," and the humor derives from its probable truth.

(3) The Court sometimes performs a protective function. As argued above, a participatory democracy is possible only where the procedural affirmations of the First Amendment in particular and other pertinent amendments in general (e.g., Fifth and Fourteenth), or their equivalent counterparts, are comprehensively incorporated into and made a continuing part of the political process. The review function of the Court *may* operate to protect these procedural requirements and to extend their coverage (e.g., using the Fourteenth Amendment to extend the Bill of Rights to the states). [8]

But the Court "in its wisdom" may also restrict these affirmations by formulating a "clear and present danger" doctrine to put constraints on free speech, [9] by showing considerable ambivalence regarding what is symbolic speech and thus protected by the First Amendment, [10] and by narrowing its view on when freedom of assembly is to be protected. [11]

In short, the companion principles and institutions of judicial review and judicial supremacy are quite undemocratic on their face. The near total absence of accountability, of mechanisms for holding their oracular judgments responsible and responsive precludes any other conclusion.

In the United States, however, where veneration of the Court (not necessarily a particular bench of judges) is very high, efforts should continue to convert the Supreme Court into a reinforcing structure for participatory democracy. Some gains are made directly by exercising continuing hard-nosed vigilance in the Senate over Supreme Court appointments. The denial of approval to G. Harrold Carswell and Clement Haynsworth, thought by many to be ill qualified nominees of

8. Ibid., pp. 199-203.
9. Ibid., pp. 209-14.
10. Ibid., pp. 215-20.
11. Ibid., pp. 217-22.

the Nixon administration, were bitter struggles of a kind that can only with difficulty be repeated. Some gains are also made indirectly by public scrutiny and debate of the judgments rendered by the Court. But these will not suffice. Structural reform to establish accountability is required if the "Platonic graft" is to be accommodated to the democratic "trunk." Perhaps improved selection processes, shorter terms, and instating additional members on the Court are worthy of consideration. A counterargument is that this would convert the Court into a mini-legislature with accountability little improved.

A major hazard resides in the dislocative effects of any change in this venerated institution. These effects are not to be dismissed lightly, especially in a time when the community is already anxious and divided by inadequate efforts to cope with heavy pressures for change in areas of revolutionary unrest. Even so, a participatory democrat must have a firm notion of "which direction is forward" in this context as well. We cannot live as "members one of another" if nonaccountable elites are given ultimate discretion over important public questions. A participatory democrat would revamp the United States Supreme Court.

Chapter 13

OBLIGATION AND POLITICAL ACTION

In moments of crisis, the professionals often can't cope; or, given new perceptions of injury and injustice, they seem to be coping badly. Then the democratic system offers a standing invitation to the rest of us to enlist in political life, an invitation to commitment and participation.

MICHAEL WALZER*

The democrat turns his back resolutely on the temptation to divide men into pursuers of happiness and bearers of responsibility. He summons every man to his place in the public forum. To "life, liberty, and the pursuit of happiness" he adds the "dignity" which is found in sharing the colleagial life of the rulers of the human city. The threat to that conception of human dignity takes many forms. But none is more deadly than the temptation of the marketplace.

JOSEPH TUSSMAN**

*Michael Walzer, *Political Action*, Quadrangle Books, Chicago, 1971, p. 15.
**Joseph Tussman, *Obligation and the Body Politic*, Oxford University Press, 1960, p. 121.

The political function is continuous and developmental; political structure is discontinuous and replacemental. The foregoing exploration of the structuring of discretion in quest of participatory democracy elaborated this distinction between function (process) and structure (institutions). As Edmond Cahn observes,

> Unlike a man's body, the "body politic" cannot be conceived or generated once for all. Its destiny must depend on continual acts of new generation and new revelation.[1]

We noted some "new creation" of institutions to extend and enhance discretionary dignity of people generally in references to, for example, the extention of the franchise and the assurance of its practical availability, the development of research support agencies for legislators, and the continuing reform of the Democratic Party and its convention structure to make them more accessible to people previously excluded. We noted some "new revelation" concerning the meaning of participatory democracy in references to, for example, the educative, non-broker character of democratic leadership, the erosion of dependency on equational justice, and the recognition of the infirmities of compromise. Our provisional sketch of a theory of participatory democracy, however, has not so far focused upon the discretionary democrat—this agent-actor, participant-observer—the accuracy and adequacy of whose decisions and judgments ultimately determine the success or failure of experiments in self-rule. The citizen is the "ultimate decision maker" in a participatory democracy. As Joseph Tussman reaffirms for us,

> The essential feature of a democratic polity is its concern for the participation of the member in the process by which the community is governed. It goes beyond the insistence that politics or government be included among the careers open to talent. It gives to each citizen a public office, a place in the sovereign tribunal and, unless it is a sham, it places its destiny in the hands of that tribunal. Here is the ultimate decision-maker, the court of last appeal, the guardian of the guardians, government "by the people." The significance of democracy as an ideal rests on the significance of participation in the sovereign tribunal; *for the democrat, being tribunal-worthy is what being a rational animal means,* and the character we bring to the office of the citizen is the crucial test of culture.[2]

The "office of the citizen" is where political action occurs. The foregoing theories of political process and analyses of political structure can become guides to experience and political action only if the obligations and activities of men and women serving in that "office" are made to be

---

1. Edmond Cahn, *The Predicament of Democratic Man*, Dell Publishing Co., New York, 1961, p. 23.
2. Tussman, *Obligation and the Body Politic*, op. cit., pp. 105-06. (Emphasis added.)

compatible with the assumptions and characteristics of participatory democracy. Joseph Tussman rightly contends that,

> Democratic political life turns upon the office of the citizen and upon the demands of that office. The citizen is, in his political capacity, a public agent with all that that implies. He is asked public, not private questions: "Do we need more public schools?" not "Would I like to pay more taxes?". He must, in this capacity, be concerned with the public interest, not with his private goods. His communication must be colleagial, not manipulative. He must deliberate, not bargain. This is the program. And it is simply the application of tribunal manners to the electoral tribunal. Nothing is more certain than that the abandonment of this conception spells the doom of meaningful democracy.[3]

This "citizen . . . in his [or her] political capacity" must thus engage in some serious reflection on what participatory involvement means, on how to meet the demands of "the office of the citizen," on what being an agent-actor entails. Consider now three aspects of political commitment and obligation of the citizen. We pose them as questions:

(1) To whom and what is a citizen obligated?
(2) What is the extent and character of political obligation?
(3) What is the justification for political obligation?[4]

I.   CITIZEN OBLIGATIONS

The citizen has a life-long dual obligation as a member of a democratic polity—an obligation to one's community and an obligation to oneself.[5]

The obligation to one's community is implied in the affirmation that "we are members one of another." The citizen, as we noted earlier, is not, contrary to capitalist belief, primarily a hedonistic, egoistic, atomistic, and quietistic organism. Neither is the citizen the class-conditioned product of a Marxist system, nor the survival-bent, force-imposer of a fascist system. The citizen is a member of a *community* in which social, economic, and political activities are carried on by conjoint involvement of persons in communal and cooperative institutions. The "homogeneous globule of desire" is a fiction. The "self-made man" is a fiction. Orthodox economics' analogue of a self-sustaining Robinson Crusoe is a fiction. The "rugged individualist" of the American frontier is a fiction. The "great-man theory of history" is a fiction. Those who, in describing their work, make obsessive use of the first person singular— "*I* did this on my own," "*I* accomplished that," "By myself, *I* . . ."—are perpetrating fictions.

3. Ibid., p. 108.
4. Adapted from Hannah Pitkin, "Obligation and Consent—I," *The American Political Science Review*, Vol. 59, December, 1965, pp. 990-99.
5. See in this connection, E. Cahn, *The Predicament of Democratic Man*, op. cit., pp. 45-89, in which limits on the extent of moral obligation of a citizen are explained.

As members and residents in a community, people are constantly in interactive, interdependent relations with others to carry out tasks thought by some to have merit. From the moment a person draws the first breath, he or she relates to, depends upon, draws sustenance from others. People's personalities, identities, conceptions of their own character derive from that interaction. Surely there can be no argument here.

Accordingly, the continuing obligation of a citizen is to recognize that dependency and interdependency and, with that recognition, to participate as extensively as time, wit, energy, and resources will permit in helping to determine what a community shall perceive as purposes and how it will go about achieving those ends-in-view.

Abandoned here is the capitalist dualism and dichotomy between the individual and society. There is, as Tussman contends, an intra-individual tension between private interests and public obligation. But there is no acceptable bracketing of the individual vs. society in a participatory democracy. A democrat's basic obligation is to community —its creation and its continuity. That obligation is not contraindividual; such interactive involvement is the mechanism through which individuality, personality, and self-identity are created. Capacity for self-rule can only arise in a social context which encourages and provides the material means for the development of individual capacities to reason, to think, to relate, to reflect, to analyze, to invent, to create, to judge, to choose, to organize, and to love.

But the communal obligation of the citizen does not end here. He or she shares in the responsibility of attempting to bring those who see themselves as marginal persons (outside of the system) to a recognition that the political process can also be made to serve their goals and purposes in life, that they too can grow and benefit from participation as public citizens. Those who are alienated from the community, those to whose needs and purposes the community has not responded, those who have things done to them and for them but who are denied the right to do for themselves, those who have been deliberately or unknowingly injured (physically or mentally) by malicious and/or mistaken judgments of community leaders, those whose apathy dulls interest in the electoral process are "outsiders" and constitute some forty per cent of the adult American community. "The 40 [per cent] abstain because the present system will not entertain the alternatives that meet their needs."[6]

But people can be encouraged to move from being marginal members to being participating members of the community. Unless the political system can be made to respond to their communal needs—can respond to their defeats, their cynicism, their alienation, and their illnesses—their indifference will continue to blight their own lives and prospects, and the community will be the poorer—morally, politically,

6. John H. Schaar, "Insiders and Outsiders," *Steps*, Vol. I, No. 2, November, 1967, p. 6.

and materially—because of their disinterest. The citizen must face and respond to this cleavage between those inside and those outside the system. The cleavage can be resolved or reduced only where the agenda for government is rewritten. Unlike past practice, it will not do for the sixty per cent inside the system to rewrite the rules allegedly on behalf of the forty per cent outside the system. The forty per cent *themselves* must discover that they can in fact participate in ways to remake the system more in accord with their own sense of priority and pertinence.

Much of what in preceding pages has been discussed as revolutionary unrest arises from failures of the insiders to permit the system adequately to respond to the poverty of the outsiders, to the racism which ethnic members face, to the political hostility shown by established power-brokers when minimal political participation is permitted (e.g., in the Community Action Programs), and to the visual, moral, and physical blight and pollution associated with life in the inner-city ghettos and barrios.

Finally, the citizen is obligated to himself or herself. This public person has the continuing task of self-growth and self-development in order to become and remain "tribunal-worthy"—that is, to acquire the capacity to think critically and coherently and to communicate capably on public issues. This citizen must continuously develop his or her talents for reasoned reflection and coherent discourse to the end that his or her contribution to communal deliberations and to electoral processes will make a difference in the way the community perceives its problems and goes about seeking solutions.

Such self-development is advantaged in a participatory democracy because the question of individual worth as a human being is not at issue. It is settled. All persons are worthy! Democracy means non-invidious determination of public policy. To whatever degree an existing community treats people in a discriminatory manner such that individuals develop serious doubts about their own self-worth, to that degree that community is engaged in its own destruction. Whether the assault on human worth is grounded in ism-ideologies as analyzed above or in other undemocratic formulations, the effect is the same—the community is gravely crippled. And those who are engaged most aggressively in the crippling of others are engaged in an equally devastating assault on their own sense of their own self-worth. Demeaning the self-image of others to inflate one's own is transparently invidious—and fascistic. We really are "members one of another." As such assaulters create "outsiders" via discrimination and alienation, they destroy their own capacities to be participating decision makers, because once the shallowness and callousness of their judgments are observed, their credibility is dissipated. Invidious judgments increase tensions, generate unrest, magnify differences, abort consideration of alternatives, and becloud reasoned judgment concerning "which direction is forward." The obligation of the citizen is to strip one's own deliberative and judgmental activities of all invidiousness. One's capacity to deal with the distinction and tensions between one's own private interests and one's public obligation will be therewith materially improved.

II.   EXTENT OF POLITICAL OBLIGATIONS

Given the citizen's obligation to the community and to himself or herself for political participation, and the obligation to assist in bringing outsiders inside the system, or in extending the system to include the concerns of the outsiders, it will be helpful next to examine the scope of the citizen's obligation and a sampling of the roles which can be undertaken as a participatory democrat.

The question of the extent or scope of obligation is not difficult. As a general rule, the citizen will want to involve himself or herself as much as possible in the deliberative processes on public policy at all points where such policies significantly impinge upon his or her life and that of the larger community. Given limited time, energies, and resources, every citizen must, of course, often make very difficult judgments about which issues are critical and how one can most effectively bring one's capacities to bear on them.

With reference to the political process itself, this normally involves the citizen in pressure politics or electoral politics or both as a political activist. [7] The citizen's roles in electoral politics (choosing candidates and among candidates) are generally familiar. People become party and campaign organizers, fund raisers, precinct walkers, public speakers, coffee-klatch holders, media arrangers, voter registrars, election-day drivers, literature distributors, and voters. They may become campaign managers, expert policy advisors, appearance schedulers, speech writers, delegates to party conventions, and candidates.

The citizen's roles in pressure politics are also generally familiar. People become letter-writers, petition-circulators, "bird-doggers" at committee hearings, option-pushing visitors to legislators and executives, demonstrators, marchers, organizers of communities and publics, researchers of performance of officials, and cataloguers and publicizers of lobbyists' influence.

In all such roles, the intent is clear: to preserve and extend the reaches of participatory democracy, to achieve a system that is demonstrably responsive and responsible. So much is evident.

But the scope of political processes extends beyond these overtly governmental areas; so also, accordingly, does the obligation of the citizen. This is why the democratic form is frequently referred to (sometimes piously) as "a way of life." Indeed, it is! Public-policy formation

---

7. See Michael Walzer, *Political Action, A Practical Guide to Movement Politics*, Quadrangle Books, Chicago, 1971. Also, Donald K. Ross, *A Public Citizen's Action Manual*, Grossman Publishers, New York, 1973.

(in the broadest definition) occurs in other institutional complexes as well. We mention three such areas out of a much larger number that might be cited: the family, the school, and the enterprise.

A family is a microcosmic political unit. The structure and decision making within that unit, especially because of its strategic bearing on child raising, produces significant consequences well beyond that unit. The citizen's role in his and her own family is thus of more than casual interest.

Here, too, the argument is for noninvidious determination of the rules and arrangements which govern life in a family. The remarks in chapter 3 concerning "considerate parenthood" in personality formation will be found to be consistent with and supportive of the principle of noninvidious democratic participation. Indeed the thrust of those remarks is to describe an attitude and an approach to child rearing which will, among other things, assist the young to become reflective, self-confident, capable agent-actors willing and able to assume their obligations as public citizens.

In passing, it should be noted that such noninvidious determination of family rules is not in conflict with the fact that minority is and must remain a dependency status. The fact of parental authority over children is not at issue; the extent and character of that authority is. Considerate parents are not laissez-faire types; neither are they mechanical democrats (every member votes on every issue). The object is to rear children in a way which progressively removes parental authority coincident with the development and maturation of capacities for self-guidance, effectual choice, and social responsibility. Parental authority is used to make parental authority increasingly unnecessary.

In addition, the women's liberation movement of the late 1960s and 1970s advocates a rethinking of the family roles of men and women as husbands and wives. Clearly among the sources of disenchantment for women has been the traditional conception of marriage as a master-servant, superior-inferior relationship in which the wife is the subservient member. [8]

A school is a microcosmic political unit. Policies determined there, or by a governing board, define the nature of inquiry, apply theories of learning, specify curriculum, inculcate attitudes and beliefs concerning the social order, provide skill training, and the like. The citizen's role extends well beyond perfunctory involvement in a PTA or a vociferous protest at a school-board meeting against sex education in the schools or a tax override. The citizen's role includes a continuing concern to help organize publics to insure that schools *function* as microcosmic *participatory* institutions.

8. For example, see Simone de Beauvoir, *The Second Sex*, Bantam Books, New York, 1961, pp. 400-55.

John Dewey began early in this century[9] to argue for democracy in education. [10] His efforts and that of others generated the much-maligned but often ill-understood Progressive Education Movement of the 1930s. It constituted, in the hands of its more able practitioners, a "revolt against formalism" in instruction and an approach in which the learner took on significant responsibility for his own growth and development. That tradition, or variants of it, is reflected more recently in the writings of Harold Taylor, in which universities and colleges are encouraged to bring students into important policy-making responsibilities. [11] At the public-school level, the writings of William Glasser and Herbert R. Kohl suggest new ways in which the authoritarianism of the classroom, the suspension of curiosity, and lack of relevance of the curriculum can be reduced. [12] The conduct of the office of the citizen might well include, then, activities which help to move additional numbers of schools away from being enclaves of institutional racism, of psychic manipulation and oppression, of near-penal attitudes toward behavior, of nonpertinent instruction, to centers of vitality, hope, and learning. This will require courageous support for adequate funding, for neighborhood ethnic and income integration, for intellectual freedom for teachers, and for models of school operation which affirm the worth and dignity of students and teachers and demonstrate that affirmation by an eyeball-to-eyeball acceptance of a substantial role for students and teachers in policy making.

An enterprise, a place of work, is a microcosmic political unit. [13] Policies determined there stipulate the terms and conditions of employment—wages paid, fringe benefits available, pensions provided, safety procedures enforced, stability of employment connections, and the like.

We have already noted in another connection the respects in which collective bargaining brings representatives of workers organized in unions into negotiation with organized managements over the contractual terms and conditions of employment. A citizen will support such measures and extend them, so long as they show promise of providing workers with a substantive voice over the working rules which organize their work experience. But over the last several decades in the United States, the increasing size and bureaucratization of trade unions have frequently produced entrenched self-perpetuating leadership far

9. John Dewey, *Democracy in Education*, Macmillan, New York, 1916.

10. For a historical perspective, see Rush Welter, *Popular Education and Democratic Thought in America*, Columbia University, New York, 1962.

11. Harold Taylor, *Students Without Teachers*, op. cit., 1969.

12. William Glasser, *Schools Without Failure*, Harper and Row, New York, 1969, and Herbert R. Kohl, *The Open Classroom*, New York Review Book (Vintage), New York, 1969.

13. Work is a place where politics can be pursued as a "performing art." See H. S. Kariel, *The Promise of Politics*, op. cit., pp. 62-69.

removed from popular control of its members. Elites appear in trade-union circles even as they appear in public governments, large corporations, churches, and colleges.

Accordingly, a citizen's role at work may involve in addition either or both of the following: First, the citizen at work can take on the role of what Ralph Nader calls the "whistleblower." [14] That is, where a worker sees in his own organization a blatant pursuit of pecuniary gains or amassing of private power, or a substantial disregard of public obligation (e.g., racist or sexist hiring practices, pollution of streams, falsification of reports to public or government, production of adulterated or worthless goods, price gouging, demeaning personnel practices), he or she may feel compelled to "blow the whistle" on the enterprise, to "go public" and report his or her knowledge to the press, the appropriate regulatory agency, or other agencies of the government. If the "enterprise" were a public government agency, then of course the reporting would have to be to review agencies and/or the press and public. Such behavior certainly will tend to put one's job in jeopardy; the whistleblower may win few supporters among coworkers.

Perhaps, even more importantly, whistleblowing will confront the individual with a conflict of personal loyalties—inside associates and organization vs. outside community. The resolution of such conflicts is always difficult and highly personal. However, whistleblowing does represent a serious concern with the effects of policy on the community, and presumably a participatory democrat would approve. The community must find ways of protecting individuals who "blow the whistle" from economic reprisals including job severance. The point is not to encourage "rat finks" or to create martyrs; it is to encourage the disclosure of information, especially when it is obviously vital to the public's well-being.

Second, a citizen as a worker may undertake an equally difficult task—that of seeking with others a more fundamental revamping of a production unit to increase worker control over that enterprise. [15] Such "industrial democracy" has long been a goal of socialists of various persuasions. For a good part of this century such ideologists believed that the nationalization of industry would assure industrial democracy. Experience with such industry in Western Europe and elsewhere has not borne out the hope. Some scholars find the Yugoslav experiment with "decentralization and self-management" an interesting and promising attempt to establish worker control of individual plants in a context

14. Ralph Nader, Peter J. Petkas and Kate Blackwell (eds.), *Whistleblowing*, Grossman Publishers, New York, 1972.

15. See James Gillespie, "Toward Freedom in Work," in C. George Benello and Dimitrios Roussopoulos (eds.), *The Case for Participatory Democracy*, Viking Press, New York, 1971, pp. 73-94. See also Seymour Melman, *Decision-Making and Productivity*, Blackwell, Oxford, England, 1958.

where general political policy is not particularly democratic. [16] But the transplanting of institutional structure from culture to culture is even more hazardous than the transplanting of organs of the body between humans. Structure indigenously developed in one area normally will not thrive in another area where the culturally conditioned expectations are substantially different. Accordingly, systems of worker control pertinent for the United States will have to derive from and be compatible with the American experience.

III.   JUSTIFICATIONS FOR POLITICAL OBLIGATION

When a person contemplates the role of citizen in the community, becomes aware of his or her political obligations to the community and to himself or herself, and gains some notion of the sweep and character of that obligation, the query will probably arise: Why should I be obligated at all? Why must I obey authority? Why must I abide by rules even if they are determined through popular deliberative processes?

The last question is easily dispatched. Living in a community *means* abiding by the rules which give identity to that community and which pattern behavior in pursuit of human purposes and tasks. There really is no live option to abandon community generally or to live in the presence of others in the absence of rules. So much is obvious.

But the other questions do not have obvious answers. Above, in these pages, we have argued that the legitimacy of a government, and the rules it enforces, derives from that government's having been approved by those who live under its jurisdiction. The consent of the governed is required if legitimacy is to be accorded. It bears repeating here also that virtually all existing governments *purport* to rule by consent (with the possible exception of some fascists). This means that there really is a kind of world-wide acquiescence in this meaning of legitimacy. We here continue to affirm the contention that consent is the basis for legitimacy.

More precisely,

> The theorist founding political obligation in consent responds . . . in this way: you are obligated to obey if and only if you have consented. Thus your consent defines the limits of your obligation as well as the person or persons to whom it is owed. Legitimate authority is distinguished from mere coercive power precisely by the consent of those subject to it. And the justification for your obligation to obey is your own consent to it; because you have agreed, it is right for you to have an obligation. [17]

16. See, for example, Gerry Hunnius, "The Yugoslav System of Decentralization and Self-Management," in Bennello & Roussopoulos (eds.), ibid., pp. 141-77.
17. Hanna Pitkin, "Obligation and Consent—I," op. cit., p. 993.

The matter does not end there. Two conceptual difficulties arise: (a) Whose consent is to be taken into account? One's ancestors', one's own, or that of one's community? (b) How is consent to be shown? By overt act, by tacit acquiescence, or otherwise? [18] Clearly our understanding of the meaning and significance of political obligation hinges on resolving these difficulties or upon finding another way of perceiving consent and obligation.

First, from the point of view of a participatory democrat, the consent of ancestors probably can be dismissed as not binding in the obligatory sense. That would constitute a near-total deference to tradition and *as such* is not a persuasive reason for obligation.

Requiring the timely and continuous consent of the individual to establish obligation is also difficult to sustain. It would seem to gut the meaning of public obligation if on any issue or policy personal consent were withdrawn and obligation ended. In this case, presumably, an individual, without reference to prior commitments, communal needs, public consequences, or consistency, may cut away, may disobey, and no recourse could be justified. Obligation would become intermittent; it might appear or in fact be capricious.

Past consent of an individual as a basis for obligation seems no more adequate. Must past promises and commitments bind one for the whole of one's life? Do not changed circumstances and changed governments alter or end public obligation? We have defended a continuing obligation to community; can we defend a past promise to a government? Long-past consent would seem unduly to constrain and inhibit persons as agent-actors from deliberating on policy when that policy touches upon a fundamental revamping of governmental institutions.

Contemporary consent of one's fellow citizens as a basis for obligation of an individual puts that individual in a position where he or she may have to obey a majority of which he or she is not a member and which is not correct in his or her view. Would not this rule out the right to dissent from a majoritarian government which had become authoritarian? Is the obligation to obey a majority incurred without regard to the purposes being served?

Secondly, and finally, how is consent of an individual or a majority to be shown? Except for aliens, who take out papers and become citizens, most do not sign pledges or contract agreements which declare and record this consent. Neither is there evidence of social contracts being actually drawn up by persons living in a *pre*-governmental, that is, pre-civilized, state of existence. One might argue the case for consent having tacitly been given, but that seems to be a tenuous grounding for obligation.

18. In this and the following paragraphs we draw extensively on the work of Hanna Pitkin.

> . . . it appears to be extremely difficult to formulate a notion of tacit consent strong enough to create the required obligation, yet not so strong as to destroy the very substance and meaning of consent.[19]

In short, efforts to ground obligation in consent of the governed, where inquiry probes beyond the cliché, have become difficult and analytically unsatisfying, at least to a participatory democrat.

The formulation of a "doctrine of hypothetical consent" seems to offer elements of an alternative approach. According to this doctrine, the meaning and significance of consent really hinges upon "the nature of government" as a perceptive agent-actor views that government.

> . . . your obligation depends not on any actual act of consenting, past or present, by yourself or your fellow-citizens, but on the character of the government. If it is a good, just government doing what a government should, then you must obey it; if it is a tyrannical, unjust government trying to do what no government may, then you have no such obligation. Or to put it another way, your obligation depends not on whether you have consented but on whether the government is such that you *ought* to consent to it, whether its actions are in accord with the authority a hypothetical group of rational men in a hypothetical state of nature would have . . . to give to any government they were founding.[20]

When the question is put as to whether or not "you *ought* to consent to it" the agent-actor citizen must pose the normative question —the value question. Here the question of "Shall I obey?" becomes a question of "Is the government *worthy* of my commitment?" If it is worthy, I am obligated; if it is not worthy, I am not obligated. Obligation hinges, then, on the character of the government.

The "doctrine of hypothetical consent" would suggest that a government is worthy if "its actions are in accord with the authority a hypothetical group of rational men in a hypothetical state of nature would have to give to any government they were founding." Such a government, negatively speaking, must not be "unjust" or "tyrannical." Ambiguity remains, however, as to the substantive character or the distinguishing nontyrannical traits of such "authority" conferred by "a hypothetical group of rational men." Our citizen, without an applicable principle of *appraising* "authority," will not know whether one "ought to consent" or whether, for example, one should start a movement for radical reform. A reasonable inference at this point is that the idea of democracy itself might well function as the criterion of worth.

The consent of the governed is sustained as the test of legitimacy. Consent is not to be accorded on the basis of past or present promises or

---

19. Hanna Pitkin, "Obligation and Consent—I," op. cit., p. 994.
20. Hanna Pitkin, "Obligation and Consent—II," *The American Political Science Review*, Vol. 60, March, 1966, p. 39.

contracts individually or collectively assumed or conjectured. Consent is to be accorded and obligation incurred only where a government is *worthy* of such a commitment. We suspect that utilitarian ethics and tyrannical power will not serve as measures of worth. Democracy is implied as that standard in terms of which choices could be made, but no specific formulation of an alternative criterion by which to judge worthiness has yet been made. The following three chapters on social value and social goals are expressly addressed to that concern.

In sum, elements of a theory of participatory democracy have been sketched out in the foregoing five chapters. We have affirmed the capacity for self-rule of people generally. We have attested to their capacity for rational, deliberative reflection. We have insisted upon their educability. We have acknowledged their interest in participating in the formulation of rules which govern their lives. We have advocated placing ultimate discretion over public policy in the hands of people generally. We have detailed the political functions which are necessary to participatory democracy. We have provided examples of institutions which aid and abet and others which pervert or destroy the effective implementation of these political functions. We have suggested means for conflict resolution. We have examined aspects of political obligation the better to inform political action.

An analytical dilemma remains.

IV. POLITICAL ACTION AND FEDERALISM

In the previous section, entitled "Economy," we discussed at length a theory of an evolving, functional economy, and now we have just concluded an examination of a theory of a participatory, democratic polity. As perceptive readers may already have sensed, something of a dilemma emerges initially as an attempt is made to join or tie these two segments together into an evolutionary and normative theory of political economy.

On the one hand, much of the institutional structure of an evolving, functional economy may well continue to consist of large-scale, bureaucratic organizations: industrial corporations, many of which are multinationals; trade unions whose memberships are counted in the thousands; large government departments and agencies that have achieved considerable de facto autonomy of operations; financial institutions with discretion of considerable magnitude; and economic interest groups able to marshall many dollars for candidates and many letters to senators. Most such institutions, and those who run them, appear, and to some extent are, remote and out of reach.

On the other hand, a participatory democracy calls for individual participation in determining the rules and restraints (public and private) under which people collectively live. Individual participation for many will seem to be "small potatoes." How does a vote in an election or a caucus, a discussion or a protest statement at a hearing, or a week spent "pushin' doorbells" for a candidate have any significant bearing on what happens in the major institutional power systems—private and public—which organize much of our lives? Are we suggesting that chicks can make up and enforce the rules for playing (economic) games with elephants? How can we expect a democratic polity effectively to manage an evolving, functional economy? How do we relate the third section of this work to the second?

Two interrelated answers may be suggested. No one should suppose that implementing answers will be easy, but the following may suggest elements of a citizen's agenda for the near future: (a) Invigorate and democratize the political process. Continue vigorously to perfect mechanisms for holding *public* power wielders accountable. (b) Use political processes when and as necessary to hold *private* economic power to account to seek convergence of private policy judgments and the public interest. [21]

With reference to the first response, it is clear that private power can be effectively regulated by public authority only if the political system itself is renovated to increase the responsiveness and responsibility of political figures to the general public as their constituency. Holding political figures to account is as crucial as it is for polical power to hold private power to account.

The fact is, denigrations notwithstanding, that votes do matter; caucus participation does make a difference; participation in party-platform construction can be effectual; political organization through parties does determine which candidates emerge. Politicians do listen to constituents. If the earlier-mentioned reforms (especially, perhaps, the public funding of congressional and other campaigns) were operative, they should actually free political candidates from dependency on special-interest support and increase their obligation to and leadership for a general constituency.

As Dewey remarked, publics can be created; constituencies can be identified; new leadership can be found both from within existing party circles and from without. But success hinges on raising the levels of dedication to political involvement and activism. Increasing the citizens' degree of commitment to become, as Tussman suggested, "tribune-worthy" should be encouraged. But participation is not to be made contingent on formal schooling or status. A participating democracy's success is a function of communicating the conviction that self-governance is possible and that it is important to the lives of participants.

Implicit in the second response is the recognition that people cannot look to the natural laws of the market nor the historical laws of class conflict nor the laws of the survivalistic emergence of great leaders to

---

21. Fresh insights on the question of accountability will be found in Bruce L. R. Smith (ed.), *The New Political Economy: The Public Use of the Private Sector*, John Wiley & Sons, New York, 1975.

spare the community the continuing burden and obligation of refashioning its political economy. Also implicit is the recognition that the formulation and application of a principle of democratic federalism is required. Federalism connotes a division of function, structure, and authority among constituent political units.

For present purposes, that principle of federalism can be stated as follows: Political mechanisms to hold economic power to account must be commensurate in scope with, and must exceed the power and authority of, the institutional power systems whose judgments are at issue. Elephants must cope with elephants; chicks with chicks. This means that the public review of nonpublic decisions must occur at the level of inclusiveness where the power in fact resides and where the decisions' determinants are found to exist.

If one is concerned about garbage in the streets, inadequate zoning controls, or police protection in the parks, custom and common sense refer these to local governmental jurisdiction, and properly so. If one is concerned with monetary policy, control of inflation, or military defense, again, custom and common sense declare these to be national-level concerns. That problems sometimes exist at more than one level and require response at more than one level is obvious, for example, as in funding public education. Local, state, and federal jurisdictions are all currently involved. As causes of problems change, jurisdictions and functions must evolve accordingly.

But what are the appropriate jurisdictional areas regarding the price-setting powers of the steel or auto industry, the control of developmental technology for nonfossil fuels by oil companies, the jurisdictional struggles of major national unions, the setting and enforcement of environmental-protection standards, the protection and restoration of scenic and heritage areas, the protection of consumers from commercial fraud, the prevention of intimidation and abuse by public agencies, the preservation of personal privacy and First-Amendment guarantees from violations by public and private agencies? In these and other instances, the jurisdictional levels of regulatory authority, if needed, are not so obvious. Multilevel approaches may very well be needed.

But we would be less than candid if we failed to recognize that holding private economic power systems accountable will now typically require new and revised regulatory initiatives of the national government. It doesn't matter whether or not the situation was intended; the American economy is an integrated *national* economy. Most important economic policy is now and must continue to be made at the national level. There will be exceptions to this assertion; economic problems with determinants less inclusive should be dealt with through smaller political jurisdictions.

There appears to be, accordingly, a residual case for federalism—for the retention wherever possible of political interest and action in smaller jurisdictions. The extensive debates starting with *The Federalist*

Papers on the distinction between federal government (divided sovereignty) and national government (unitary sovereignty) are not necessarily passé. It might even be possible to take seriously (and cautiously) the conservative request to reduce the scale and size of national government. What these advocates normally fail, however, also to recommend is the corollary reduction in scale and size of private industrial governments. Federalism cannot survive easily in a context where private collectivism has already occurred. Ideological references to "free enterprise" and "competitive restraints" as descriptive of such private, concentrated, frequently national or international industrial governments are of course a smokescreen.[22] Private concentration of economic power appears to have been the chief saboteur of the credibility of the ideology of capitalism. The community should not be deterred by diversionary ideological references from gaining control over its own economic destiny.

Fundamental to the whole matter, however, is the recognition that the development of political mechanisms to hold political and economic power to democratic accounting will require constant inquiry and creative and normative institutional invention.

In the application of the principle of democratic federalism, a number of approaches to inquiry and policy may be suggested. The following are examples:

1. Public Information. Evidently, since the seventeenth-century judgments of English courts,[23] English law has affirmed that enterprises "affected with the public interest" may be regulated in the public interest. Effective regulation requires knowledge. The political economy must be operated in a goldfish bowl. Decisions that materially affect the public's economic and political welfare may not be kept secret by public or private institutions. Needed is a vigorous continuation of the pursuit of "freedom of information" legislation to open up governmental business to public purview. Needed also are rules which require the release of information about private-industrial-government operations and decisions. Even the federal government seems to have had difficulty in getting full disclosure of cost figures and other information from such industries as steel, drugs, autos, and petroleum in recent years.[24] As we noted above, choice without knowledge is a fraud. The bright sunlight of disclosure appears to have a salutory impact on behavior. The public

---

22. See Robert B. Seidman, "Contract Law, the Free Market, and State Intervention: A Jurisprudential Perspective," *Journal of Economic Issues*, Volume III, No. 4, December, 1973, pp. 553-75.

23. Munn v. Illinois (94 U.S. 113, 1876) in H. S. Commager, *Documents of American History*, II, 4th ed., Appleton-Century-Crofts, New York, 1948, p. 92.

24. For example, James Nathan Miller, "They're Giving Us Gas, All Right," *The New Republic*, February 12, 1977, pp. 15-17.

should not be denied the benefits of that impact. "Do not block the way of inquiry."

2. Public Penetration. One approach which has been suggested here and abroad and which is implemented occasionally is to place public representatives on private decision boards. Generally, this means putting public members on boards of directors and other directorates. It might mean placing such individuals in high- or middle-management levels, on executive boards of unions, cooperatives, interest groups, professional associations, or wherever substantive economic and political policy decisions are being made. The purpose served is not to legitimate private power centers or simply to provide a public representative voice in private decision making. The purpose, rather, is to provide a watchdog role to apprise public agencies of private performance and judgment and to recommend inquiry and public action as required. Public representatives might more frequently be placed in adjudicatory roles, as they were in the tripartite (labor, management, and public members) regulatory boards of World War II and the Korean conflict (OPA, WPB, etc.).

3. Public Parallelism. Parallelism applies the yardstick principle. Here, a public enterprise would be established as one of a few or several private corporate enterprises carrying out the function of making steel, autos, or tires; running a railroad or an airline; and the like. The purpose is to give the public government direct and continuing information on the adequacy and character of judgments made on prices, costs, mix of outputs, etc. in the industry paralleled. The purpose is not to supplant private with public enterprise to pursue some ideological goal. Rather, the point is to secure and release appraisals on performance not often otherwise available.

4. Public Planning. The American political economy is one of the few major systems without a national agency to engage in medium- and longer-term economic planning. Historic antipathy to the idea of planning is grounded in ideology-based apprehensions. Institutions of democratic economic planning can be created to conduct inquiry, collect and collate information, make specific recommendations concerning desired levels of employment, growth, price levels, and the like. No regular and effective mechanisms exist for making extended-period recommendations on the civilian-military product mix, the levels and character of public and private investment, rate of utilization of productive facilities, shifts in patterns of income distribution, problems in resource creation and allocation, [25] etc. We already have considerable planning experience

25. In this connection, see proposals of the National Commission on Supplies and Shortages, *Government and the Nation's Resources*, U.S. Government Printing Office, Washington, D.C., December, 1976; and National Commission on Supplies and Shortages, *Additional Views of Commissioner Weinberg on Indicative Planning*, U.S. Government Printing Office, Washington, D.C., December, 1976.

and structure for other purposes and in other political jurisdictions, as with county planning commissions which suggest policy on land use and state planning bodies which recommend on environmental protection, but national economic planning is still underdeveloped.

5. Public Regulation of Prices and Wages. In addition to an invigoration and renovation of existing independent regulatory commissions as an attempt to reverse the trend of commissions' becoming beholden to those allegedly regulated, there are other areas for exploration. If, as we suggested above, most important prices are already administered by private industrial governments, there is every reason seriously to consider the creation of a continuing long-term wage-and-price-control board to regulate those prices and wage settlements which demonstrably broadly affect the general level of prices and wages. Such selective wage-and-price controls can work effectively to restrain administered price inflation.

6. Public Financial Regulation. Such regulation might well extend beyond reform of the Fed and its controls to categories of interest rates, where differential rates might be associated with different categories of investment. Such controls would not affect the economy uniformly, however. Large corporate enterprises tend to be less affected by monetary policy than small or medium enterprises. First, large enterprises are able to finance much capital formation out of retained earnings. Second, as John Kenneth Galbraith long ago suggested, large enterprises have the power to administer prices and thus are able to pass on in higher prices whatever increases in costs they have from paying higher interest rates. [26] Accordingly, restrictive monetary policy, including higher interest rates, falls differentially and adversely on small and medium-sized firms. The tailoring of interest rates to encourage some kinds of investment in preference to others may, even so, be a useful regulatory device.

7. Public Tax Controls. The United States has not often used tax policy overtly and directly for the purpose of regulating economic behavior. The focus has been, rather, on revenue generation for public functions. Whether intended or not, even so, tax policy has often had a regulatory impact. But, assuming integrity in the administration of tax laws, there is no reason in principle for not using the power to tax more generally as the power to regulate on the public's behalf. It is now routine to try to manipulate the *level* of investment with tax writeoffs or rebates, and accelerated-depreciation allowances; extractive industries are sometimes accorded depletion allowances. Why should not public bodies participate more generally in the determination of the *character* of investment? Tax rates could vary with the kind of investment expenditure made. Might not investment in geriatric clinics and child-

26. John Kenneth Galbraith, "Administered Prices and Monetary-Fiscal Policy," in Lawrence Ritter (ed.), *Money and Economic Activity*, (3rd ed.), Houghton Mifflin, Boston, 1967, pp. 317ff.

care centers be encouraged and investment in dog tracks and casinos be discouraged, for example?

8. Public Experimentation. A very great deal of public-policy experimentation has been characteristic of the American experience. Wisconsin early in this century and California and Oregon in recent decades have, for example, served informally as laboratories of experimentation in economic and social policy. What is needed is a considerable expansion and invigoration of such efforts coupled with a greater measure of understanding and acceptance when experiments fail.

Public programs that fail—some public housing, community-action plans, welfare schemes, for example—get a bad press because they are and must be public and conspicuous. What we sometimes seem to forget is that there are also private failures. There remains an illusion that consequences of private failures are borne mainly by the immediate workers, the financial backers, owners, and managers. There are more, and often more significant, public consequences than these, of course. The larger community is adversely affected also. Any traveler in the American West who has viewed ghost towns or visitor to Europe and elsewhere who has witnessed the deterioration of community when the main industry in a town fails is aware of the employment, income, and personal costs paid by flawed private judgments.

Withall, what is suggested here is more experimentation and greater acceptance of a public responsibility to minimize the negative consequences on individuals when such experimental approaches sour or fail. Accordingly, subsidy programs to local and state governments and federal agencies to set up pilot programs to test theories and prove out adjustments before they are implemented on a larger scale are obviously recommended. Such experimentation should also include exploration of ways of increasing public accountability of those making economic decisions.

9. Public Rationalization. There are areas in which both public and private institutions function where the structural character is so complex and the level of overall performance so unsatisfactory that a fundamental overhaul under national aegis—a rationalization—of jurisdictions and institutions seems absolutely essential. Those areas already moving in this direction are medical care and welfare programs. In each instance, though not to the same degree, institutional innovations have been made on a piecemeal basis in the past in response to one or another momentary concern. The overall design, the removal of contradictory features, the erosion of bureaucratic power systems, and the like have not been major concerns. Environmental protection, energy-resource development, and control of pricing power would appear to be possible candidates for future rationalization.

10. Surrogate Citizenship. Finally, the difficulties of finding avenues for participatory citizenship in a world of remote and large-scale organizations have fostered the appearance of surrogate citizens—organizations that purport to represent citizens in settings and levels of

political action that may otherwise not be accessible. While no one supposes that Ralph Nader's Public Citizen group or John Gardner's Common Cause organization can take the place of activistic, direct involvement of individuals in the political process, these and other citizen-lobbies do perform valuable functions of disclosure, of providing reform proposals, of engaging representatives, and the like.

In this connection, we should remind ourselves that in no model of participatory democracy can any citizen be effectively involved in more than a very few public issues and/or political jurisdictions at any one time. People must choose where to use their limited time and energies as citizens. Organized surrogate-citizen lobbies offer one way of extending a citizen's influence.

That citizen-lobbies can have a salutory impact is reasonably well demonstrated in the last decade. Ralph Nader's activities as a consumer advocate have come to symbolize this surrogate citizenship. Under his aegis a large number of investigative studies have been completed concerning the performance of public and private institutions at mainly the state and national levels. His public appearances have provided opportunity for raising questions about the adequacy of private and public decision making. Common Cause has contributed evidently to efforts to reform election procedures. This kind of activity can usefully be expanded. The "bird-dogging" function, keeping an eye on public and private bodies framing and implementing policy, will absorb a very large number of persons in ways that are both publicly fruitful and personally rewarding.

In the foregoing, the issue is policy judgments—their character, their consequences, and their accountability. The making of judgments, choices, involves the application of criteria or value principles. Remaining in this study is one major area to which all of the analysis and discussion thus far have been pointing—that of social value and social goals.

How does one decide about the virtue of these proposals concerning federalism and economic regulation? How does one determine the worth of a government? we asked above. He does one decide "which direction is forward"? we asked earlier. How does one choose among alternative recommendations for ending inflation and poverty, ending elitism and political alienation, ending racism and sexism, and ending environmental pollution and degradation? How can one translate "we are members one of another" into some judgmental criterion that will permit citizens, as participants, to make judgments and therewith make a difference in their behavior and thus with their lives?

In addressing next the value problem directly—the problem of formulating and applying a warrantable criterion of judgment—and in discussing the corollary and derivative social goals of freedom, equality, and justice, we provide a provisional response to these questions.

VALUE
AND GOALS

Chapter 14

IS, OUGHT, AND UNDERBRUSH

. . . a rigorous adherence to the "fact-value dichotomy" renders intelligence cautious just where it must be bold, dumb where it should be articulate . . .
JOHN H. SCHAAR*

. . . to eliminate value judgments from the subject-matter of social science is to eliminate the subject itself . . .
JOAN ROBINSON**

What is positive depends on a prior determination of the normative.
SIDNEY S. ALEXANDER†

A public or social value system is essentially a logical necessity.
KENNETH J. ARROW‡

*John H. Schaar, "Some Ways of Thinking About Equality," *The Journal of Politics*, Vol. 26, 1964, p. 868.

**Joan Robinson, *Freedom and Necessity*, Vintage/Random House, New York, 1971, p. 122.

†Sidney S. Alexander, "Human Values and Economists' Values," in Sidney Hook, *Human Values and Economic Policy*, New York University, New York, 1967, p. 107.

‡Kenneth J. Arrow, "Public and Private Values," ibid., p. 10.

The continuing brooding, gnawing, consuming awareness of multi-faceted revolutionary unrest across the country and around the globe reflects a profound and comprehensive moral crisis. This moral crisis is manifested in atypical, sometimes threatening, behavior of people, in the way people view their common human condition, and, accordingly, in the way people perceive ideas of social value and social goals. This chapter and those which follow are addressed to this moral crisis and to the concepts of social value and of social goals—freedom, equality, justice—the violation or abandonment of which is thought to delineate the substance of that crisis.

Having observed the canyon-wide hiatus between ism-ideologists and evolutionary theorists on questions of knowledge, human nature, the economy, and the polity, no reader will be surprised to find a similar chasm in this realm of social value and social goals.

At the outset note that some of the dimensions of this moral crisis are not at all obscure:

No serious appraiser of the economic process is advocating that high inflation, malnutrition, abject poverty, or involuntary unemployment is a public good—what ought to be.

No serious contender for public office is publicly insisting that media opinion manipulation, credibility gaps in official pronouncements, de facto disenfranchisement, or elitist political control is a public good—what ought to be.

No outspoken representative of minorities or women is supporting continued exhibition of attitudes and actions of racial discrimination, male chauvinism, religious prejudice, or ancestry derogation as a public good—what ought to be.

No sensitive environmentalist is proposing that atmospheric pollution, water-course poisoning, disappearance of life forms, or resource squandering is a public good—what ought to be.

Each such condition, attitude, or action is an acknowledged moral outrage.

Revolutionary unrest is a product of moral outrage. Such unrest arises from a failure of people with discretion either to see the difference between "what is" and "what ought to be" in these (and other) areas of experience or, what is more likely, from an inability to formulate and apply relevant principles of social choice, to find ways of moving effectively from "what is" to "what ought to be." "The cost of revolutions must be charged up to those who have taken for their aim arrest of custom instead of its readjustment. . . . [to those] who having power refuse to use it for ameliorations."[1]

---

1. John Dewey, *Human Nature and Conduct*, Modern Library, New York, 1930, pp. 167-68.

I. "OUGHTS" OF ISMS

Ideologists are likely to have ready answers for both the faulty perception and the immobilized behavior. Each of the ism-ideologies contains a distinction between "is" and "ought"; each contains a principle of social value, and thus can offer guidance to believers in determining "which direction is forward" and how to get there. And given a value principle, each ideology is able to offer, in addition, derivative ideas concerning freedom, equality, and justice in response to the ancient quest in Western civilization for these corollary goals.

Consider briefly how the "what ought to be" questions are responded to by the ism-ideologies. What are their normative premises?

In the classical and neoclassical tradition in political economy and in the derivative capitalist ideology, the satisfaction of wants, notably consumer wants, has been and remains the basic criterion of judgment, the standard of value, the distinction between good and bad, proper and improper, and desirable and undesirable. *Utility*, the ability or capacity of goods and services to satisfy wants, has been and continues to be the value referent.

Utility is the meaning of capitalist value, and price is its measure. Prices paid are "objective" data which indicate and measure the "subjective" worth of what is acquired. Economists in their courses sometimes talk about maximizing "utils"—units of satisfaction—but students are reminded that since "utils" are imaginary (like Al Capp's Smoos), prices serve as surrogate indicators of value. Indeed, orthodoxy is often described simply as "price theory." Price represents real worth and hence is the main object of inquiry in mainstream analysis. The credibility of capitalism as an economic system hinges on its claims to efficiency in maximizing utility as value. As most students know, that system itself is often used as a criterion of choice. The competitive model is used as a normative standard. The closer behavior approximates the ideologically defined system, the *better off* we all are, we're told.

But, as Joan Robinson remarks,

> *Utility* is a metaphysical concept of impregnable circularity; *utility* is the quality in commodities that makes individuals want to buy them, and the fact that individuals want to buy commodities shows that they have utility.[2]

Since capitalist theory affirms that *all* behavior is to maximize utility, it cannot explain any *particular* behavior whatsoever; it cannot distinguish or discriminate among or between behaviors. The moral relativity of utility renders it impotent as a construct for inquiry. Orthodoxy does not and cannot distinguish among or between wants; it does not

---

2. Joan Robinson, *Economic Philosophy*, Aldine Publishing Co., Chicago, 1962, p. 47 (emphasis in original).

address the character of wants. For the ideology, one want is .as good or bad as another. Accordingly, the utility ideologists are ambivalent; their position is inapplicable. Orthodoxy contains no principle with which to make choices among alternative institutional arrangements and therefore is fatally flawed. [3]

For the Marxists, moral concerns are conspicuously primary. Marxists are endemic appraisers, judgers, and critics of what is. But their own social-value theory is not clearly set forth. Even so, it is possible to formulate and approximate their general position: The criterion of judgment—the principle of social value—for the Marxists appears to be "fulfillment of the Marxist design." The "Marxist design" is the deterministic historical sweep of succeeding modes of production and exchange. The "ought" is thus encompassed in the dialectically formulated Marxian theory of history.

Marxists are saying that you ought to do that (1) which, in general creates products through the use of nonalienated, unexploited proletarian labor; (2) which, under capitalism, intensifies the class struggle; (3) which, in the socialist phase, contributes to the appearance of socialist structure of public ownership, comprehensive planning, and the dictatorship of the proletariat; and (4) which, in the communist stage, ends alienation and creates an esthetically oriented society. The grand design of Marxism is fulfilled with the use of these criteria in their respective areas of applicability. The third and fourth versions represent, respectively, the normative use of the Marxist socialist and communist models.

The difficulties with this criterion and its components are many. We mention a few: The first, (1) above, tends in application to identify productive labor as an exclusive province of the proletariat. This class alone is identified with the forces of production; it has a monopoly on economic virtue. We see here again the invidious use of class membership in determining worth and value.

Furtherance of the class struggle, (2) above, sees the end as the demise of capitalism; any means are legitimate which serve that end. This divorcement of means and ends, as we explain later in this chapter, cannot be accepted. As the means are chosen, so are the ends determined. Finally, the normative use of ism models elevates *particular* structures into the role of criteria. One cannot rationally use a *structural* criterion to choose among alternative institutional *structures*. It is an exercise in reaffirming that with which you began.

For the fascists, who, as advocating ideologists, also wish to wrap their normative notions in attractive covers, there is an identifiable value principle. Behind fascist references to spiritual growth, ethical idealism, male virility, national aggrandizement, hero-worship, racial

3. See also, Melville J. Ulmer, "Human Values and Economic Science," *Journal of Economic Issues*, Vol. VIII, No. 2, June, 1974, pp. 255-66.

purity, historical reverence, and the like is a basic criterion of judgment. That principle is the acquisition and retention by an elite (or its leader) of total power, including the power to apply coercive violence to inferiors. The coercive hold on and invidious use of political, economic, and military power is the standard or principle of judgment for fascism. Basically it is simple: The fact of attaining power is a sufficient justification for its exercise.

Claims to morality shrink with reflection, however, into superficial immorality. The fascist position is an absolutist one; neither inquiry nor experience will induce revision by its practitioners. This is no appeal to reason; it is a "retreat from reason." Efforts to apply this criterion are often seen as the normative use of the fascist model. Reservations concerning this use of isms have already been noted.

With the underlying value premises which have just been discussed, ism-ideologies offer ready-made accounts of and solutions for the problems generating revolutionary unrest, the moral crises of our day:

Capitalists: A free competitive enterprise system produces goods and distributes income on the basis of economic worth or contribution of utility; poverty is a result of indolence. Government should minimize its interference with free competitive markets. Free markets provide for maximization of utility and equality of opportunity. Pollution is an externality.

Marxists: Capitalism generates poverty; it forces the proletariat to live in a condition of increasing misery. Government as superstructure is an instrument of oppression. Racism is a product of capitalism; racism ends with communism. Capitalist profit-mongers are indifferent to the environmental impact of their pursuit of gain.

Fascists: The economy must first serve the goals of the state and the leader. Those goals are to secure and to retain total power. Those who support the leader will live well. Democracies are impossible; the cry is "give us a leader." Race mixing is an abomination; Aryans are responsible for culture; male dominion is natural. Miscegenation is pollution; resource seizure assures growth.

But these proffered "explanations" and "solutions" and their counterparts are nearly everywhere irrelevant, incomplete, mistaken, or perverse. These maxims from yesterday's isms do not offer an adequate response to the contemporary moral crisis because the *normative* content of that crisis is nowhere made a sufficient object of scrutiny or inquiry. Each offers recommendations for moving from "is" to "ought," but their respective approaches preclude a warrantable and adequate consideration of how the "ought" is to be defined, of how the "public good" is to be identified, of what the "public interest" consists. None of the ism-ideologies seems able to provide a criterion of judgment for choosing among alternative policy options which is credible, which is not subject to major analytical or experiential criticism. Accordingly, the derivative concepts of freedom, equality, and justice are also seriously flawed. A fully adequate theory of value may indeed not yet be available, but a preliminary formulation is suggested below.

Admittedly, such an undertaking is presumptious; it may not succeed. But the quest is, in our view, critical. There is no more urgent conceptual problem on the frontier of economic and social inquiry. The tolerable quieting of revolutionary unrest, indeed the erosion of its *raison d'etre*, hangs on measurable success in the undertaking.

At the outset, it will be helpful to examine two sets of ideas which have made inquiry into social value, in particular, so very difficult. What follows immediately, then, is an exercise in underbrush clearing.

II.   POSITIVE-NORMATIVE DICHOTOMY

Although the insistence upon ethical aloofness, of avoiding the making of social value judgments, has characterized the work of major political economists for over a century, that aloofness is breaking down. Scholar-teachers have been forced to be relevant; they have had to respond to moral crises. In consequence, they have begun to bring questions of purposes, of what ought to be, of what structural changes would constitute reform, *within* the inquiry process. [4] And the "breaking down" has proceeded far enough for such scholarship to be of assistance to contemporary political activists seeking increasingly significant and generally nonviolent participatory involvement.

Even so, it is still the case that a perverse and historically crippling blockage continues to forestall much serious study of the social-value problem as it relates to economics and politics. That blockage is the largely uncritical acceptance even yet of the positive-normative dichotomy.

The basic dichotomy is simple enough. Posited is a construct which divides and divorces some kinds of inquiry, knowledge, and activities from other kinds (see figure 14-1). Separation is alleged to be complete between the positive and the normative, between matters of "is" and matters of "ought," between means and ends, between the study of

4. See, for example, Paul Streeten (ed.), *Value in Social Theory: A Selection of Essays on Methodology by Gunnar Myrdal*, Routledge and Kegan Paul, London, 1958; Clarence E. Ayres, *Toward a Reasonable Society*, University of Texas, Austin, 1961; Joan Robinson, *Economic Philosophy*, Aldine, Chicago, 1962; T. W. Hutchison, *"Positive" Economics and Policy Objectives*, George Allen & Unwin, London, 1964; Adolph Lowe, *On Economic Knowledge*, Harper & Row, New York, 1965; Sidney Hook (ed.), *Human Values and Economic Policy*, New York University, New York, 1967; Robert L. Heilbroner (ed.), *Economic Means and Social Ends*, Prentice-Hall, Englewood Cliffs, New Jersey, 1969; Gunnar Myrdal, *Objectivity in Social Research*, Random House (Pantheon), New York, 1969; Kenneth E. Boulding, *Economics As a Science*, McGraw-Hill, New York, 1970; Lewis Mumford, *The Pentagon of Power*, Harcourt, Brace & Jovanovich, New York, 1964, 1970; Benjamine Ward, *What's Wrong with Economics?*, Basic Books, New York, 1972; "Does Economics Ignore You," (6 essays), *Saturday Review*, January 22, 1972, pp. 33ff; Robert L. Heilbroner, "Economics as a Value-Free Science," *Social Research*, Spring 1973, pp. 129-43; E. Ray Canterbery, *The Making of Economics*, Wadsworth Publishing Co., Belmont, California, 1976.

IS	MIDDLE	OUGHT
MEANS		ENDS
SCIENCE		ART
FACT		VALUE
REAL		IDEAL
DESCRIPTION		PRESCRIPTION
ECONOMICS	MISSING	ETHICS
TRUE OR FALSE		GOOD OR BAD
MATTERS OF MIND		MATTERS OF HEART
EXPLANATION		EVALUATION
ANALYSIS		POLICY

Figure 14-1 Positive-Normative Dichotomy

science and that of art, between matters of the mind and matters of the heart, between questions of fact and questions of value, between that which is real and that which is ideal, between exercises in description and admonitions of prescription, between the disciplines of economics or politics and that of ethics, between the realm of the true or false and the realm of the good or bad.

This dichotomy, to repeat, is a divorcement of the one set of categories from the other. It is perceived as a missing-middle construct. Characteristics of the allegedly positive have virtually no common content with those of the normative; they are separated by divergent epistemologies. Not only are they different, each from the other; they are mutually exclusive. To affirm the one is to deny the significance of the other in that context. Or so it is claimed.

For example, Nassau Senior insists that "the political economist as such has nothing to do with any of the other physical or moral sciences or with any of the physical or moral arts."[5] John Stuart Mill argues that "Science is a collection of truths; art a body of rules, or directions for conduct."[6] Lionel Robbins affirms that "Economics deals with ascertainable facts; ethics with valuations and obligations . . . Between the generalizations of positive and normative studies there is a logical gulf fixed which no ingenuity can disguise and no juxtaposition in space or time bridge over."[7] Milton Friedman contends that "positive economics is in principle independent of any particular ethical position or normative judgments . . . it deals with 'what is,' not with 'what ought to be.'"[8]

5. Nassau Senior, *Industrial Efficiency and Social Economy*, S. Leon Levy (ed.), Henry Holt, New York, 1928, p. 13.

6. John Stuart Mill, *Essays on Some Unsettled Questions of Political Economy*, John W. Parker, London, 1954, p. 124.

7. Lord Robbins, *The Nature and Significance of Economic Science*, (2nd ed.), Macmillan and Company, London, 1952, p. 148.

8. Milton Friedman, *Essays in Positive Economics*, University of Chicago Press, Chicago, 1953, p. 4.

The positive-normative dichotomy can no longer be sustained for two major reasons:

First, if scholars and writers on political economy are to be significant, that is, are to have something constructive to say about the real problems facing the community, the positive-normative dichotomy must be ignored. Belief in this dichotomy is incompatible with the formulation of analysis to explain causal linkages. Such formulation derives its significance from its diagnostic role in problem solving. Affirmations of the dichotomy sound increasingly hollow. Students have observed that text writers who profess to "eschew value judgments" in an introductory chapter in support of descriptive analysis, often become, in later chapters, prescribers, advisors, and recommenders of policy on grounds that such policies are more rational, more efficient, more productive of more consumer satisfaction, or will "improve the workings of the price system."

Compare this claim to value avoidance

> Basic questions concerning right and wrong goals to be pursued cannot be settled by mere science as such. They belong in the realm of ethics and "value judgments." The citizenry must ultimately decide such issues. What the expert can do is point out the feasible alternatives and the true costs that may be involved in the different decisions. But still the mind must render to the heart that which is the heart's domain.[9]

. . . with this advocacy of "proper" policy:

> Is there no hope for limiting monopoly and oligopoly? Yes, there is.
>
> For one thing, . . . make sure that barriers to entry are kept to a minimum . . .
>
> For a second thing, [see that] government antitrust policy bears down hard on the slightest sign of collusion designed to keep prices firm and to control supply . . .
>
> For a third thing, some economicsts—such as George J. Stigler— would argue that large firms should be broken up into many small pieces...
>
> Government regulation and government antitrust laws are the principal weapons a mixed economy uses to improve the workings of the price system.[10]

Thus, the basic questions "concerning right and wrong" are not simply left to the citizenry. Paul Samuelson's positivistic economic science includes the *advocacy* of competitive institutions and solutions as being *better* than monopolistic or oligopolistic institutions or solutions on grounds of efficiency, utility maximization, and the like. In proposing policy to curtail monopoly and oligopoly, he is applying a value premise inherent in his positivistic science. Orthodoxy, it would appear, disclaimers notwithstanding, has heart as well as head.

9. Paul A. Samuelson, *Economics* (8th edition), McGraw-Hill, New York, 1970, p. 6.
10. Ibid., p. 498.

Such writers should not be too heavily criticized, however. Their inconsistency, though troublesome, does also reveal that, pretentions to positivism notwithstanding, such scholars *do* recognize in their recommendatory moments that the significance of their work is a function of its relevance for problem solving. They implicitly, if not explicitly, recognize that problems exist, that solutions as institutional adjustments are required, and that serious inquiry can be of instructive help to the community in its task of determining the propriety, worth, or wisdom of proposed changes. The foregoing does not, however, excuse Paul Samuelson's normative use of the competitive price system as the recommended criterion of judgment. The discussion does suggest that with increased recognition of the inherently advisory role of political economists, the defense of the positive-normative dichotomy may very well dissipate.

We say again, if inquiry is purposeful, it is value laden. And inquiry addressed to real problems is by common consent purposeful. [11] Problems stated incorporate a difference between "is" and "ought"; *no problem can be conceived or perceived except as value theory provides a distinction between "is" and "ought."* Thus, on grounds of significance the dichotomy between the positive and the normative must be disallowed. So much is elementary.

Second, the positive-normative dichotomy is logically flawed. Consider the means vs. ends dimension of the conceptual divorce. Many students are already aware that the missing-middle separation of economics and ethics, of means and ends, is a catechismal tenet of Establishment political economy. The positivist economist will say such things as, "Economics is a study of means, not ends," or "The ends are given by society; economists advise on suitable means to attain such ends," or "Economists explain consequences of using particular means to achieve given ends," or "Economics is the study of efficient allocation of scarce means among unlimited and alternative ends," or "Tell us what you want to achieve (what ought to be), and we will tell you how to get it" (but not whether or not you ought to get it).

In all such cases, means and ends represent different realms or orders of being and knowing. Analysis of means, allegedly, is possible through scientific, factual inquiry; analysis of ends is nonscientific, idealistic inquiry. [12] From the point of view of individuals or groups, means are discretionary; ends are nondiscretionary. Means are chosen; ends are given by society, Nature, or God. One realm or dimension is mutually exclusive of the other realm or dimension.

11. Hans Jonas, "Economic Knowledge and Critique of Goals," in Heilbroner (ed.), *Economic Means and Social Ends*, op. cit., pp. 67-87.
12. In this connection, see Charles K. Wilber and Jon D. Wisman, "The Chicago School: Positivism or Ideal Type," *Journal of Economic Issues*, Vol. IX, No. 4, December, 1975, pp. 665-79.

The trouble is, from the point of view of social and economic inquiry, the divorcement of means and ends is indefensible, non-applicable in fact to real problems, and delusive in its implications where application is attempted.

Look at it this way:

By common consent, inquiry purporting to be rational, and in later times, scientific, is concerned with explaining observable regularities of nature and experience in causal terms, for example, in terms of cause and effect. Over the years, we have moved beyond the confines of seeking "first causes" and of viewing cause-effect relations as singular (monocausal) and as necessarily linear. But we retain in modern inquiry the idea of explaining or accounting in "if-then" terms, for example, if this and this and this occur, then that and that will occur. Such is an if-then proposition.

Students learn early to distinguish between causation and correlation, recognizing that correlation does not explain, although it may suggest where to look for an explanation. Students also learn early that the captions of "cause" and "effect" are supplied by the inquirer and affixed to elements of the phenomena observed. Accordingly, what is "cause" and what is "effect" is designated as such by the inquirer where linkages of "if-then" are disclosed or where it can be asserted that "because of this, that occurred."

Such labeling clearly does not necessarily end with a singular cause-effect connection, however. What is an effect in a continuum becomes in turn a cause engendering still further effects. Accordingly, observed regularities are manifested as linked chains of multiple cause-and-effect connections. *Effects become causes of subsequent effects.* What is under examination is a process or a *continuum of causal linkages*, which for the inquirer's purposes (his or her normative concern or interest) are under scrutiny.

Now for "causes," read "means," and for "effects," read "consequences," (see figure 14-2). Means-consequence connections are synonymous with cause-effect relations. With a simple transposition of language, given the foregoing, it is clear that consequences become means to further consequences. Indeed, *the means chosen determine the consequences.*

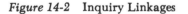

→ CAUSES ———→ EFFECTS (CAUSES) ———→ EFFECTS (CAUSES) ———→ETC. →

→ MEANS →CONSEQUENCES (MEANS) →CONSEQUENCES (MEANS) →ETC. →

→ MEANS ———→ ENDS (MEANS) ———→ ENDS (MEANS) ———→ ETC. →

→ MEANS → ENDS-IN-VIEW (MEANS) → ENDS-IN-VIEW (MEANS) → ETC. →

———→ — — — INQUIRY CONTINUUM ——→ — — — ——→ — — — ——→

Figure 14-2   Inquiry Linkages

No case of notable achievement can be cited in any field (save as a matter of sheer accident) in which the persons who brought about the end did not give loving care to the instruments and agencies of its production. The dependence of ends attained upon means employed is such that the statement just made reduces in fact to a tautology.[13]

Again, although the designation of what are "means" and "consequences" is a judgmental action reflecting inquiry purposes, the fact that means determine consequences and that those consequences constitute means which induce further consequences can scarcely be in dispute.

And now, finally, for "consequences," read "ends-in-view" (Dewey's phrase). Means are chosen to produce *particular* consequences; they determine those consequences. Since these ends-in-view are consequential and a part of the continuum or process under study, they are provisional and transitional; they are intermediary and instrumental; they are "temporal and relational." Here, then, following Dewey, we can distinguish between "ends" (or better, "Ends") and "ends-in-view." "Ends" may originate outside the inquiry process; they are not necessarily the product of inquiry; they are not affected or modified by inquiry. "Ends" are antecedently given, fixed, usually static, and not normally modified by experience or reflection on experience. Examples of Ends are the capitalist's pure competition, Marx's communism, and Hitler's "1000-year Reich." "Ends-in-view" are sought-after outcomes of human action; they are reflective of human purposes as inquiry and experience inform and modify such purposes. Says Dewey,

> . . . all "effects" are also "causes," or, stated more accurately, . . . nothing is *final* in the sense that it is not part of an ongoing stream of events. If this principle, with the accompanying discrediting of belief in objects that are ends but not means, is employed in dealing with distinctive human phenomena, it necessarily follows that the distinction between ends and means is temporal and relational. Every condition that has to be brought into existence in order to serve as means is, *in that connection*, an object of desire and an end-in-view, while the end actually reached is a means to future ends as well as a test of valuations previously made. Since the end attained is a condition of further existential occurrences, it must be appraised as a potential obstacle and potential resource. If the notion of some objects as ends-in-themselves were abandoned, not merely in words but in all practical implications, human beings would for the first time in history be in a position to frame ends-in-view and form desires on the basis of empirically grounded proposals of the temporal relations of events to one another.[14]

13. John Dewey, *Theory of Valuation*, University of Chicago Press, Chicago, 1939, p. 27. Copyright © 1939 by The University of Chicago. All rights reserved.
14. Ibid., p. 43.

The appraisal for which Dewey calls affirms the need for the perception and use of a principle of value with which to choose among ends-in-view or alternative consequences. In selecting some ends-in-view in preference to others, we apply and exhibit a criterion of judgment reflecting the purposiveness of inquiry. All purposeful inquiry is value laden, we have insisted.

But the foregoing analysis of a distinction between means and ends-in-view as an attribute of deliberative inquiry does not provide a value principle. It does not suggest which ends-in-view *ought* to be sought as consequences; it does not distinguish a "potential obstacle" from a "potential resource." The identity of an adequate value principle remains undisclosed so far. What the distinction does suggest is that the divorcement of means and ends, and the positive-normative distinction associated therewith, is logically flawed because it denies the provisional and processional character of inquiry and denies that human purposes can be conceived through the rational apprehension and analysis of human experience.

Most readers already understand perhaps the paramount infirmity of the means-ends divorcement: When people say "Use any means to achieve the end you want," most students recognize that this admonition reflects the means-ends divorcement, and they are prudently suspicious of its qualities as a maxim to guide conduct. The reason is clear: Use *any* means? Hardly. The suggestion is that morality applies to ends but not to means. Students correctly suspect that the matter of morality, if applied at all, must logically be applied to means as well as ends. Means determine consequences; means determine ends and ends-in-view. Immoral means will produce immoral consequences; immoral means produce immoral ends or ends-in-view.

Consider the following:

Doing things for and to the poverty-ridden (means) will not end destitution (end-in-view); it will perpetuate it. Increasing the volume of savings among the rich (means) will not "trickle down" as augmented incomes for the poor (end-in-view).

Fascist means will not produce democratic results; fascist means produce fascist consequences. A dictatorship of the proletariat does not produce the interest, capacity, or opportunity for self-rule. Official lying will not preserve a climate of mutual trust; it will destroy it.

Anti-Caucasian bias or female chauvinism will not help terminate the invidious use of race and sex differences; either of these biases will magnify it. Tokenistic support for "black capitalism" will not contribute materially to a reduction in black unemployment (which is typically twice that of whites).

Unenforced environmental protection legislation will not slow degradation of the environment; it will provide the illusion of action without the substance of structural reform. The auto industry created the demand for high-horsepower polluting engines; it did not merely respond to it.

The choosing of means is also the choosing of ends-in-view. Value theory (principles of morality) must be applied to each. Divorcement of means and ends does not resolve the value problem; it evades it. And, since people must make normative judgments, must choose among alternative means and ends-in-view, must apply some criterion of judgment, those adhering to the positive-normative dichotomy have not accepted responsibilities as professional scholars and teachers to assist the community with its normative, that is, its moral, judgments. The positive-normative dichotomy has been used as a device to divert inquiry from an extensive examination of the character of the moral crises of the age. But, since judgments must be made, criteria will be, and are being, applied. Are these criteria the object of inquiry in economics and political science? In recent decades, evidently, they have not been to the degree called for by the prevailing revolutionary unrest.

III.   ETHICAL RELATIVISM AND ETHICAL ABSOLUTISM

Ideologists and evolutionary political economists who work their way out of the entrapments of the positive-normative distinction may yet encounter a second formidable and entangling clump of conceptual underbrush—the dichotomy of ethical relativism and ethical absolutism. This blockage, too, can prevent the formulation or clarification of a perspective on social value and social goals which is relevant to the moral crises of the day.

Advocates of yesterday's isms find themselves on either side of this dichotomy: Capitalists are normally ethical relativists. Marxists and fascists are in different ways generally ethical absolutists. In anticipation of an argument developed below, evolutionary political economists will find it necessary to locate a third and different position from that of the ideologists. In any case, the dichotomy of ethical relativism and ethical absolutism, while no newcomer to social inquiry and debate, generates a stunting and arresting impact on the effort to think clearly about "which direction is forward."

At the outset, it is important to recognize that relativists and absolutists alike, tacitly or expressly, assume that value judgments will be made. Operationally they are all normativists; the ethical (moral) question of "what ought" is acknowledged as both legitimate and significant. The dichotomy arises from their differing conceptions of what kind of a normative principle may be used.

Ethical relativists insist that all values and all criteria of judgment are relative to the individuals who express them or to the culture from which they emerge and which espouses them. Ethical relativists see a vast divergency among peoples and cultures with regard to human purposes and social goals. Patterns of thought and behavior are so diverse, so lacking is cross-cultural commonality, that it is thought to be presumptuous for any person, a product of a particular culture, to judge his or her counterpart from a different culture. Values are relative to the sponsoring culture. Ethical relativists *defer* to the tastes, habits, customs, mores, and folkways of people and affirm that ideas or principles of morality, of value, are particular and unique, not general and comprehensive.

Ethical relativists develop a pan-cultural tolerance; they attempt to avoid imposing their ethical principles and standards on others. (Few religious missionaries, it appears, have been practicing ethical relativists.) They would express normative ambivalence to the expression that "pushpin [a child's game] is as good as poetry," that beer is as good as Bach, or that deer hunting and head hunting are merely culturally divergent ways of demonstrating prowess.

Ethical relativists as anthropologists are cataloguers of divergent customs; as economists, they are ethically indifferent to the character of people's wants.

> So far as we are concerned our economic subjects can be pure egoists, pure altruists, pure ascetics, pure sensualists . . . Our deductions do not provide any justification for saying that caviar is an economic good and carrion a disutility. . . . Individual valuations : . . are outside the sphere of economic uniformity . . . from the point of view of economic analysis these things constitute the irrational elements in our universe of discourse.[15]

As political scientists, ethical relativists are pluralists; as sociologists, they are pushers of the "situational ethic," that is, each situation may call for the application of a discrete ethical principle.

Ethical relativists do see the need for ethical judgments, for social-value principles, but their response is, "To each his own [values]," then, "Who can say naught agin' him."

Ethical absolutists, on the other hand, will buy none of this proffered cultural and ethical relativism. They, in differing ways, profess to see ethical principles which transcend existing culturally conditioned views both temporally and spatially. Ethical absolutists differ dramatically with one another, however, concerning the identification and source of these inclusive and continuing absolutists principles of morality and value.

Some profess to see cross-cultural universals in thought and behavior. These ethical absolutists advocate particular criteria as having validity because of this universality. Behaviors affirmed and recom-

---

15. Lionel Robbins, *An Essay on the Nature and Significance of Economic Science*, op. cit., p. 106. Quoted by Walter A. Weisskopf, *The Psychology of Economics*, University of Chicago, Chicago, 1955, p. 248.

mended because of this alleged commonality might include recourse to market price systems, affection for children, reverence for the dead, or the aggressive quest for power over others. However, the margin between such contentions as these and ethnocentrism (a habitual disposition to judge others by one's own cultural or ethnic standards) is small indeed. Elevation and projection of one's own mores and folkways, acquired tastes, wants, and preferences into a criterion of judgment is most difficult to avoid. The probable inadvertent drift of an ethical relativist into the role of an ethical absolutist via the route of ethnocentrism will already have occurred to many students.

Other absolutists profess to find ethical absolutes in metaphysical forces or phenomena. Such *outside*-human-experience sources of idealistic absolutes include deference to an all-encompassing Reason, an all-knowing God, or an omnipresent Nature. Here, the appeal of ethical absolutists is an appeal to faith—to a belief in nondemonstrable realms of being and power, and to a state or condition of mind which is often intrinsically introspective, deferential, intuitive, and submissive. The contents of such a faith may well be virtually noncommunicable.

Still others profess to find ethical absolutes *within* the realm of human experience, yet *outside* the domain or control of particular persons. Pan-temporal and pan-cultural insistence upon blood lines and race as an index of worth, the furtherance of "the law of motion of society" embodying class conflict, the affirmation of sex differences as an index of capacity, the deference to age as the source of communal wisdom are examples of ethical absolutes for which demonstrability may be claimed.

Whatever the source of the ethical absolute, however, all such positions share a common abhorrence of ethical relativism. Each absolutist is supremely confident of the ethical adequacy of his or her position and may well be prepared to extend its hegemony where opportunity permits or force ensures.

Regrettably, for purposes of fashioning a defensible and applicable criterion of judgment for economic and political policy making, an evolutionary theorist is not likely to find guidance or solace with ethical relativism or ethical absolutism. He or she will reject each (and the dichotomy of the two) because they are too confining, of doubtful relevance, and insufficiently demonstrable to serve as sources of social-value theory. [16]

16. Note, however, that this does not imply necessarily a rejection of these views in other contexts and for other purposes. Neither is it to be understood as an attack on the fact of belief as such nor on the integrity and wisdom of those holding ethically relative or ethically absolute views.

This analysis is addressed to the formulation of a principle of judgment of public policy which does not uniquely rest upon constructs of either ethical relativism or ethical absolutism. It is hoped therewith to avoid the sterility of relativism when arguments reduce to "about tastes there is no disputin'" and the futility of absolutism

An evolutionary theorist rejects ethical relativism for its professed ambivalence regarding behavior and criteria for judging behavior. Customs and criteria do, of course, vary widely, but the fact of that variation does not preclude consideration of their merit when applied to or incorporated into experience.

Everywhere people make value judgments. Those judgments produce consequences. Such consequences are in principle examinable. Examination permits reflection on the character of the consequences and upon their bearing on future events. Such reflection will almost inescapably involve application of criteria which define pertinence and which permit appraisal of such consequences. Appraisers are not likely to be ambivalent about consequences. And when those doing the appraising have discretion over policy and are thus able to reorder the rules following such an appraisal, there will be even less ambivalence regarding consequences. There will be little deference shown to belief and custom merely because it is habitual and commonplace. Evolutionary political economists cannot accept ethically relative criteria because to do so would place them in the position of having to use what is (existing custom and belief) as a standard or criterion in judging what ought to be. The effect is a circular reaffirmation and reinforcement of the status quo! That would be acceptable *only* in the unlikely event that the status quo were in no sense problematic or troublesome, if there were no revolutionary unrest. And the test of what is "problematic" and why it is problematic must necessarily arise from outside settled convention and habit, that is, from outside ethically relative criteria.

Evolutionary political economists must reject the other half of the dichotomy, ethical absolutism, as well. The primary appeal to faith in lieu of an appeal to reason will have little attraction. Being asked to accept value principles on grounds which are not amenable to scrutiny, which do not include appraisal of experience, which have little or no evidential base (and for which in principle none could be generated), and/or which dampen rather than encourage reflective capacities and the exercise of judgment is unacceptable.

Indeed, whether the source of the ethical absolute is cultural commonalities, metaphysical forces, or deterministic social phenomena makes little difference. Each source denies discretion over principles of discretion. Each denies a choice over principles of choice. There is no evolution of insight contemplated; there is no growth in understanding;

reflected in reciprocal efforts to convert others to our own articles of faith.

That some readers will find commonality, corollaries, or parallels between the value principle developed below and that of those who regard themselves as relativists or absolutists is not to be denied. There are, after all, Utilitarian, Marxian, Christian, Moslem, Hebraic, and other approaches to perceiving human dignity and to defining the good, the true, and the beautiful. Divergent routes may sometimes converge.

no movement among or refinement of value principles in consequence of experience, or of inquiry and reflection.

Ethical absolutists are not on the way; they have already arrived. Evolutionary theorists are always enroute; their destination is always provisional and intermediary; their destinations or arrivals are departure points for further reflective travels.

A criterion of judgment must be sought elsewhere than in the either-or boxes of the relativists and the absolutists. The ambivalence of the former and the certitude of the latter are in differing ways crippling.[17]

What is required is a criterion of judgment which draws on and is reflective of experience, which recognizes the fact that life is a process, which acknowledges that the human animal is both a product and producer of culture, which is a continuously refined product of reasoned reflection, which clearly distinguishes "what is" from "what ought to be," and which is demonstrably applicable to the problems which generate, in our day, areas of revolutionary unrest. Neither relativists nor absolutists offer criteria with which to cope with poverty, elitism, racism and sexism, and pollution.

An alternative criterion is given provisional formulation in the following chapter. With this formulation, we can then address the corollary and derivative questions concerning the social goals of freedom, equality, and justice.

17. On these and related matters, see Rick Tilman, "Value Theory, Planning, and Reform: Ayres as Incrementalist and Utopian," *Journal of Economic Issues*, Vol. VIII, No. 4, December, 1974, pp. 689-706.

Chapter 15

VALUE AND ITS COROLLARIES

A *"disinterested" social science has never existed and never will exist. For logical reasons, it is impossible. A view presupposes a viewpoint. Research . . . must have a direction. The viewpoint and the direction are determined by our interest in a matter. Valuations enter into the choice of approach, the selection of problems, the definition of concepts, and the gathering of data . . .*

GUNNAR MYRDAL*

A *value premise should not be chosen arbitrarily: it must be relevant and significant in relation to the society in which we live. It can, therefore, only be ascertained by an examination of what people actually desire. People's desires are to some extent regularly founded on erroneous beliefs about facts and causal relations. To that extent a corrected value premise—corresponding to what people would desire if their knowledge about the world around them were more perfect—can be construed and has relevance.*

GUNNAR MYRDAL**

---

*Gunnar Myrdal, *Asian Drama I*, Pantheon/Random House, New York, 1968, p. 32.

**Gunnar Myrdal, *An International Economy*, Harper & Brothers, New York, 1956, p. 336.

Throughout this work, with occasional exceptions, we have been suggesting that yesterday's isms are not pertinent enough for use in contemporary problem solving. Ideological recommendations for coping with dimensions of revolutionary unrest are derived from social philosophies which are in varying ways inappropriate to the task. In some instances, recourse to ideology seems to exacerbate rather than moderate or remove the causes of unrest.

We have attempted in each major area of political economy and social philosophy so far examined to provide an alternative position to that of the belief systems of capitalism, Marxism, and fascism. We have called this alternative "a normative and evolutionary theory of political economy."

Absolutely at the core of this, or any, perspective on political economy, is the theory of social value and the formulation of social goals. We here reject the capitalist value theory of utility, the Marxist value theory of fulfillment of the Marxist design, and the fascist value theory of power and its invidious defense. We must also reject, as will be evident below, the corollary views of freedom, equality, and justice derived therefrom.

What sets off the following formulation of instrumental-value theory from the social-value theory of other belief systems is that it is derived exclusively from the experience continuum of people and that it articulates what often has historically been meant by progress, reform, or betterment. This "new" principle will be seen by some as an old principle, restated.

The following value theory is different in kind; it is a product of inquiry; it may be modified or replaced by subsequent inquiry. It is not an unexamined postulate to be asserted; it is a distilled principle which has given and will give direction to conduct. It does not draw on or defer to idealistic views of what ought to be, but it may generate recommendations for changes in structure or performance similar to recommendations emerging from other belief systems (humanism, Christianity, neo-Marxism).

The formulation here is thus provisional and exploratory. The nature of scholarly inquiry is not to settle matters "once and for all," but to create and to open new doors of insight into settled conventions and habitual views of economic and political "ills." Inquiry into value principles must move to center stage.

I. SOCIAL VALUE IDENTIFIED

Throughout the foregoing, we have repeatedly asked "which direction is forward" in a societal setting in which protracted problems seem not to yield to ism-ideology answers. We posed therewith the problem of choice and inevitably the problem of criteria of choice. We have now arrived at a point at which we can (1) provisionally advance a nonideological principle of social value, (2) offer some account of its explicit and implicit elements and referential content, and (3) draw distinctions and contrasts with other value principles. We then suggest in the following part of the chapter some corollary concepts of the instrumental value principle and representative applications to areas of contemporary revolutionary unrest.

(1) We now affirm that that direction is forward which provides for *the continuity of human life and the noninvidious re-creation of community through the instrumental use of knowledge.* [1] We consider the foregoing to be a criterion of judgment, a social-value principle, which is general in its relevance to the universe of the social process, to the functional components of that process (economy, polity), and to choices among institutional forms which organize that process. We suggest further that the resolution of political and economic problems in particular (in the sense in which "resolution" can be held to have rational meaning) probably requires the use of this criterion in lieu of other proffered theories of value. We remind ourselves that the only serious grounds on which political economists for centuries have claimed significance for their work have been its alleged relevance to the resolution of real problems facing real people in real political economies. We respectfully acknowledge and join that tradition.

(2) Consider now some explicit and implicit elements of this instrumental principle of social (economic and political) value. *Explicit* aspects include the following:

"Continuity": The whole of the human experience is with process, the social process. There is no human history except of evolutionary movement of human organisms and of the culture such persons create and preserve. "Continuity" in the value premise is grounded in this fact and asserts the obvious as an "ought"—that the continuance of human life is a precondition for the pursuit of all earthly concerns including the creation and use of all social and value theory. As Sidney S. Alexander has observed, "effectiveness is the first virtue [of social institutions]. The social system must work, it must permit at least the physical survival of the society. The evolutionary, if not the moral, priority of effectiveness . . . is illustrated in the history of mankind." [2]

Providing for continuity implies, beyond the obvious, an awareness of conditions which positively foster human life, indeed which reflect a

---

1. Adapted from J. Fagg Foster, "The Relation between the Theory of Value and Economic Analysis," (mimeographed), University of Denver, (no date), and "Current Structure and Future Prospects of Institutional Economics," (mimeographed), University of Denver, 1975. Modified versions of the next few pages appear in my article, "A Social Value Theory in Neoinstitutional Economics," *Journal of Economic Issues*, Vol. XI, No. 4, December, 1977, pp. 823-46, and in my article, "Constructs of Value, Freedom and Equality in Institutional Economics," *The Social Science Journal*, Vol. XV, No. 1, January, 1978, pp. 27-38.

2. Sidney S. Alexander, "Social Evaluation through Notional Choice," *Quarterly Journal of Economics*, Vol. 88, No. 4, November, 1974, p. 605.

this-worldly reverence for human life. Included is a deference to human potential and developmental capabilities. The social process is the locus of value;[3] it does not define social value. Asserting continuity of the social process is nevertheless critical, if commonplace.

Reflect again on the debates upon and the implications of the Cuban missile crisis in the early 1960s, when the game of missile "chicken" was played almost to "the point of no return." Think again about the consequences of bringing an economy virtually to a halt with an uncontrolled inflation (Germany, China) or the reoccurrence of a Great Depression. Reflect further on the energy crisis and the food crisis of the 1970s and the prospects for the 1980s and beyond. Consider the hazards and implications if the nuclear club expands to include twenty or thirty or forty nations, many of which are nursing ancient and current manic grievances. Because of the global interdependency of our time, destruction of one community will necessarily have destructive effects on many other communities. Value theory must take cognizance of that fact.

"Re-creation of community": Here the intent is to make very clear that human life is feasible only in the context of culture. "We are members one of another" in a community in which institutions pattern (prescribe and proscribe) our lives. Re-creating community means reconstituting the structural fabric of that social order to provide for continuity by utilizing effectively the stock of human wit and wisdom. Since all people already reside in community, the task is to re-create. No human starts from ground zero socially or culturally; individuals are born into communities which are going concerns with language, custom, and order already affirmed in some definitive form.

Implied also is that this criterion is intended for use in choosing among and between institutional forms. Which prescriptions are now understood to be obsolete in view of current knowledge? Which patterns of correlated behavior have abandoned their original instrumental functions and have become vehicles for the retention of status or the exercise of power? Does not the negative connotation of *bureaucracy* derive from this circumstance?

Thus, "re-creation of community" delimits the universe of applicability of this instrumental value principle to the realm (mainly) of *social* choice. Under review here is a principle of social value. We are concerned with the character of the community and the impact it makes upon the lives of its constituent members. The principle may be found also to have relevance as a criterion in judging personal or individual conduct, but that is not our central concern at this point.

"Noninvidious": This term speaks to the character of community just mentioned. Recall, Veblen used the term *invidious* (as we have been

3. See Clarence E. Ayres, *The Theory of Economic Progress*, University of North Carolina Press, Chapel Hill, 1944, chapter 10.

doing elsewhere in these pages) to refer to "a comparison of persons with a view to rating and grading them in respect of relative worth or value. . . . An invidious comparison is a process of valuation of persons in respect of worth."[4] We at various points have remarked about the invidious use of race, sex, ethnicity, color, wealth, ownership, rank, age, power, etc., in one or another of yesterday's isms. Here we are saying that the invidious use of any distinction is to be avoided in the application of reliable knowledge to the re-creation of community to assure continuity. Here the inherent potential and worth of every human being is affirmed. We are confirming the fact of human reason and the fact of the historic concern for continuity and community as elements in an alternative value principle.

Although definitions of what is evil vary over time and place, evil persons are not usually celebrated or revered. They may be feared or despised. Evil men act invidiously, denying worth, judging capriciously, destroying life, threatening economic livelihood, or waging war. In recent decades, only the fascists have celebrated warfare as an ennobling human experience. We recognize the world-wide propensity, when warfare or street violence evolves from whatever cause, to dehumanize the "enemy" with invidiously conceived epithets of "gook," "Jap," "gringo," "nigger," "honky," "wog," "Kraut," and the like, in order to make it easier to use physical violence against such persons. This dehumanization is incompatible with the value principle here advanced.

Noninvidiousness permits qualitative judgments. Does a proposed structural change enhance dignity and a sense of self-worth of individuals[5] or does it erode or destroy by denigration and discrimination? Where the latter occurs, the opportunities for instrumental involvement of such persons are seriously curtailed or eliminated. Their capacity to help re-create community is impaired. We return to this point below.

"The instrumental use of knowledge": This phrase is intended to incorporate the idea that knowledge which is reliable is instrumental to

4. Veblen, *Theory of the Leisure Class*, op. cit., p. 34.

5. *Dignity* and *a sense of self-worth* are difficult terms to extricate from their sometimes invidious use. We often tend to associate dignity with royalty and "breeding." And we remember that the Nazi SS troops had *a* sense of dignity and self-worth. Some effort to provide referential content or meaning is required in this context.

We intend a noninvidious meaning to include all of the following: growing knowledge of and trust in self, including capacities, sensitivities, commitments, and limitations; integrity as a willingness to adhere to principles rationally held and to honesty in their revision and application; decision capacity as indicated by an assertive claim to the right to decide in personal matters and to participate with others in social and public choices; self-confidence which derives from the approving feedback of others prompted by one's own confidence in others; reflective capacity as willingness to seek truth and to expose fruits of one's reflection; ungraded view of others which recognizes that one's own dignity is not diminished by another's, that dignity is not a scarce or finite good, and that it is not a product of status, rank, position, class, power, or income.

an understanding of social reality and ought to be employed efficiently to relevant areas of human problems and experience. [6]

Reliable knowledge, recall, is a product of rational inquiry. Through recourse to factual subject matter and the imaginative and guiding use of hypotheses, causal relations in phenomena are explained when "conjugate correspondence"[7] is established between theory and fact, between concept and evidence. Such correspondence yields tentative truth.

Reliable knowledge includes the whole fund or stock of evidentially grounded, logically consistent recognitions of means-consequence connections evolving incrementally as a knowledge continuum. It includes warrantable knowledge of the natural and social sciences, of such folk wisdom as reason and evidence confirm, of cognitive recognitions in and out of libraries. It is the aggregative, cumulative product of tool and idea contributions running back beyond written records. Recognized is the fact that new knowledge represents recast and/or reconstituted old knowledge to which a modest additional fragment of demonstrable fact or insight has been added. [8] Such knowledge is reliable not because it is unchanging or absolute, but because it is credible in the sense that it is logically cohesive and evidentially warranted.

The reference to "instrumental use" of reliable knowledge in the value principle affirms the relevance of such knowledge in the identification and resolution of human problems. We call on the reliable knowledge of the medical doctor when bodily pain appears. We seek the reliable knowledge of economists when price levels vault up at rates of two to five per cent per month. We request the reliable knowledge and council of political scientists and jurists when Constitutional crises confront the community and threaten the basic acceptance of the specified structure and function of governmental institutions. However, there is no implication from this use of knowledge that something ought to be done simply because it can be done, scientifically and technologically. We do not intend the intrusion of any kind of technological determinism. We would disallow all such inferences. The fact that an H-bomb could be built does not necessarily infer that it should have been built.

Reference to "instrumental use" conditions and constrains the use of reliable knowledge to that which is pertinent and compatible with the remainder of the principle. At issue is the fittedness or appropriateness of means chosen to serve ends-in-view, recognizing that means determine ends-in-view. One does not repair a watch with a sledge hammer or enhance political democracy by campaign sabotage. There is no

6. C. E. Ayres, *Theory of Economic Progress*, op. cit., chapter 10.

7. John Dewey, *Theory of Valuation*, University of Chicago Press, Chicago, 1939, pp. 40-50.

8. C. E. Ayres, *Theory of Economic Progress*, op. cit., chapter 6.

presumption, moreover, of perfect knowledge or foreknowledge. Rather, the principle embodies an insistence that economic and political problems be identified and approached as a matter of a difference between what our reliable knowledge indicates is possible and desirable and what current practice shows is going on instead. Having been expelled from the front door, no positivism is to be permitted to sneak back in through an unguarded rear door. We suggest that reliable knowledge can and does include material usually characterized as normative. Again we reject the fact-value dichotomy.

Implicit in the principle of social value identified as "the continuity of human life and the noninvidious re-creation of community through the instrumental use of knowledge" are two additional elements:

First, it must be evident that this instrumental value principle assumes that human beings in the social dimensions of their lives do indeed have genuine problems of choice to which a social value principle is pertinent. We dissent from the view that people are wholly conditioned organisms for whom real choice is an illusion. [9] People do think and choose, and their choices make a difference. Their judgments are not wholly preconditioned or predetermined. No great defense is needed for the proposition that every legislative body in (say) the United States is in fact engaged in rewriting the rules with which people's lives are ordered. The judgments of legislators, governors, and presidents do make a substantive difference. The rules enacted may or may not be blatantly invidious, but they are the result of decisions overtly made. Volition is assumed to exist. Men and women demonstrably are discretionary agent-actors.

Second, it must also be evident that this principle of social value draws upon and is designedly relevant only to the realm of existential fact and experience. No recourse is made anywhere to special kinds of intuitive knowledge, to divine presence or revelation, to ideal and unknowable essences and powers.

This instrumental value principle purports to be the formulation of a criterion which in fact has been used historically since time out of mind. As a minute-long exercise, think back over the normative terms used to characterize leaders and led, and countries and communities. What has been meant by labels of "wise," "able," or "just," applied to leaders? What has been meant by captions of "reform," of "progress," or of "development"? Did not the "reforms" of the New Deal, the "progress" of the New Frontier, and the "development" of emerging nations in recent decades refer at bottom to the quest for continuity and instrumental effectiveness of policies to cope with real problems in ways to restore community and enhance human dignity? It would seem so.

---

9. Consider human beings as represented in B. F. Skinner, *Walden Two*, Macmillan, New York, 1962.

In one sense, then, what is being proposed here is scarcely novel at all; it may in the minds of some be regarded as commonplace or even as conservative. In any case, it is to be reviewed and tested in the bright sunlight of stated assumptions, of open analysis, and of testable conclusions. It draws not at all on nonpublic realms of knowing or nonreasoned patterns of defense. It has little to suggest to those seeking psychic trips, introspective revelations, or "getting one's head on straight." There is no recourse to anyone's guru. We seek a principle drawn from existential fact about human experience. We submit that a revision and replacement (when it is necessary) will have to be drawn from the same universe of reason grounded in hard evidence.

(3) Consider next some contrasts and distinctions between social value as "the continuity of human life and the noninvidious re-creation of community through the instrumental use of knowledge" and other approaches and formulations. Our intent is to characterize and distinguish, and to stimulate and provoke.

First, of great importance is the recognition that this instrumental value principle, unlike the normative ideologies of capitalism, socialism, communism, or fascism, contains no particular institutional structure. It neither directs nor implies movement in the *direction* of a preconceived set of institutional forms. The oft used expression here of Walton Hamilton's—"Which direction is forward"[10]—refers to the need for making and remaking institutional choices. As he makes very clear, the expression does not suggest change to approximate an ism; exactly the contrary is intended. The social-value principle differentiates an approvable *condition* from one that is not.[11] It does not specify nor imply the structural changes that will be required to resolve problems and re-create community. This principle permits analysis of what has gone "wrong" with existing prescriptive or proscriptive arrangements; it does not impose an ism-defined adjustment as the solution. In consequence, this value principle is fundamentally different from those grounded in yesterday's isms; it is intended for use in lieu of ism criteria.

As a corollary, the "constants" which are implied in this alternative value principle have to do with procedures—open inquiry, honest reporting, public testing, empirical checks, tentative status of truth seeking, etc.—not with the elevation of favored institutional forms into the role of criteria. For example, this principle of value, as such, neither supports (as do the capitalists) nor attacks (as do the Marxists) the institution of private ownership of productive plant and equipment. The "ought" is not perceived as the fuller achievement of a free-enterprise capitalism nor of a public-ownership socialism. We can stand outside all

10. Walton Hamilton, *The Politics of Industry*, Alfred A. Knopf, New York, 1957, pp. 165ff.

11. Adapted from J. Fagg Foster, "Notes on the Character of the Process and the Specific Identification of the Theory of Value," (unpublished), University of Denver, 1948.

of yesterday's isms and begin to make judgments of *condition* looking to functional performance or its lack instead of *direction* toward or away from somebody's ism.

Second, this social-value principle neither defers to nor depends upon wants, tastes, preferences. It enshrines none; it permits judgments among and between them by permitting examination of their character and of the consequences when they are satisfied—a blockage classical or neoclassical theorists or ideologists seem not to have been able to surmount. There is no elevation here of given wants, whatever they are, into a value referent. There is no ethical relativism of "about tastes there is no disputin'", nor indifference to what it is that "makes people happy" (harassing blacks, putting women down, community organization, listening to Beethoven's Seventh Symphony).

Third, although the matter is arguable, this value principle is designed to be general and inclusive in the universe of its intended use— problem solving in political economy. Although the principle obviously does assume an achievement motivation and human concern about problems, it is not meant to be provincial or ethnocentric. It would seem to cater to no particular nation or people or subgroup. Invidious discrimination exists within the American, French, British, German, Russian, etc. communities; also within the black community, within the women's movement, within the Establishment middle class, within the East-Coast-educated elite, within church circles, trade unions, and fraternities. The social-value principle here recommended is not the product of a singular national group. The United States has no monopoly on "virtue" so conceived. The principle raises the power and status of no group at the expense of another group.

Fourth, social value as "the continuity of human life and the non-invidious re-creation of community through the instrumental use of knowledge" will not serve, we think, as a mask or screen concealing the desires of a few to rule the many. We intend to offer no glib apologia for an elitist economic and/or political power system. On the contrary, the reverse is intended, that is, to provide a criterion of appraisal which will assist with the unmasking and unmaking of power centers which remain unaccountable to those touched significantly by such power.

Fifth, clearly this instrumental value principle offers no utopian solution; it is no panacea. It is no magic elixir which if taken in prescribed doses will clear up economic and political aches and ills without inquiry and vigorous social action. There is no End in sight and none that can be brought into view. There are no ultimate "goods" implied and no "once-and-for-all" ideal solutions recommended. Indeed, one of the several purposes of this work is to argue the irrelevance of any such effort. Economic and political analysis which employs this non-ism value principle will be very mundane, not necessarily ordinary, but decidedly impure in the ritualistic academic sense. Practitioners will chew their pencils, risk ulcers, experience anguish and despair, get sore feet, and probably get their hands dirty. They may also experience the exhilaration that results from purposeful work that makes a difference.

Sixth, and finally, this value principle offers no escape from hard, arduous inquiry; it compels intellectual tool creation, theory building, and evidence compiling and evaluating. It offers no shortcuts, easy answers, or simple solutions. It is no recipe of ingredients which can be combined to produce the perfect product. It has no answer page at the end of the book. This criterion of judgment is a principle to use as a tool of inquiry; it is fashioned to perform the function of serving as a vehicle which allows choices to be rationally and evidentially made. Its universe of application is the social process; it is of central significance in economic and political analysis.

As with all conceptual tools, the test of the principle's adequacy is not a matter of the status or standing of its proposers, nor of its longevity, nor of its ism-ideological correspondence or lack thereof. The test, rather, is one of determining whether or not this value principle will function to identify problems which are instances of breakdown in the instrumental functioning of existing institutions—blockages, disjunctions, obsolescences, disruptions, terminations, violent outbreaks, and the like. Further, will this principle suggest avenues of inquiry which will enable creative minds to recommend revisions to re-establish some measure of functional effectiveness in ways which restore community and enhance the discretionary dignity of those affected? Treating people noninvidiously enhances discretionary dignity. The proof of the pudding is in the eating, 'tis said. The significance of this social-value principle will be determined in the context of its use.

II.   VALUE COROLLARIES AND APPLICATIONS

Consider now some extensions and applications of the social-value theory herein proposed:

Understanding of our alternative value principle, the continuity of human life and the noninvidious re-creation of community through the instrumental use of knowledge, will be enhanced if we explore some derivative and corollary criteria which, we believe, are pertinent to the making of choices in the several areas generating revolutionary unrest— poverty and the economic revolution, elitism and the political revolution, discrimination and the racial and sexual revolutions, and environmental degradation and the ecological crisis.

(1) A corollary ethical concept for the economic revolution is the criterion of *instrumental efficiency*.

The term *efficiency* may immediately come under some heavy criticism by persons who see in it a shorthand caption for an amoral, computerized, dehumanizing, technological economy that is indifferent to human interests and compassion. Such an inference is not unreasonable as one reflects on the character of some recent use of nuclear technology, military technology, and computer technology which may appear intimidative and threatening. But *efficiency* can be recast and salvaged in a way which, we think, need not engender the bitterness and blanching its use has sometimes evoked. With the introduction below of certain constraints and clarifications, the term can be salvaged and its use as a derivative criterion delineated.

Interest here focuses especially upon the relevance of instrumental efficiency as a criterion in determining the level, character, and distribution of production. Whatever and wherever the economy, ideological characteristics notwithstanding, the economic function of producing and distributing real income must be performed tolerably well. "Tolerably" means acceptable or endurable to the people involved; "well" means effective use of resources as the latter are defined by currently available knowledge and its application as technology.

In determining the *level* of output of real income and the technological manner of its creation, *instrumental efficiency* utilizes, but harnesses and constrains, technical efficiency and directs its use to the service of inclusive human and humane purposes including problem solving through structural change in the economy. The harnessing and constraining of technical efficiency is accomplished by the override role of continuity, community re-creation, and noninvidiousness in the general criterion of social value described above. Technical efficiency is sought *provided* it is compatible with, nonsubversive of, these components of instrumental value theory.

Technical efficiency denotes extracting maximum output from resource inputs (physical, financial, institutional, technological). Recourse to technically efficient means of making steel via the oxygen process; technically efficient means of extracting maximum BTUs from coal; technically efficient means of macro-management of the economy for full utilization of the available labor force; technically efficient means of organizing workers in productive teams; technically efficient means of distributing incomes, taxing incomes, or providing continuity in receipt of incomes illustrate the point. Economies ought to operate efficiently in this sense so long as the overriding criteria are not violated.

The concern here is with the appropriateness of means or tools used in achieving ends or results. What is the "right" tool (physical or conceptual), the instrumentally efficient tool, to accomplish the task at hand? At issue is the matter of pertinence. Is a hand saw useful in repairing a pocket computer? Is Say's Law (supply creates its own demand) an admissible conceptual tool in explaining determinants of aggregate income and employment? Is the positive-normative dichotomy mandated as a philosophical tool in addressing the normative problems of choice? The instrumental efficiency of the tool is determined in the context of its use by answering two questions: Were anticipated consequences in fact realized? Are the consequences approvable with reference to instrumental value theory?

In determining the level of output, then, the instrumental efficiency criterion calls for the most skillful use of appropriate conceptual tools in defining problems (e.g., of structural unemployment and/or administered inflation) and of formulating options as institutional change to correct for such problems.

However, this concept of instrumental efficiency does not, for example, validate the "growth of output at any cost" position. It is not exempt from judging the environmental consequences. To be so would violate the continuity principle as an overriding constraint. The efficient mining of the soil's fertility, efficient clear-cutting of timber, efficient exhaustion of fossil fuels, although feasible in a technical sense, may not in a larger context be tolerable at all. One must judge the *consequences* of such efficient use of knowledge and technology not on a short-term particularistic and/or pecuniary basis, but on a longer-term, cultural continuity, general community basis.

Similarly, the instrumentally efficient use of human resources does *not* connote the "scientific management" of people as developed by Frederick W. Taylor and his more recent devotees. [12] To do so would violate the continuity and noninvidiousness principles as overriding constraints. Treating people as machines, fragmenting work into simple chores and defining jobs thereon, making and insensitively applying time-and-motion studies of work requirements, denying workers' participation in determining rules governing work, psychologically manipulating workers into conformist roles, and the like tend to dehumanize work and alienate workers.

Instrumentally efficient use of labor means, in contrast, a catering to and encouragement of the fullest development of thinking skills, manipulative abilities, self-directing inclinations, and other distinctively human potentialities in the production process. [13] The human being is the premier resource. Creativity, imagination, motivation, and sense of achievement and of communal commitment ought to be enhanced by the work experience, not suppressed by it.

The instrumental efficiency criterion applies also to judgments in the realm of the *character* of production. What goods and services will be produced? What is to be the composition of the output mix? What array of occupations shall constitute the labor force?

Most are familiar with the conventional version of this problem: determining the civilian-military product mix and the consumer-producer good mix. Even these conventional judgments, of course, compel the application of normative principles. When, if ever, is it

12. See, for example, David Jenkins, *Job Power: Blue and White Collar Democracy*, Penguin Books, New York, 1974, pp. 25-35.

13. Ibid., pp. 282 ff and passim.

instrumentally efficient to produce war goods? What pattern of capital-goods formation is optimum? What kinds of consumer goods should be made available? The answers will not necessarily come easily.

When, for instance, communities are compelled to set priorities in the character of production because of substantial interruptions in the flow of real income occasioned by natural disasters, warfare, political upheavals, and the like, the application of the instrumental-efficiency criterion would suggest that, for example:

(a) basic foods be provided before goods for ceremonial display or invidious emulation
(b) auto factories be rebuilt before gambling casinos and race tracks
(c) skilled medical technicians be trained before bond salespeople
(d) military production be confined to literally defensive operations only
(e) houses and apartments be rebuilt before luxury second homes
(f) social overhead capital expenditures (transport, communication and educational facilities, for example) be given a higher priority than display edifices for political elites[14]

The extent to which the foregoing sounds approvingly common-place is an indication of the degree to which the instrumental-efficiency criterion is already a part of judgmental habits.

Occasionally, the community has more extensive knowledge on which to draw in applying the instrumental-efficiency criterion to consumer goods' composition judgments, however. There are now available indices of optimum space requirements for individuals at work and in homes, nutritional and caloric indices suggesting recommended forms and amounts of food for consumption,[15] recommendations of products with which to maintain health, and the like. The instrumental-efficiency criterion underlies these familiar recommendations.

Further, the criterion will apply to the determination of whether some goods should be produced at all (hazardous toys, nonbiodegradable agricultural chemicals, neutron bombs) and whether the availability of goods produced should be restricted in some manner (habit-forming drugs, hand guns, radioactive substances). The instrumental-efficiency criterion forces consideration of the *character* of the consequences ensuing from the *character* of production. The political question of who is to exercise discretion over the character of production of course remains. The following section bears on this question.

Finally, the subsidiary criterion of instrumental efficiency applies also to the *distribution* of production. This criterion will not sustain or defend marked inequality of income distribution. As most are aware, in

14. Readers of Veblen will recognize adaptations here of the fundamental Veblenian dichotomy. See the author's "A Social Value Theory in Neoinstitutional Economics," *Journal of Economic Issues*, Vol. XI, No. 4, December, 1977, p. 827.

15. For example, Food and Nutrition Board, National Research Council, *Recommended Dietary Allowances*, National Academy of Sciences, Washington, D.C., 1974.

any exchange economy, money-income receipt largely determines the extent and character of individual economic choices. Deprivation of income means deprivation of genuine economic choices. Since effective choice is essential for effective economic participation, the nonavailability of adequate flows of money income to significant portions of the community dramatically impairs their instrumental efficiency. Their capacity to secure minimally adequate housing, sustenance, education, health care, and recreation to permit their most effective productive involvement on a job and the fullest development of their latent physical, mental, and motivational capacities will be obstructed. [16] It is instrumentally *inefficient* to cripple any fragment of the community by deprivation, discrimination, or alienation. As Clarence E. Ayres often remarked, to cripple a part is to cripple the whole of a community. [17] The crippling results from the fact of pervasive interdependency. One person's injury is another person's burden. Consequences of individual and group behavior impinge on and extend or constrain other persons' behavior. Community means interdependency.

Few need to be reminded that income distribution in the United States *is* markedly unequal. For a generation and more the bottom fifth of family income recipients has received some 4 to 6 per cent of total money income; the top fifth has received around 41 to 45 per cent of such income. [18]

To illustrate further: In the United States in the mid-1970s almost 26 million people, or 12.3 per cent of the total population, were living in poverty according to official Census Bureau definitions of poverty. [19] In 1969, when the poverty component evidently was roughly comparable, some 14.4 million Americans were facing outright hunger and malnutrition in the absence of food grants or assistance, and only 44 per cent of those later *did* actually receive any food assistance. [20] Finally, if

16. On this and related matters, see, for example, Oscar Lewis, "The Culture of Poverty," in *On Understanding Poverty*, Daniel P. Moynihan (ed.), Basic Books, New York, 1968-1969, pp. 187-200; also, Winifred Bell, Robert Lekachman and Alvin Schorr, *Public Policy and Income Distribution*, Center for Studies in Income Maintenance, School of Social Work, New York University, New York, 1974.

17. Ayres, *Theory of Economic Progress*, op. cit., p. 233 and *The Industrial Economy*, Houghton Mifflin, Boston, 1952, pp. 268-69.

18. Jonathan H. Turner and Charles E. Starnes, *Inequality: Privilege and Poverty in America*, Goodyear Publishing Co., Pacific Palisades, California, 1976, p. 51. See also, Morton Paglin, "The Measurement and Trend of Inequality: A Basic Revision," *American Economic Review*, Vol. LXV, No. 4, September, 1975, pp. 598-609.

19. *New York Times*, September 26, 1975, pp. 1 & 36. See also, "Money Income and Poverty Status of Families and Persons in the United States, 1974-1975," United States Department of Commerce, Bureau of Census, U.S. Government Printing Office, Washington, D.C., 1976; Michael Harrington, "Hiding the Other America," *The New Republic*, February 26, 1977, pp. 15-17; and "Big Increase in 'Officially' Poor," *San Francisco Chronicle*, July 14, 1977, p. 9.

20. U.S. Congress, Senate Select Committee on Nutrition and Human Needs, *The Food Gap: Poverty and Malnutrition in the United States*, U.S. Government Printing Office, Washington, D.C., 1969, pp. 20-21.

one may assume that the level of real income specified by the Bureau of Labor Statistics (BLS) as an "intermediate level of living" (a modest but not luxurious level)[21] is the minimum level necessary for continuing instrumentally efficient productive work, somewhere between one-third and one-half of the population falls below this threshold. For example, for an urban family of four, the median income in 1976 was $16,336; the BLS intermediate income in 1977 was $17,106.

Not only is the larger community deprived of the economic contribution which this eighth, or third, or half might otherwise be able to make (a concern shared presumably with the orthodox capitalists) but, more importantly, to reiterate, a paucity of income shrivels life's choices generally to the point where intellect, creativity, compassion, and commitment are stunted or destroyed for those denied. We then live in a layered or tiered community suffering from elitism and privation alike. [23] This would appear to be inefficiency of really monumental proportions.

Finally, a qualification (or disclaimer) needed in reflecting on the adequacy of instrumental efficiency as an economic criterion involves the recognition that all ism-ideology economies claim to be efficient— especially so perhaps with the capitalists, who have insisted for a century that an unfettered free-market system is the most efficient economic order conceivable. That such insistence is no longer credible should now be apparent to the most casual observer of the economies of self-proclaiming capitalist countries. Recall that President Nixon, who appeared to cater to an ideological constituency, was driven by the evident failures of two and one-half years of deference to market mentalities to the introduction of wage and price controls beginning in August 1971. [24] The recourse to direct controls must have been ideologically unpalatable; he had been denigrating such controls through most of his political career.

Competitive market economies are not instrumentally efficient for a number of reasons:

(a) They provide no way, ideologically or institutionally, for wants and preferences to be appraised in the market. The question of the

21. We do not intend to imply that BLS estimates of city worker budgets are necessarily ideal or that they are necessarily sufficient measures or standards with which to judge the adequacy, on instrumental-efficiency grounds, of various levels of money and real income. They are rough approximations, indicative but not definitive.

22. U.S. Department of Commerce, Bureau of the Census, Consumer Income Reports, Series P-60, #110, U.S. Government Printing Office, Washington, D.C., March, 1978. U.S. Department of Labor, Bureau of Labor Statistics, "Autumn 1976 Urban Family Budgets and Comparative Indexes for Selected Urban Areas," U.S. Government Printing Office, Washington, D.C., 1978.

23. See also, Ben B. Seligman, Permanent Poverty: An American Syndrome, Quadrangle Books, Chicago, 1968, chapter 2; and David Hamilton, "The Political Economy of Poverty: Institutional and Technological Dimensions," Journal of Economic Issues, Vol. I, No. 4, December 1967, pp. 309-20.

24. Leonard Silk, Nixonomics (2nd ed.), Praeger, New York, 1972.

character of wants is excluded from consideration. This is an abandonment of a normative responsibility which the community in some other way must cover. In the United States, often producers themselves make the judgment on the character of product and then, through media advertising, condition the public to concur. [25]

(b) Competitive market economies do not address the fact of inequality of income distribution as a problem. The combination of functional distribution through competitive factor markets and personal distribution through nonmarket mechanisms is thought to suffice. Inequality allegedly generates the monetary savings which many of the orthodox still regard as determinant of investment and growth.

(c) Competitive market economies do not provide for the introduction of nonpecuniary criteria in economic decision making. Prices are surrogates for real, utility values. Adjustment of prices or output to maximize profit is a sufficient indicator of the adequacy of judgments. Profits are the primary success indicator. The irony of some such expression as "Oh, the factory was destroyed? No matter; it was insured" is a reflection of our unease with the illusion that pecuniary values "stand in" for social value. Profits are not an indicator of instrumental efficiency.

(2) A corollary ethical concept for the political revolution is the criterion of *democracy*.

At an earlier point we suggested that in deciding the extent and character of political obligation, one might ask whether or not a particular government was worthy of support. We may now affirm that to the degree that the political process is organized to provide for participatory democracy, a government is worthy. That is, the idea of democracy itself may be used as a criterion, a standard in terms of which to make choices among institutional and candidate options. Does what is contemplated as structural change increase or decrease the ability and the opportunity of people to determine the rules governing their own lives? Does the candidate favor or oppose participatory involvement in determining policy? Democracy, recall, means self-imposed restraints. If a system does provide for self-rule, it is worthy; if a system does not, it is without legitimacy.

Democracy as a term does not define a given, rigid, and substantive set of political institutions as such (e.g., tripartite government, multiple-party system); it identifies the locus of responsibility for political decision making and suggests procedural conditions (e.g., free speech, due process, majority rule) through which it may be exercised. Thus, democracy is not an "ism" on a par with, say, capitalism or socialism; it offers no final institutional package or recipe; it is a continuing means, not a structurally defined End. Democracy defines a set of conditions for bringing reasoned judgment to bear on public problems; it does not

25. This is John K. Galbraith's "revised sequence," as we noted above.

specify a priori the institutional forms which ultimately may constitute the proposed solution.

Democracy is a necessary, but not a sufficient, criterion in choosing among alternatives, however. The fact that an institutional choice (e.g., to establish a national medical-insurance program, to reimpose the death penalty, to expand nuclear-fission energy installations) is made by a majority vote, directly or indirectly, does not necessarily mean that the "continuity of human life and the noninvidious re-creation of community through the instrumental use of knowledge" is therewith being served. Majorities may be "wrong," as we are often reminded by the elitists. Factually, such may well be the case. But the "rightness" or "wrongness" of majorities is not to be decided by elitist criteria nor, for that matter, by majoritarian criteria. The democratic contention is that the greater the degree of popular participatory involvement in the making of public judgments, the greater will be the interest in determining whether or not a decision is or will be "right."

In a democratic order, when a judgment is "mistaken," when in an instrumental sense the action taken does not resolve the problem, those who bear the incidence of the mistake are the ones typically who will be most interested and vigorous in seeking a correction. Those who most directly bear the human costs and dislocations of breakdowns—disruptions or distortions in the operation of existing institutions—are, in an open society, most likely to take a lively interest in the use of reliable knowledge to modify structure and resolve the problem. Even so, the reactions of some to a shortfall may be reasoned or irrational, instrumental or ceremonial, deliberative or violent, insight seeking or scapegoat hunting, but so long as the incidence of the problem remains unresolved, there will be a continuing stimulus to define mistakes and to formulate corrections.

There is, in democratic orders, an inherent tendency to subject public decisions to scrutiny and revision leading to real, if not final, solutions for problems. It is this process of deliberation and appraisal which warrants the contention that democratic orders are efficient. They are efficient in achieving needed institutional change to restore instrumental effectiveness to important areas of human endeavor.

Democracy, then, as an addendum criterion assists with the pursuit of that ancient political "Holy Grail"—the public interest. Every politician defends his or her votes and actions on grounds of "serving the public interest"; that is a part of the rhetoric of legitimacy. Why? Because obviously he or she seeks support (consent) from those he or she allegedly represents. The instrumental value theory advanced above does indeed identify the public interest, and democracy is the most efficient process thus far conceived through which to achieve some approximation thereof.

(3) A corollary ethical concept for the racial and sexual revolutions is the criterion of *noninvidiousness* itself.

Readers are well aware that much use has already been made of this criterion at several points in the presentation this far. Some additional explication of the idea in this context should help remove remaining obscurities.

We begin with an affirmation of some comfortable and generally settled conclusions about men and women as social beings. Evidently it is everywhere the case that people wish to be well thought of; they seek the recognition and esteem of others for the fact of their being and for the fruits of their labors and activities. Cultures and customs pattern the ways and means of seeking and exhibiting such recognition and esteem. Physical prowess, control over others' behavior, creation of art objects, reflective capacities, decoration of the human body, engaging in sports, acquisition of material possessions, demonstrated skills with tools, ordering and coordinating capacities, to mention but a few, are all areas in which and by which recognition and esteem have been and are being sought. The "psychology of ego involvement"[26] affirms this quest for identity, for notice, for recognition, for acceptance by others.

In addition, there is the obvious fact that everywhere human beings are different—frequently observably different—from one another on literally scores of divergent indexes. As we remarked above, such categories of difference include, among others, race, creed, national origin, sex, ethnicity, age, rank, parentage, wealth, income, religious belief, attained education level, stature, height and weight, intellect, sibling order, skin color, facial configuration, hair texture, color and styles of attire, power over others, temperament, aggressiveness, blood type, etc., etc. So much is a recitation of the obvious, but there is a reason for the reminder.

Invidiousness means the use of one or several of these distinctions among persons to challenge or assault the basic worth of human beings; it means to denigrate and demean people; it means to deny dignity *because* of the observed or assumed presence of such differences without regard to a context in which the distinction might or might not be significant or make an instrumental difference. To judge invidously, then, is to denigrate the worth of particular individuals or classes of individuals.

Given recognition manifested in the way, as individuals, we do differ from one another, we seek, when we judge invidiously, to enhance our own egos, our own importance, our own conception of self-worth by demeaning those without our own traits simply because they are without such traits. Invidious judgments are unfairly discriminatory.

---

26. Muzafer Sherif and Hadly Cantril, *The Psychology of Ego-Involvement*, John Wiley, New York, 1947.

In the case of racial and sexual discrimination, no extensive catalog of examples is required. [27] Although gains have been made in eroding discrimination in recent decades, it still appears that politicians will sometimes use overt or covert appeals to racism in their campaigns; that women continue to have more difficulty than men in gaining access to loans and credit (credit cards, mortgage loans, etc.); that busing school children to achieve racial balance remains a source of intense domestic conflict; that differential pay for women for work identical to that done by men may still be found on occasion in education, business, and government. The Bakke case, involving the denial of admission to a white student at the medical school at the University of California at Davis, tested in the courts the right of universities to establish particular types of compensatory admission practices to overcome in part past exclusion of minorities on invidious grounds. Federal Affirmative Action programs were deemed necessary to interdict racism and sexism in hiring and promotion policies of universities receiving federal assistance. The Equal Rights Amendment to seek an end to sexism through Constitutional mandate has been blocked in a number of states. [28]

Not quite so evident, however, is the fact that the invidious use of distinctions as a criterion directly conflicts with the more inclusive principle of social value set off above. Invidious judgments, by fostering interpersonal and intergroup conflict, directly threaten continuity of instrumental economic, political, and social functions. Race riots, religious conflict, terrorist tactics by aggrieved minorities, overt discrimination, political intimidation of ethnics, and other major and visible manifestations of invidiousness are ugly and dislocative; frequently they promote physical violence. When such conflicts become consuming and/or violent, the instrumental effectiveness of people to think and to act in a reasonable and rational manner is markedly impaired. Such conflict-engendered enmity makes the task of "re-creating community" virtually impossible. And, as was suggested by the discussion in chapter 11, part VII, there is an instrumental-value rationale for the use of force to prevent violence and terrorism. A democratic noninvidious community does enforce the law and maintain civil peace. But the character of law and the nature of civil peace remain open as areas of discussion and discretionary action.

Community building means cooperative exploration of problems and the formulation of agreed-upon responses to such problems. Community building provides a vehicle for people to express and act on their

---

27. See Edythe S. Miller, "Veblen and Women's Lib: A Parallel," *Journal of Economic Issues*, Vol. VI, Nos. 2 & 3, September, 1972, pp. 75-86.

28. A general assessment appears in Kenneth B. Clark, "The Costs of Discrimination," *Challenge Magazine*, Vol. 20, No. 2, May-June, 1977, pp. 33-39.

commitments to each other, to children, families and friends, and to the physical environs which are familiar. Racism and sexism, for example, preclude community creation because they disintegrate conceptions of common purpose, or forestall the creation of common purposes, and convert resolvable differences of opinion into challenges of the right to life, to income, to have identity, to make a difference, to be "somebody" in one's own eyes as well as those of others, to be worthy and to be recognized by one's peers as such! But invidious judgments make such discretionary involvement difficult if not impossible, thus stripping people of their dignity. Where such conditions exist, there can be no real community.

(4) A corollary ethical concept for the ecological crisis is the criterion of *environmental compatibility*.

As most students are aware, social inquiry is concerned with person-person relations; person-thing relations are significant but are normally the purview of scholars in disciplines other than the social sciences (e.g., natural sciences). While person-thing relations are not the object of social inquiry, obviously they often set the terms or conditions within which social inquiry occurs. Similarly, a social community differs from a biotic community; the latter sets conditions in which the former occurs and operates.

A biotic community is composed of the interdependencies (mainly, energy-exchange and food-chain relations) of life forms with each other and of life forms with the physical environment. [29] The biotic community of interdependencies is a reflection of no doctrine of design. What environmental conditions do not favor, they prohibit. "Nature selects nothing; it simply eliminates or absolves." [30] A biotic community simply *is*. If there are momentary or enduring balances, that is a matter of fact, not of purpose. Such a community is neither pro nor con of life forms specifically or generally, including human life; it is neither virtuous nor insidious; it exhibits "neither grace nor right, but only displacement." [31] As such, it is amoral or nonmoral; it merely and profoundly is. "Nature flows carelessly, according to its monstrous insensate habit, impassive and undisturbed, whether or not men institute political relations among themselves." [32]

A social community must exist and seek continuity within the ecological limits of the biotic community. People are dependent upon and interdependent with other life forms. The biotic community sets conditions, but it provides no judgments. People alone make judgments.

29. One version is that of Aldo Leopold, *A Sand County Almanac*, Sierra Club/Ballantine, New York, 1970, pp. 251ff.
30. John F. A. Taylor, "Politics and the Human Covenant," *The Centennial Review*, Michigan State University, East Lansing, Michigan, 1962, p. 3.
31. Ibid.
32. Ibid., p. 5.

People as actor-agents define social community, affirm its purposes, delineate its relations, and live out its constraints and obligations. A social community can exist only when individuals perceive themselves as mutually committed to one another. As we have seen, democratic communities accept the obligation to observe rules which have been introduced by popular consent. A biotic community knows nothing of obligation or commitment, or consent.

The environmental ethical principle, then, is the criterion of compatibility—compatibility between the social and biotic communities. The social community, through its political judgments, must assure that it continues to function within constraints of the biotic community. The principle of compatibility corresponds with the more inclusive criterion introduced above—the continuity of human life and the noninvidious re-creation of community through the instrumental use of knowledge.

Logical and ethical implications of the foregoing would include the following:

(a) Preserve the biotic community *and* preserve the social community. The continuity component of the general criterion above cannot otherwise be met.

(b) Conserve life forms and the physical environs which sustain them. A principal reason is that knowledge of the complexities and interdependencies of life forms is not, and probably never will be, sufficiently complete to foresee the consequences of the extinction of any life form. For many, the esthetic reasons are equally compelling, of course.

(c) Conserve technologically defined resources; avoid pollution of air, water, and soil; forestall despoilation of forest, stream, and ocean— not because nonhuman life generally takes precedence over human life, but because the continuity of the social community is dependent on the continuity of biotic life.

Environmental compatibility of the social with the biotic community is, then, an applicable principle of judgment. There are implications and applications of this principle.

Perhaps nowhere in our quest for warrantable normative precepts in political economy is the ethical dilemma for an individual more sharply drawn nor easier to see. To an individual pursuing his or her private interests, following capitalist traditions, the land, including the flora and fauna, is an exploitable resource to turn to one's own economic (pecuniary) advantage. One "mixes his labor with the soil" and thereby gains a right to the fruits of that labor. To an individual as a member of a community, however, such pursuits by oneself and others similarly engaged may well seriously impair or destroy the biotic community, including now oneself. Accordingly, much of the literature on the ecological crisis affirms the need for the supremacy of public obligation to community (social and biotic) over private economic advantage. [33] It now appears that the creation of a viable social community, including the jettisonning of ideologically grounded beliefs, may well be a precondition, or at least a concurrent condition, for preserving a biotic community.

Economists of the traditional, Establishment, neoclassical kind have sometimes had difficulty relating their explanations of pricing phenomena to the crises of environmental degradation. Committed to utility-value theory, the efficacy of free markets, and private enterprise, they have suggested that air and stream pollution, land-form emasculation, plant and timber eradication, and the like be viewed as "externalities" [34] —consequences outside the normal operations of supply-and-demand market processes. Such theorists and ideologists have attempted to apply their analytical models through efforts to "internalize externalities," that is, to bring the community's peripheral ecological costs (resulting from pollution and the like) within the market process by, for example, taxing firms that pollute for the full costs of repairing the damage their activity creates. [35] In this way the full costs (including costs to the environment) would be paid for by product users, and the market mentality would continue to reign supreme. A difficulty, of course, is that the pollution itself may very well continue even where policy is based on these premises.

A variant from the same general theoretical and ideological source would seek "the proper balance between the utility of [resource-using] activities to the individual and the disutility they impose, via the environment, on others." [36] Recourse is also made to Pareto optimality [37] and other utility-based criteria in attempts to find analyses to permit the identification of such balances.

But the problem of social value in the ecology crisis is not a matter of full-cost charges to private enterprise or of finding a balance of utilities and disutilities. The problem concerns the refinement and use of a criterion of ecological judgment which affirms the necessity of interdependent compatibility of the social and the biotic communities. This criterion would serve as an alternate principle to benefit-cost equivalencies, internalized externalities, utility-disutility balances, and the like. Our roles as public citizens seeking such compatibility must

33. Leopold, A Sand County Almanac, op. cit., pp. 258-61. Also, Barry Commoner, The Closing Circle, Bantam Books, New York, 1972, pp. 249ff; and Harold Wolozin, "Environmental Control at the Crossroads," Journal of Economic Issues, Vol. V, No. 1, March, 1971, pp. 26-41.

34. Discussed in Robert Staaf & Francis Tannian, Externalities: Theoretical Dimensions of Political Economy, Kennikat Press (Dunellen), Port Washington, New York, 1973.

35. See, for example, Commoner, The Closing Circle, op. cit., pp. 249-91.

36. Robert Dorfman & Nancy S. Dorfman, Economics of the Environment, W. W. Norton, New York, 1972, p. xix.

37. For example, new condition A is better than new condition B, if in A at least one person would be "better off" without making anyone "worse off."

supplant, in this area, our pursuits as private citizens as necessary—especially, the "conquering of nature" for personal pecuniary gain. [38]

Consider the following: With regard to standing redwoods, evidently it is a question of whether commercially marketable supplies are exhausted within another quarter-century or so at current levels of extraction, or whether remaining stands are preserved now for their significance to the biotic community.

With regard to fossil fuels, it is, evidently, a question of whether known high-yield coal beds will be strip-mined clean in the next one hundred years or so with attendant environmental havoc (witness West Virginia, Kentucky, and Tennessee currently), of whether domestic petroleum reserves will be drained in the next thirty to fifty years with attendant pollution and land scarring, or whether additional research energies will be diverted now to find suitable and environmentally acceptable alternatives (solar, fusion, geothermal, wind, tidal energy sources).

With regard to ocean waters, it appears to be a question of whether oil and chemical pollution will destroy most sea life in the next half-century with accompanying monumental dietary curtailment and environmental deterioration, or whether adequate constraints applied internationally can be introduced promptly to provide for biotic continuity in that area.

The conclusion seems apparent: Literal biotic disaster and further environmental degradation are virtual certainties unless a viable ecological ethic is applied to problem areas now known to require its use.

It is important to note that there may well be times when conflict will occur between the economic criterion of instrumental efficiency and the ecological criterion of biotic and social community compatibility. [39] The application of the economic criterion, it should be understood, is generally to be conditioned by and subject to the constraints of the ecological criterion. Economically productive and equitably distributed real income probably can continue in most areas without extensive environmental degradation. There is no economic law which compels the production of nonbiodegradable materials, for example, or the production of plastic containers and their disposal at sea or by noxious burning. There is no economic law which compels the profligate waste of existing energy capacities, for example, use of fuels (four per cent of national total?) for the illegal bombing by B-52s of Cambodia from

38. Regarding control of externalities, see Ralph C. d'Arge & James E. Wilen, "Governmental Control of Externalities, or the Prey Eats the Predator," *Journal of Economic Issues*, Vol. VIII, No. 2, June 1974, pp. 353-72.

39. In this connection, see K. William Kapp, "Development and Environment: Towards a New Approach to Socioeconomic and Environmental Development," in R. Steppacher, B. Zogg-Walz, and H. Hatzfeldt, *Economics in Institutional Perspective*, Lexington Books/D. C. Heath, Lexington, Massachusetts, 1977, pp. 205-18.

January to August 1973, or building codes which fail to specify adequate insulation in new construction. There is no economic law that precludes the massive diversion of scientific and technical research personnel from military weaponry to the development of more environmentally compatible production methods and output. Even though rhetoric on the subject of environmental protection may be faddish, it cannot be dismissed; the "opaque facts" of the problem and its potentially disastrous consequences remain.

From the principle of social value and its illustrative applications, we now turn to the derivative social goals of freedom, equality, and justice in order to complete the formulation here of a normative and evolutionary theory of political economy.

Chapter 16

FREEDOM, EQUALITY, AND JUSTICE

A humane economy requires more than prosperity and economic growth, more than efficient allocation of resources. It demands changes in the framework of economic institutions to achieve greater equality and freedom. It requires dispersal of the economic power and governmental authority that support the present disposition of income, wealth, and power. It requires a social environment that brings a sense of community and fellowship into human relationships. It demands compatibility among man, his technology, and the natural environment. And all of these things must be done on a worldwide scale. These are the goals of the future, to which economists and everyone else will have to devote their energies.

DANIEL R. FUSFELD*

Just because the "rightness" of a political decision cannot be proved—because its consequences, short- or long-range, cannot be predicted with certitude nor its ultimate ethical supremacy demonstrated—are we obligated to construct a decision-making procedure that will leave the way open for new ideas and social change . . .

Do not block the possibility of change with respect to social goals.

THOMAS LANDON THORSON**

---

*Daniel R. Fusfeld, "Post-Post-Keynes: The Shattered Synthesis," *Saturday Review*, January 22, 1972, p. 39 © 1972 *Saturday Review*. Reprinted by permission.

**Thomas Landon Thorson, *The Logic of Democracy*, Holt, Rinehart, Winston, New York, 1962, p. 139.

Wherever revolutionary unrest becomes manifest, wherever existing arrangements are thought to constitute a moral crisis, there will be found disputants who are pressing their cases by calling for freedom, equality, and/or justice. For centuries, at least in the West, these captions—freedom, equality, justice—have signified the ongoing quest for human betterment. As with the term *democracy*, these social goals generally connote human conditions to be assiduously sought and for which death is frequently not thought to be too high a price to pay.

What would people have us accept as the defensible and applicable concepts of freedom, equality, and justice? One's impulsive response is suggestive but insufficient. In a general way, perhaps, we associate freedom with options and choices, equality with sameness and fairness, and justice with scale-balancing and noncapriciousness. But vagueness and ambivalence, and consequent uncertainty, plague efforts to think clearly about these social goals. The seeming confidence and certitude of the ideologists appear to offer clarity and certainty. We shall suggest that increasing clarity and greater confidence are possible for an evolutionary political economist, but only if yesterday's isms are abandoned. That is a good part of the case that remains here to be made.

I. SOCIAL GOALS THROUGH ISM WINDOWS

Advocates of yesterday's isms display, in their roster of conceptual materials, reasonably definitive ideas of freedom, equality, and justice. A brief examination of these ideas will set the stage for a reformulation which follows. (See figure 16-1 for a summary of these ideas.)

For capitalists, freedom has long meant the absence of restraint. The fewer the restraints, short of anarchy, the freer one is. Freedom here connotes choice to participate or not in markets as consumers, workers, and entrepreneurs. Choices are reflections of unexamined preferences—spontaneous and hedonistically rational. The competitive

	Freedom	Equality	Justice
Capitalism	absence of restraint	equality of opportunity	equational justice through market
Marxism	obedience to authority— general will	true equality only comes with communism	equational justice with socialism— beyond with communism
Fascism	obedience to authority— leader & party	deny equality— favor invidious inequality	dispensation by leader
Normative Theory of Political Economy	expanding area of genuine choice	right to be and to belong	provision for instrumental involvement

Figure 16-1 Isms and Goals

market provides the only *kind* of restraints on choice that is allowed. They are natural; no individual introduced them. Government policies are the wrong kind of restraints; they are "arbitrary" and unnatural. Thus in orthodoxy it is freedom vs. order, freedom vs. authority, and freedom vs. planning.

This view is flawed by its deference to natural-order restraints, by its narrow noncultural idea of choice, and by its recourse to utility as the criterion of choice.

The capitalist view of equality is reflected in its advocacy of equality of opportunity, which consists of having and retaining equal *access* to participation in a competitive economy. The capitalist view of equality does not imply equal incomes or equal participation in, or equal satisfaction from, market involvement.

This view is flawed by the "opaque fact" of pervading income inequality, as was noted above. In any exchange economy, income determines choices and defines opportunity. Equality of opportunity mistakenly assumes that participants start even. Because they do not, market participation gives those with a differential advantage a differential opportunity. Markets "reward rewards"; equality of opportunity generates greater inequality. [1]

The capitalist view of justice is also troublesome for an evolutionary political economist. Accepted uncritically is the ancient dictum of the equational theory of justice. Justice is done, it is said, when something is brought into equality with something else: when income received equals contribution made; when "a life for a life" or "a tooth for a tooth" is the principle of settlement. For capitalists, competitive markets become justice-dispensing instruments as marginal productivity theory "explains" the balancing of wage received and the market value of product supplied. Linked and balanced are effort and reward, pleasure and pain, utility and disutility, benefits and costs. For John Bates Clark, the principle was a natural law and a moral imperative. Weighing scales are the symbol. This ideological doctrine fuels the antipathy towards welfare programs and those who "get something for nothing," and the disenchantment for progressive taxation, which imbalances taxes paid and benefits received.

The principle of equational justice, too, is flawed: There is a conspicuous absence of substantive or normative meaning in balance or equilibrium. The principle rests on the archaic psychology of hedonism. Practically, it is not applicable or available; the dispensing competitive free markets do not in the main exist. [2]

1. John H. Schaar, "Equality of Opportunity, and Beyond," in de Crespigny and Wertheimer (eds.), *Contemporary Political Theory*, op. cit.
2. In this connection, see David Hamilton, "Reciprocity, Productivity, and Poverty," *Journal of Economic Issues*, Vol. IV, No. 1, March, 1970, pp. 35-42.

For the Marxists, freedom means obedience to the authority of Marxist analysis and to the obligations which a commitment thereto imposes. A free person for the Marxists is one who has knowledge of necessity as disclosed by historical materialism and identifies his total behavior with that knowledge. Knowing that Marxism is "true," a person who conforms to the constraints which that knowledge generates is free. Such a person then fulfills his or her obligation to Marxian "truth" by acting to implement the Marxist design. In the socialist transition stage, when knowledge of necessity is the special competence of the elite vanguard of the proletariat, freedom means obedience to the authority of the dictatorship of the proletariat, which defines and imposes its conception of the general will on the community. Conformity to the general will, so conceived, may well require suppression of political speech and behavior of those who do not yet perceive the "truth" of the Marxist "knowledge of necessity." Only with the communist phase does the "realm of freedom" fully flower, when the withering of the state, the end of economic classes, and the end of alienation will have occurred.

Such an authoritarian view of freedom has little appeal here. Generally absent is the idea of freedom as choice over the restraints under which one lives. Opportunities to inform choice are constrained. "So everyone must think alike—the Maoist way—to attain true freedom."[3] And, on means-determine-ends grounds, freedom as obedience to authority which, under socialism, suppresses dissent, will hardly evolve into a discretionary freedom under communism.

On equality, the Marxists have little to say. They acknowledge the significance of the quest for equality under the capitalist mode. They join in voicing complaints over capitalist inequality. But equality, like freedom, is only attainable with the final ism shift to communism.

With regard to social justice, Marxists are somewhat ambivalent. Although the capitalist *system* in their view is unjust, Marx did not argue, pursuing equational justice, that labor should have the whole product of labor. Funding of public functions like education would require holding back part of the total output. Yet Marxists use bourgeois equational justice in the socialist period, as is reflected in the expressions: "He that does not work, neither shall he eat;" and "for an equal quantity of labor, an equal quantity of products."[4]

Even so, Marxists, sensing its inadequacy, wish to "get beyond" bourgeois equational justice. Under communism, the dictum, "From

3. John W. Gurley, "The New Man in the New China," *The Center Magazine*, Vol. III, No. 3, May, 1970, p. 28. Reprinted with permission from *The Center Magazine*, a publication of the Center for the Study of Democratic Institutions, Santa Barbara, California.

4. N. Lenin, "State and Revolution," in the *Essential Left*, Barnes and Noble, New York, 1961, p. 231.

each according to ability, to each according to needs"[5] would prevail. Here equational justice would be abandoned.

While the Marxist ambivalence is understandable, the use of equational justice in socialism and the absence of an identified alternative principle of justice in communism contributes little to our search for applicable formulations of goals.

For fascists, freedom means obedience to the authority of the totalitarian state and its leader; freedom is "a concession of the state." One is free to the extent that one submerges one's own identity and individual discretion in the interests of the state as these interests are defined by the leader and party. "For Fascism, society is the end, individuals are the means and its whole life consists in using individuals as instruments for its social ends."[6] Freedom means obedience to fascist restraints as these are determined by heroic great men—messianic leaders emergent from the raw survivalist struggle of life. One is most free when one enthusiastically conforms.

That this view is a total rejection of the historic meaning of freedom as effectual choice is obvious. In denying discretion to people generally, fascism asserts the pre-emptive superiority of the judgments of invidiously constituted elites. The view contributes to revolutionary unrest; it is a part of the problems, not of their solution.

Fascist equality is a contradiction of terms. Fascists deny that equality in any useful sense exists or can exist. Fascism ". . . affirms the fertilizing, beneficent, and unassailable inequality of men, who cannot be leveled through an extrinsic and mechanical process such as universal suffrage."[7] Equality is a myth; fascists celebrate invidiously conceived inequality. Worth is identified by race, origin, ethnicity, sex, and prowess. Such inequality is natural and given; it is to be exploited.

The fascist conversion of human differences into criteria of relative worth and designations of role and function need not detain us. Its credibility as an analytical construct is absent.

Fascist justice is a matter of dispensation by those who hold coercive authority. Legal systems stipulating individual rights and protections do not necessarily govern. Justice is what those who hold power say it is. That such "justice" may well be capricious, vindictive, retaliatory, equational, or expedient comes as no surprise. Leaders dispense justice in the name of the state. There is no obligatory appeal to reason, principle, or code. Capriciousness, arbitrariness, and invidiousness are

5. Marx, "Critique of Gotha Program," in Marx and Engels, *Selected Works, II*, Foreign Languages Publishing House, Moscow, 1958, p. 24.

6. Alfredo Rocco, "The Political Doctrine of Fascism," in Carl Cohen (ed.), *Communism, Fascism and Democracy*, Random House, New York, 1962, p. 343.

7. B. Mussolini, "Doctrine of Fascism," in University of Colorado Philosophy Department, *Readings on Fascism and National Socialism*, Swallow, Chicago, (no date), p. 17.

elevated into maxims of social judgment. Surely the human experience deserves better.

Consider now some alternative views of freedom, equality, and justice.

II.   FREEDOM AS GENUINE CHOICE

In contrast to these isms, freedom does mean "options and choices." The concept of freedom for an evolutionary political economist, drawn from and consistent with instrumental value theory, may now be brought into view. Freedom, we suggest, must come to mean *an expanding area of genuine choice*. This meaning has both an individual and a social dimension.

In the social sense, freedom is a product of culture. It is established by restraints (albeit of a particular variety). It requires the creation of prescriptive rules for enlarging discretion over prescriptive and proscriptive rules. ". . . the most basic form of liberty," writes John Maurice Clark, "is the liberty to choose how much liberty one will exercise and what guidance one will accept." "The really unfree system," he continues, "is not the system without guidance and direction, but the system which deprives the individual of this basic liberty of choice."[8] Freedom requires the development and perfection of institutional forms to expand the spheres of discretionary involvement—genuine choice.

In the individual sense, freedom means the progressive enlargement of the rational, means-consequence-perceiving capacity of people and of opportunities to choose among alternative ways of organizing structural aspects of the political and economic processes. The exercise of freedom requires the development in individuals of self-directive capabilities. To be effectual, freedom must be grounded in reliable knowledge. To survive and thrive, it must be communally shared. It presumes that all human beings are in principle educable. It is the condition *sine qua non* for the attainment of human dignity.

Freedom, to repeat, must come to mean an expanding area of *genuine* choice. But when is choice genuine? Choice is genuine if, when one course of action (or institutional option) is chosen over another, the consequences resulting will be discernibly and significantly different than would have been the case had another course or option been selected. Voting, for example, can be meaningless if genuine alternatives are not on the ballot, as is normally the case in plebiscites. Choice can only be genuine, moreover, when the chooser is really able to understand the means-consequence relations involved; when the person can with some confidence predict and appraise the probable course of events

8. John Maurice Clark, *Economic Institutions and Human Welfare*, Knopf, New York, 1957, pp. 85-86.

that will ensue following his or her choice. Such perception and capacity to predict and appraise consequences are an inherent part of the process of making rational choices. Indeed, that is what we normally mean by rational choice when we operate outside the narrow, ideology-serving assumptions of capitalistic orthodoxy.

In sum, for choice to be genuine, it must be informed; it must be based on knowledge. Freedom means both the opportunity to choose among genuine alternatives and ready access to knowledge that will function to make the selection an informed one. Choice without knowledge is a fraud. Knowledge without choice is sterile. Free societies are those which understand this necessary linkage and provide prescriptive and proscriptive arrangements (e.g., the First Amendment) to assure access to knowledge and the right to employ it in guiding choice making. [9]

Consider now some of the assumptions and implications of these assertions. If, as we contend, freedom is established by restraints of a particular sort, attention must now be invited to the matter of the restraints.

Since all institutions are restraining, were we to join the capitalists and view freedom as the absence of restraint, we would be suggesting that institutional restraints are the antithesis of freedom. But not even the capitalists can really opt for this position. They are compelled to allow for market restraints (institutions) so that there can be economic coordination. And these market restraints are legitimate because they are allegedly a component of a natural order.

Actually, as now must be clear, the issue of freedom does not hinge on the presence or absence of restraints nor on the amount of restraints as such. Rather, it hinges on the character of restraints, by whom they are imposed, and the purposes for which they are instituted. Of course institutional restraints are indispensable to civilized existence. It is not the fact of restraints that endangers freedom as genuine choice; it is the kind of rules, codes, statutes, and customs—their scope and their consequences—that is at issue.

In a literal sense, as we have several times remarked, organized life requires prescriptive and proscriptive stipulations. Such prescribed patterns specify how a people shall organize themselves to accomplish various social, economic, and political functions. To repeat, there is no human life outside of community. To have community requires organization. Organization consists of institutional arrangements. Such belaboring of the obvious seems yet needed in order to continue undercutting the habituated tendency to see freedom as the antithesis of

---

9. See Francis M. Myers, *The Warfare of Democratic Ideals*, The Antioch Press, Yellow Springs, Ohio, 1956, pp. 236-41. We do not assume, of course, that "knowledge" is gained only through formal schooling.

order, organization, authority, or even planning. A chief infirmity of yesterday's isms is their inability to permit genuine choice over the restraints which do give order and pattern to our common lives.

What kinds of restraints, then, are required in order to provide for an expanding range of choice over restraints, an expansion which we now affirm to be the defensible meaning of freedom? The answer is clear. All economic, political, and cultural prescriptions and proscriptions which actually function to provide all individuals with the opportunity, the stimulation, the education, and the reinforcing support to develop their rational, reflective, discriminative capacities, their emerging self-consciousness, their capabilities for discrimination among options, their stock of cognitive meanings, their skills of meaningful communication, are restraints which create conditions of freedom for the individual.

Similarly, all restraints which operate to foster and encourage the application of such capabilities and capacities to the problems of choice in organizing the functions of producing and distributing real income and of determining and administering public policy serve the purpose of expanding freedom.

Structural arrangements and rules of behavior as diverse as (a) progressive-income taxation, minimum-wage laws, and income transfers; (b) the First Amendment, "one-man-one-vote" reapportionment rulings, and open primaries; (c) Fair-Employment-Practice laws, abandonment of separate-but-equal doctrines, and the Equal Rights Amendment; (d) Environmental-Protection-Agency controls on auto emissions, rules governing disposal of radioactive wastes, and surface-restoration mandates on strip miners are, it would appear, generally oriented toward the expansion of the range of freedom as genuine choice for individuals as members of a self-governing community.

Conversely, any restraints or rules or laws which impair the individuals' development of reflective, self-conscious, discretionary capabilities or deny individuals the opportunity to exercise such capabilities are enemies of freedom. Further, any restraints which find their sanction in the perpetuation of power, of status, or of position are nearly always inhibitive of freedom.

Accordingly, restraints (rules, practices, codes, laws, etc.) which tend generally to inhibit freedom as an expanding area of genuine choice might well include the following examples: (a) private "governmental" control through multinational nonaccountable corporations, self-perpetuating nonresponsive trade-union leadership, wholly "other-directed" working conditions; (b) loyalty oaths, brokerage politics, bureaucratic secrecy, "managed" news, and political lying; (c) restrictive covenants (de facto or de jure), institutional racism, chauvinistic or authoritarian marriages; (d) profit-maximizing urban development, public-regulatory-agency manipulation or control by ecologically insensitive industries, and nonenforcement of pollution-control regulations. [10]

Freedom as an expanding area of discretion is intimately tied to and interdependent with the more inclusive value position discussed above—the continuity of human life and the noninvidious re-creation of community through the instrumental use of knowledge. The instrumental value principle provides the criterion for the exercise of choice—freedom. Freedom to choose restraints is the freedom to choose, with others, the *character* of rules, codes, and regulations that organize and give meaning to our lives. The instrumental criterion provides a means of identifying what is wrong and what the *character* of rules and codes should be; the condition of freedom as an expanding area of genuine choice provides for the exercise of rational will in reconstituting structure to correct what is wrong.

Freedom is essential for instrumental-value judgments to be implemented in experience. Freedom is the instrument through which judgments of relative worth of programs and structures are made, unmade, and remade. Instrumental value guides the exercise of freedom; expanding freedom assures the vitality and viability of the value principle. Indeed freedom sets the context for continuing scrutiny of that principle itself.

Thus, the superior restraints that may be freely chosen are precisely those which are judged *worthy* through the application of the value principle herein advocated. We do indeed act freely when applying this criterion; as members of a community we become participants in the re-creation of institutional fabric. No ism-ideologist can afford to allow this prerogative.

We are now in a position to view the relation between freedom and government in an altered light. It is true, of course, that governmental

10. A possible initial reaction to this listing of examples of prescriptions and proscriptions which extend or shrink freedom is that it is merely pouring old "liberal-left" wine into new "instrumentalist" bottles, that what is being presented here is not much of a departure from policy views of more conventional approaches after all. A similar reaction may occur in discussions of equality and justice below.

Such a reaction is partially correct. To the extent that the "liberal-left" draws its rationale from democratic philosophy, including its applications to the economy, commonality will be observed in the two positions. But much of the "liberal-left" position (as reflected, e.g., in the Democratic Party and the Peace and Freedom Party) continues, apparently, also to reflect dependency on and deference to elements of the ideologies of capitalism and Marxism. In these respects there is conspicuous divergence. The problem may well lie in ambiguity over what the "liberal-left's" basic position really is and ought to be.

Our concern here is to contribute, if possible, to the formulation and clarification of a philosophic base for social action that is more relevant to problem solving, more humane, more stimulative of creativity, more dependent on recourse to reason, and more open to further inquiry and reconstitution than are other perspectives and paradigms. The exploration of convergence with or divergence from other positions is a useful, and should be a continuing, inquiry exercise for students.

institutions have a somewhat unique position in any community. Normally, they possess police powers; they have, as noted above, nearly exclusive powers of mandamus and injunction. They do, therefore, obviously represent repositories of power and authority. But the capitalists, we are reminded, confuse authority with authoritarianism. All governments possess power and authority; they may or may not be authoritarian. As we have seen, authoritarian systems confer rule-making authority upon some fragment or elite element of the community at large. Such governments were and are quite properly condemned by the orthodox capitalists and participatory democrats alike. What the capitalist ideologists fail to appreciate is that governmental authority may be used (in participatory-democratic systems it will be used) to expand the range of effectual choice for its citizens. If governmental authority is actually held accountable to the community generally through representative institutions and otherwise, that community will find governmental processes to be a most important instrument (sometimes the only instrument) through which to provide alternatives. Government may also provide the mechanisms and guarantees to assure that choices made will be effectual and that all individuals may participate without invidous discrimination.

However, the laws and restraints emanating from government are to be judged no differently from restraints emanating from any other source. What is their character? What is their purpose? What consequences may reasonably be expected? Are those consequences contributive to or destructive of opportunities for future choice making? Does the community retain the right to repeal or modify the restraints? Is the effect to enhance the development of capacities for all to make rational choices? Answers to such questions will give a useful index of whether a society is open or closed.

Certainly restraints, including governmental restraints, are directive. But in a literal sense, people must create and self-impose restraints which promote and condition for freedom. Actual political participation in a democracy includes such creation and self-imposition of restraints. Such participation, however, should not be denied to or reduced for adult individuals because of some test of literacy, years of schooling, or measure of intellect. The continuing exercise of freedom as genuine choice, the fact of participation, is itself a sufficient, but perhaps not optimal, educative experience. Democracy, because it promotes freedom, is, in principle, the most efficient form of policy making, whatever the level of attained skills or knowledge of the people involved.

But the development and improvement of lingual, reflective, and cognitive capacities is typically on the continuing agenda of democratic communities to invigorate and extend the range of effectual choice. Compulsory-school-attendance laws are intended to help assure the development of such capacities. Becoming reasoning and rational choosers is, of course, a life-long pursuit which, one hopes, is aided by formal education, but by no means confined thereto. Increasing compliance with the canons of rational and normative inquiry is expected to improve the quality of judgment. Freedom can be expanded most rapidly and pervasively where there is acceptance of the procedural canons which distinguish reasoned discourse and open-ended inquiry from affirmations of ideology and myth.

A free society is one which encourages the development of the latent capabilities for reasoned, discretionary involvement of its members in clear recognition that such capacities will be subversive at times of received doctrine, established custom, and ideological belief. Such perpetual ideamongering is the basis for all reformmongering.

But let no one be deceived. Reformmongering will be resisted. Institutions become habitual, and people (liberal or conservative, instrumentalist or Marxist) who see their identities and careers as being contingent on existing structure and its continuance will look with no kindness upon those who would challenge or threaten that structure. As Robert H. Montgomery has observed, "The Ancient and Honorable Order of Flint Workers" will not look with favor upon the inventor of the "bronze ax" because he or she threatens their status and power preeminence based on "the art of chipping flint to a cutting edge and shaping it to implements of war and peace."[11] Every age develops its vested interests. The "Beaters of Bronze" doubtless in due course displaced "The Ancient and Honorable Order of Flint Workers."

Free societies are those which expect and understand institutional rigidities and find educational and democratic ways of generating change and of minimizing the personal destruction and communal dislocation generated by such change.

Effective reformmongering societies are those which maximize free involvement in democratic processes. Those to be affected by contemplated change may *themselves* participate in the decisions determining initiation, timing, scope, duration, and character of proposed changes. Such participation will not eliminate resistance, nor should it necessarily. The burden of proof is on those pushing the modification. But such participation does provide an opportunity for a learning process to guide and shape such change, if any, as it is undertaken.

How, then, does the companion social goal of equality relate to what has been said here about social value and freedom? To this important matter, we next turn.

III.   EQUALITY AS DISCRETIONARY DIGNITY

The concept of democratic equality effectively eliminates the lament which ism-ideologist elitists of one kind or another have offered over the

11. R. H. Montgomery, *The Brimstone Game,* Vanguard Press, New York, 1940, pp. 28-29.

years. The Darwinist doctrinaires have insisted that ". . . advantages which are shared cease to be advantages at all" and that ". . . when everybody is somebody, nobody will be anybody."[12] The concept of equality here advanced affirms precisely that "everybody *is* somebody" —a somebody who, in the interests of re-creating community, deserves respect from himself or herself and from his or her peers.

Accordingly, democratic equality refers to a condition in which, through participatory (choice-making) involvement of all persons, *"the being and belonging"*[13]*—hence the dignity—of each member is affirmed.* The affirmation is precisely that "advantages"—political prerogatives, real income, communal responsibilities, educational access —shall be shared, not based on indexes of who is deserving, or by application of evaluative principles, but on the basis of mutuality, interdependence, and common humanity.

As John Schaar has remarked, equality affirms that

> . . . "the poorest he that is in England hath a live to live as the richest he." There is the heart of the matter: each man has a *life* to live, not a role to perform; that life must be *lived*, not acted out according to some prefixed pattern; and *he* must live it, not give over the responsibility for it to someone else. It is this common and ultimate responsibility that each has for the living of his own life, this understanding that in the end each is responsible before himself and before all others for making his life one worthy of a man, that has always stood at the heart of the idea of a common humanity as the ground of a claim for a minimal equality of treatment.[14]

Equality of treatment, so perceived, is the ultimate basis for human dignity. Such dignity is impossible in the absence of effective democratic involvement in determining the character of life in a community. As Schaar argues elsewhere:

> . . . insofar as any man does not participate in forming the common definition of the good life, to that degree he falls short of the fullest possibilities of the human vocation. No man can assign to another dominion over how he shall live his life without becoming something less than a man. This way of thinking about political action leads to an idea of equality whose tone and implications are very different from those of the equal opportunity formulation.[15]

12. R. H. Tawney, *Equality*, Capricorn Books, New York, 1961, p. 33. Copyright © 1952, George Allen and Unwin, Ltd., London, England. Reprinted by permission of the publisher.

13. John H. Schaar, "Equality of Opportunity, and Beyond," in de Crespigny and Wertheimer (eds.), *Contemporary Political Theory*, op. cit., p. 151.

14. John H. Schaar, "Some Ways of Thinking About Equality," *The Journal of Politics*, Vol. 26, 1964, p. 877.

15. John H. Schaar, "Equality of Opportunity, and Beyond," in de Crespigny and Wertheimer (eds.), *Contemporary Political Theory*, op. cit., p. 151.

Indeed, this view of equality is not only "very different from," it is fundamentally in conflict with the whole idea of equality of opportunity —of equal chances to become invidiously unequal. The whole competitive ethic, at least from Horatio Alger to today, is a basically undemocratic elitist notion grounded in nineteenth-century conceptions of life as a jungle, or survival of the fittest, of the virtues of winners and successes over losers and failures.

The more conservative minded will no doubt insist that any sizeable achievement of equality connoting affirmative acceptance of "being and belonging" must be accompanied by a leveling down of performance, of the expansion and concurrence in mediocrity, of the loss of that measure of intellect and leadership which only an elite (unequally treated) can provide. But this ancient "the-sky-is-falling" dictum confuses, putting it gently, the meanings of superiority and excellence. As John Livingston has shown, the distinction between superiority and excellence parallels the distinction between equality of opportunity and democratic equality:

> . . . excellence simply describes the standards which define all our aspirations in the development of our talents, while superiority is a judgment of the relative worth of human beings. Equality resents superiority; it only resents excellence when men have been induced to test their own worth in a contest in which superiority rather than excellence is the objective.[16]

He continues,

> The clarification of this confusion is to be found in examining the meaning of standards. To be without standards (that is, institutionally sanctioned and enforced criteria for measuring the relative worth of individuals) is not to produce normless individuals (that is, individuals who lack standards of excellence for judging their own and others' work). Real achievement and excellence do not require standards of the first sort, though they obviously require the latter. For that reason, the protection of the incompetent does not imply the protection of incompetence.[17]

The core of the matter is that democratic equality does not admit of "superior" or "inferior" persons. "Everybody is somebody." Individual worth—"being and belonging"—is not at issue in a participatory-democratic order. Standards of excellence do not question the contention that the "poorest he . . . hath a life to live as the richest he."

Acculturated patterns of inequality tend to deny this contention with untoward effects on both the allegedly superior and inferior categories. R. H. Tawney's delightful prose provides an example of how:

16. John C. Livingston, "Tenure Everyone?" in Bardwell L. Smith and Associates, *The Tenure Debate*, Jossey-Bass Inc., San Francisco, 1973, p. 63.

17. Ibid.

> One of the regrettable, if diverting, effects of extreme inequality is its tendency to weaken the capacity for impartial judgment. It pads the lives of its beneficiaries with a soft down of consideration, while relieving them of the vulgar necessity of justifying their pretensions, and secures that, if they fall, they fall on cushions. It disposes them, on the one hand, to take for granted themselves and their own advantages, as though there were nothing in the latter which could possibly need explanation, and, on the other hand, to be critical of claims to similar advantages advanced by their neighbours who do not yet possess them. It causes them, in short, to apply different standards to different sections of the community, as if it were uncertain whether all of them are human in the same sense as themselves.[18]

And such "standards" are precisely those which challenge the "being and belonging" of those deemed inferior. But democratic equality does not enshrine incompetence; it protects people from having their participatory dignity eroded by application of criteria impuning their worth and their membership in the community. Racism and sexism, for example, rest exactly on just such efforts to impune worth and membership!

Moreover, democratic equality does not presume the absence of differences of ability or achievement. An example used by Schaar will be helpful:

> The paradigmatic case is that of the relation between teacher and student. The teacher's superior knowledge gives him a just claim to authority over his students. But central to the ethic of teaching is the conviction that the teacher must impart to students not only his substantive knowledge but also the critical skills and habits necessary for judging and contributing to that knowledge. The teacher justifies his authority and fulfills his duty by making himself unnecessary to the student.[19]

Thus, a democratic view of equality "still leaves wide scope for the existence of necessary and just . . . differences, but it brings a different mentality to their appraisal."[20] It denies the politician the "claim to superior rights on the ground of special merit."[21] It also denies to the participatory democrat the absolution of "partial responsibility for public policies" and from "shared responsibility and guilt." No participatory democrat can say "Somebody else rules; I just live here." Ordinary citizens carry "the burden of caring for the public good." On the other hand, the "doctrine of equality of opportunity, tied as it is to the principle of hierarchy, [struggle up the ladder] easily leads to moral

18. R. H. Tawney, *Equality*, op. cit., pp. 24-25.
19. John H. Schaar, "Equality of Opportunity, and Beyond," in de Crespigny and Wertheimer (eds.), *Contemporary Political Theory*, op. cit., p. 151.
20. Ibid.
21. Ibid.

arrogance on the part of the winners and to the taking of moral holidays by the losers." [22]

Some implications of this principle of democratic equality are nearly, but perhaps not quite, self-evident. In the polity, democratic equality requires the affirmation of "being and belonging" through, for example, noninvidious access to procedures and institutions for the resolution of disputes (equality before the law), noninvidious access to information sources and deliberative processes in political debates, and full participatory rights in electoral processes.

In the economy, democratic equality requires the affirmation of "being and belonging" through, for example, continuous receipt of money (and real) income shares sufficient to sustain the life of individuals and families at (minimally) a rising "health and decency" level, noninvidious access to meaningful work, full participatory rights in setting community economic policies (priorities, wage rates, growth levels, etc.), and the provision of protection from the discriminatory use by any fragment of the community of the power to grant or withhold real income.

The most casual reflection will indicate that democratic equality as discretionary dignity fits, as hand in glove, with the principle of social value as the continuity of human life and the noninvidious re-creation of community through the instrumental use of knowledge, and with freedom as an expanding area of genuine choice. But democratic equality stands in stark contrast to the equality of opportunity of the capitalists, to the incomplete abandonment of bourgeois equality of the Marxists, and to the denial of equality of the fascists. In our view, those seeking insight into the revolutionary concerns of our day can in no way afford to abandon to the ism-ideologists the effort to conceive equality in a pertinent way. Democratic equality can serve as a tool of inquiry and of social action.

We complete our quest for an evolutionary and normative theory of political economy by moving, finally, to a recasting of a principle of social and economic justice.

IV.   JUSTICE AS INSTRUMENTAL INVOLVEMENT

As freedom denotes the right of choice, as equality denotes the right of "being and belonging," so also does justice denote the right to be treated fairly. Justice as fairness [23] helps to assure the availability of freedom and equality so perceived.

22. Ibid.
23. A somewhat divergent formulation of the idea of fairness appears in John Rawls, "Justice as Fairness," in de Crespigny and Wertheimer (eds.), *Contemporary Political Theory*, op. cit., pp. 192 ff.

Social justice, we suggest in what follows, should come to mean *the assurance to all of instrumental involvement in the social process.* [24] Instrumental involvement results from noninvidious, democratic determination of laws, rules, and codes and noncapricious, nonmalicious, and nonsubversive administration of such laws, rules, and codes. Social justice, in short, is a product of the conduct of the political process—the determination and administration of public policy—in a manner consistent with the instrumental value principle herein advanced. Judging among institutional restraints with the criterion of the continuity of human life and the noninvidious re-creation of community through the instrumental use of knowledge will tend to assure social justice; it will give meaning to the idea of fairness—of fair treatment.

Politically, the achievement of social justice—provision for instrumental involvement—requires that in the establishment of restraints, no arbitrary or capricious distinctions be made among individuals or groups. It means that in determining and administering democratically determined rules, the principle of even-handedness must prevail. No one's discretion is to exceed that of another unless such differential extension has been popularly determined and is continuously subject to accountability requests and recall provisions. Justice as fairness denies the extension of special privilege on invidious grounds. Those denied discretion or rendered politically impotent are denied justice as fairness.

Accordingly, a political system is unjust—denies instrumental involvement—if a significant segment of the electorate is effectively disenfranchised because the system fails to convince them that the system can be made to respond to their problems. [25] A political system is unjust which prevents publics from being constituted where real grievances remain unattended, and from seeking political relief at the neighborhood, city, state, and national levels.

A political system is unjust—denies instrumental involvement—if one's own possession of substantial wealth (and access to other people's wealth) is a precondition for consideration of a leadership role in standing for political office.

A political system is unjust—denies instrumental involvement—which permits capricious, vindictive, or malicious enforcement of agreed-upon restraints. "Selective" law enforcement is reflected at times in the failures to cite the privileged or the wealthy for traffic or drug-law violations, in the differential allocations of police resources for various categories of crime (street crime vs. white-collar crime), in the corruption of enforcement agencies themselves by organized criminal syndicates, and the like. Have federal enforcement agencies pursued

---

24. This formulation comes from the work of J. Fagg Foster, professor of economics, University of Denver.
25. John Schaar, "Insiders and Outsiders," op. cit.

with equal vigor violations of federal civil-rights laws and violations of federal income-tax laws?

A political system is unjust—denies instrumental involvement—when the structures of government have themselves become impediments to the noninvidious recasting of prescriptive and proscriptive rules. Practices of seniority, nonrecording and nonreporting of representatives' votes, manipulative control of bills by committees, the closing of hearings, the withholding of information through classification and allegations of executive privilege, the deliberate failure to take up some kinds of issues at all, bureaucratic rivalries and internacine interagency conflicts, all represent impediments to the realization of social justice as fairness. Instrumental involvement in self-government is denied when political custom and practice exhibit marked elitist, aristocratic, or bureaucratic characteristics.

Economically, the achievement of social justice—provision for instrumental involvement—requires that every human being have access to the education, training, skills, employment connections, and income required to make an effective and continuing contribution to the community's production and distribution of real income. Justice as fairness here does not mean "opportunity" to become competitive in a survivalist jungle; it means that equality as "being and belonging" must be translated into genuine options/connections for meaningful and significant involvement in the economic process. For involvement to be meaningful, such economic connections must permit and encourage self-realizing growth of insight and capacity (in contrast, e.g., to Charlie Chaplin's *Modern Times* assembly-line nut-tightener). For involvement to be significant, such economic connections must be a source of esteem from the community because of their instrumental contribution to the economic well-being of that community (unlike the hapless inventor of a non-wearing and non-soiling fabric, played by Alec Guiness, in *The Man in the White Suit*). Few readers need detailed examples of mentally stupifying, physically exhausting, personally degrading, emotionally devasting employments which deny that sense of significance and esteem. [26] The dreary labor history of factory child labor, of twelve- to fourteen-hour work days (seven days a week), of dangerous and cramped work at coal faces, of totally "other-directed" and senselessly redundant white-collar work, of maiming and crippling and killing by unsafe factory machines, of violent war-like reprisals against labor dissenters and organizers, is familiar enough to students of the American and European labor movements.

Economically, the achievement of social justice—provision for instrumental involvement—requires a catering to people's most distinctive

---

26. See Studs Terkel, *Working*, Pantheon/Random House, New York, 1974.

human capabilities: their reasoning capabilities, their impulses, to compassion, their recognition of community and the need for its continuity, their growing sensitivity and awareness of their impact on others, and their sense of workmanship. Social justice requires the creation and operation of an economy that fairly is life enhancing, that is community creating, that is nondiscriminatory for all.

Accordingly, an economic system is unjust—denies instrumental involvement—when in quest for an illusive balance of contribution and payment, deference is given to a market allocation of income without regard to its real- and money-income effects upon individuals. The capitalists' insistence upon seeking an equivalence between effort extended (disutility) and income received (utility) through the unfettered competitive price system tends to condone patterns of inequality in income receipt which may be judged, by social justice standards here recommended, to be bordering on the scandalous.

Similarly an economy is unjust—denies instrumental involvement—when individual means tests [27] are used in deciding upon the social or public provision of income (in dollars or in kind) to individuals and families not otherwise receiving a liveable income. Means tests tend to be unjust because, at bottom, they appear to represent the imposition of the economic power of the rich (those that have "made it") upon the poor in a manner to deprive the poor of their discretion, hence their dignity, and therefore of their capability and interest in emerging from their state of economic privation. For a half-century and more there has been agonizing over welfare grants and levels and over the question of entitlement. The imposition of a means test to determine entitlement may well be an invidious use of economic power by the few through the agency of the state.

An economy is unjust, further, when it tolerates significant or protracted involuntary unemployment. Since, as nearly everyone knows, in an exchange economy availability of a job to provide continuous and adequate money income is a source of economic discretion, of economic freedom, those without jobs and income are economically, and to some extent politically, disenfranchised. It is no accident that the "economic royalists" of any age are reluctant to see full employment conditions; their capacities to coerce the labor force into accepting their terms of employment are materially reduced at full employment.

An economy is unjust—denies instrumental involvement—which permits racial and sexual discrimination (e.g., de facto school segregation, core city-suburb segregation, trade-union racial exclusion, sex segregation by profession, position, and income) because it perpetuates caste, class, and sex differences, thereby tending to destroy the image of

27. A meticulous examination of the financial circumstances of a person as a condition precedent to receiving public grants of money as welfare payments or other forms of transfer payments.

self as a significant person among those against whom such discrimination is practiced. Such destruction of self-images, of self-worth, erodes the interest and capacity of people to seek and sustain significant economic connections.

An economy is unjust—denies instrumental involvement—which tolerates a tax structure, the burden of which is borne by those less able to pay. Indeed, to cite a specific case, Philip Stern has shown that the United States has a tax system which provides "welfare payments averaging some $720,000 a year . . . *to the nation's wealthiest families*—those with annual incomes of over a million dollars."[28] The total cost of such "welfare payments" to the rich comes to about $77 billion per year at recently current rates.

As most students know, the overall tax system in the United States (federal, state, and local) is not progressive; it is, over most income ranges, proportional.[29] In some areas it is conspicuously regressive (sales taxes on consumer goods). A tax system which is not organized primarily on the ability-to-pay principle does not meet social-justice criteria here advanced.

If social justice, in its economic dimension, is to mean assurance of instrumental involvement, how then, for example, ought income to be distributed consistent with the value principle we have recommended above?

Justice as instrumental involvement is a "needs" concept, but not in the means-test sense of needs where, grudgingly, subsistence income is provided by those having income to those without income. Nor is it to be taken to mean "needs" in the want-satisfaction, utility-disutility sense, where ethical relativism is incapable of distinguishing between the "need" for a polo pony and the "need" for surgical treatment. Instrumental justice is not concerned with the "needs" of the leisure class for conspicuous display, nor the "needs" of an elite to exercise intimidative control over the led, nor of the "needs" of an economy for the unspent incomes of the well-to-do (voluntary savings) to finance investment and promote "progress."

Rather, justice as instrumental involvement calls for patterns of income distribution (in money or in kind) which are sufficient to permit a person to secure that level of product and services which will enable him or her to secure, for example, as much formal education as he or she has the capacity to absorb; to maintain mental and physical health and that of one's family; to develop latent talents, skills, and capacities to equip oneself to make a significant instrumental contribution to the life process of the day. Critical is the idea that "needs" are not to be

---

28. Philip M. Stern, *The Rape of the Taxpayer*, op. cit., p. 5 (Emphasis added.)
29. Joseph A. Pechman and Benjamin A. Okner, *Who Bears the Tax Burden?*, The Brookings Institution, Washington, D.C., 1974.

defined by the market; rather, needs will be defined on the "presumptive-need" basis, employing reasoned judgments of what is required for individual fulfillment and social efficiency. Market mechanisms, collective bargaining, and administered-income programs (public and private) *may* be used, but the test of justice in allocation must itself be *external* to the allocative mechanisms.

Perhaps nowhere in an economy is there a more sensitive point, nor one in which the significance of doctrinal belief is more evident, than the matter of justice in allocation. Orthodox capitalists contend that market allocations *constitute* economic justice. Indeed, capitalists' aspirations to positivism and ethical relativism preclude the use of economic analysis to identify justice anywhere else. To test justice *external* to the allocative mechanisms themselves passes the ethical judgment to noneconomists. The orthodox can then focus on other aspects of the market process. Regrettably, the necessity of making a reasoned judgment—agonizing and difficult though it may be—on social justice remains. We are again reminded of the sterility of utility value theory and of the relevance of instrumental value theory.

A judgment of the level of income needed is relative not to the psychological needs (hedonistically conceived) of persons, but to their instrumental needs. It is relative not to the distribution of power and wealth, but to the actual existential requirements to make economic opportunity something more than a meaningless cliché or an ideological apologia. It is related not to the presumption of scarcity of means to satisfy unlimited wants, but to the demonstrated instrumental capacity of the economy to produce expanding volumes of goods and services.

For example, if at a given time, some are being economically deprived on invidious grounds, instrumental justice might call for a disproportionate allocation in their favor for a time to restore (or create) capacities and opportunities for significant contributions to the economic and social process. "Our invisible poor"[30] remain unattended where justice is viewed as being dispensed by market forces. They remain invisible and unattended so long as the effort-earnings linkage defines the perspective from which their condition is viewed. Orthodox capitalism, in particular, has provided a principle of justice which impairs our ability to see deprivation and aborts our capacities to think constructively regarding its removal. The quest for instrumental justice has the virtue of posing the relevant questions. It does not presume to provide automatic answers.

Although there are hazards in so doing, (note our previous "old wine in new bottles" comment), it may be useful to mention a variety of generally familiar policies, programs, and institutions which seem

30. Dwight Macdonald, "Our Invisible Poor," *The New Yorker*, January 19, 1963.

to illustrate, in good part, the pursuit of instrumental justice here introduced.

Instrumental justice is created and/or extended by

Fair-Employment-Practice laws
Tuition-free education through college level
School-lunch programs
Income-maintenance programs
Desegregation of schools and neighborhoods
Peace Corps, Job Corps, Vista programs
Manpower-training programs
Progressive tax structures
Capital gains and inheritance levies
Investment and mortgage guarantees
Public-health programs
National health service

Instrumental justice does not presume equality of income shares; neither does it sanction inequality on invidious status and power grounds, capital-fund-formation grounds, or grounds of the inherent superiorities of the elites. To inquire about equality and inequality on the utility-disutility basis is to pose the wrong kind of question. Some inequality on instrumental grounds is to be expected. Instrumental justice in the economic realm is not directed toward uniformity and sameness even in the money-income aspect. Rather, it is intended to facilitate the removal of pecuniary criteria in and pecuniary barriers to the most efficient, humane, and constructive contribution of which individuals are capable. Instrumental justice is not a matter of equivalence; it is a matter of societal provision of dignity-conveying opportunities for individual human and humane development. Attention to that problem requires the abandonment of received notions sanctioning existing patterns of money-income distribution.

The foregoing view of justice stands in sharp contrast to the deference to the capitalists' utility-disutility balancing of equational justice, to the Marxists' residue of equational justice ("he that does not work, neither shall he eat") and the ambivalent quest for nonequational justice ("from each according to ability; to each according to need"), and to the fascists' justice as dispensation of edicts by a coercively and racially constituted elite. Those who must work and live in the real world of existential fact and participate in the production and flow of real goods and services cannot afford the luxury or the apologia of the relativism of capitalist and Marxist equational theory nor the nihilism of fascist justice.

In concluding, it is worthwhile to reiterate a point made earlier. The institutional restraints—rules and regulations—introduced in search of social justice must, as Alexander Meiklejohn observes, be enforced. [31] Laws, per se, are not bondage. "Where men acknowledge no limits upon their actions, there can be no settled order of expectations among them, and where such an order is wanting, no man is significantly free." [32] Social justice requires that the rules be no more extensive, but also no less extensive, than necessary to insure instrumental participation. In America, ". . . the law of a free society permits what it does not forbid." [33]

Social justice requires, in addition, that laws be as clear as possible. The purpose, character, and universe of application should be unambiguous so that obligation can be knowingly incurred. Finally, social justice requires that laws be uniformly enforced without deference to invidious differentiation of any kind—wealth, color, race, locale, position, status. Justice as even-handedness requires equity and certainty in administration of laws.

Justice as the assurance of instrumental involvement is not a matter of bargaining, balancing, or weighing; it is a matter of maximizing the opportunities and options for individuals fully to realize their potential as human beings without invidious hindrance. Truth and justice are not bargaining chips in a poker game of elitists scrambling for prominence and position. Truth and justice are not served by ism-ideologies, but by reason, empathy, commitment, and integrity.

A normative and evolutionary theory of political economy is now in view. It rests, we believe, on humanistic, rational, and credible philosophical underpinnings. It encompasses theories of an evolving, functional economy and of a participatory, democratic polity. It incorporates normative inquiry at all stages and provides a formulation of a principle of social value as the continuity of human life and the noninvidious recreation of community through the instrumental use of knowledge. It identifies freedom as an expanding area of genuine choice; it identifies equality as the right to be and to belong; it identifies social and economic justice as the maximizing of instrumental involvement. Withall, this perspective represents a fundamental departure from the assumptions, structures and goals of capitalism, Marxism, and fascism.

We have suggested a way of pursuing the quest for discretion and dignity.

---

31. A. Meiklejohn, *Political Freedom*, op. cit., p. 14.
32. John F. A. Taylor, "Politics and the Human Covenant," *The Centennial Review*, op. cit., p. 10.
33. Ibid., p. 9.

INDEX